EVE

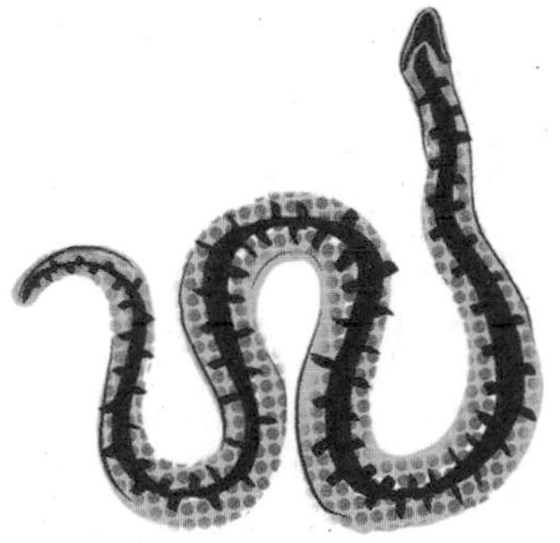

VIRAGO

First published in Great Britain in 2021 by Virago Press

1 3 5 7 9 10 8 6 4 2

A CIP catalogue record for this book
is available from the British Library.

ISBN 978-0-349-01069-4

Printed and bound in Italy by L.E.G.O. S.p.A.

Papers used by Virago are from well-managed forests
and other responsible sources.

FSC www.fsc.org MIX Paper from responsible sources FSC® C104740

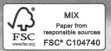

Virago Press
An imprint of
Little, Brown Book Group
Carmelite House
50 Victoria Embankment
London EC4Y 0DZ

An Hachette UK Company
www.hachette.co.uk
www.virago.co.uk

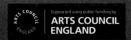

Supported using public funding by ARTS COUNCIL ENGLAND

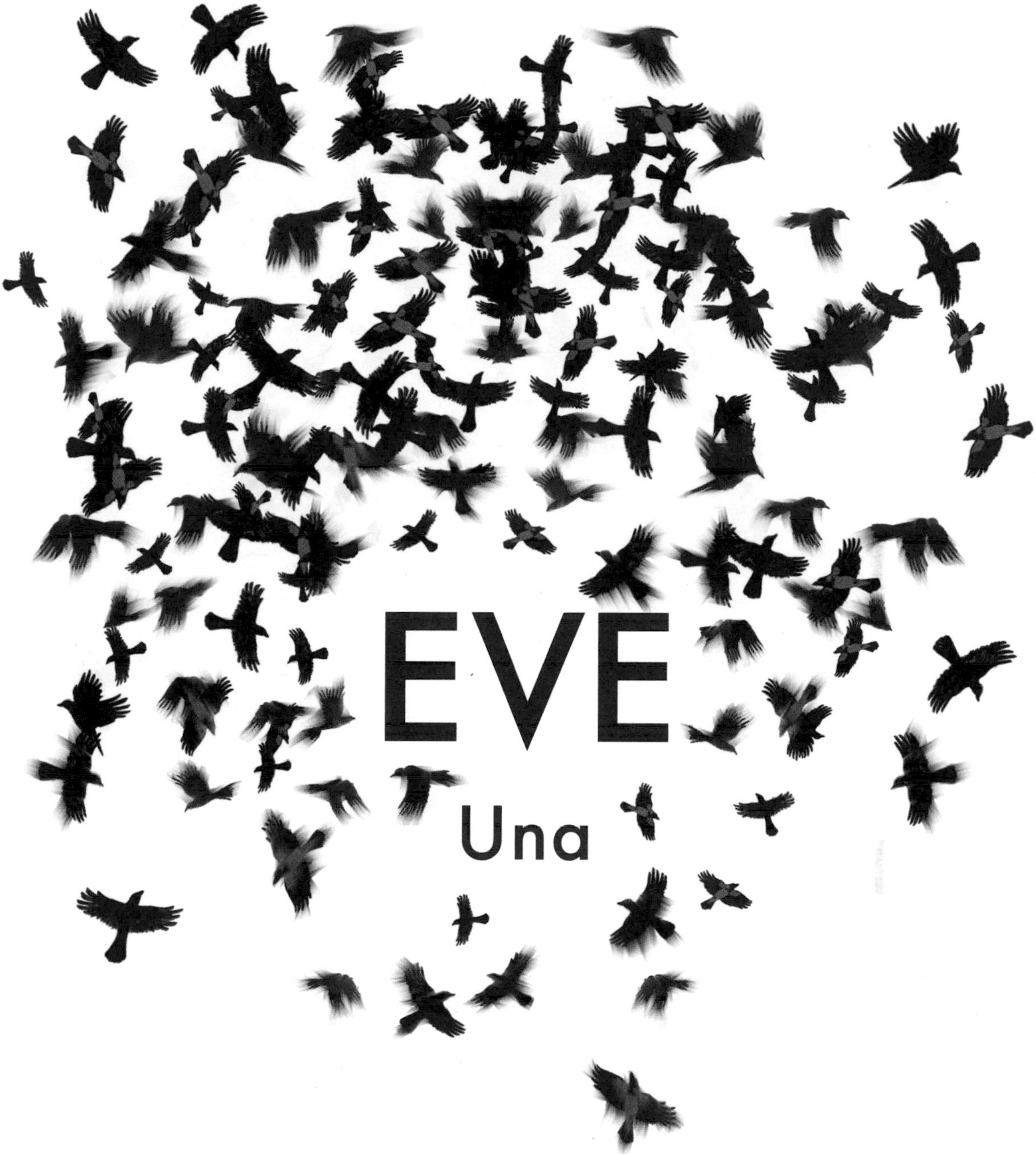

EVE

Una

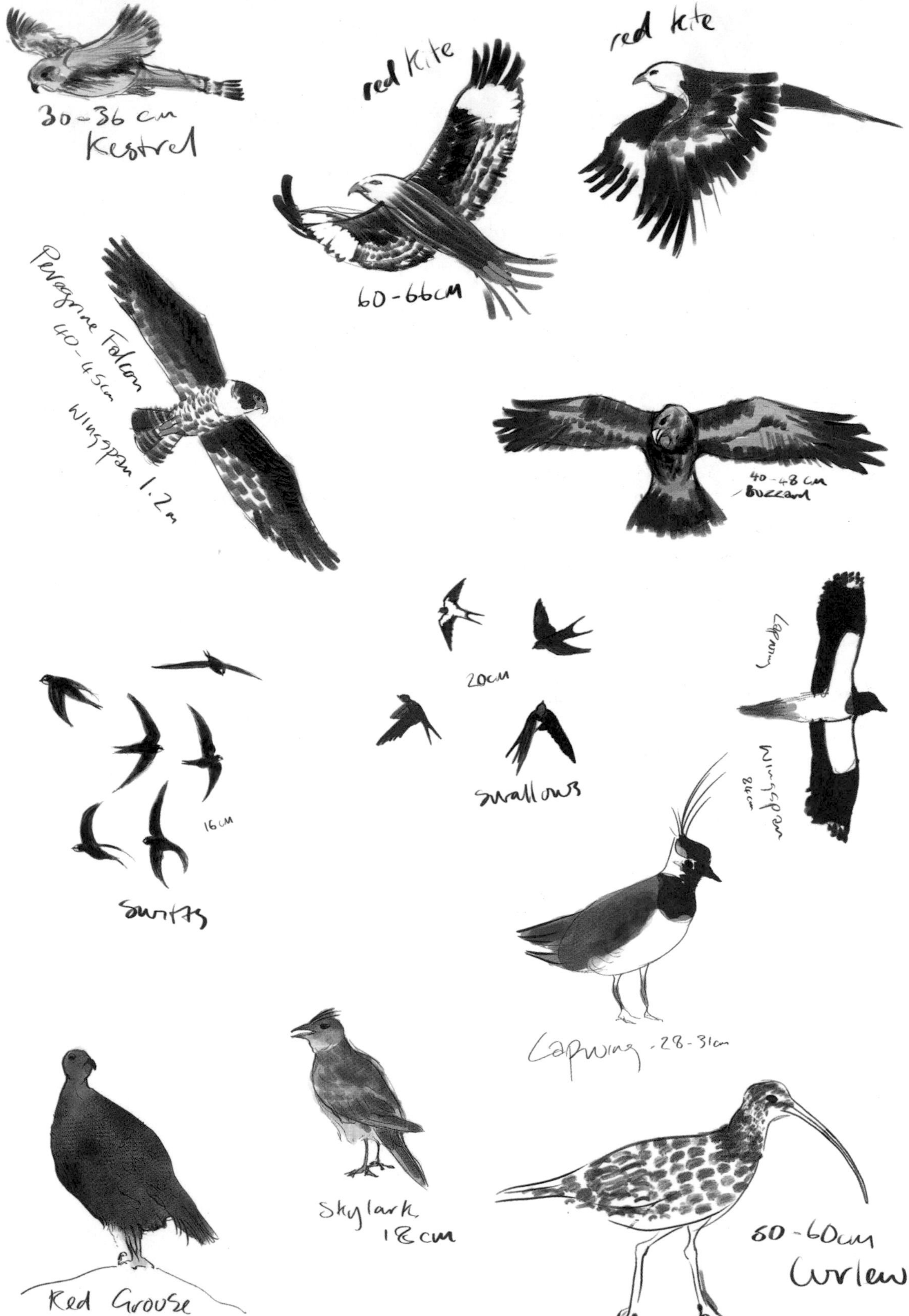

30-36 cm
Kestrel
red kite
red kite
60-66cm
Peregrine Falcon
40-45cm
Wingspan 1.2m
40-48 cm
Buzzard
20cm
Lapwing
Wingspan
84cm
16cm
swallows
Swifts
Lapwing 28-31cm
Skylark
18cm
50-60cm
Curlew
Red Grouse
40-42cm

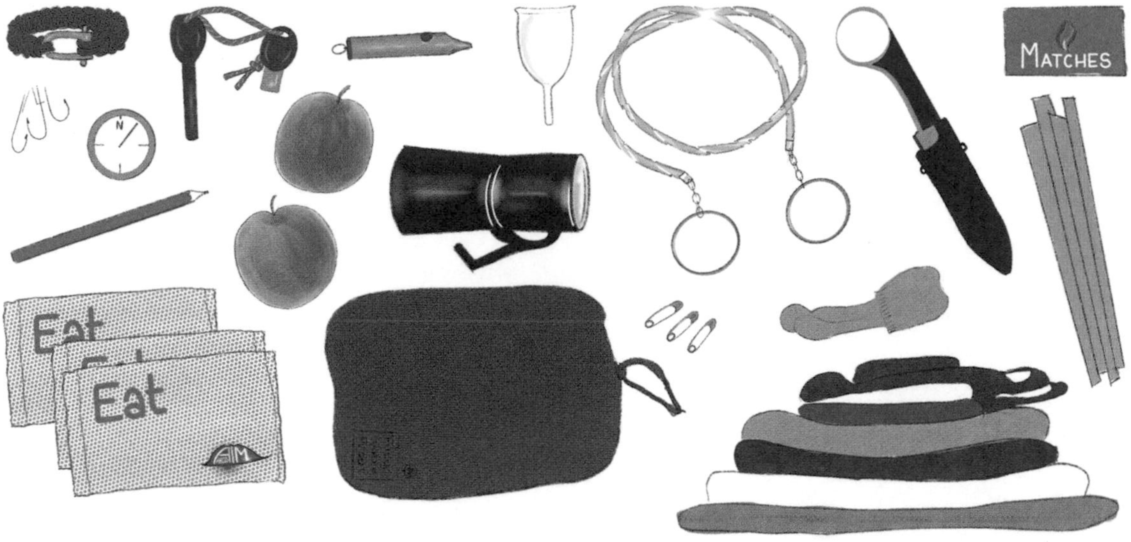
MATCHES
Eat
Eat

EVE

Una

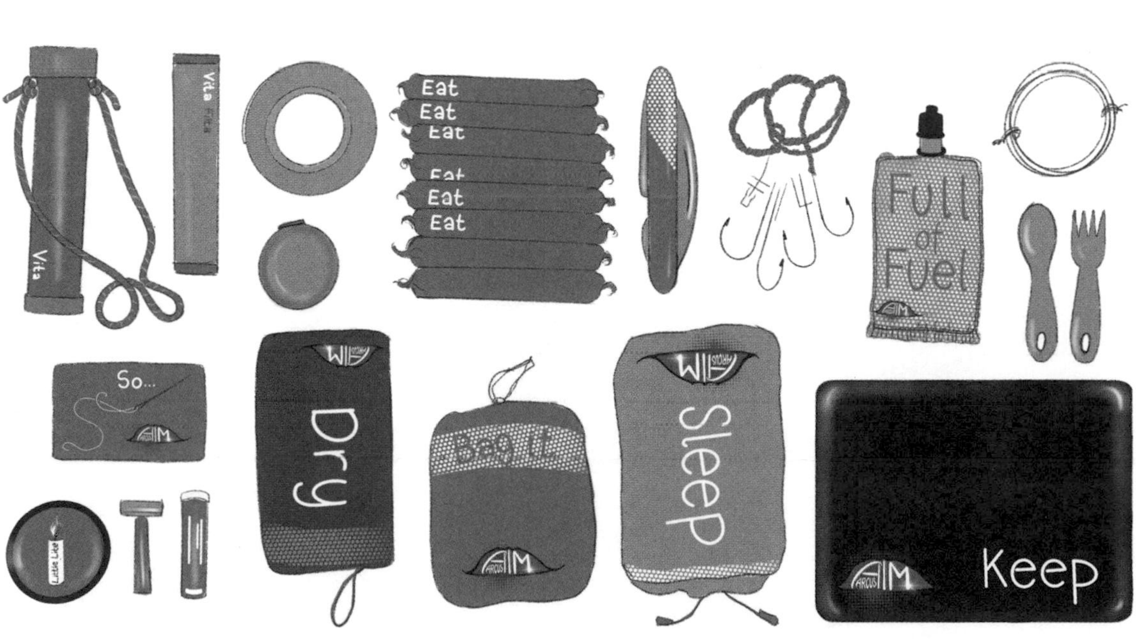
Vita
Vita
Eat
Eat
Eat
Eat
Full of Fuel
So...
Dry
Bag it
Sleep
Keep

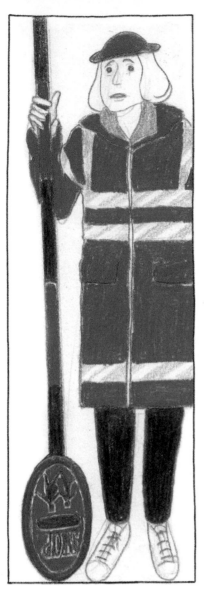

Dedicated to my children,
and all the children.

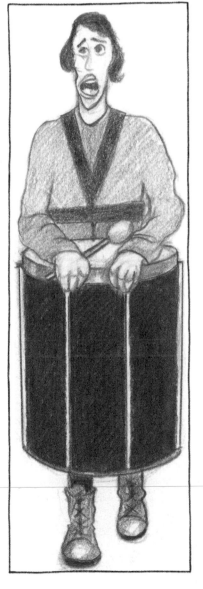

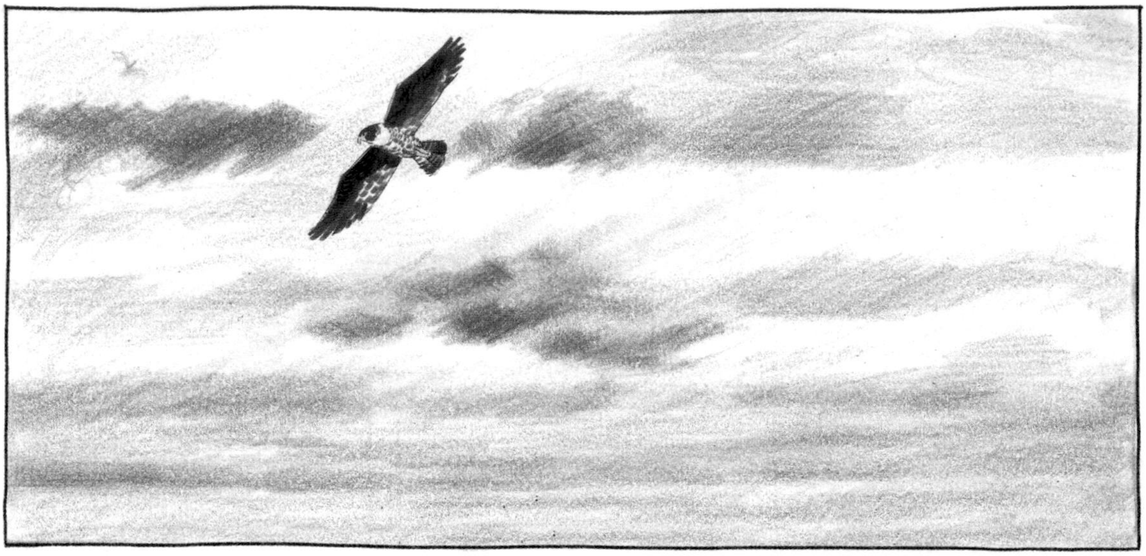

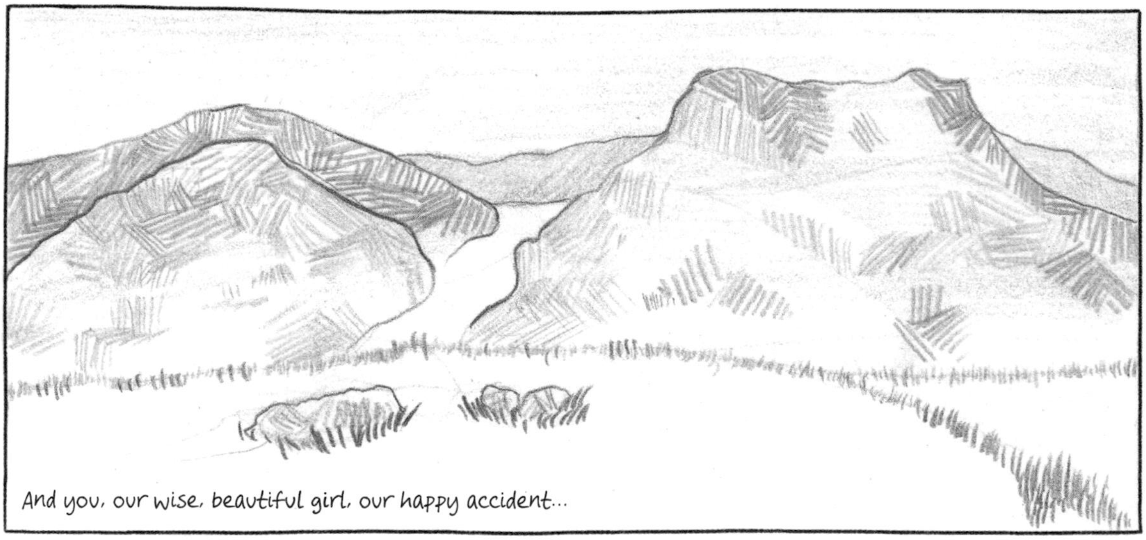
And you, our wise, beautiful girl, our happy accident...

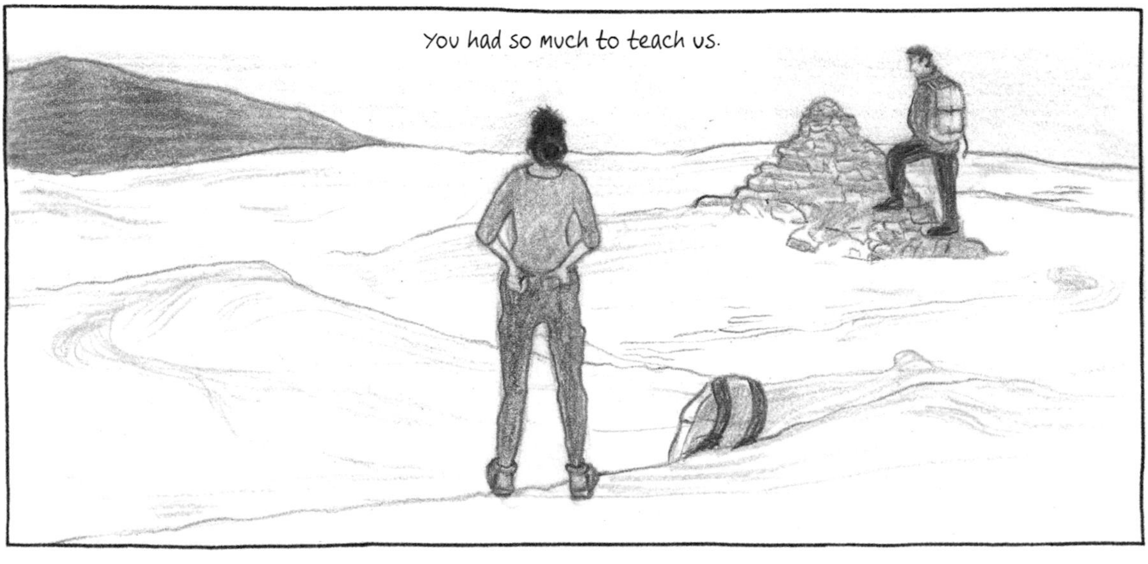
You had so much to teach us.

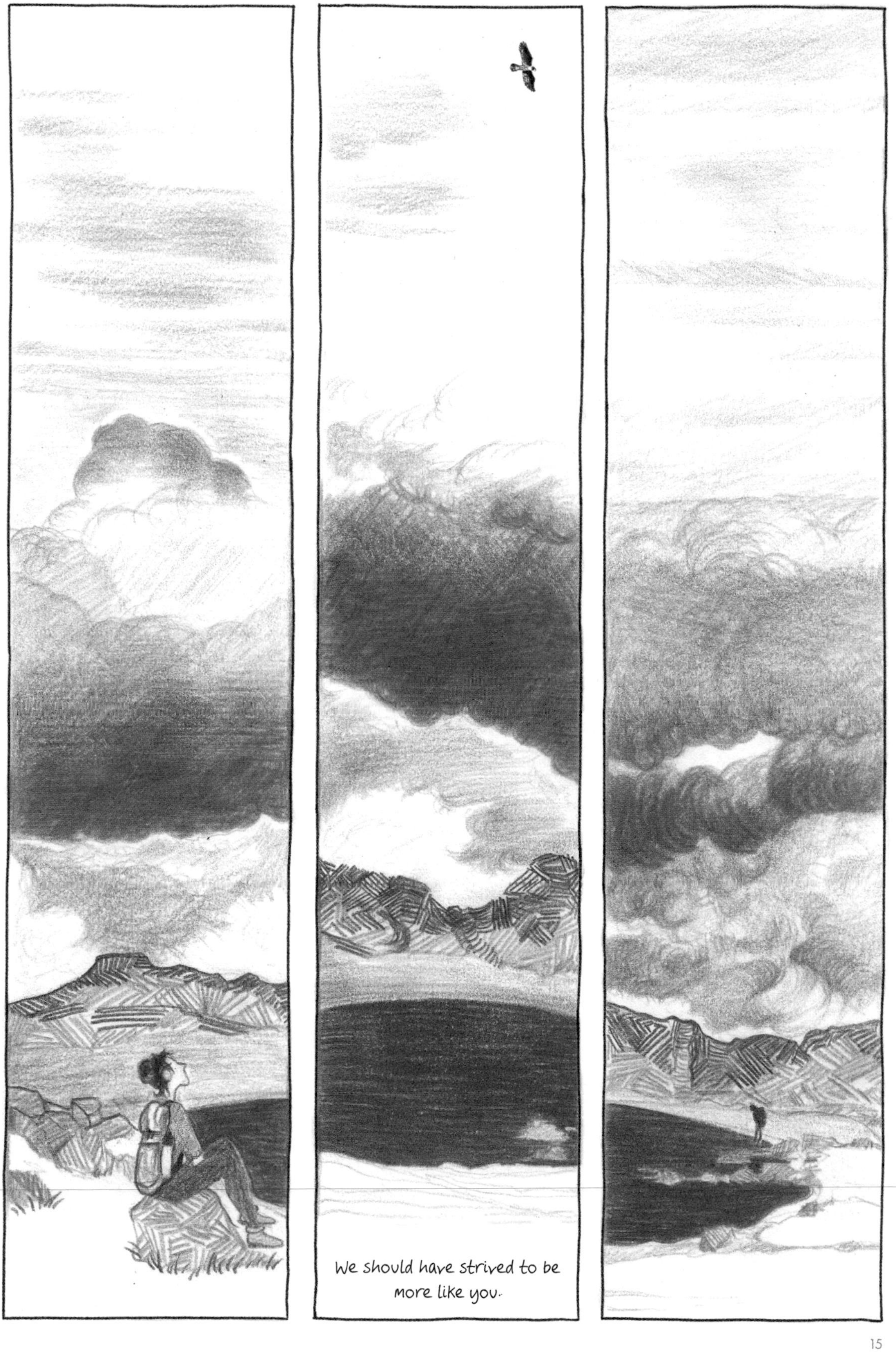
We should have strived to be
more like you.

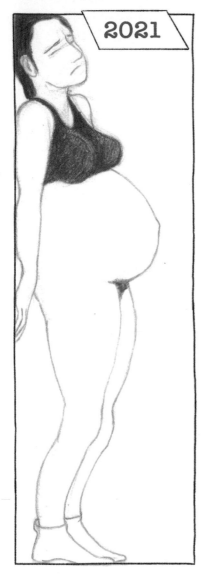

2021

It's funny...

When you've been expecting something dramatic...

But the apocalypse turns out to be...

Ha Hu Huh Ha Hu Hu Huh Hhhhh

More a slow loss of sanity than the single
momentous ruin you've heard so much about...

And you are in the middle of it.

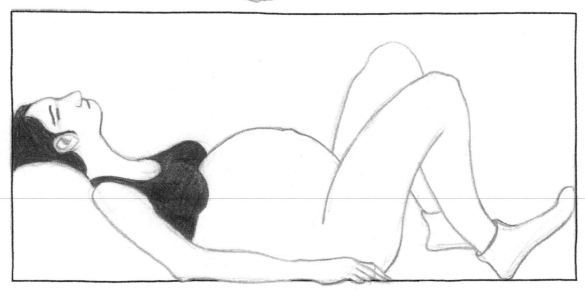

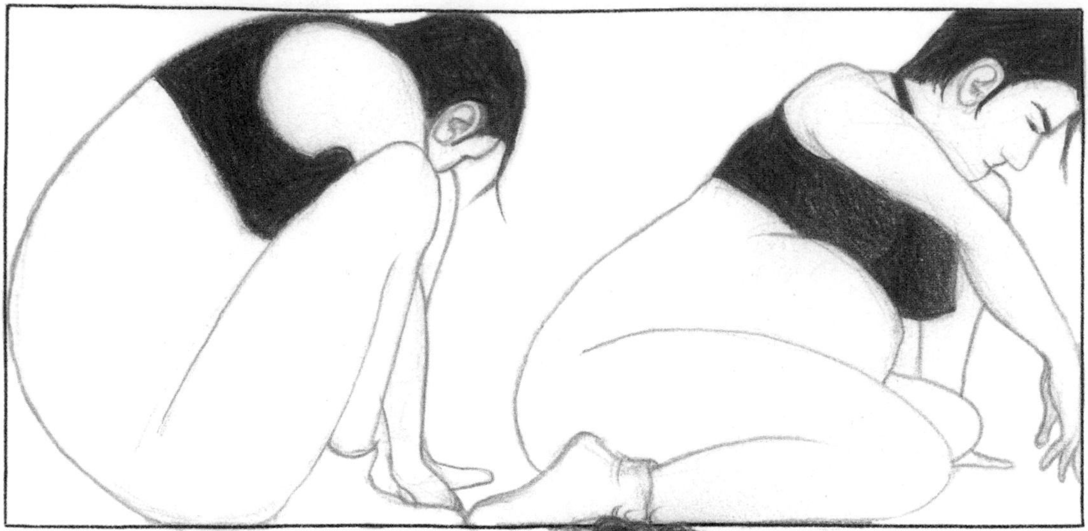

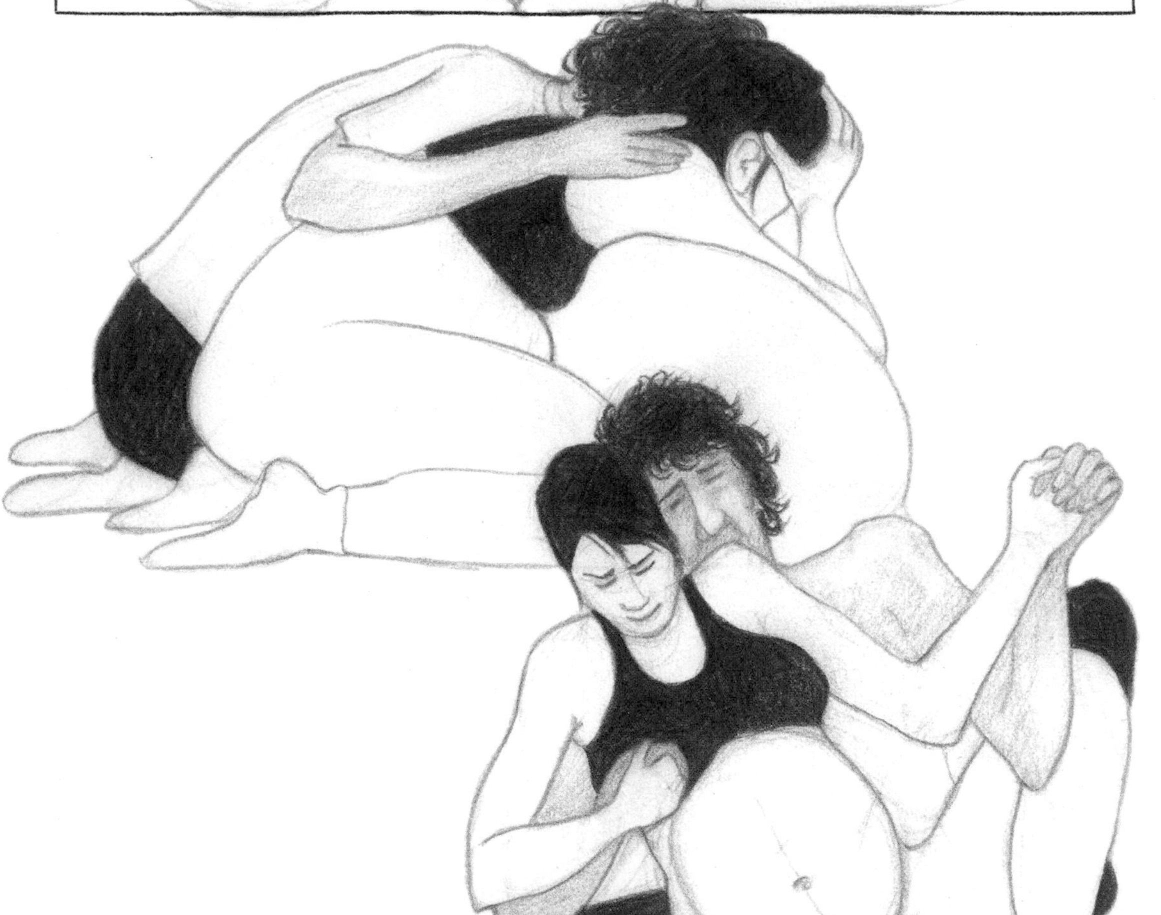

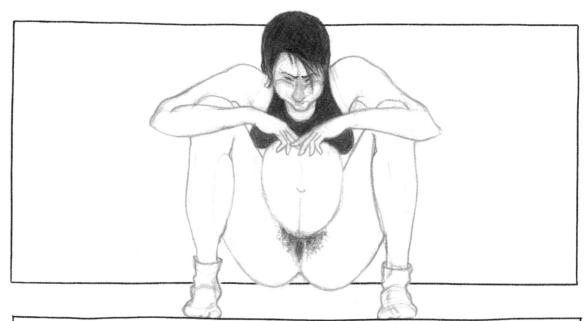

Now the news: Environmentalists *won't* gather in Helsinki next week to discuss increases in extreme weather events. The conference has been postponed due to prioritisation of global economic recovery. Yang Chen, chair of the Intergovernmental Committee for Ecological Alternatives, said a critical opportunity to discuss policy around renewable energy has been lost. Martin Prove, Secretary of State for the Environment, announced he would fight for Britain to play a leading role in any future meetings and he is determined to tackle our national dependence on fossil fuel, but the battle for the economy must come first. He added that thanks to its relatively temperate climate, the British Union is currently in a strong position to compete globally. Environmentalists said that the international committee must act immediately to stem the tide of plastic and carbon emissions killing the planet by putting in place the renewable energy and zero carbon policies agreed at the *last* summit. If they fail, the increase in incidences of extreme weather, wildfires and mass mortality of wildlife will seriously affect the geophysical environment for humans.

In trade news, the Minister for Foreign Affairs said she was hopeful an agreement could be reached for an international trade deal with the new Global Union. One of the final barriers to the deal depends on the International Committee for Cooperative Union Working-Group signing a joint agreement to continue regulatory alignment within a framework of intercontinental boundaries that a newly negotiated working-towards-unity agreement sets out. The ministry is keen to avoid further food shortages. Talks continue.

And today, proving necessity really is the mother of invention, a home-made fire storm shelter won the prestigious International Design Impact prize. The designer, Bob Harrison, patented his idea after wildfire tore through his home in Australia. Mr Harrison survived the fire in an improvised shelter in his back yard. His company began manufacturing the shelter, which he describes as a 'coffin-sized home-made kiln', for international use this year. Nicknamed the Esky, it will be manufactured as a self-build kit for ease of distribution. Made of ceramic fibre, the Esky can withstand temperatures of 1,500 degrees Celsius. Past winners of the prize include the popular, washable anti-virus hood 'Rona', the personal water filter 'Life Straw', designed to be worn around the neck, and a flat-packed flood barrier called the Kanoot. Last year's winner, the Warka Water tower, brings water to desert areas using condensation created by a small tree.

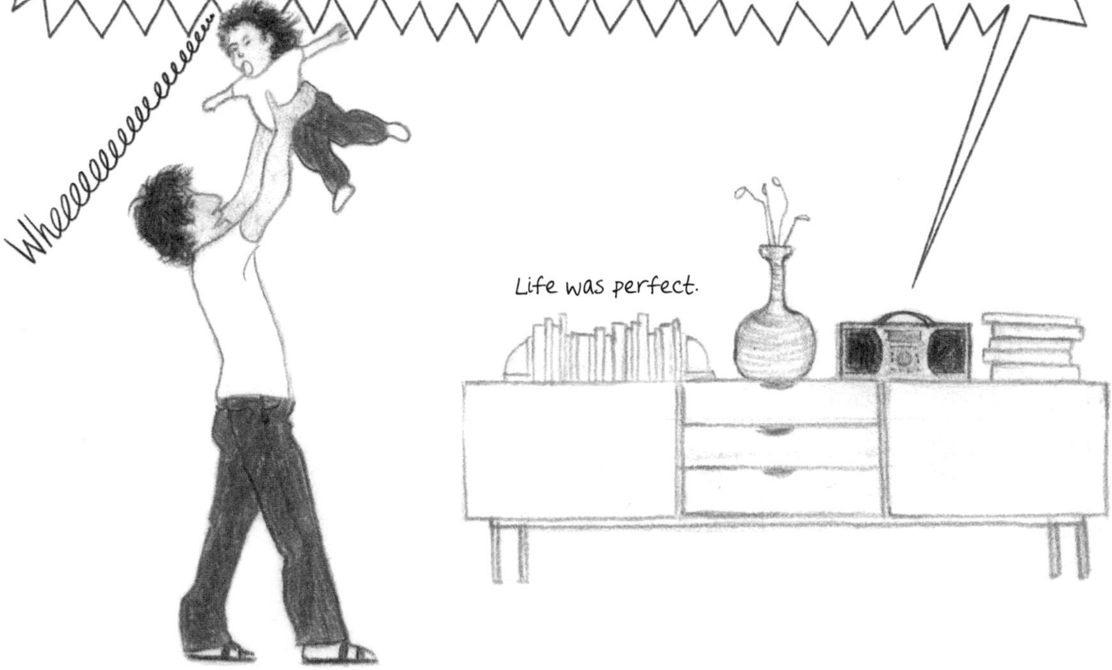

Wheeeeeeeeeeeeeeeeeeeeeeeeee
Life was perfect.

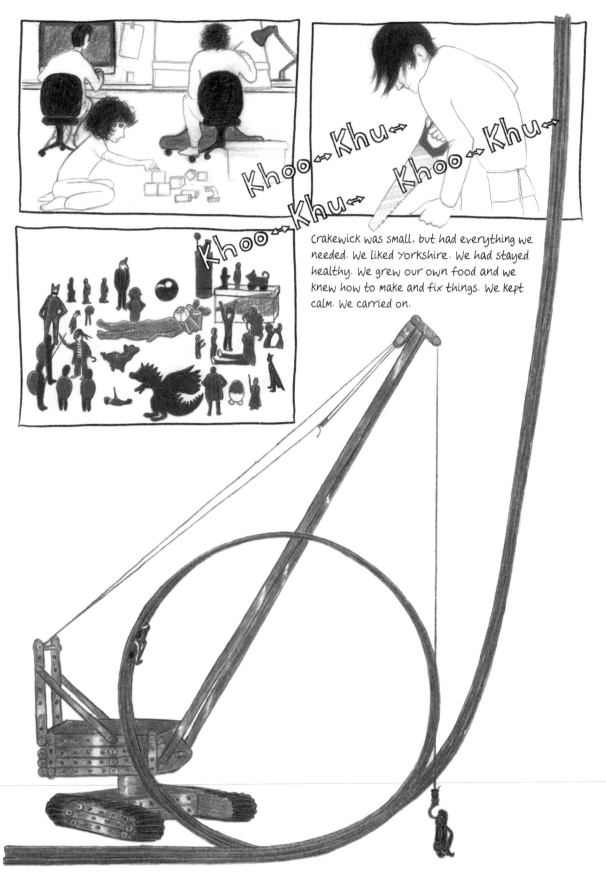

Khoo↔Khu↔ Khoo↔Khu↔ Khoo↔Khu↔ Khoo↔Khu↔

Crakewick was small, but had everything we needed. We liked Yorkshire. We had stayed healthy. We grew our own food and we knew how to make and fix things. We kept calm. We carried on.

I know it's years away, but have you thought about where Eve will go to uni? I'm saving, but I'll never be able to afford for Si to live away.

Blimey Bren, let him live a little! I don't care where or if she goes. It's a corporate racket these days. Students are rent and fees.

Gotta be her choice, D.

I hope so.

But what about the work situation, Bren? Will you keep your job?

They say we're the laziest workers in the world but I can't work any harder. I'm exhausted!

It's impossible to do a job properly in these conditions. I used to be so efficient!

Efficiency, ha! That's a racket as well. Don't be a fool!

Oh, he's off on a rant now...

I'm very good at my job!

How would you know? Most people are blind to the *futility* of their work due to the incessant cascade of *bullshit* pouring from the arse of late capitalism.

Work is never futile. It's important for all sorts of reasons. Mainly we have to stand on our own two feet...

If you ask me it's a waste of time, all of it.

I reckon they should bring back national service, but instead of soldiers, they go to art school.

Or agricultural college.

It's harder to learn to design and make things than fight, kill, destroy... plus everything should be workers' co-ops. Everything!

...

I'm sure you're right.

But it's getting late, we should get off home.

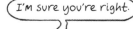

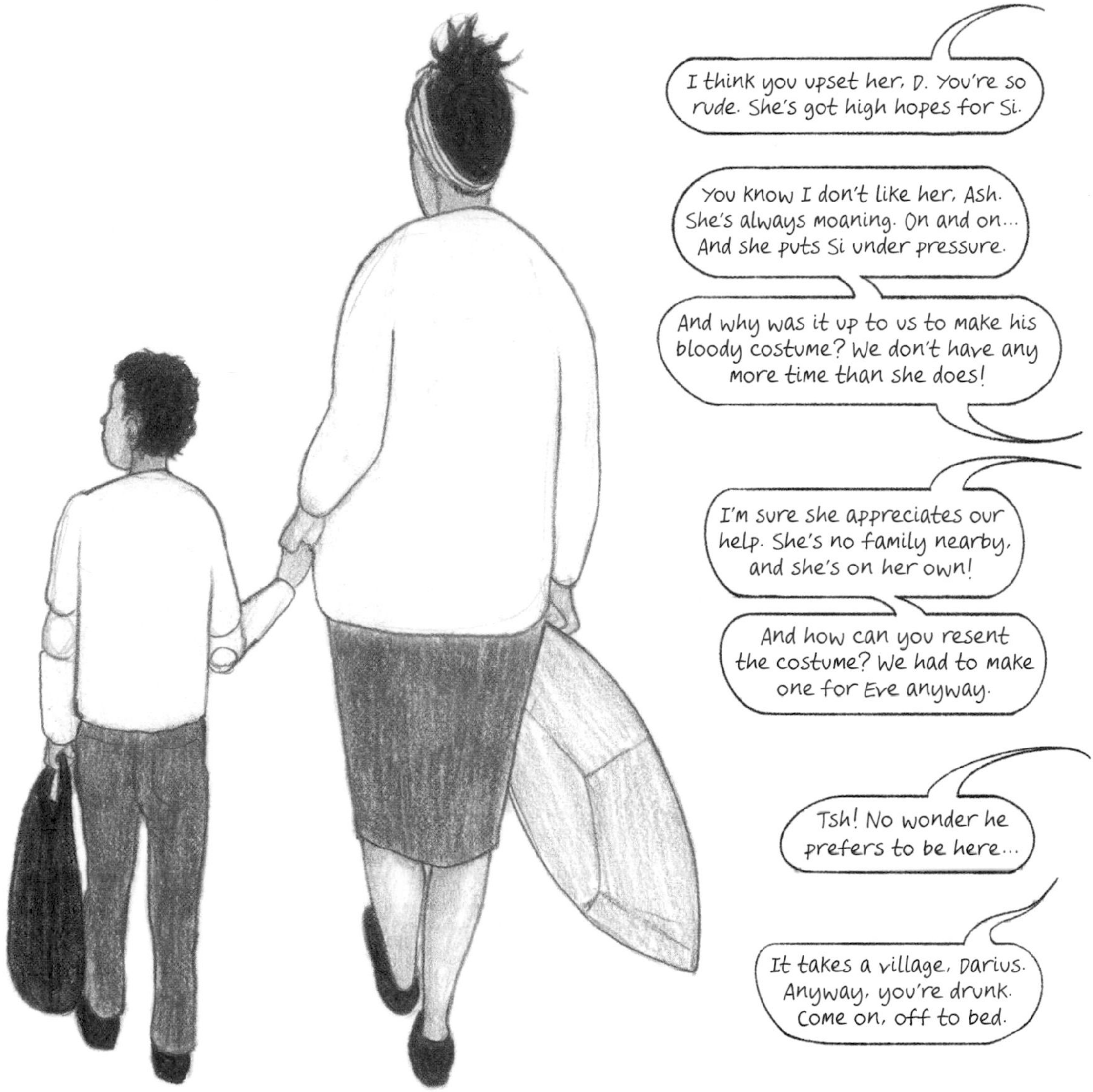

I think you upset her, D. You're so rude. She's got high hopes for Si.
You know I don't like her, Ash. She's always moaning. On and on... And she puts Si under pressure.
And why was it up to us to make his bloody costume? We don't have any more time than she does!
I'm sure she appreciates our help. She's no family nearby, and she's on her own!
And how can you resent the costume? We had to make one for Eve anyway.
Tsh! No wonder he prefers to be here...
It takes a village, Darius. Anyway, you're drunk. Come on, off to bed.

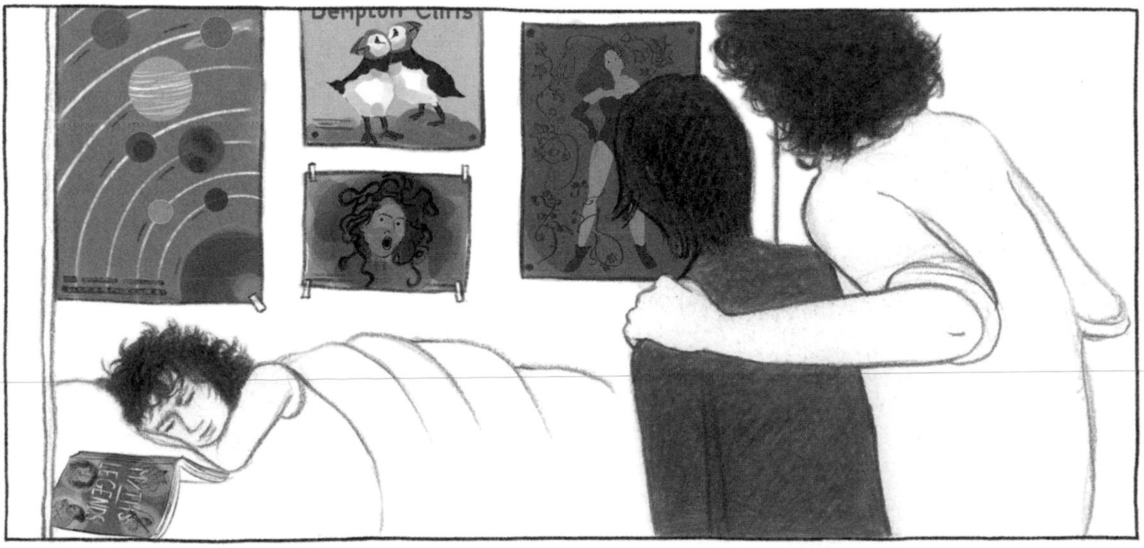

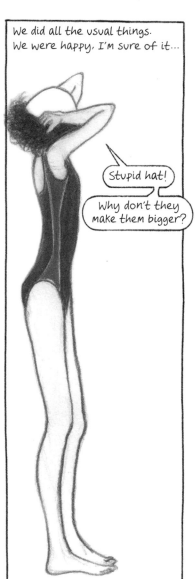

We did all the usual things. We were happy, I'm sure of it...

Stupid hat!

Why don't they make them bigger?

Do you want a hand, Eve?

I'll pull it down, you shove your hair in. Teamwork!

Fhoo Fhoo Fhoo haAa Shhhh Shhhh Shhhh
Wuu Kick, kick, kick, kick
That's great, well done.
Keep your body up in the water!

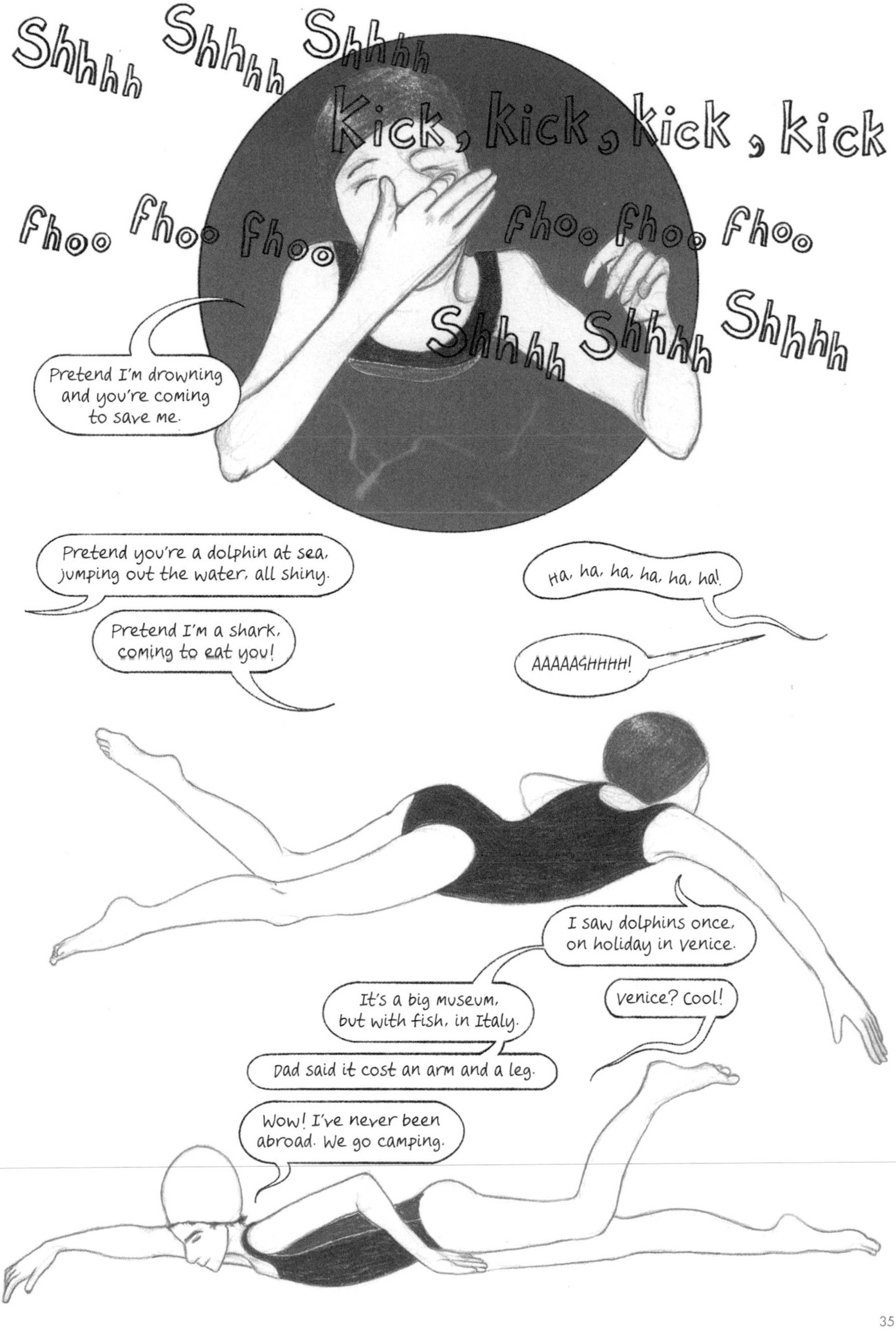
Shhhh Shhhh Shhhh
Kick, kick, kick, kick
fhoo fhoo fhoo fhoo fhoo fhoo
Shhhh Shhhh Shhhh
Pretend I'm drowning and you're coming to save me.
Pretend you're a dolphin at sea, jumping out the water, all shiny.
Ha, ha, ha, ha, ha, ha!
Pretend I'm a shark, coming to eat you!
AAAAAGHHHH!
I saw dolphins once, on holiday in venice.
It's a big museum, but with fish, in Italy.
venice? Cool!
Dad said it cost an arm and a leg.
Wow! I've never been abroad. We go camping.

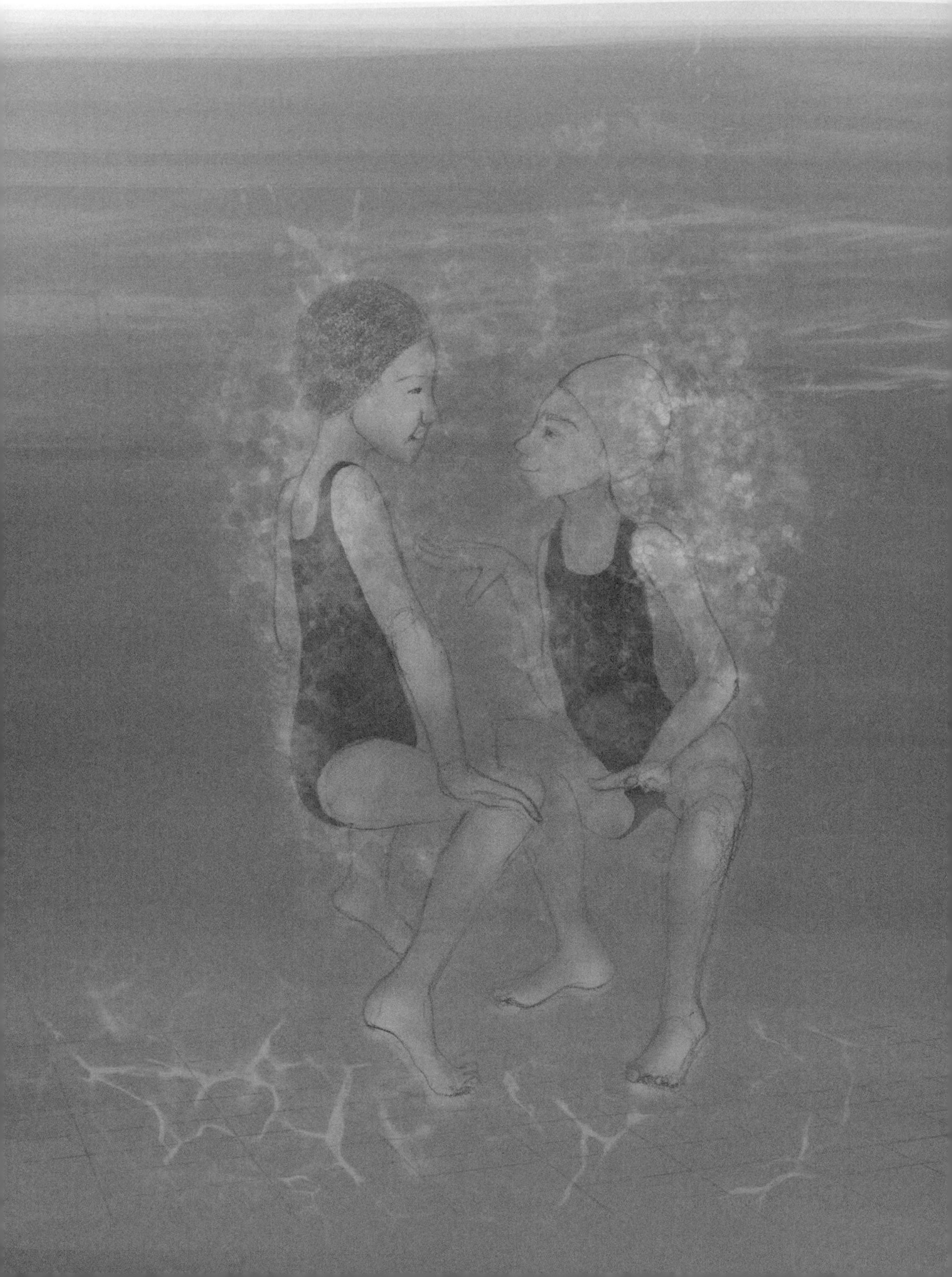

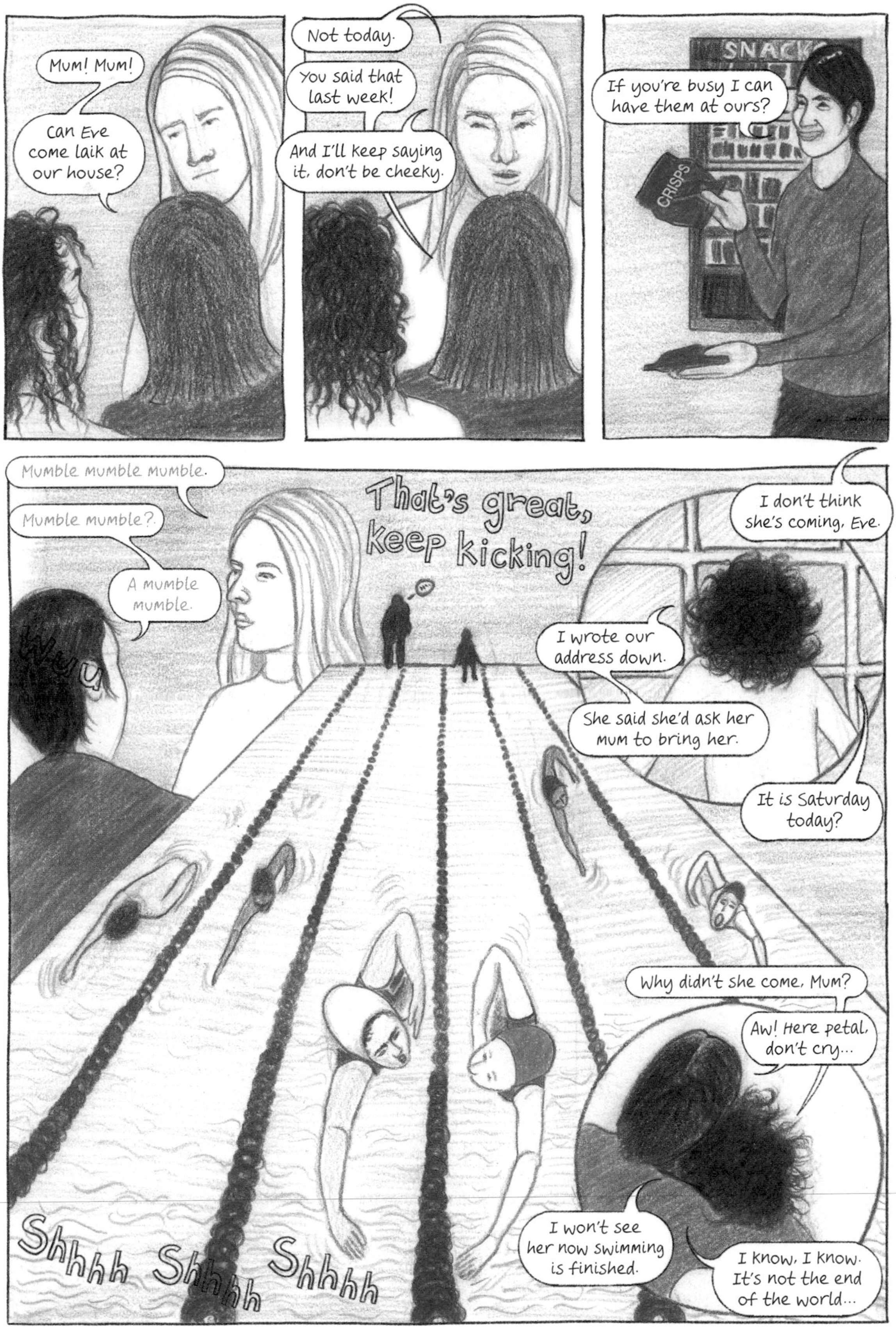
Mum! Mum!
Can Eve come laik at our house?
Not today.
You said that last week!
And I'll keep saying it, don't be cheeky.
SNACKS
CRISPS
If you're busy I can have them at ours?
Mumble mumble mumble.
Mumble mumble?.
A mumble mumble.
That's great, Keep kicking!
I don't think she's coming, Eve.
I wrote our address down.
She said she'd ask her mum to bring her.
It is Saturday today?
Why didn't she come, Mum?
Aw! Here petal, don't cry...
I won't see her now swimming is finished.
I know, I know. It's not the end of the world...
Shhhh Shhhh Shhhh

Saturday

Ruby didn't come today I waited for ages. It is raining again !
I feel sad

Tuesday

School was borin !! Stupid Leon smells like biscuits said I could
never be famous becuase who wants to look at hair like pyoobs
as if i even wanted to be famous!! Anyway He is ugly and i hate
him I have got homework for maths and english Fish pie for tea.

Monday

Mum made ice-cream, its been too hot!!! I want to go back to
swimming so I can see Ruby but mum says it finished now and we
dont know where they live. if we drive round in Haigh maybe wed
see them? Mum says Ill make new friends but i don't want new
freinds i want ruby. dhal for tea again.

MOnday

Im suposed to write this diary to improve writing but i keep
forgetin to do it. Not much goin on jus school I hate school all
about grate days of empire on and on. Chips from the chip shop
for tea cos mum and dad have got a big prodject on i like
chips from the chipshop

Sunday

Me and Dad went picking elderflowers We will make corjal later. cant go to the beach cos of flodding so we slept out last night at the Tarn looking at the Stars. i lit the Fire. We had baked taties

Wenesday

Sigh came to ours after school today he has to come every day til the hollidays. He is okay I supose but some times I wonder what ruby is doing. I wonder if she still goes to the swimming bafs? I asked mum if we can go but she says we have to do free swiming now. Ruby is funny and cool and her hair is amazing. red. Rabbit and chips for tea again Sigh wil have to get used to it. ha ha

Saturday

Went for a walk, me and sigh ran all the way up white fell and I was fastest! Mum and Dad were well inpressed. There was a ice cream van at the top I wonder how it got up there? Came back by the ridge and mum slipped and hurt her ankle and her arm Dad said she was lucky not to slide all the way to the bottom and be killed. She is feeling a bit beter now. I made her a cup of tea. One more week then no more school.

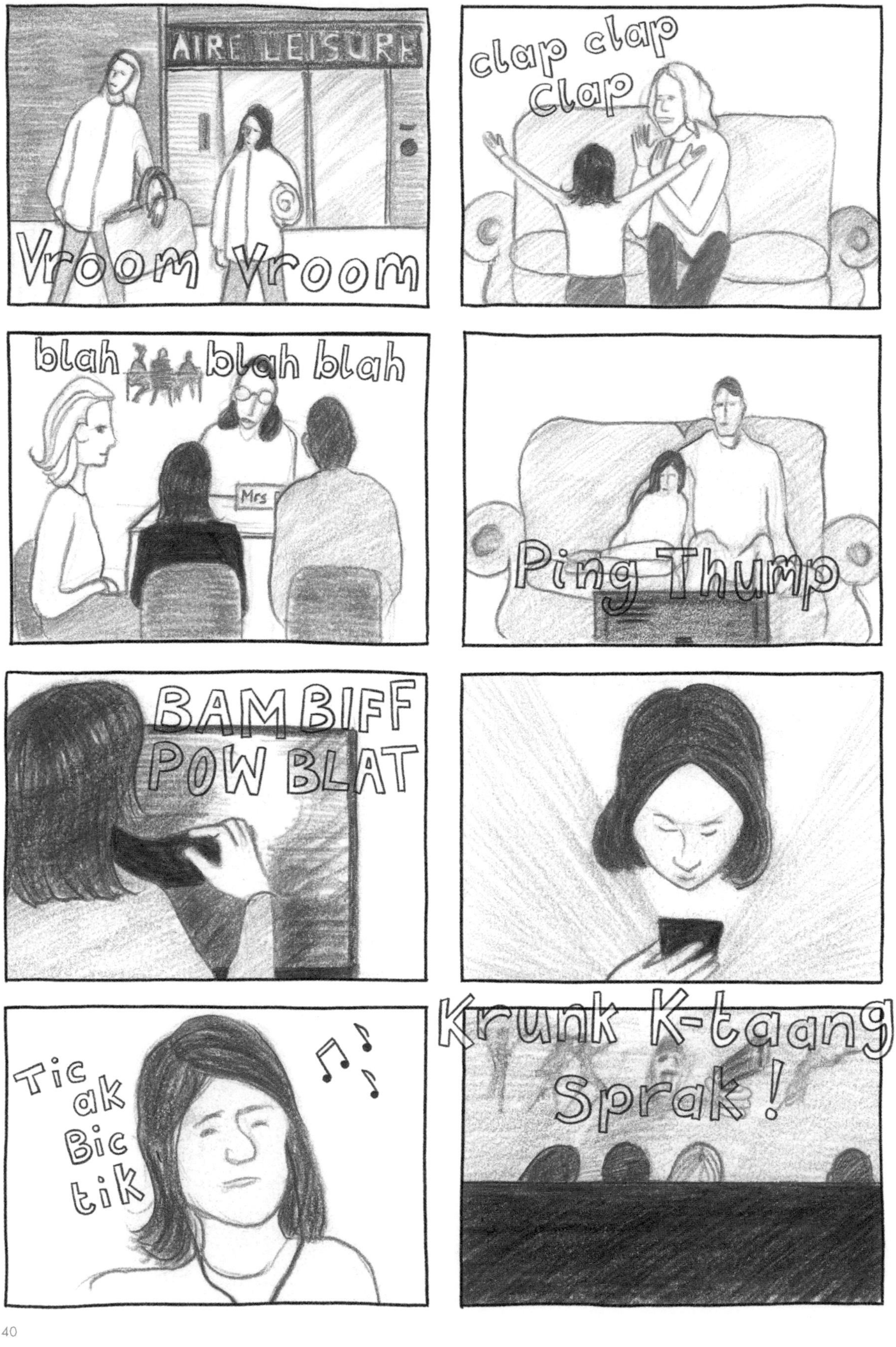
AIRE LEISURE
Vroom Vroom
clap clap
Clap
blah blah blah
Mrs
Ping Thump
BAM BIFF
POW BLAT
Tic
ak
Bic
tik
Krunk K-taang
Sprak!

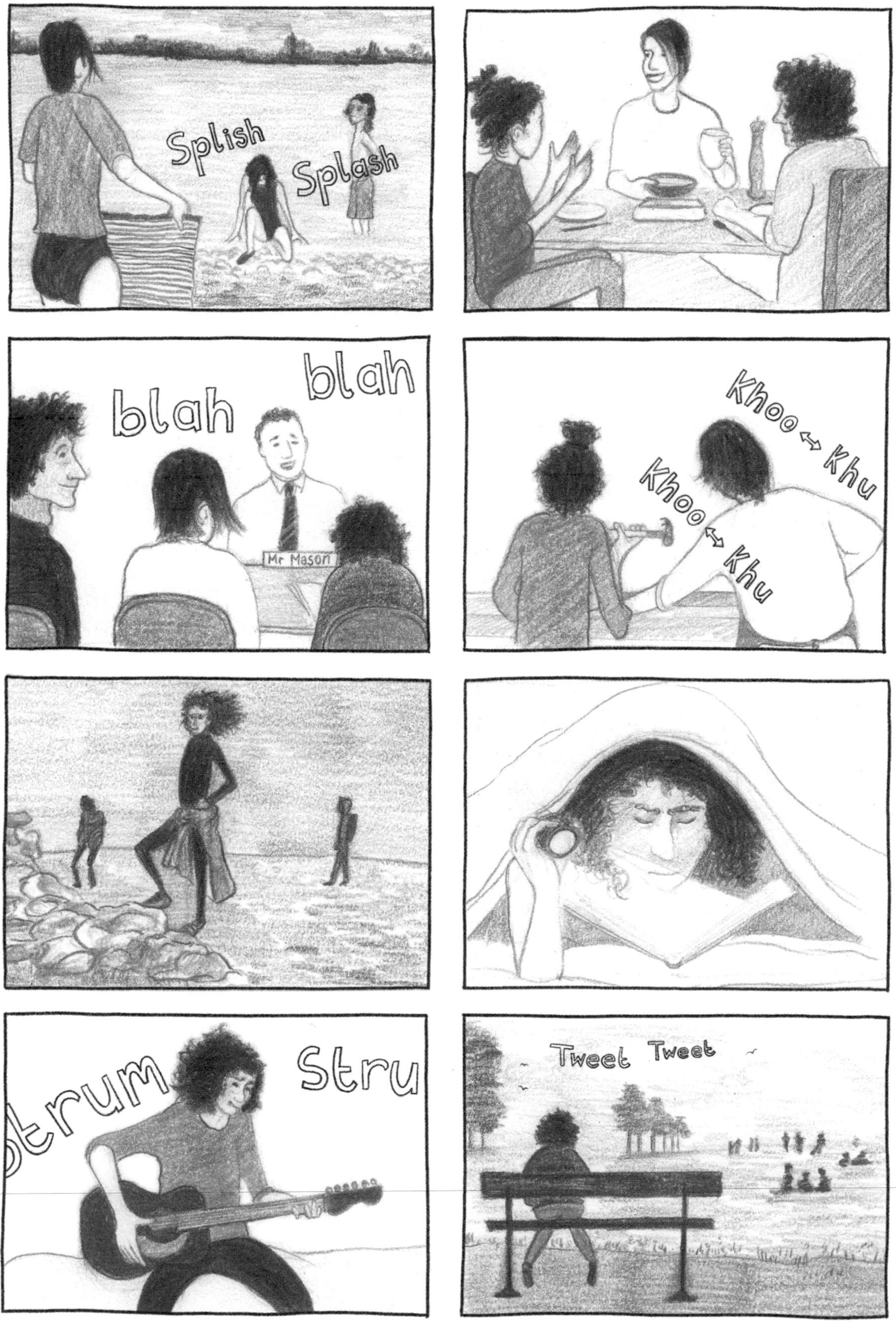
Splish
Splash
blah
blah
Mr Mason
Khoo ↔ Khu
Khoo ↔ Khu
trum
Stru
Tweet Tweet

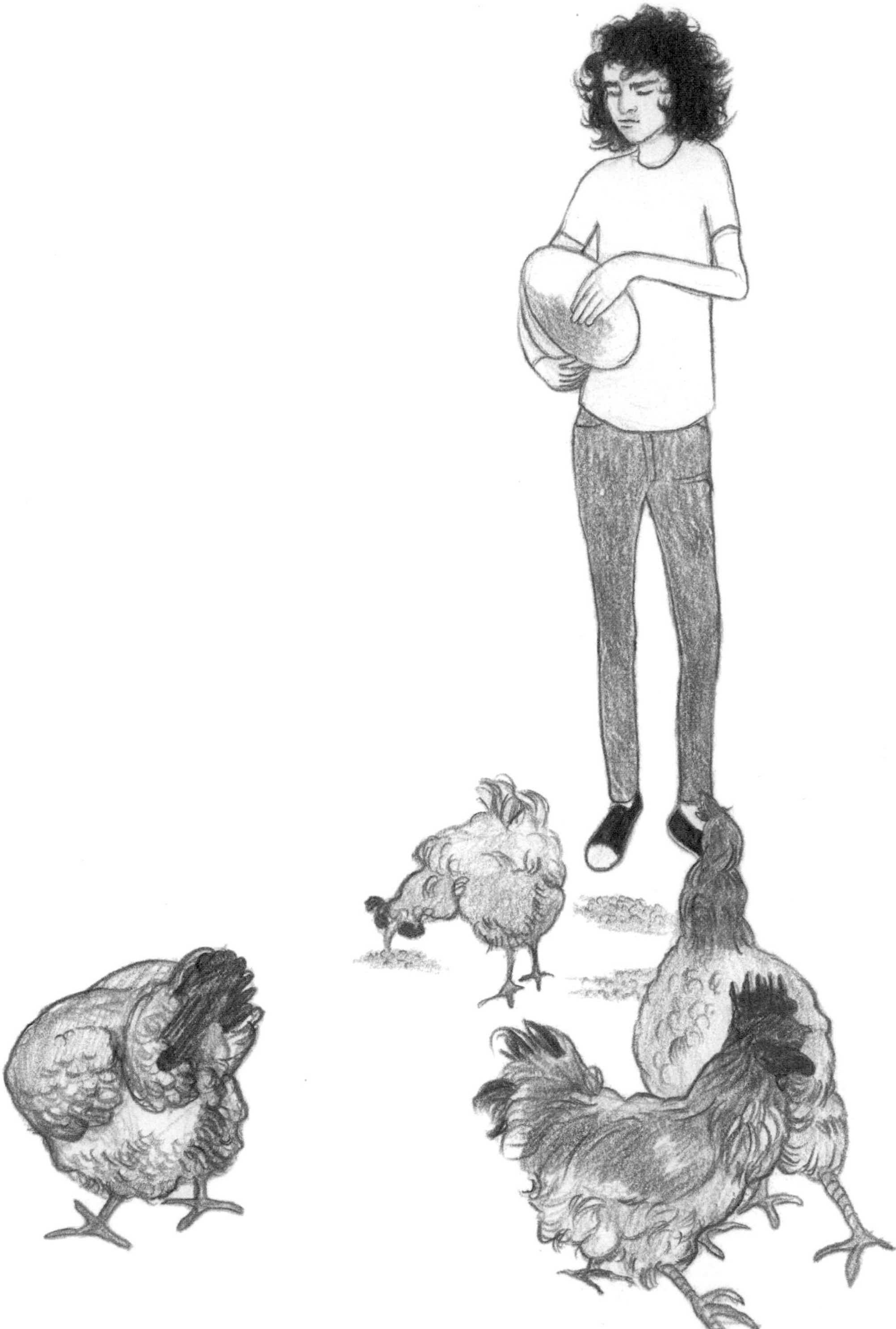

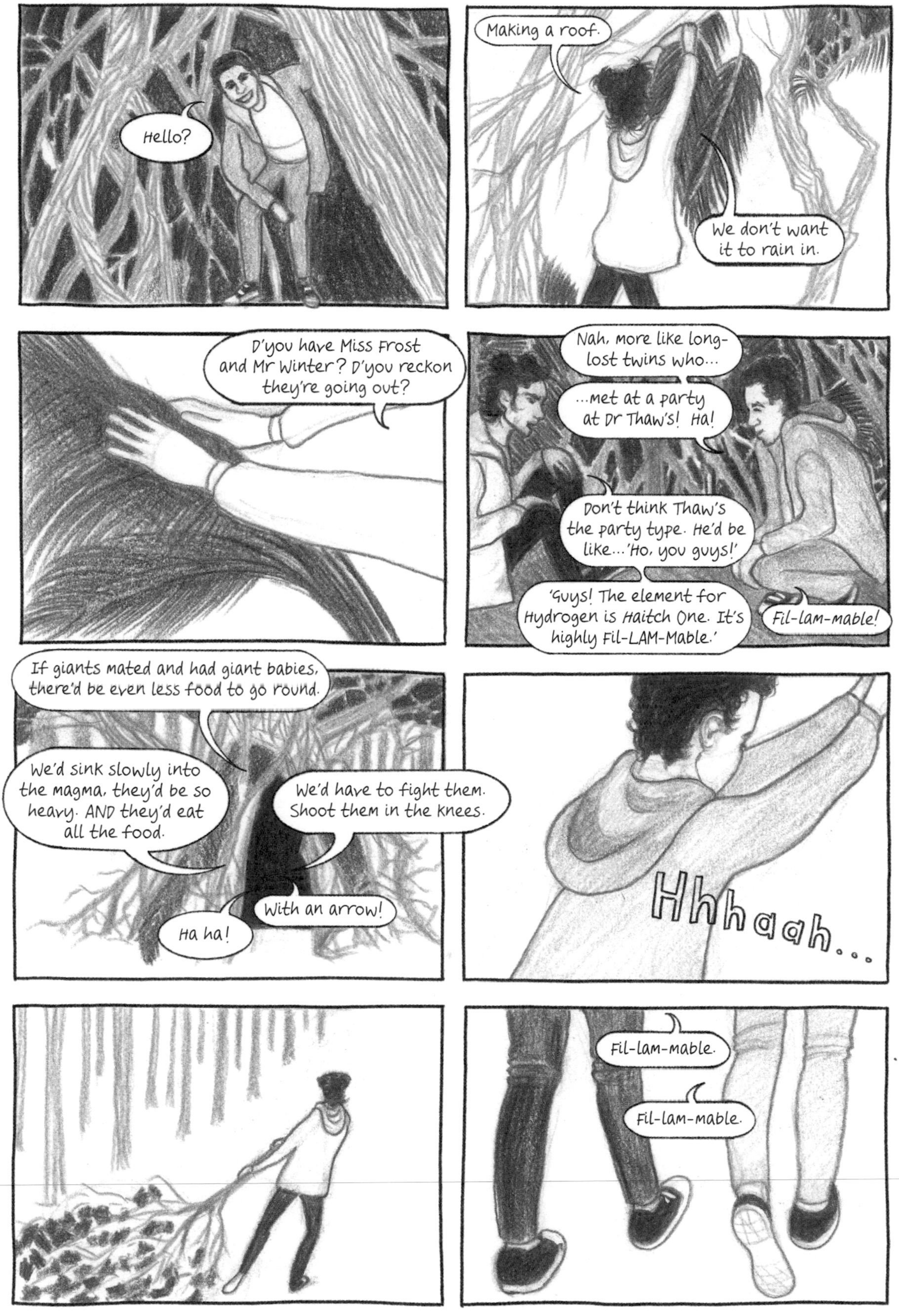
Hello?
Making a roof.
We don't want it to rain in.
D'you have Miss Frost and Mr Winter? D'you reckon they're going out?
Nah, more like long-lost twins who...
...met at a party at Dr Thaw's! Ha!
Don't think Thaw's the party type. He'd be like...'Ho, you guys!'
'Guys! The element for Hydrogen is Haitch One. It's highly Fil-LAM-Mable.'
Fil-lam-mable!
If giants mated and had giant babies, there'd be even less food to go round.
We'd sink slowly into the magma, they'd be so heavy. AND they'd eat all the food.
We'd have to fight them. Shoot them in the knees.
With an arrow!
Ha ha!
Hhhaah...
Fil-lam-mable.
Fil-lam-mable.

Thursday

High school is not as bad as i thoght but noisy. sigh is not in my class now cos he is upper maths. My form is 7TF. My form teacher is Ms Frost. No homework yet. Two weeks down 271 to go I worked it out on my scientific calculator.

Friday

me and sigh are allowed in the woods by oursleves now so we are building a den to hide there forever no school then. Only joking! I like miss frost she is nice she is pretty I like Mr winter too He teaches biology I like biology so far but was hoping chemistry would be more interesting. I like art english music drama is good Maths is ok lunch is horrible We have to queve for ages and everbod pushes Year 7 have our own area outside but it is all idiots. Next week in English we will get a offisial reading list. Dad says its nonsens and i can read what i like. theres a club after school on Mondays and wendesday called The Aim I might try it Sigh is going. Curry for tea

Monday

homework! english punctuation Miss Frost says my writing is terrible considring how much i read. She says i am in too much of a hurry and never put any capitals or commas or apostophe or full stops.

Tuesday

Girls in my form are stupid actualy, I hate them. Homework is write a newspaper article about the British character. Off camping at the weekend and ~~M~~Mum has signed me up for Junior Fell Running, so that will be good for me I think.

Thursday

There is a girl with red hair in my class, but she is not Ruby. I keep looking for her because she should come to our school, but she's not. I miss her so much. Why? Must be ages sinse I seen her. Turns out Ms Frost is head of English. She said my punctuation and capitals are getting beter.

Sunday

pancakes for breakfats with strawberries i had to pick them going to woods later with sigh

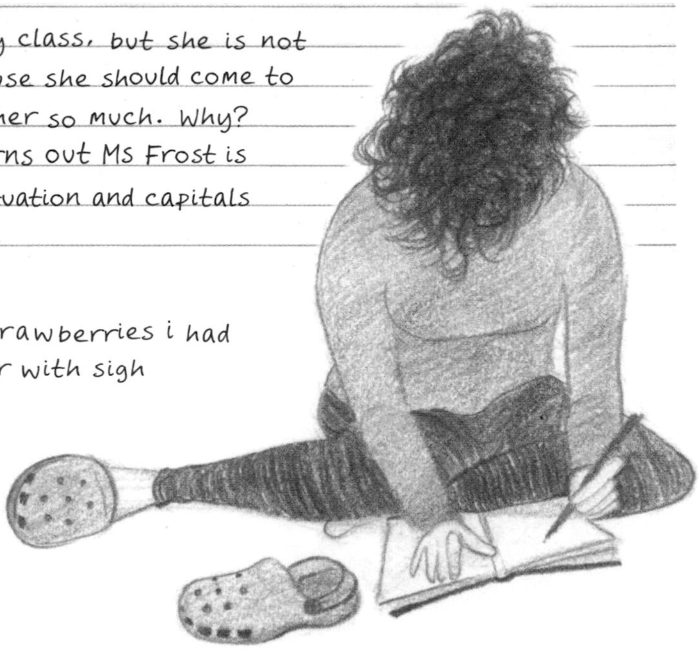

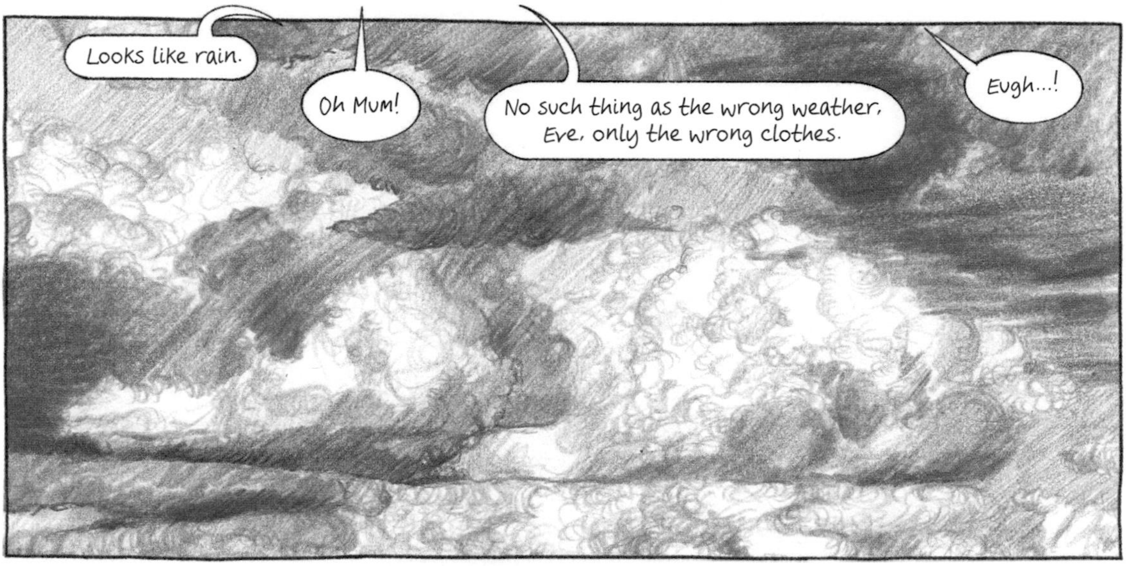
Looks like rain.
Oh Mum!
No such thing as the wrong weather, Eve, only the wrong clothes.
Eugh...!

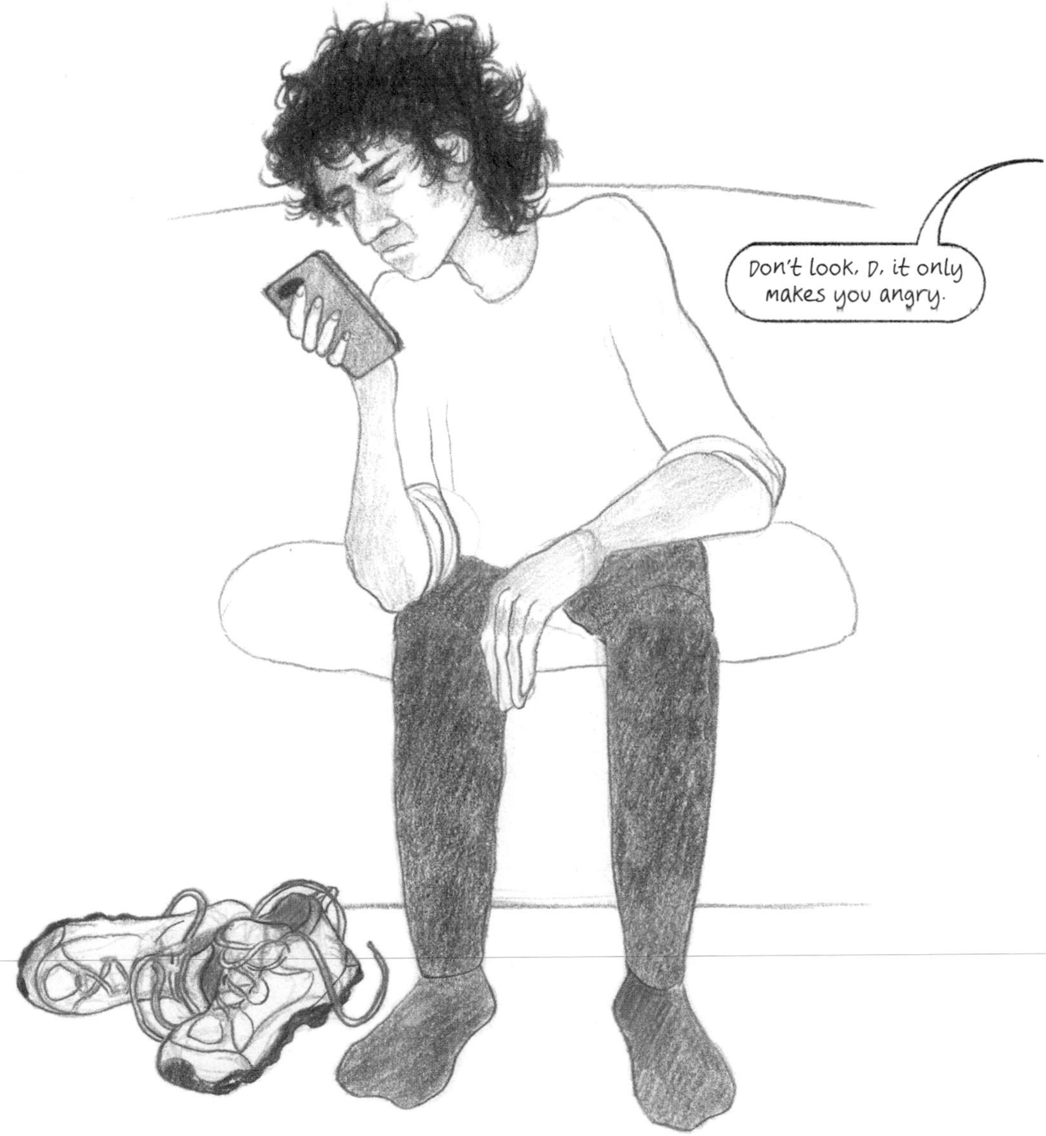
Don't look, D, it only makes you angry.

Swift, Apus apus, endangered.

Swifts spend most of their time in Africa. They need warm weather for a constant supply of flying insects and gather in large numbers to feed. Swifts used to migrate to northern Europe but stormy conditions and a lack of nesting places has led to a decline. They are remarkably fast, agile fliers. Only a diving Peregrine Falcon is faster. Swifts can cling to an upright surface like a cliff or castle wall but can't walk or perch like swallows. They are always in the air except when they nest. Swifts pair for life, meeting up each spring to build nests in cavities in buildings. Young swifts flying around buildings are checking out nooks and crannies for future use as nesting sites. They stop flying to breed, taking an equal share of the nesting duties, but eat, drink, mate and sleep in flight, resting at 10,000ft while gliding at 130 mph. Young swifts leave the nest by standing on the tips of their tiny feet, rowing their wings then pushing into the air to fall, gaining speed as they tumble. They open their wings and fly for the next four years. The swift's body is made to fly; it can't take off from the ground so if grounded, it can never be airborne again.

There you go, Evie, that's interesting, isn't it?

Mhmm...

So beautiful that she lives her whole life soaring through the sky. But so sad, that if she lands, she can never fly again.

If you'd a phone of your own you could look up all sorts of interesting things. We can afford a cheap one, like mine. It's OK!

I'm looking up right now. At all sorts of interesting things. In the sky, Dad.

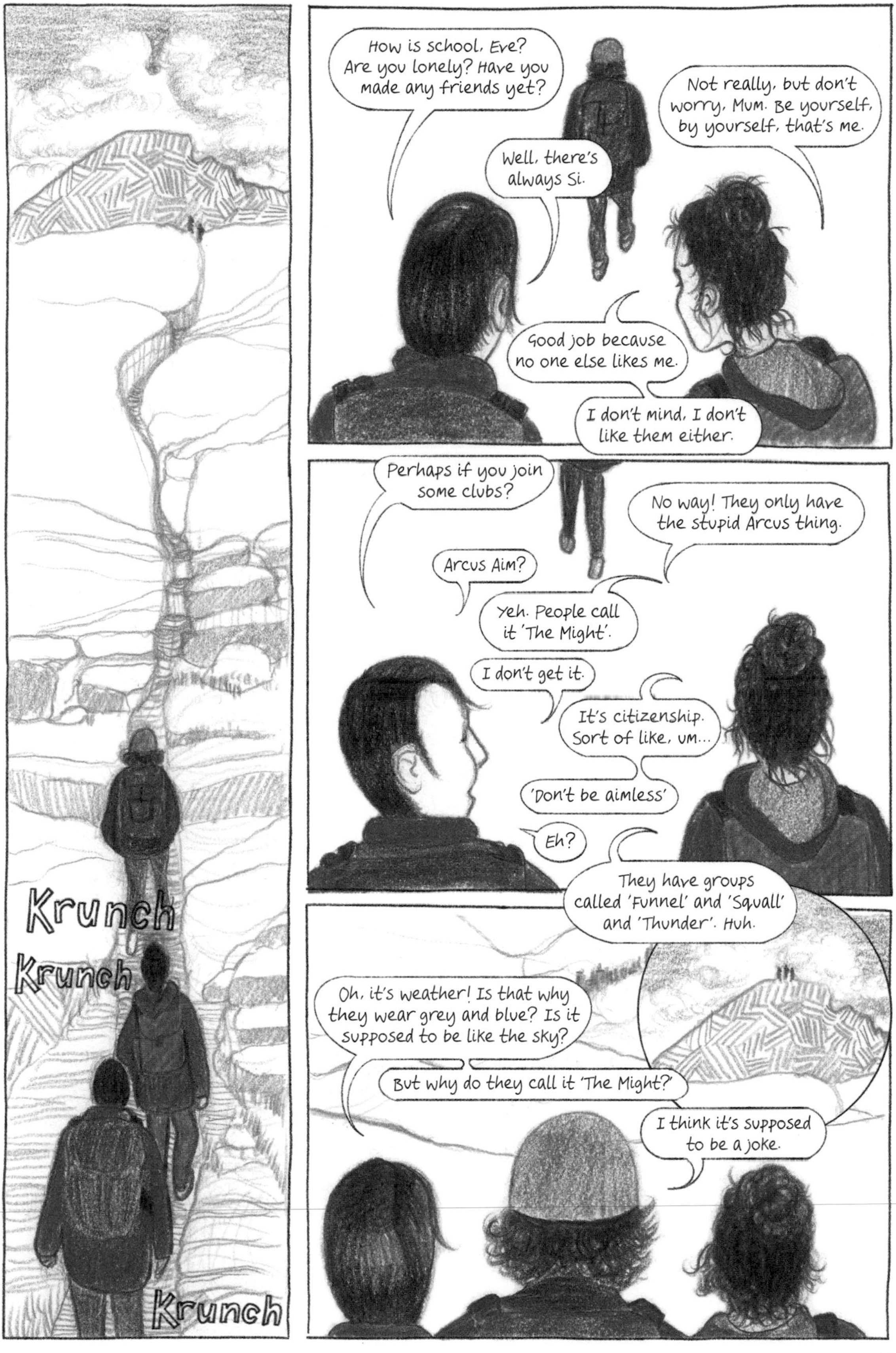
Krunch
Krunch
Krunch
How is school, Eve? Are you lonely? Have you made any friends yet?
Not really, but don't worry, Mum. Be yourself, by yourself, that's me.
Well, there's always Si.
Good job because no one else likes me.
I don't mind, I don't like them either.
Perhaps if you join some clubs?
No way! They only have the stupid Arcus thing.
Arcus Aim?
Yeh. People call it 'The Might'.
I don't get it.
It's citizenship. Sort of like, um...
'Don't be aimless'
Eh?
They have groups called 'Funnel' and 'Squall' and 'Thunder'. Huh.
Oh, it's weather! Is that why they wear grey and blue? Is it supposed to be like the sky?
But why do they call it 'The Might?'
I think it's supposed to be a joke.

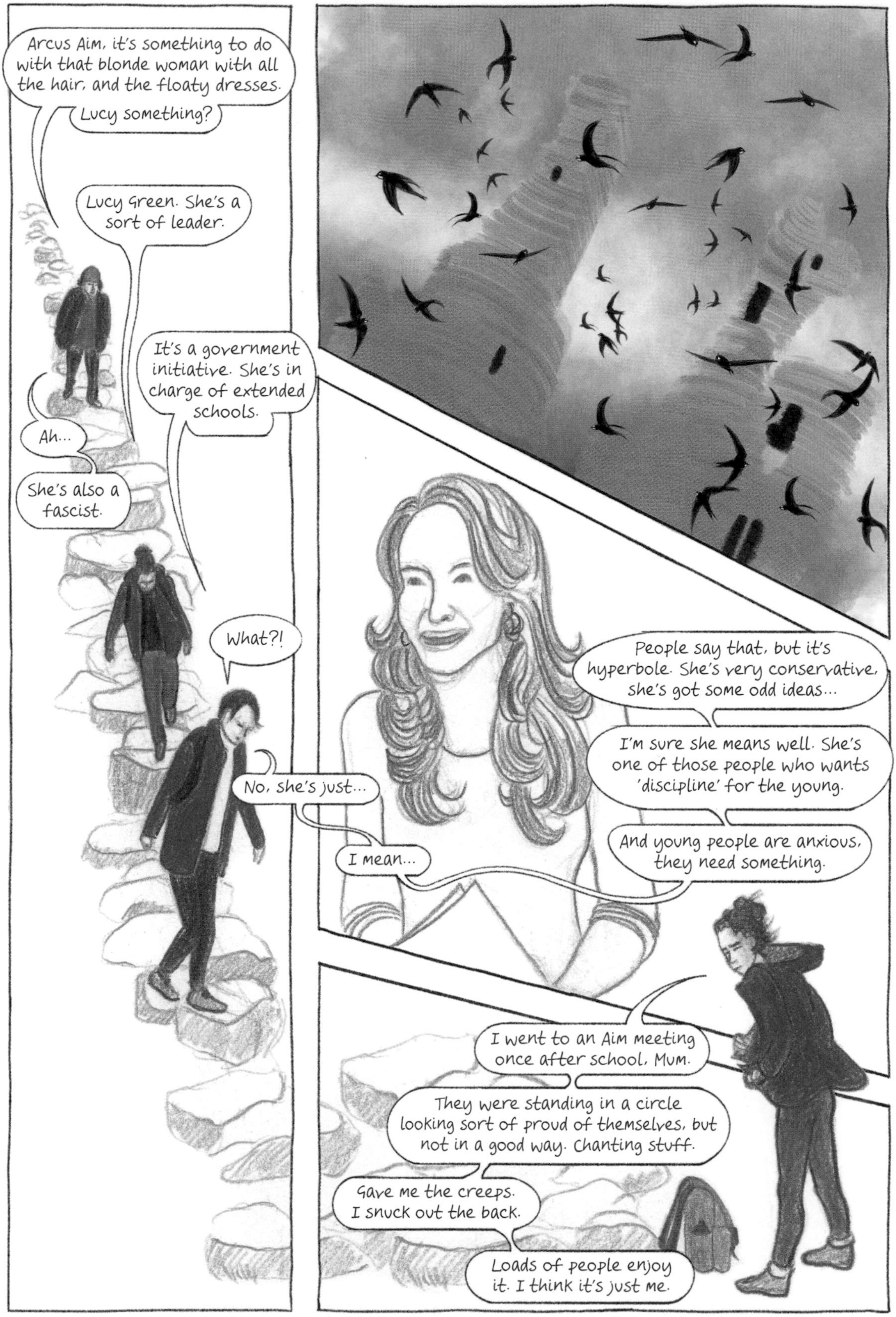
Arcus Aim, it's something to do with that blonde woman with all the hair, and the floaty dresses.
Lucy something?
Lucy Green. She's a sort of leader.
It's a government initiative. She's in charge of extended schools.
Ah...
She's also a fascist.
What?!
No, she's just...
I mean...
People say that, but it's hyperbole. She's very conservative, she's got some odd ideas...
I'm sure she means well. She's one of those people who wants 'discipline' for the young.
And young people are anxious, they need something.
I went to an Aim meeting once after school, Mum.
They were standing in a circle looking sort of proud of themselves, but not in a good way. Chanting stuff.
Gave me the creeps. I snuck out the back.
Loads of people enjoy it. I think it's just me.

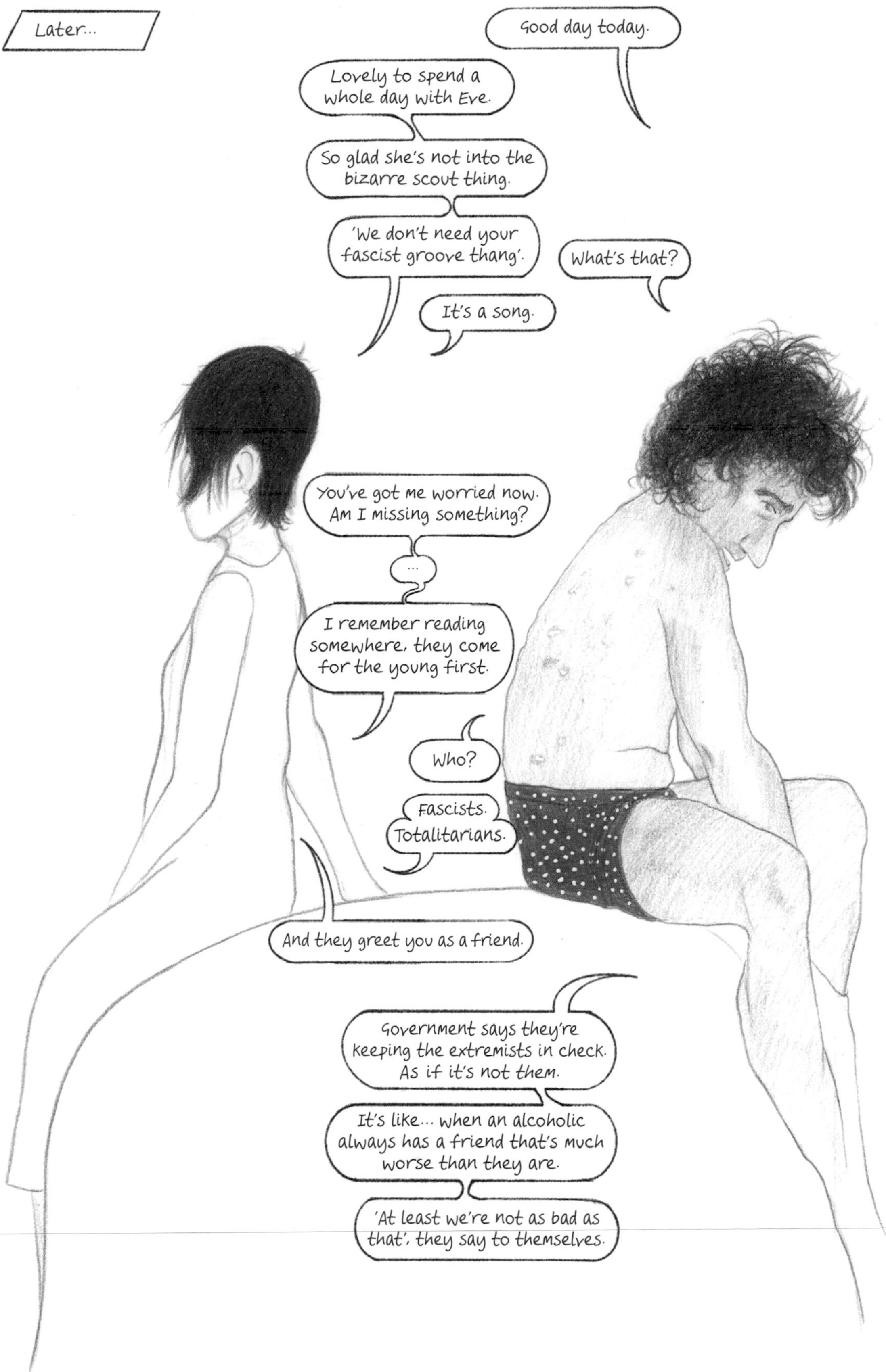
Later...
Good day today.
Lovely to spend a whole day with Eve.
So glad she's not into the bizarre scout thing.
'We don't need your fascist groove thang'.
What's that?
It's a song.
You've got me worried now. Am I missing something?
...
I remember reading somewhere, they come for the young first.
Who?
Fascists. Totalitarians.
And they greet you as a friend.
Government says they're keeping the extremists in check. As if it's not them.
It's like... when an alcoholic always has a friend that's much worse than they are.
'At least we're not as bad as that', they say to themselves.

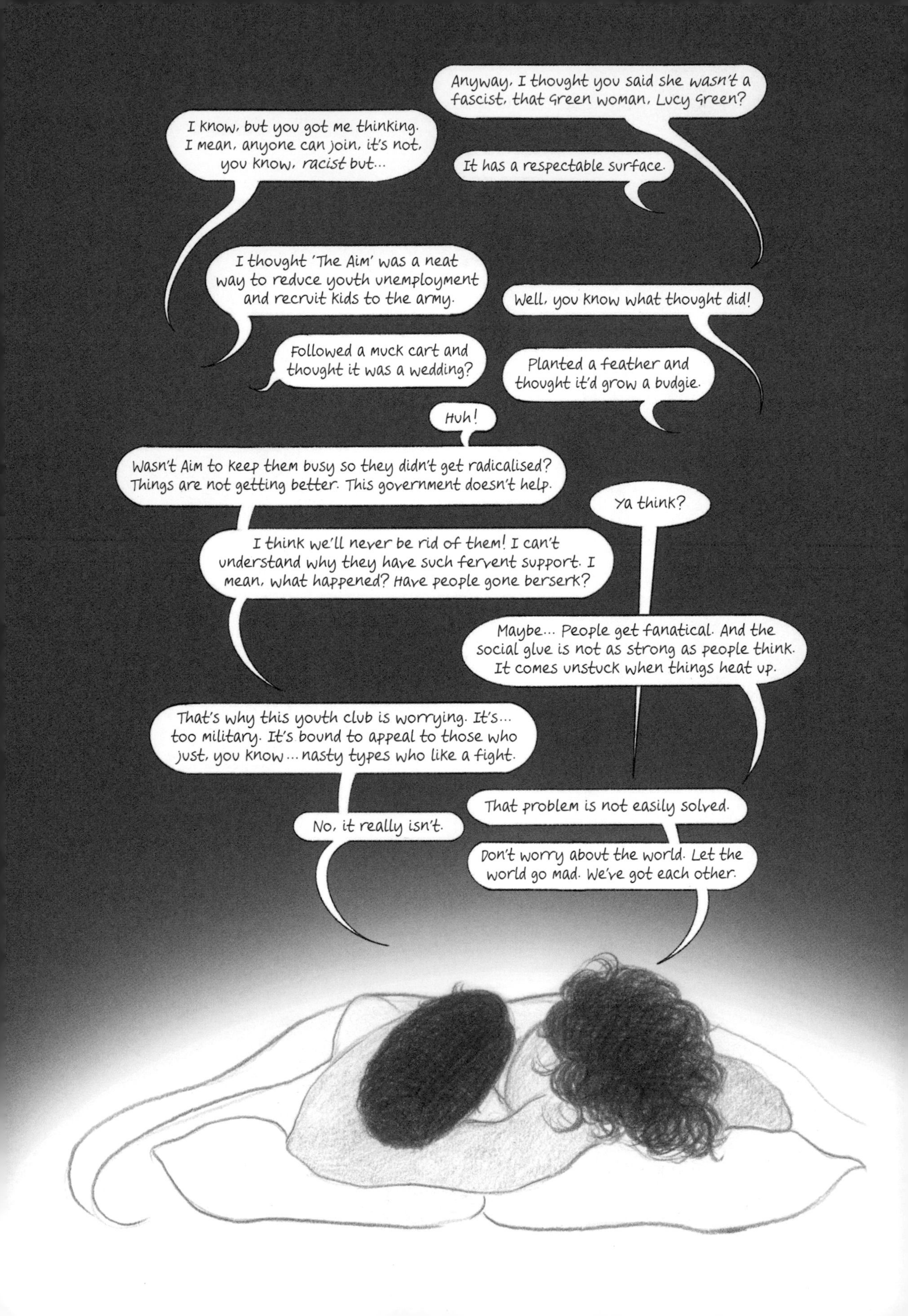
Anyway, I thought you said she wasn't a fascist, that Green woman, Lucy Green?
I know, but you got me thinking. I mean, anyone can join, it's not, you know, *racist* but...
It has a respectable surface.
I thought 'The Aim' was a neat way to reduce youth unemployment and recruit kids to the army.
Well, you know what thought did!
Followed a muck cart and thought it was a wedding?
Planted a feather and thought it'd grow a budgie.
Huh!
Wasn't Aim to keep them busy so they didn't get radicalised? Things are not getting better. This government doesn't help.
Ya think?
I think we'll never be rid of them! I can't understand why they have such fervent support. I mean, what happened? Have people gone berserk?
Maybe... People get fanatical. And the social glue is not as strong as people think. It comes unstuck when things heat up.
That's why this youth club is worrying. It's... too military. It's bound to appeal to those who just, you know... nasty types who like a fight.
That problem is not easily solved.
No, it really isn't.
Don't worry about the world. Let the world go mad. We've got each other.

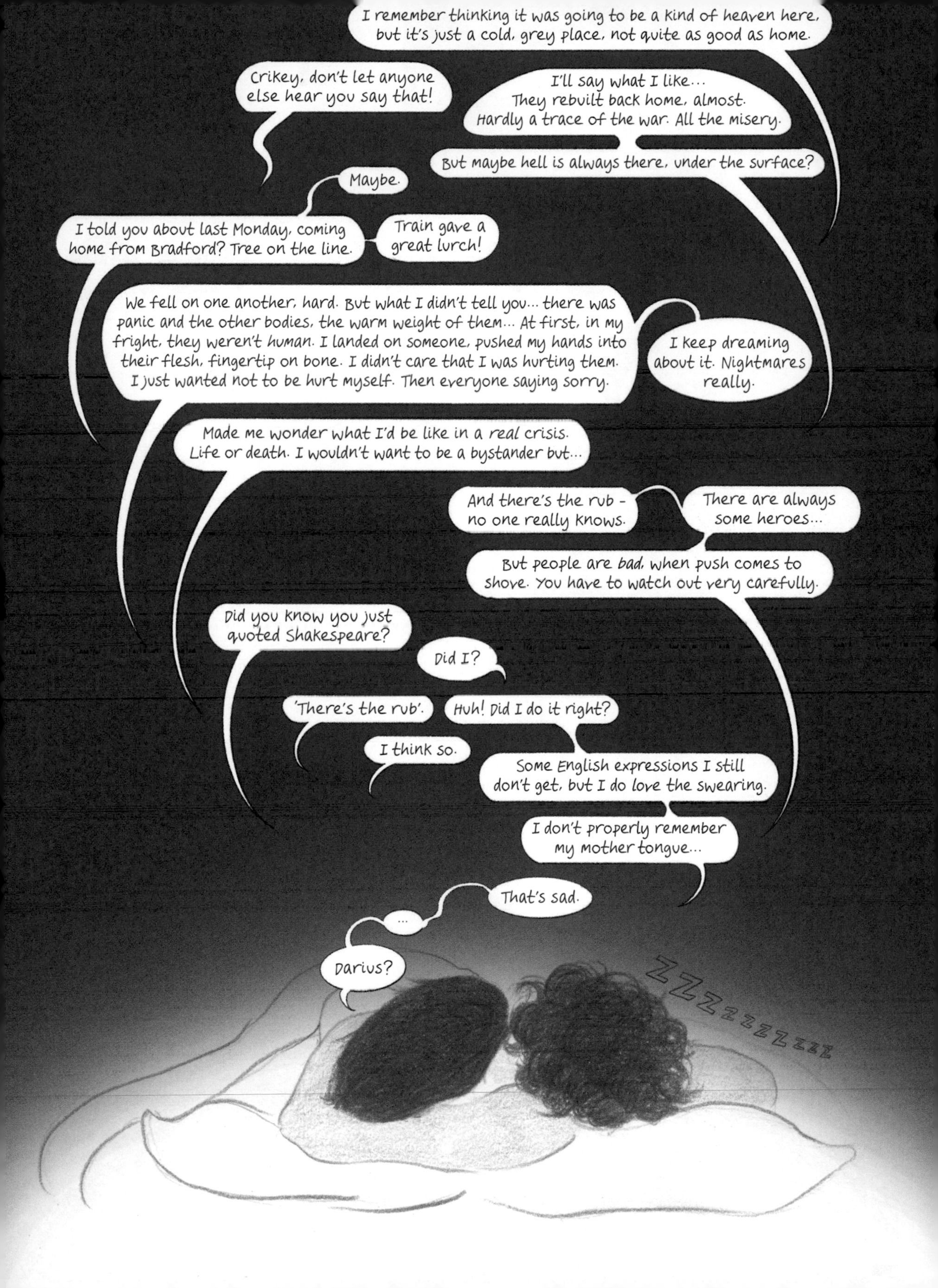
I remember thinking it was going to be a kind of heaven here, but it's just a cold, grey place, not quite as good as home.
Crikey, don't let anyone else hear you say that!
I'll say what I like... They rebuilt back home, almost. Hardly a trace of the war. All the misery.
But maybe hell is always there, under the surface?
Maybe.
I told you about last Monday, coming home from Bradford? Tree on the line.
Train gave a great lurch!
We fell on one another, hard. But what I didn't tell you... there was panic and the other bodies, the warm weight of them... At first, in my fright, they weren't human. I landed on someone, pushed my hands into their flesh, fingertip on bone. I didn't care that I was hurting them. I just wanted not to be hurt myself. Then everyone saying sorry.
I keep dreaming about it. Nightmares really.
Made me wonder what I'd be like in a real crisis. Life or death. I wouldn't want to be a bystander but...
And there's the rub - no one really knows.
There are always some heroes...
But people are bad, when push comes to shove. You have to watch out very carefully.
Did you know you just quoted Shakespeare?
Did I?
'There's the rub'.
Huh! Did I do it right?
I think so.
Some English expressions I still don't get, but I do love the swearing.
I don't properly remember my mother tongue...
That's sad.
...
Darius?
ZZZzzzzzzzz

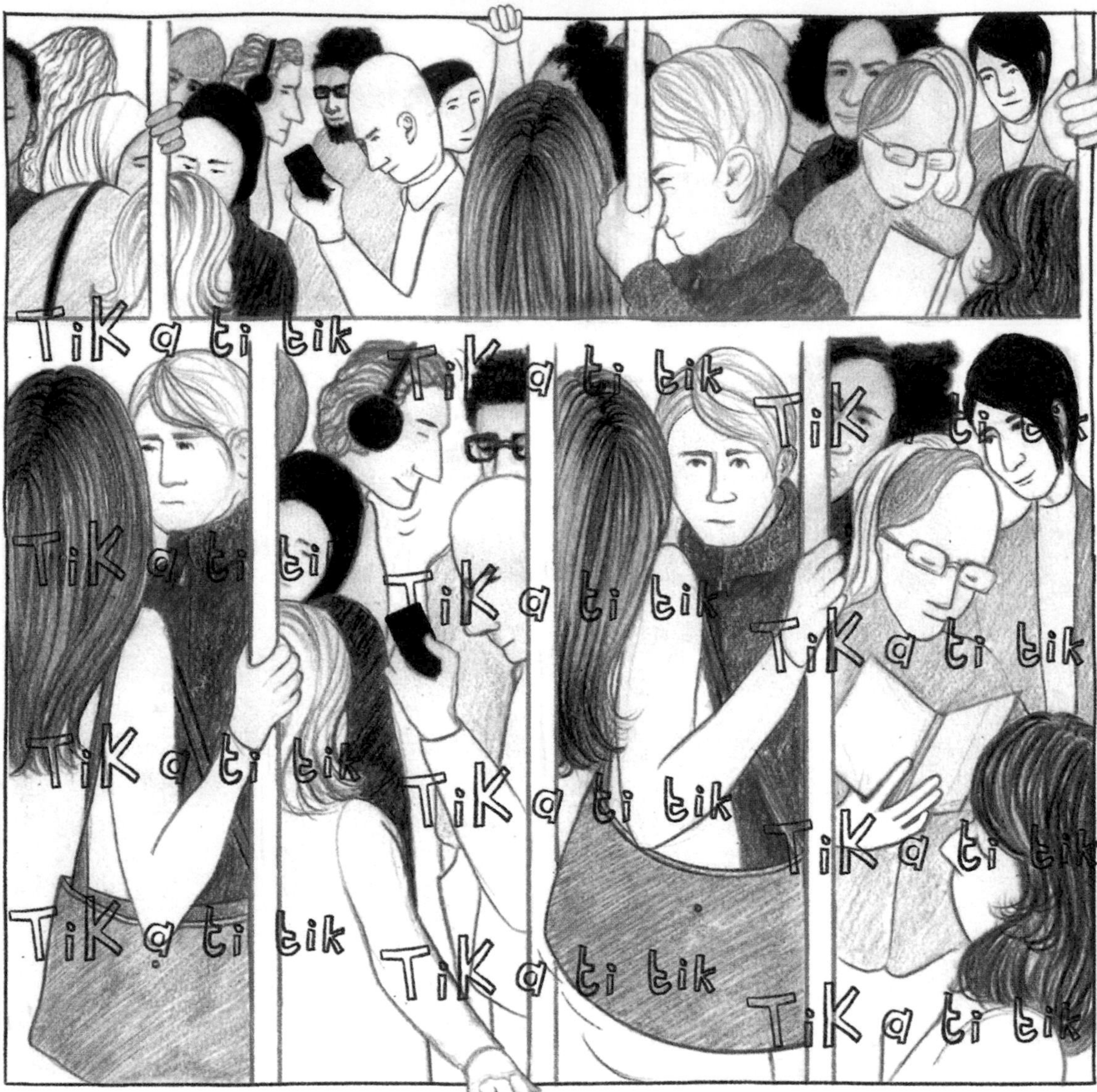
TiKa ti tik
TiKa ti tik
TiKa ti tik
TiKa ti tik
TiKa ti tik
TiKa ti tik
TiKa ti tik
TiKa ti tik
TiKa ti tik
TiKa ti tik
TiKa ti tik
TiKa ti tik

How did we ever live together like this?

So close, with such a distance between us.

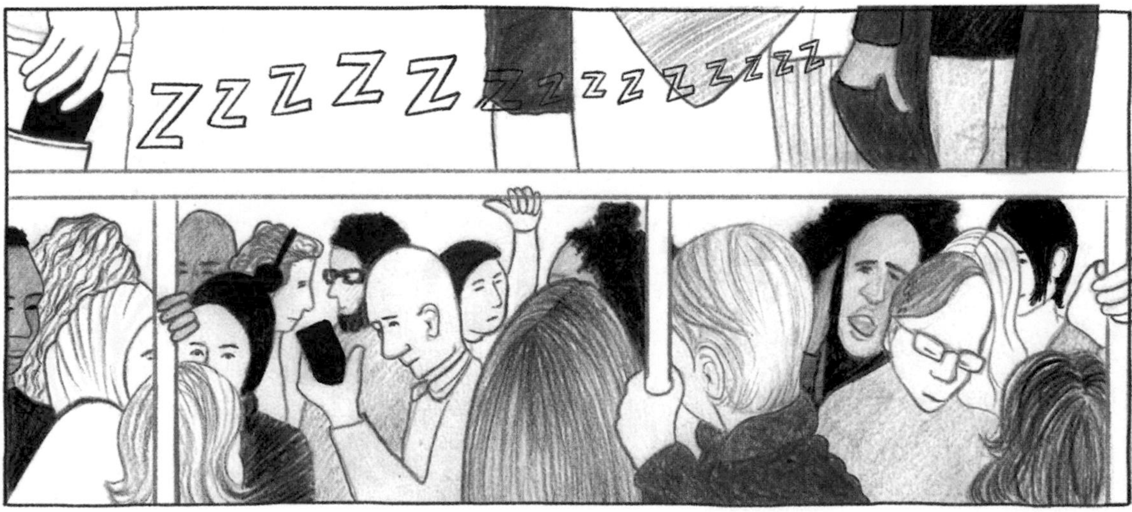
ZZZZZZzzzZZZZZ

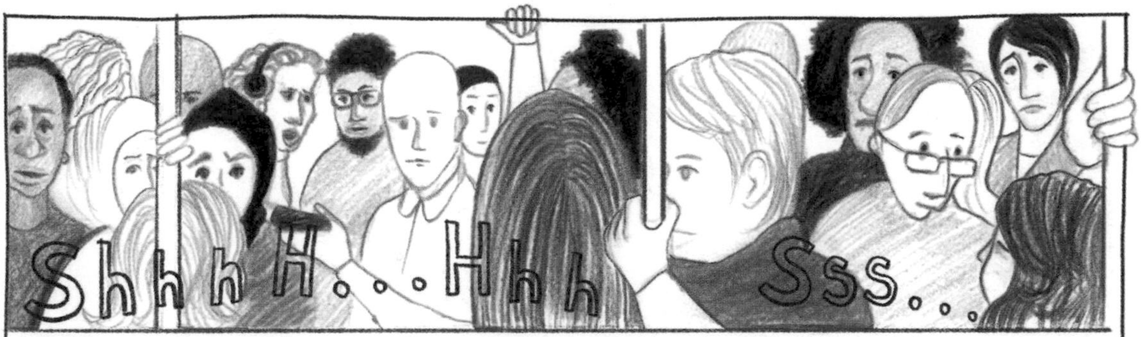
ShhhH...Hhh
Sss...

To sleep, perchance to dream - ay, there's the rub, For in that sleep of death what dreams may come
When we have shuffled off this mortal coil...

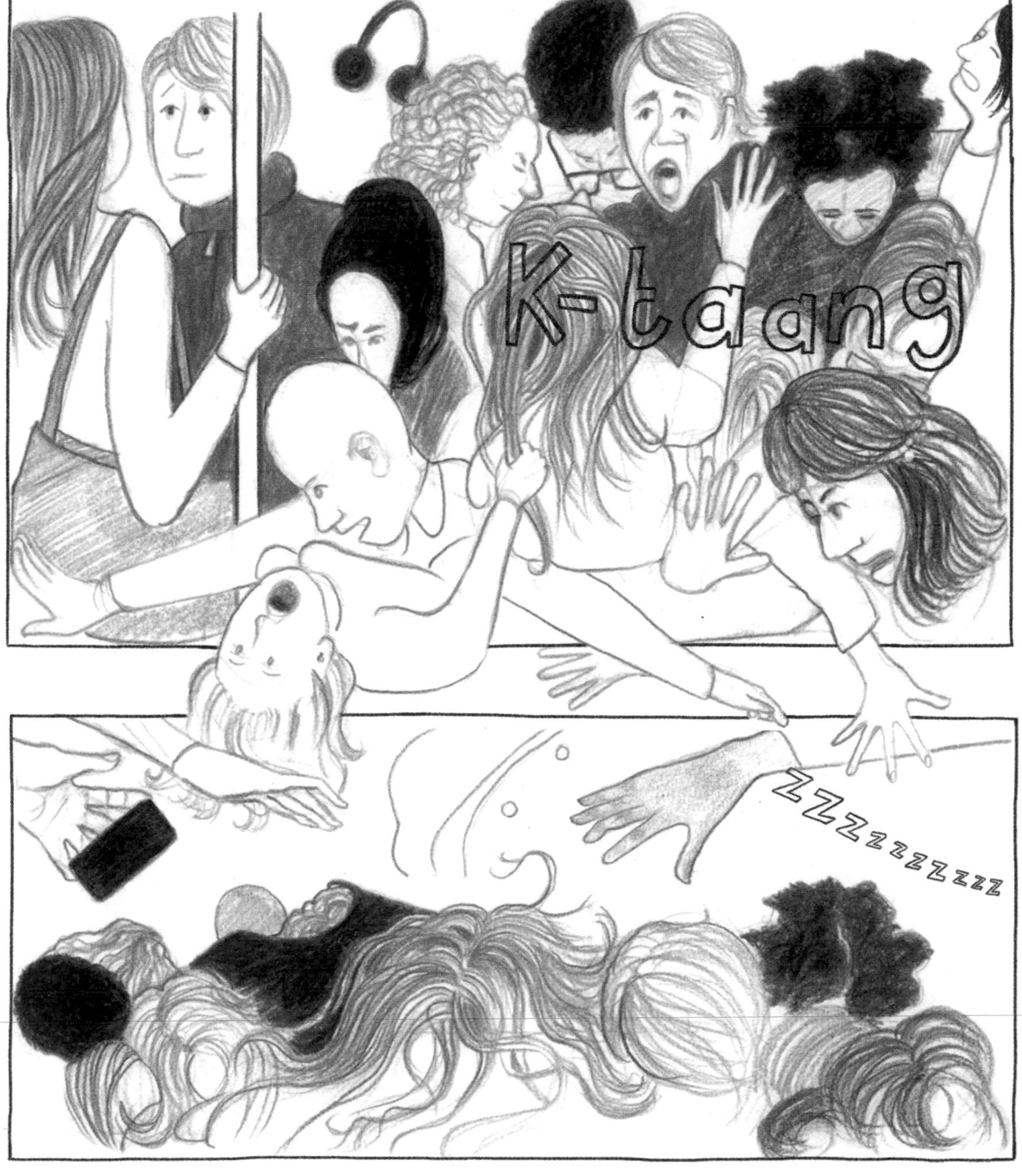
K-taang
ZZZzzzzzzz

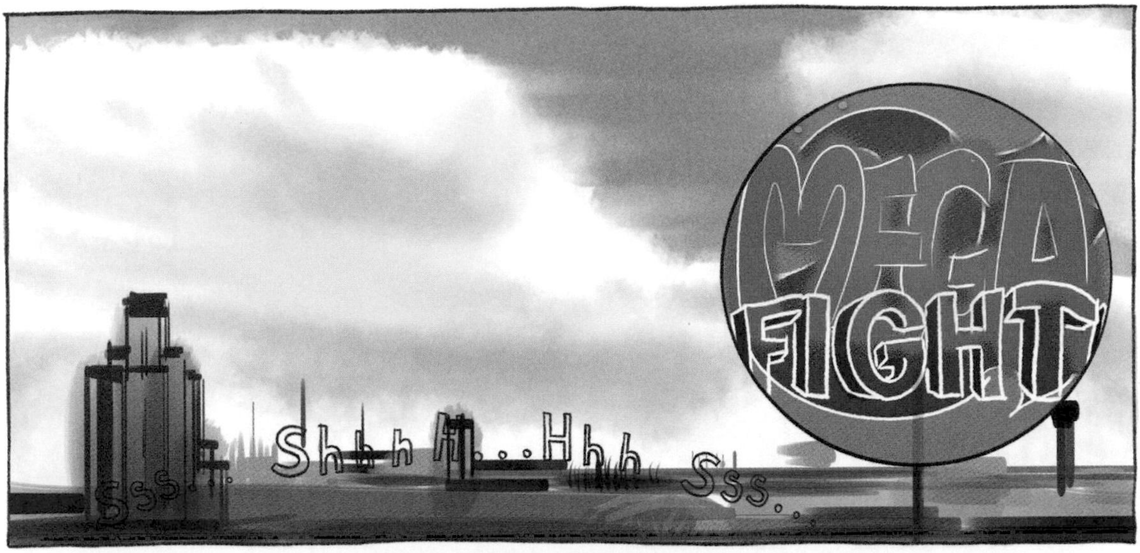
MEGA FIGHT
Sss... Shhh...Hhh Sss...

Mind - the gap. Mind - the gap.

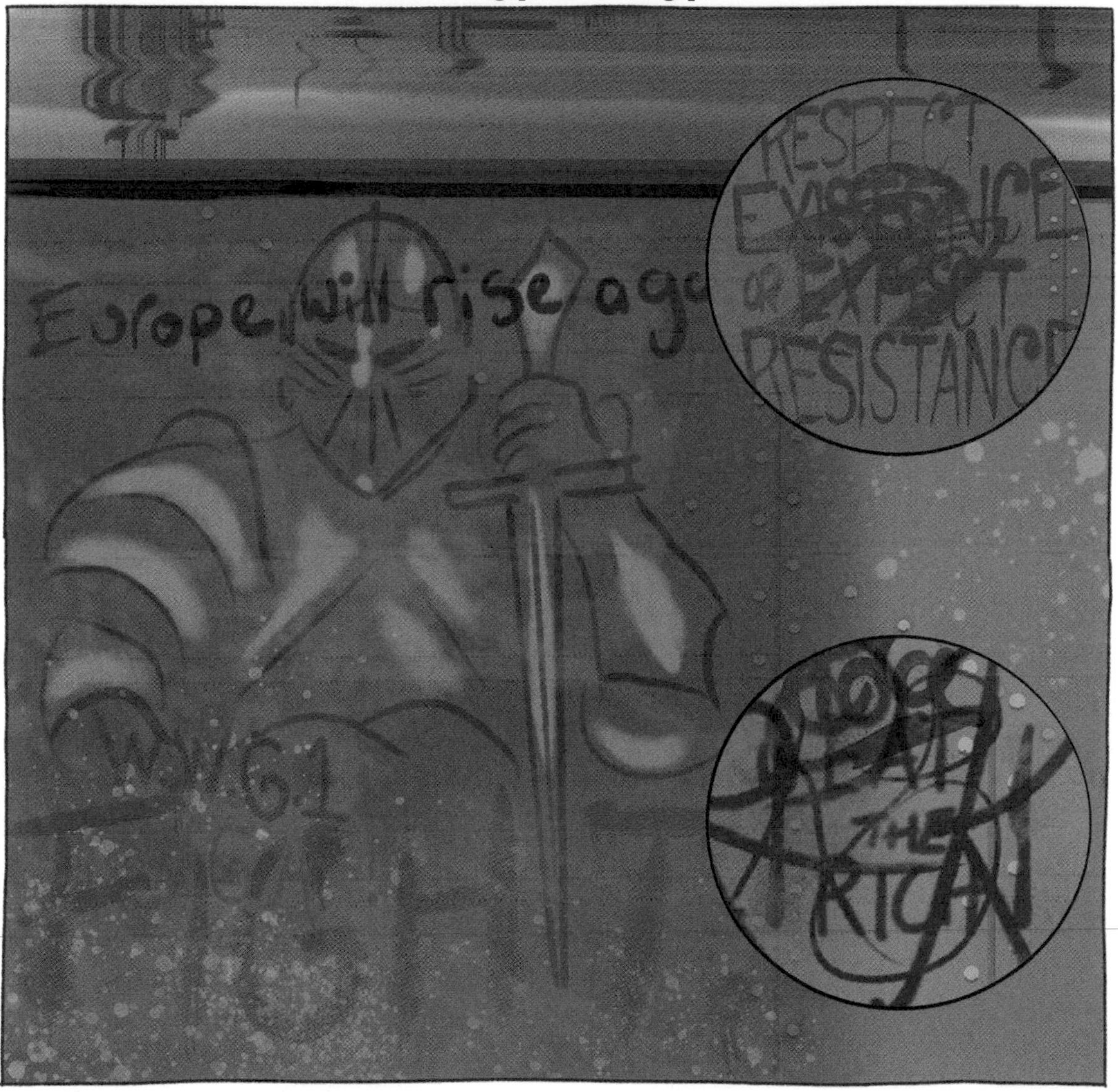
Europe will rise aga
RESPECT EXISTENCE OR EXPECT RESISTANCE
W.W.G.1
THE RICH

Don't be aimless.

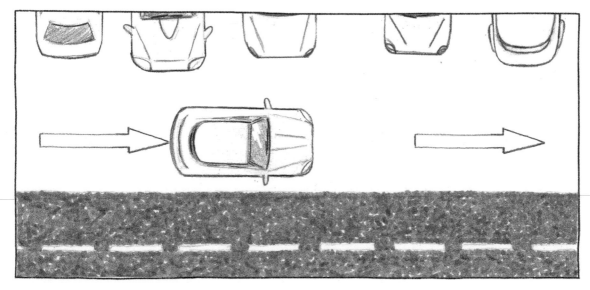

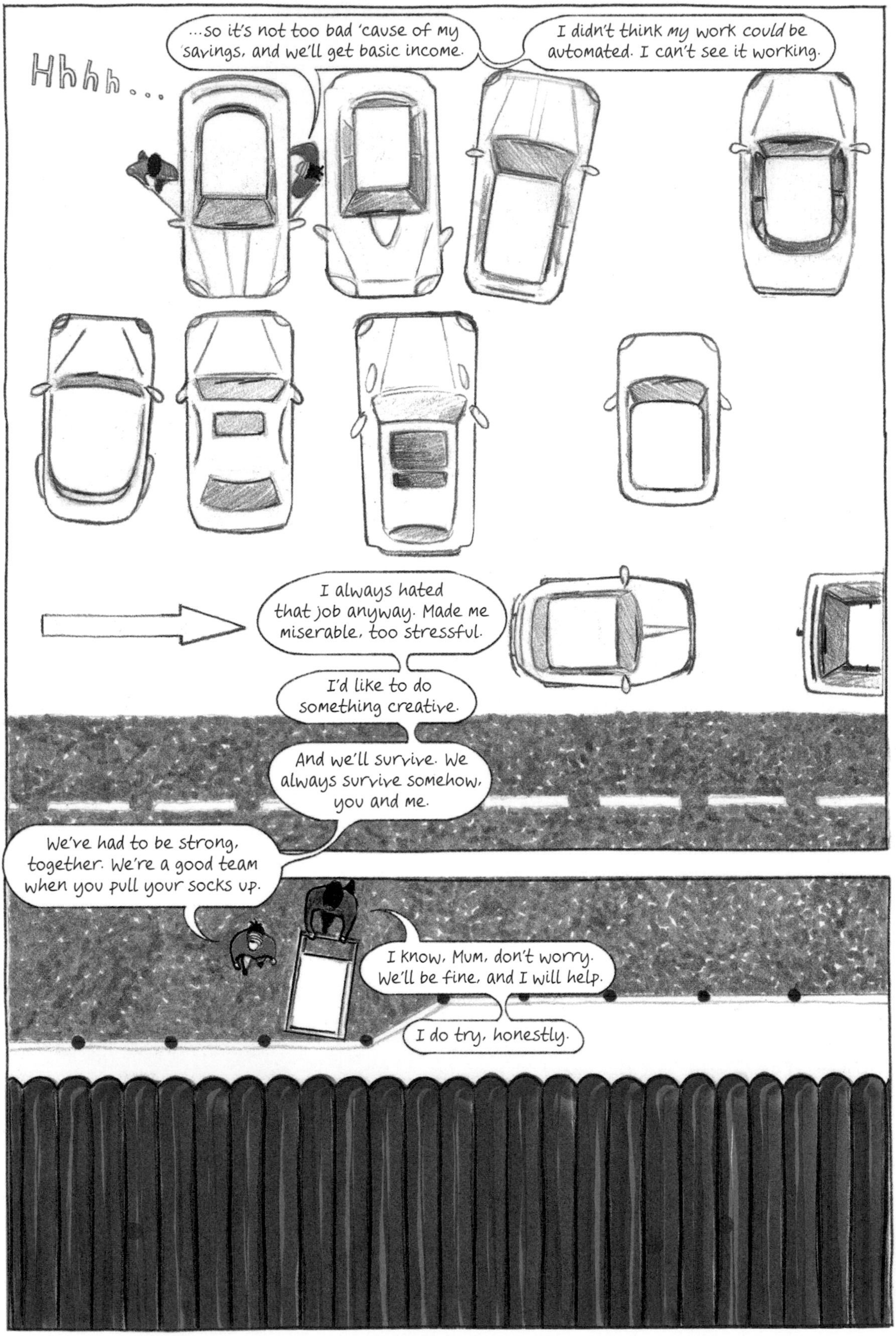
Hhhh...
...so it's not too bad 'cause of my savings, and we'll get basic income.
I didn't think my work could be automated. I can't see it working.
I always hated that job anyway. Made me miserable, too stressful.
I'd like to do something creative.
And we'll survive. We always survive somehow, you and me.
We've had to be strong, together. We're a good team when you pull your socks up.
I know, Mum, don't worry. We'll be fine, and I will help.
I do try, honestly.

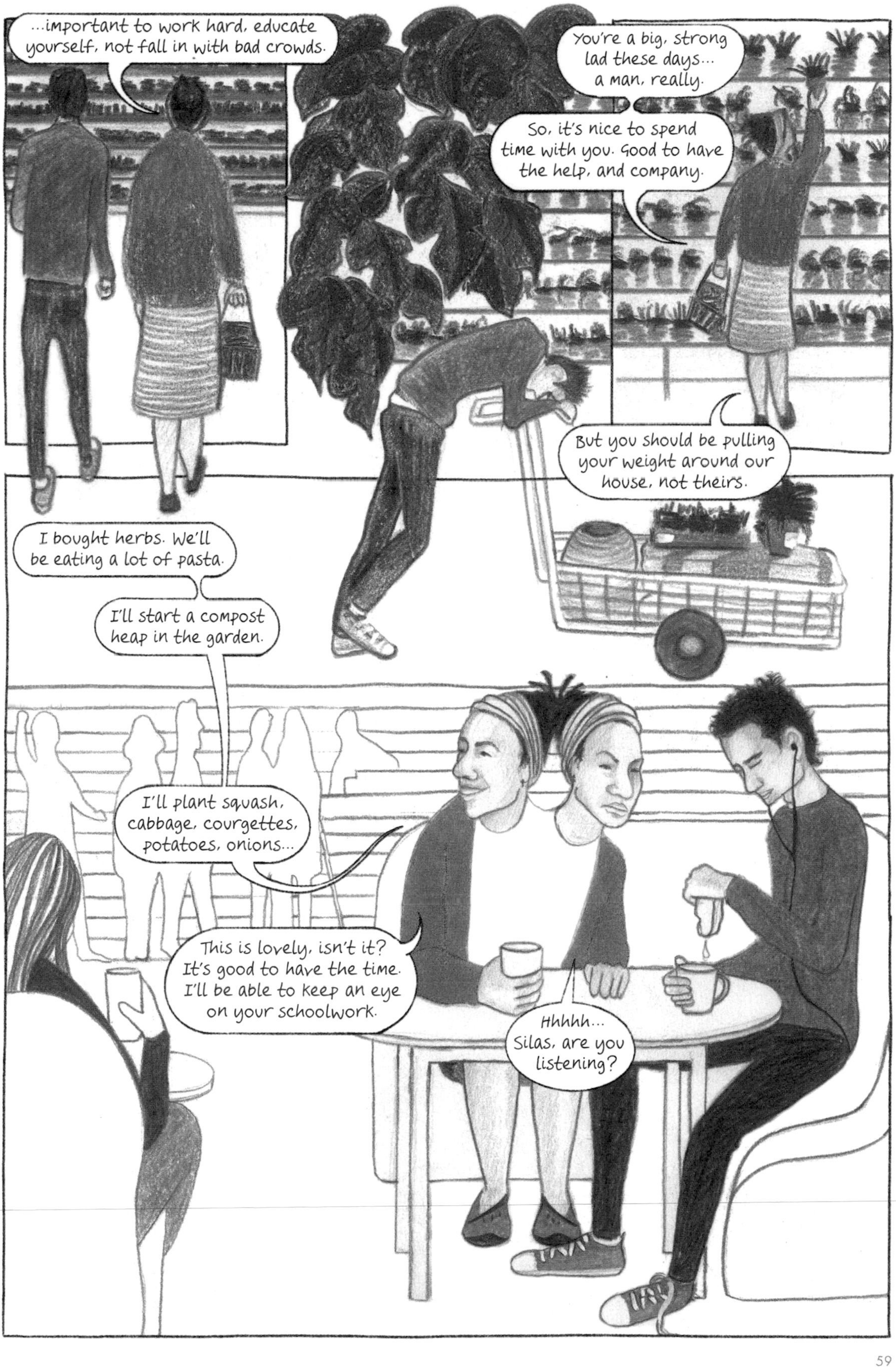
...important to work hard, educate yourself, not fall in with bad crowds.
You're a big, strong lad these days... a man, really.
So, it's nice to spend time with you. Good to have the help, and company.
But you should be pulling your weight around our house, not theirs.
I bought herbs. We'll be eating a lot of pasta.
I'll start a compost heap in the garden.
I'll plant squash, cabbage, courgettes, potatoes, onions...
This is lovely, isn't it? It's good to have the time. I'll be able to keep an eye on your schoolwork.
Hhhhh... Silas, are you listening?

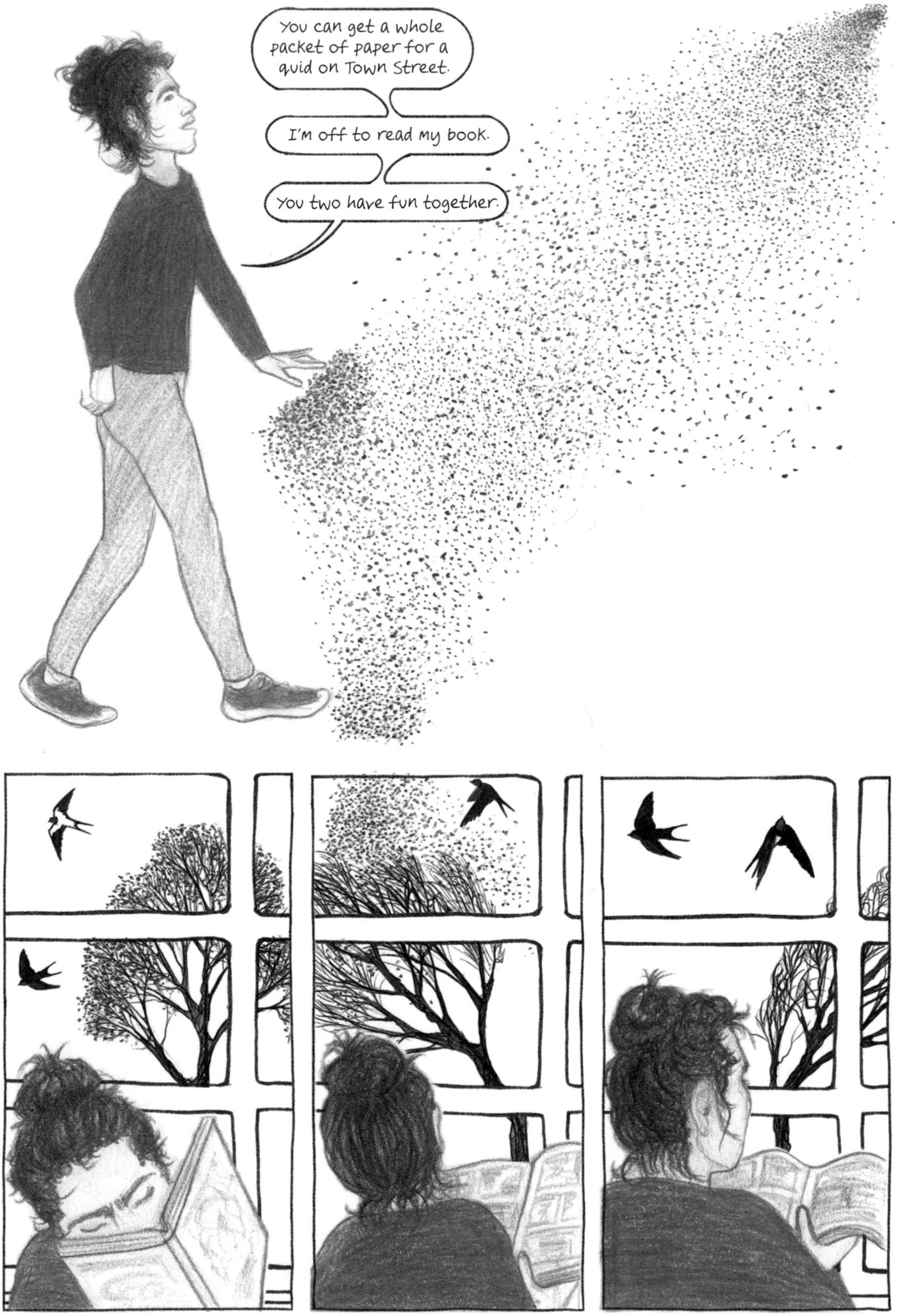
You can get a whole packet of paper for a quid on Town Street.
I'm off to read my book.
You two have fun together.

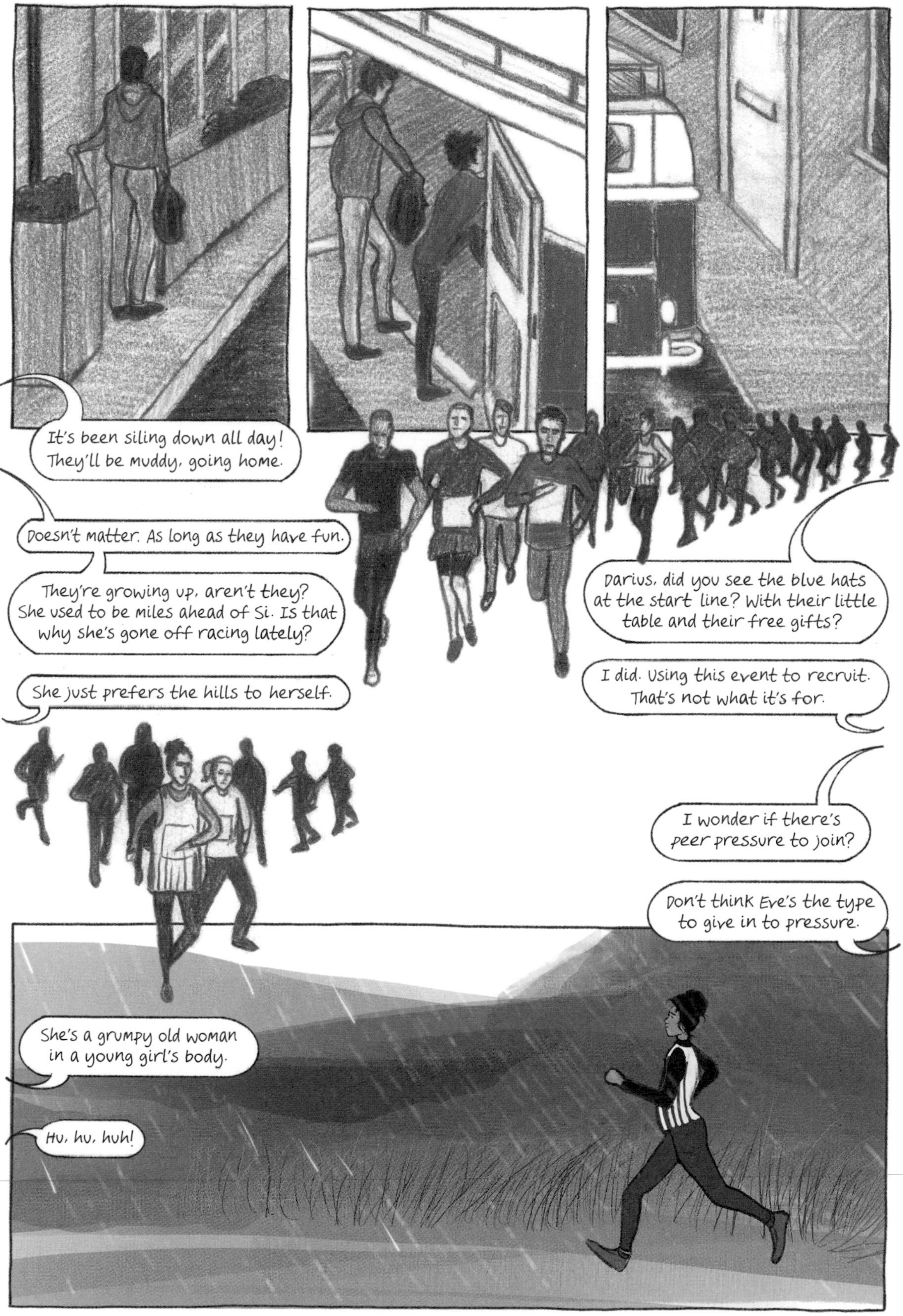
It's been siling down all day! They'll be muddy, going home.
Doesn't matter. As long as they have fun.
They're growing up, aren't they? She used to be miles ahead of Si. Is that why she's gone off racing lately?
She just prefers the hills to herself.
Darius, did you see the blue hats at the start line? With their little table and their free gifts?
I did. Using this event to recruit. That's not what it's for.
I wonder if there's peer pressure to join?
Don't think Eve's the type to give in to pressure.
She's a grumpy old woman in a young girl's body.
Hu, hu, huh!

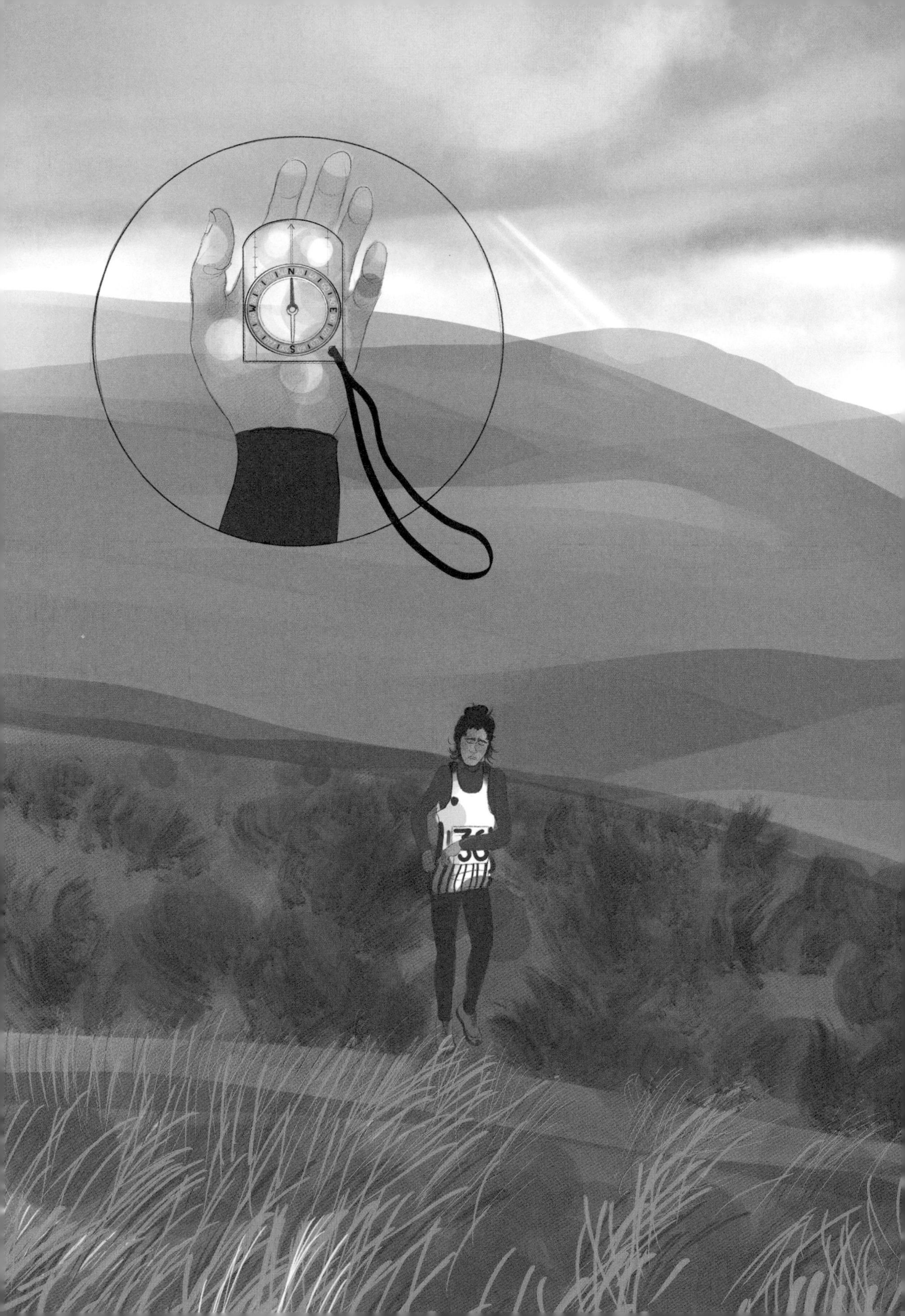

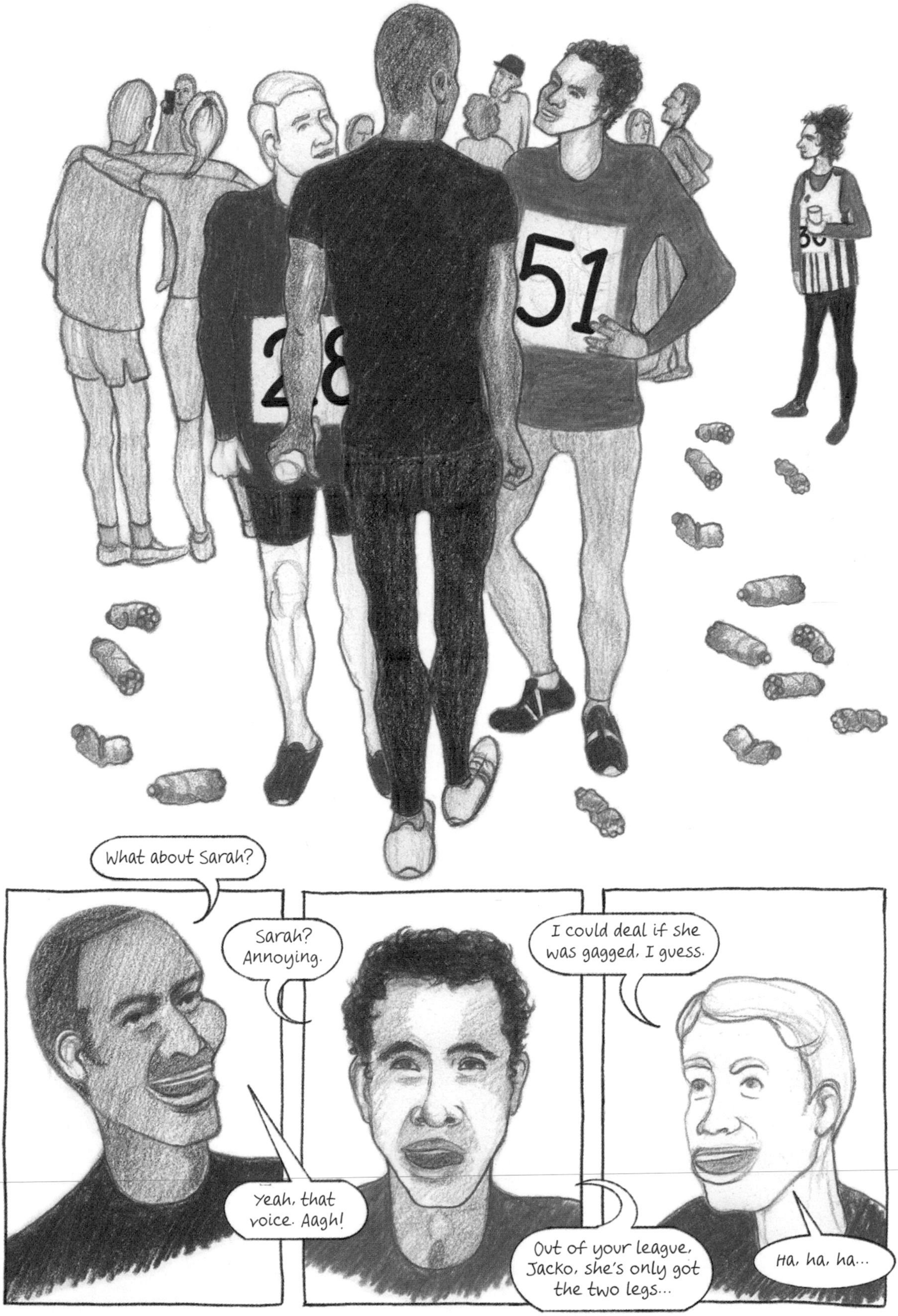
51
28
What about Sarah?
Sarah? Annoying.
Yeah, that voice. Aagh!
I could deal if she was gagged, I guess.
Out of your league, Jacko, she's only got the two legs...
Ha, ha, ha...

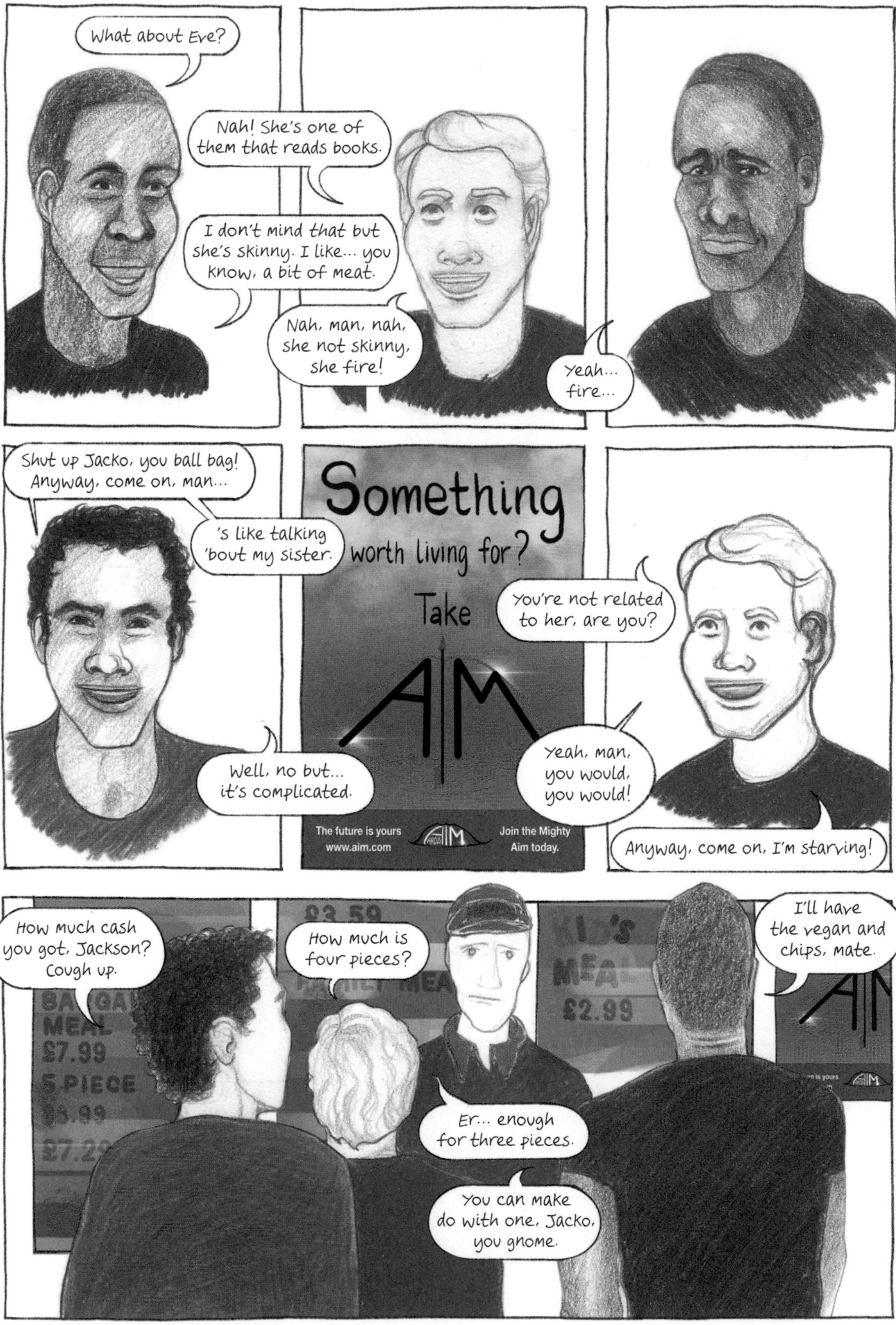
What about Eve?
Nah! She's one of them that reads books.
I don't mind that but she's skinny. I like... you know, a bit of meat.
Nah, man, nah, she not skinny, she fire!
Yeah... fire...
Shut up Jacko, you ball bag! Anyway, come on, man...
's like talking 'bout my sister.
Something worth living for?
Take
AIM
The future is yours www.aim.com
Join the Mighty Aim today.
Well, no but... it's complicated.
You're not related to her, are you?
Yeah, man, you would, you would!
Anyway, come on, I'm starving!
How much cash you got, Jackson? Cough up.
How much is four pieces?
I'll have the vegan and chips, mate.
Er... enough for three pieces.
You can make do with one, Jacko, you gnome.
£2.99
£7.99

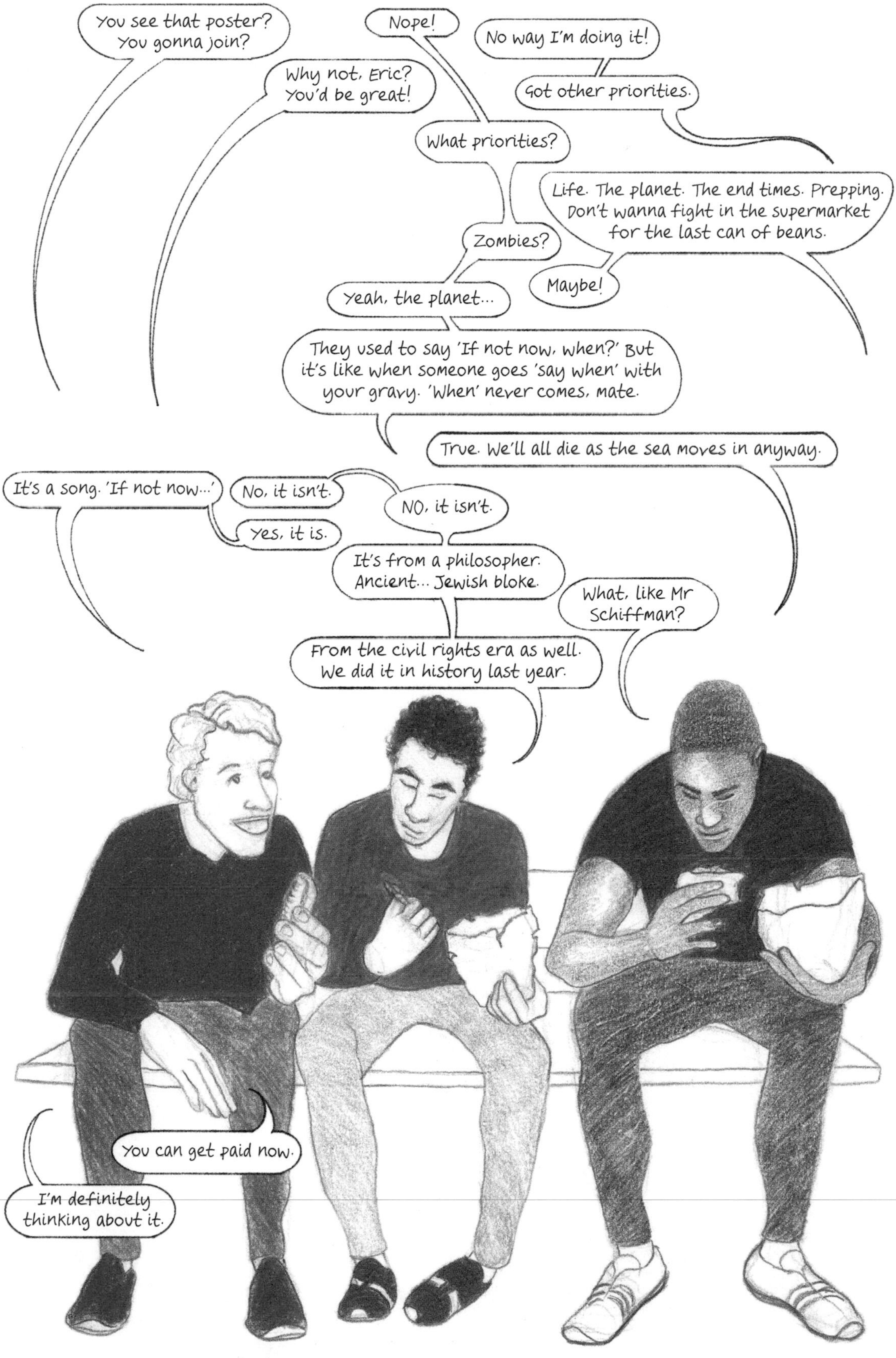
You see that poster? You gonna join?
Why not, Eric? You'd be great!
Nope!
No way I'm doing it!
Got other priorities.
What priorities?
Life. The planet. The end times. Prepping. Don't wanna fight in the supermarket for the last can of beans.
Zombies?
Maybe!
Yeah, the planet...
They used to say 'If not now, when?' But it's like when someone goes 'say when' with your gravy. 'When' never comes, mate.
True. We'll all die as the sea moves in anyway.
It's a song. 'If not now...'
No, it isn't.
Yes, it is.
NO, it isn't.
It's from a philosopher. Ancient... Jewish bloke.
From the civil rights era as well. We did it in history last year.
What, like Mr Schiffman?
You can get paid now.
I'm definitely thinking about it.

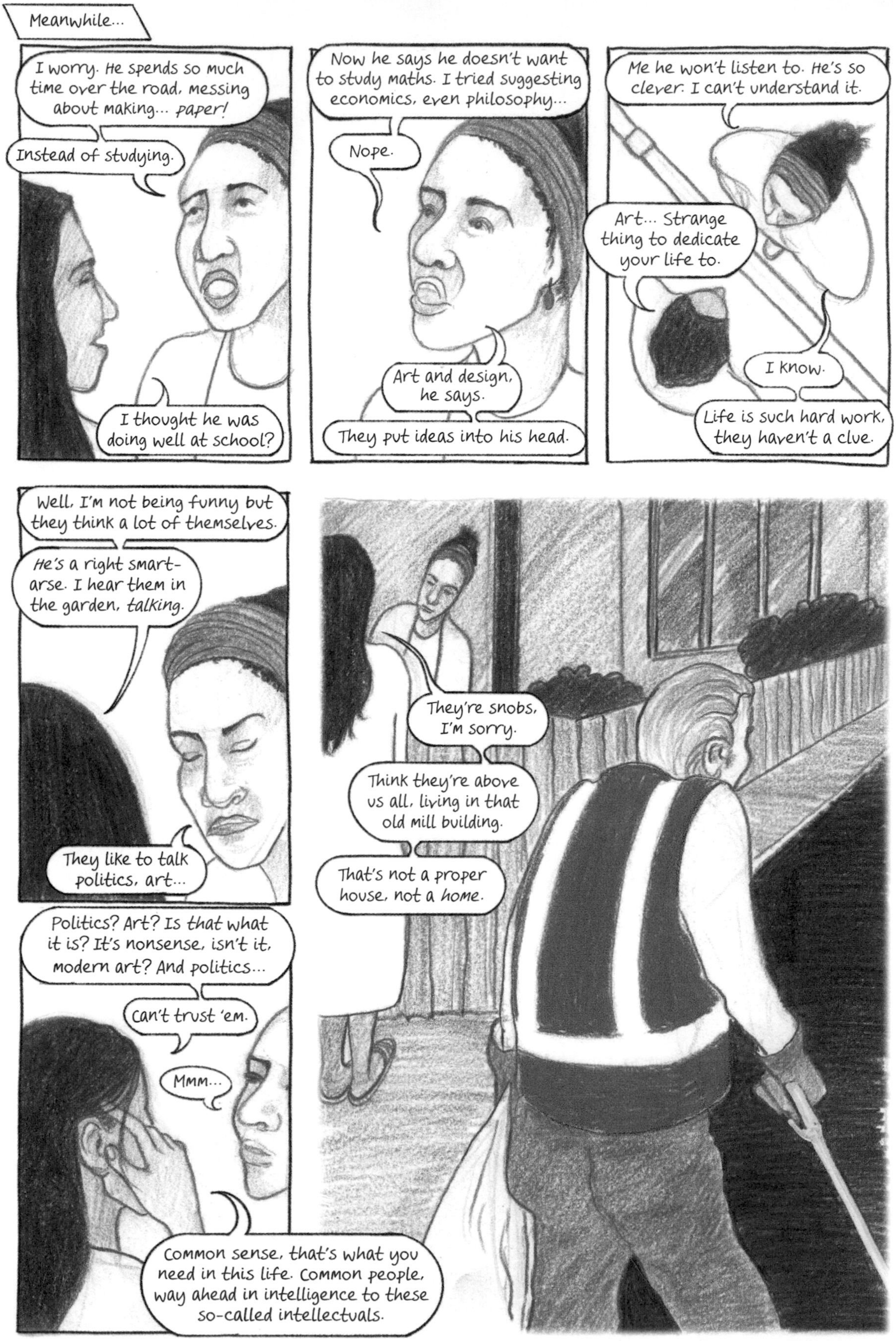

Meanwhile...
I worry. He spends so much time over the road, messing about making... *paper!*
Instead of studying.
I thought he was doing well at school?
Now he says he doesn't want to study maths. I tried suggesting economics, even philosophy...
Nope.
Art and design, he says.
They put ideas into his head.
Me he won't listen to. He's so *clever*. I can't understand it.
Art... Strange thing to dedicate your life to.
I know.
Life is such hard work, they haven't a clue.
Well, I'm not being funny but they think a lot of themselves.
He's a right smart-arse. I hear them in the garden, *talking*.
They like to talk politics, art...
Politics? Art? Is *that* what it is? It's nonsense, isn't it, modern art? And politics...
Can't trust 'em.
Mmm...
Common sense, that's what you need in this life. Common people, way ahead in intelligence to these so-called intellectuals.
They're snobs, I'm sorry.
Think they're above us all, living in that old mill building.
That's not a proper house, not a *home*.

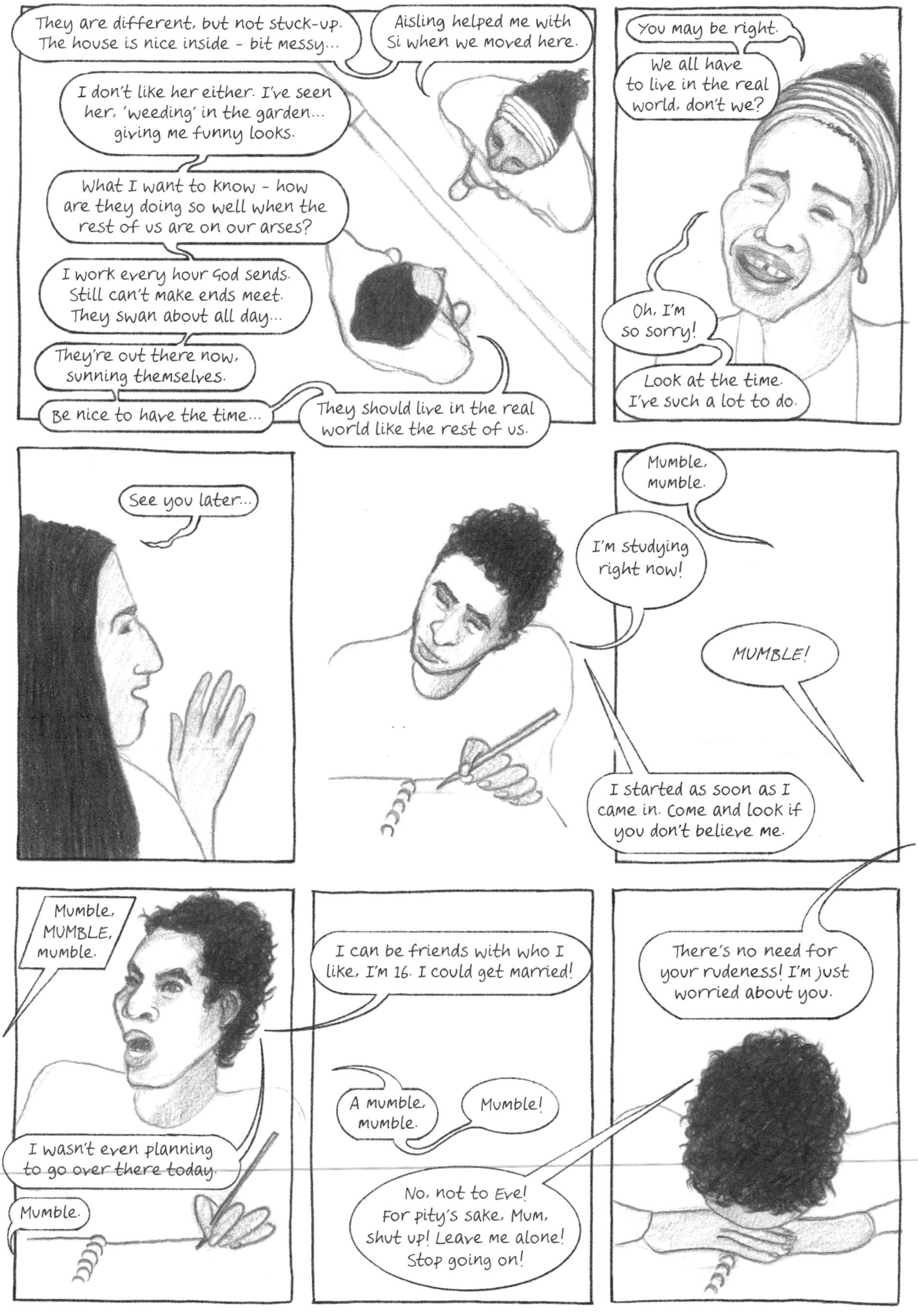
They are different, but not stuck-up. The house is nice inside - bit messy...
Aisling helped me with Si when we moved here.
I don't like her either. I've seen her, 'weeding' in the garden... giving me funny looks.
What I want to know - how are they doing so well when the rest of us are on our arses?
I work every hour God sends. Still can't make ends meet. They swan about all day...
They're out there now, sunning themselves.
Be nice to have the time...
They should live in the real world like the rest of us.
You may be right.
We all have to live in the real world, don't we?
Oh, I'm so sorry!
Look at the time. I've such a lot to do.
See you later...
Mumble, mumble.
I'm studying right now!
MUMBLE!
I started as soon as I came in. Come and look if you don't believe me.
Mumble, MUMBLE, mumble.
I wasn't even planning to go over there today.
Mumble.
I can be friends with who I like, I'm 16. I could get married!
A mumble, mumble.
Mumble!
No, not to Eve! For pity's sake, Mum, shut up! Leave me alone! Stop going on!
There's no need for your rudeness! I'm just worried about you.

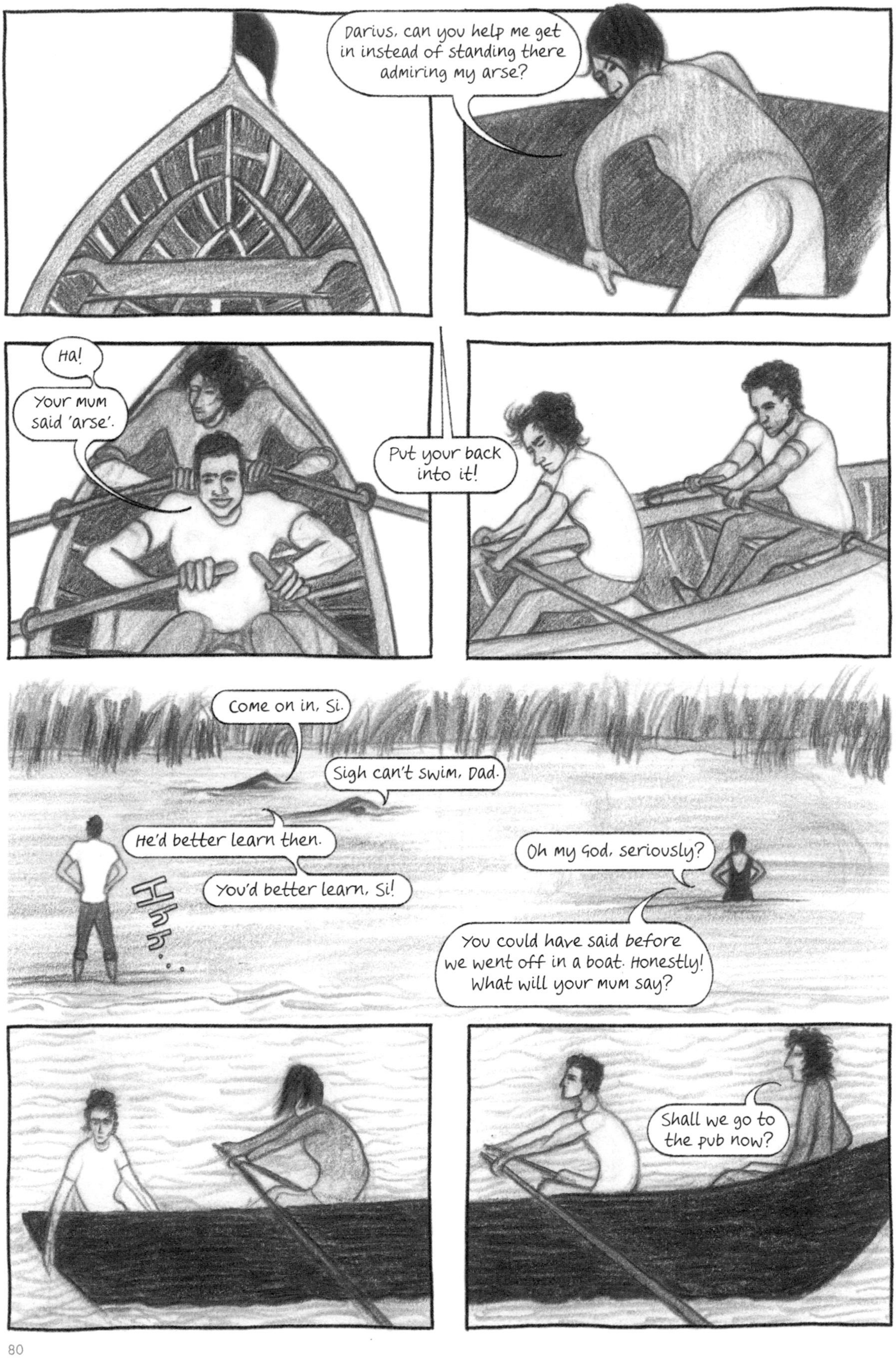
Darius, can you help me get in instead of standing there admiring my arse?
Ha!
Your mum said 'arse'.
Put your back into it!
Come on in, Si.
Sigh can't swim, Dad.
He'd better learn then.
You'd better learn, Si!
Hhh...
Oh my God, seriously?
You could have said before we went off in a boat. Honestly! What will your mum say?
Shall we go to the pub now?

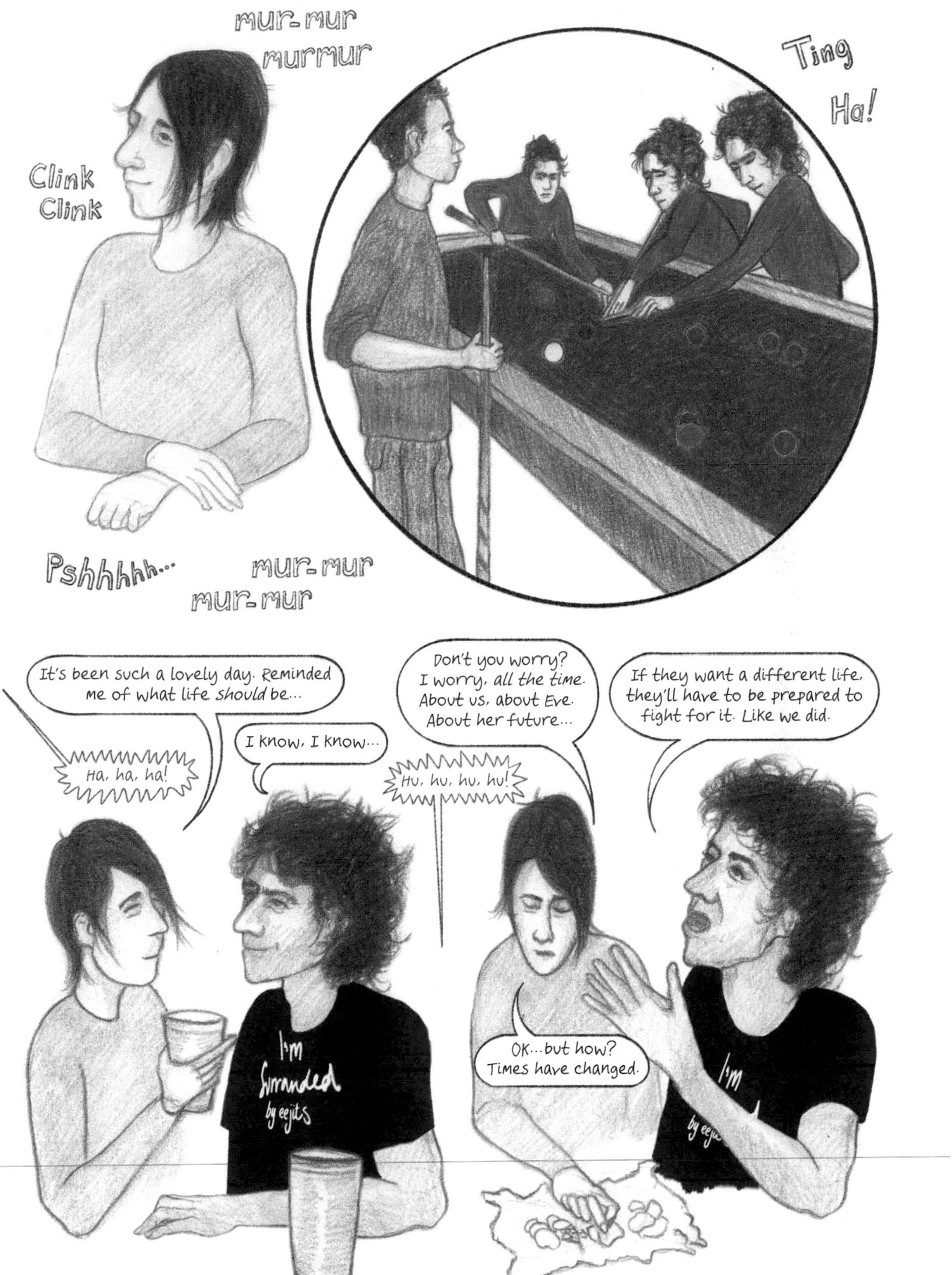
mur-mur
murmur
Clink
Clink
Ting
Ha!
Pshhhhh...
mur-mur
mur-mur
It's been such a lovely day. Reminded me of what life should be...
Ha, ha, ha!
I know, I know...
Hu, hu, hu, hu!
Don't you worry? I worry, all the time. About us, about Eve. About her future...
If they want a different life, they'll have to be prepared to fight for it. Like we did.
I'm Surrounded by eejits
OK... but how? Times have changed.

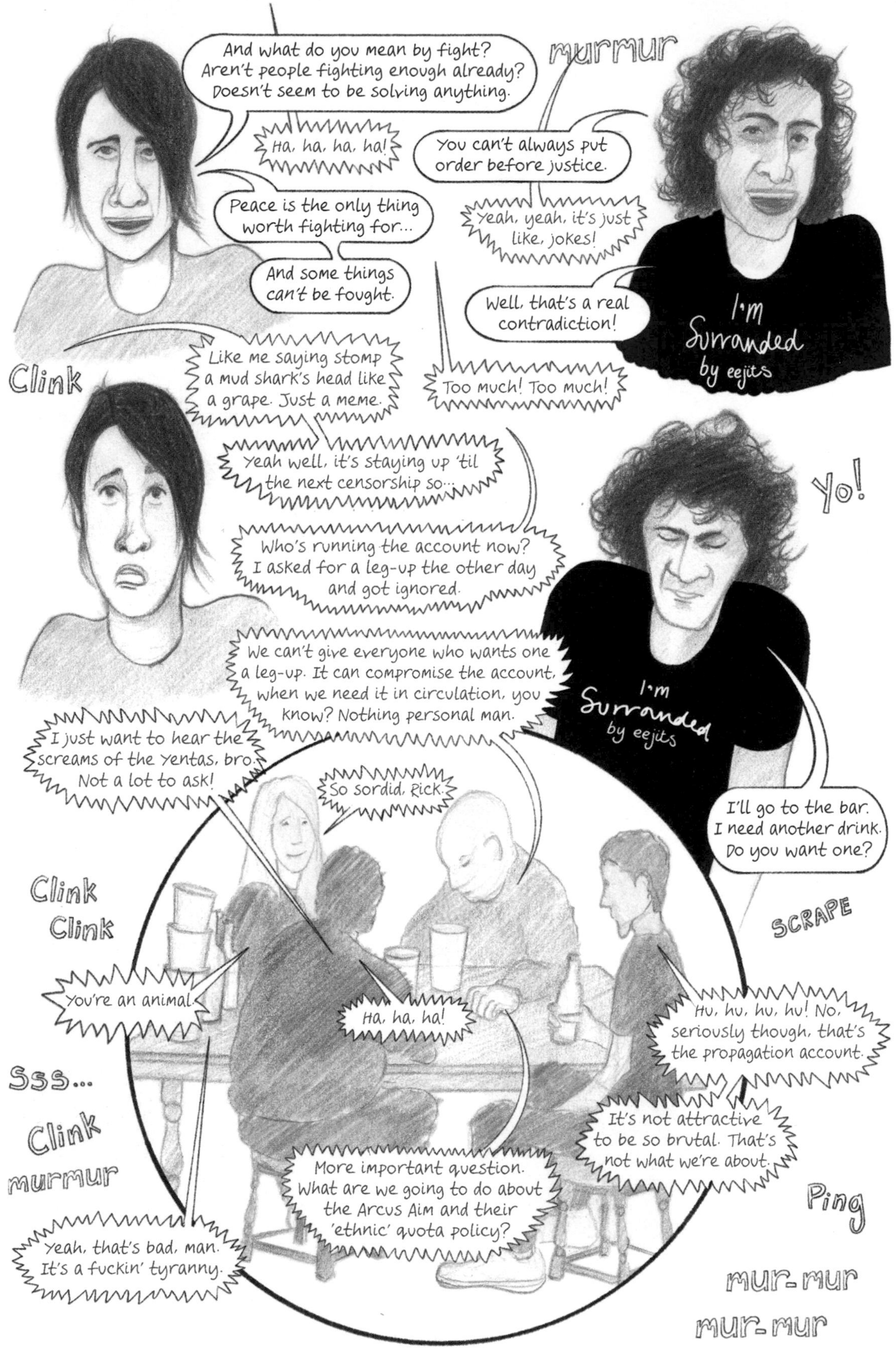
And what do you mean by fight? Aren't people fighting enough already? Doesn't seem to be solving anything.
murmur
Ha, ha, ha, ha!
You can't always put order before justice.
Peace is the only thing worth fighting for...
Yeah, yeah, it's just like, jokes!
And some things can't be fought.
Well, that's a real contradiction!
I'm Surrounded by eejits
Clink
Like me saying stomp a mud shark's head like a grape. Just a meme.
Too much! Too much!
Yeah well, it's staying up 'til the next censorship so...
Yo!
Who's running the account now? I asked for a leg-up the other day and got ignored.
We can't give everyone who wants one a leg-up. It can compromise the account, when we need it in circulation, you know? Nothing personal man.
I'm Surrounded by eejits
I just want to hear the screams of the Yentas, bro. Not a lot to ask!
So sordid, Rick.
I'll go to the bar. I need another drink. Do you want one?
Clink
Clink
SCRAPE
You're an animal.
Ha, ha, ha!
Hu, hu, hu, hu! No, seriously though, that's the propagation account.
Sss...
Clink
It's not attractive to be so brutal. That's not what we're about.
murmur
More important question. What are we going to do about the Arcus Aim and their 'ethnic' quota policy?
Ping
Yeah, that's bad, man. It's a fuckin' tyranny.
mur-mur
mur-mur

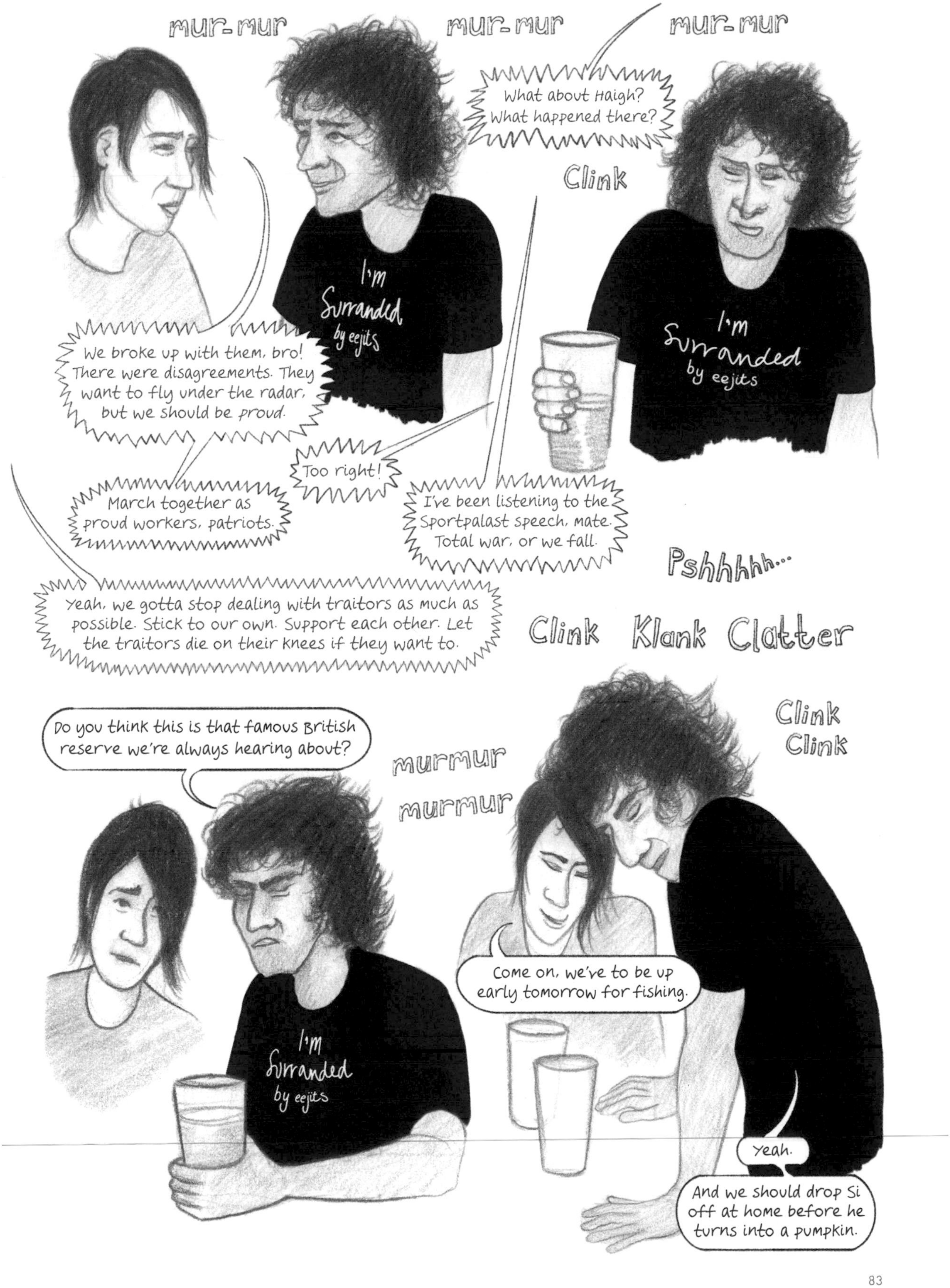
mur-mur
mur-mur
mur-mur
What about Haigh? What happened there?
Clink
I'm Surranded by eejits
We broke up with them, bro! There were disagreements. They want to fly under the radar, but we should be *proud*.
I'm Surranded by eejits
March together as proud workers, patriots.
Too right!
I've been listening to the Sportpalast speech, mate. Total war, or we fall.
Yeah, we gotta stop dealing with traitors as much as possible. Stick to our own. Support each other. Let the traitors die on their knees if they want to.
Pshhhhh...
Clink Klank Clatter
Do you think this is that famous British reserve we're always hearing about?
murmur
murmur
I'm Surranded by eejits
Clink
Clink
Come on, we've to be up early tomorrow for fishing.
Yeah.
And we should drop Si off at home before he turns into a pumpkin.

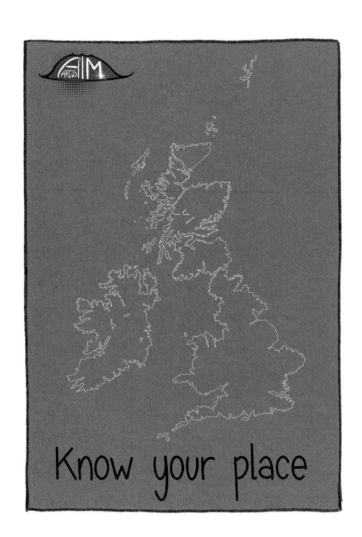

Know your place

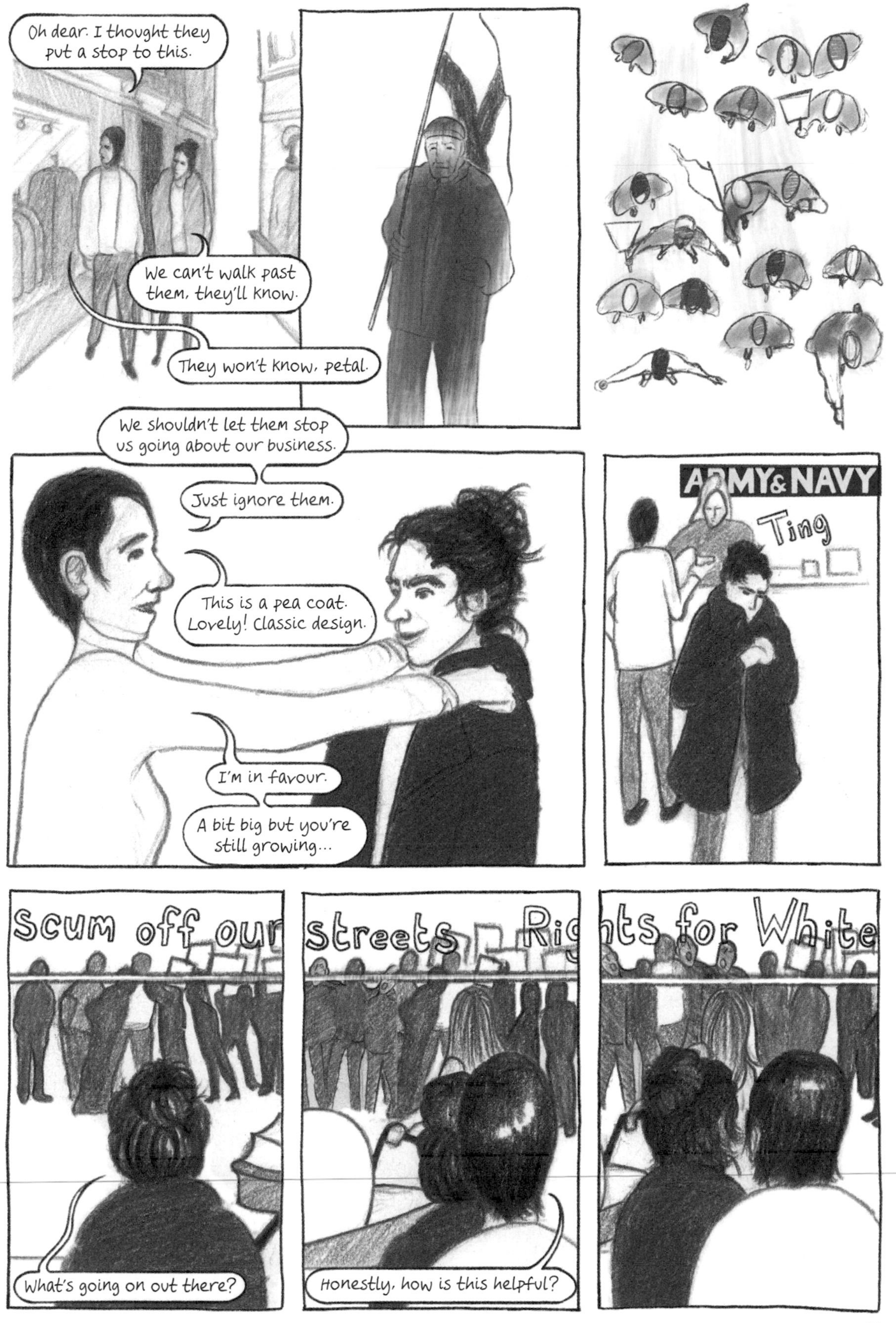

Oh dear. I thought they put a stop to this.
We can't walk past them, they'll know.
They won't know, petal.
We shouldn't let them stop us going about our business.
Just ignore them.
This is a pea coat. Lovely! Classic design.
I'm in favour.
A bit big but you're still growing...
ARMY&NAVY
Ting
Scum off our streets
Rights for White
What's going on out there?
Honestly, how is this helpful?

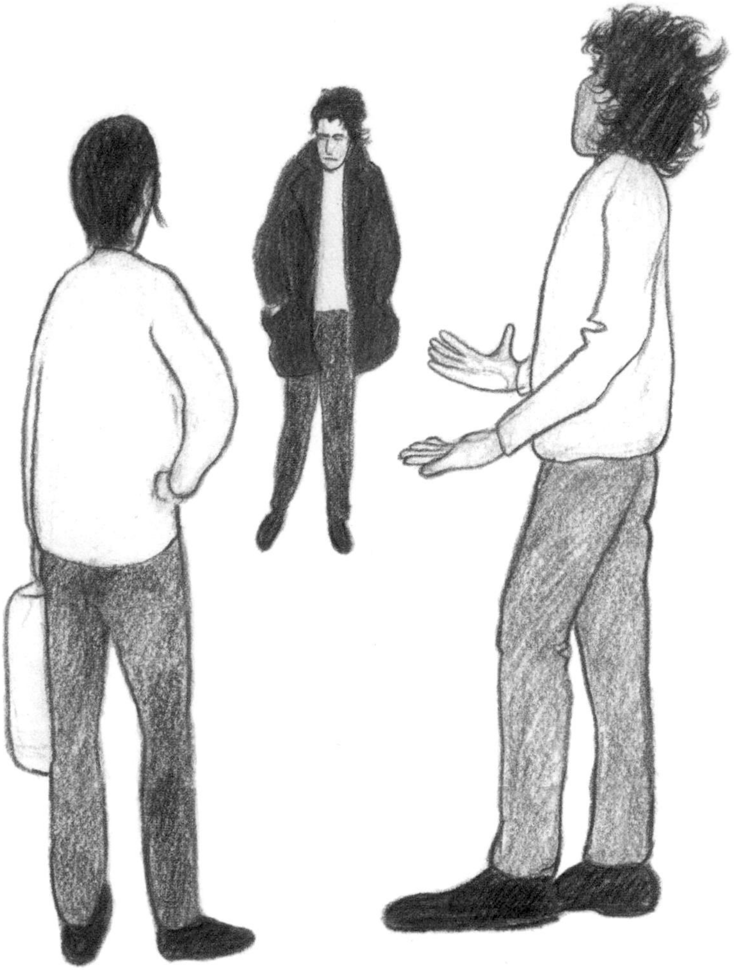

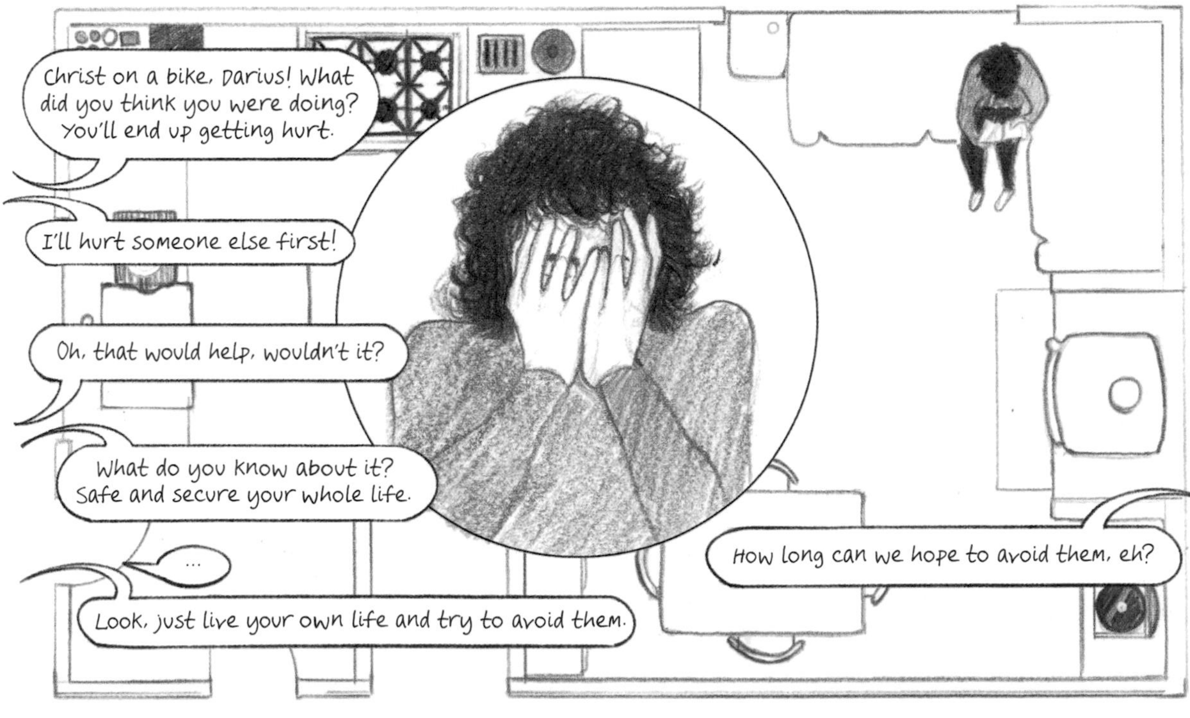
Christ on a bike, Darius! What did you think you were doing? You'll end up getting hurt.
I'll hurt someone else first!
Oh, that would help, wouldn't it?
What do you know about it? Safe and secure your whole life.
...
Look, just live your own life and try to avoid them.
How long can we hope to avoid them, eh?

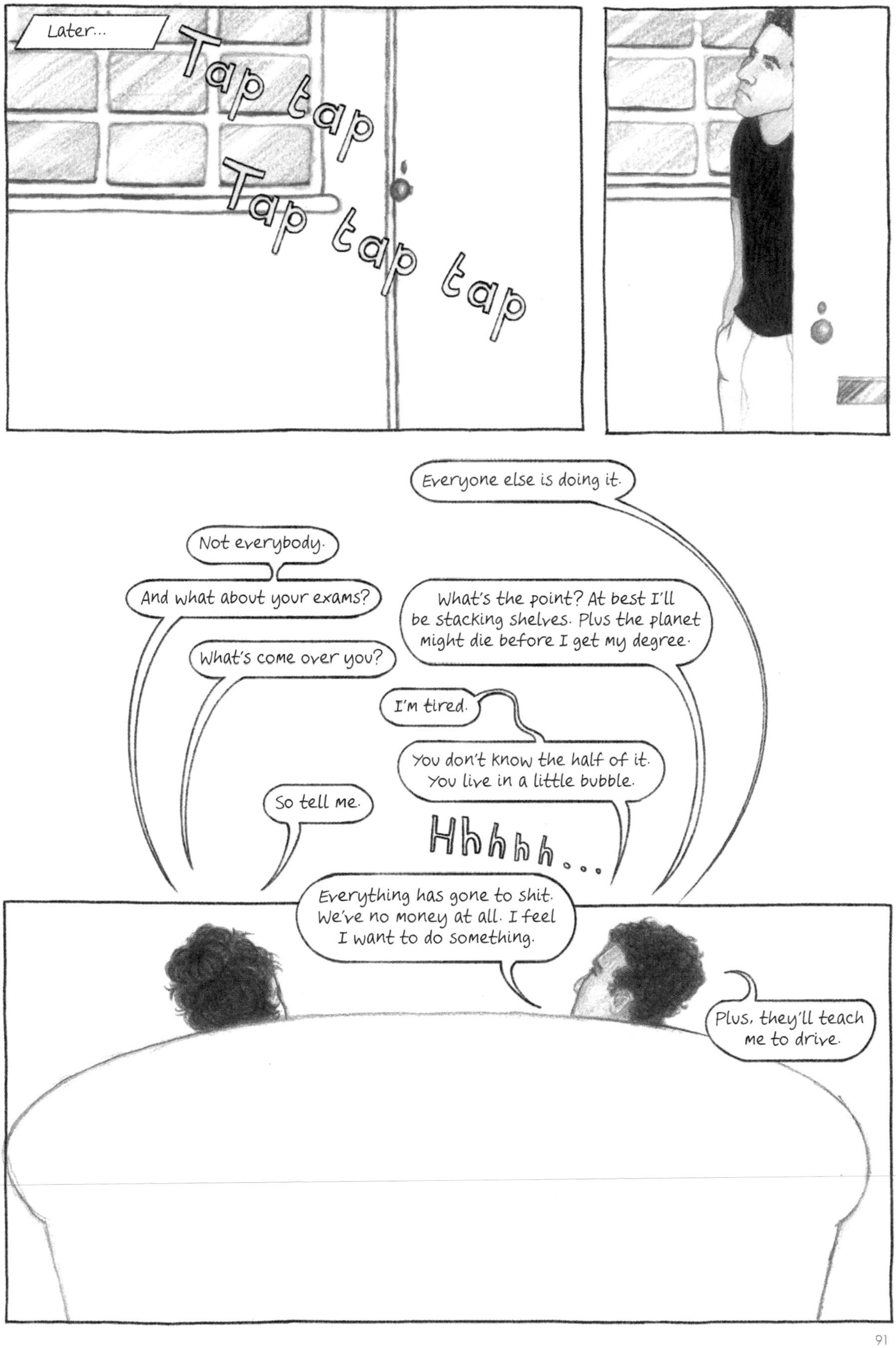

Later...
Tap tap
Tap tap tap tap
Everyone else is doing it.
Not everybody.
And what about your exams?
What's the point? At best I'll be stacking shelves. Plus the planet might die before I get my degree.
What's come over you?
I'm tired.
You don't know the half of it. You live in a little bubble.
So tell me.
Hhhhh...
Everything has gone to shit. We've no money at all. I feel I want to do something.
Plus, they'll teach me to drive.

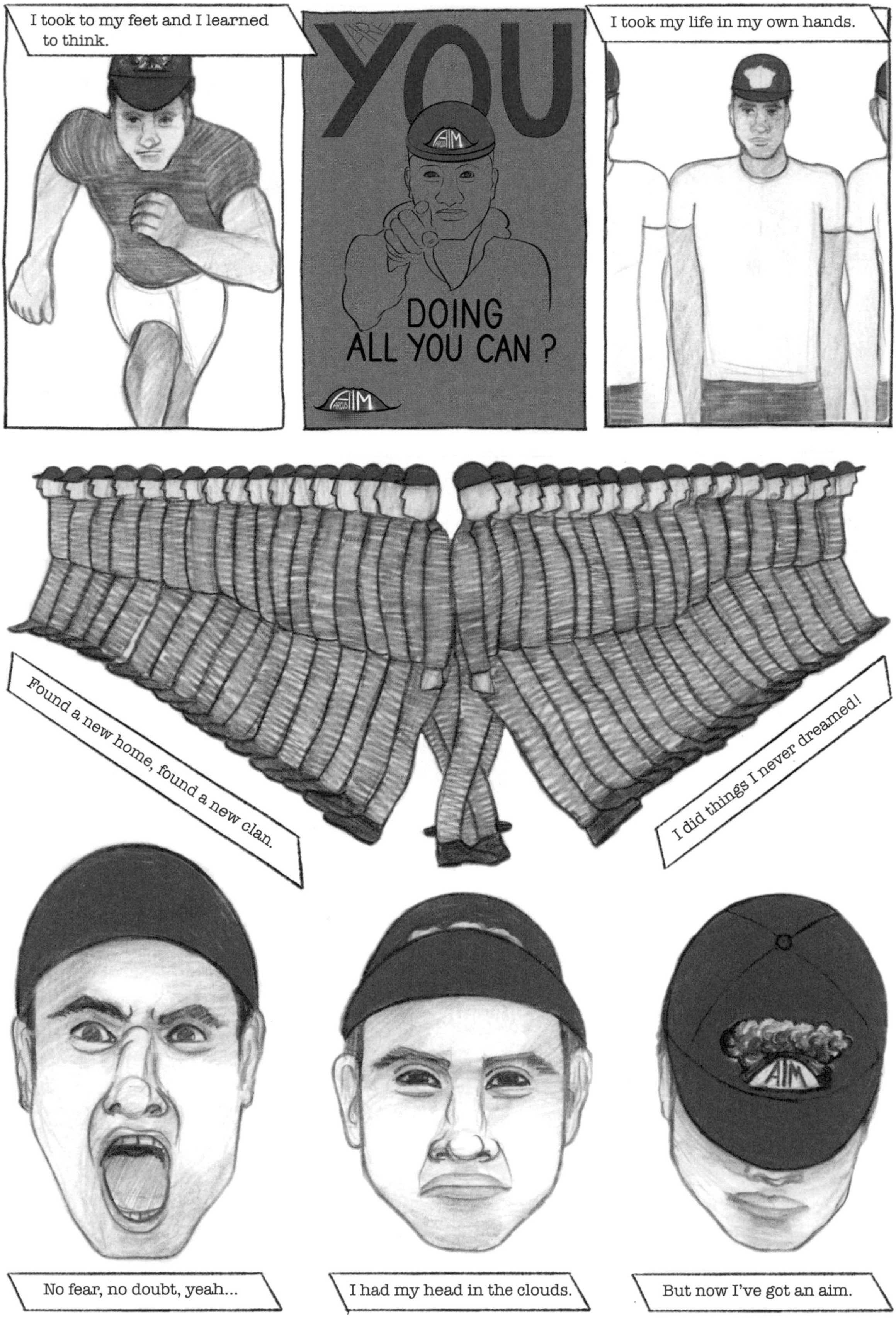

I took to my feet and I learned to think.
ARE YOU
AIM
DOING ALL YOU CAN ?
AIM
I took my life in my own hands.
Found a new home, found a new clan.
I did things I never dreamed!
AIM
No fear, no doubt, yeah...
I had my head in the clouds.
But now I've got an aim.

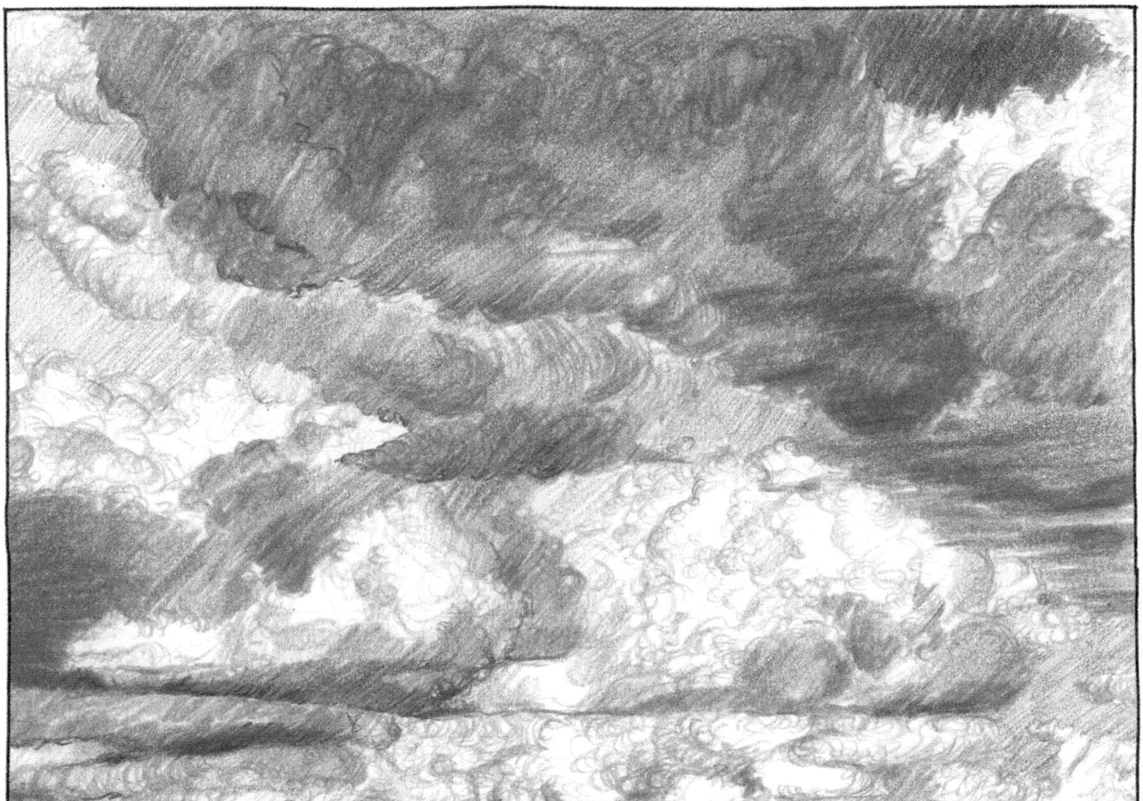

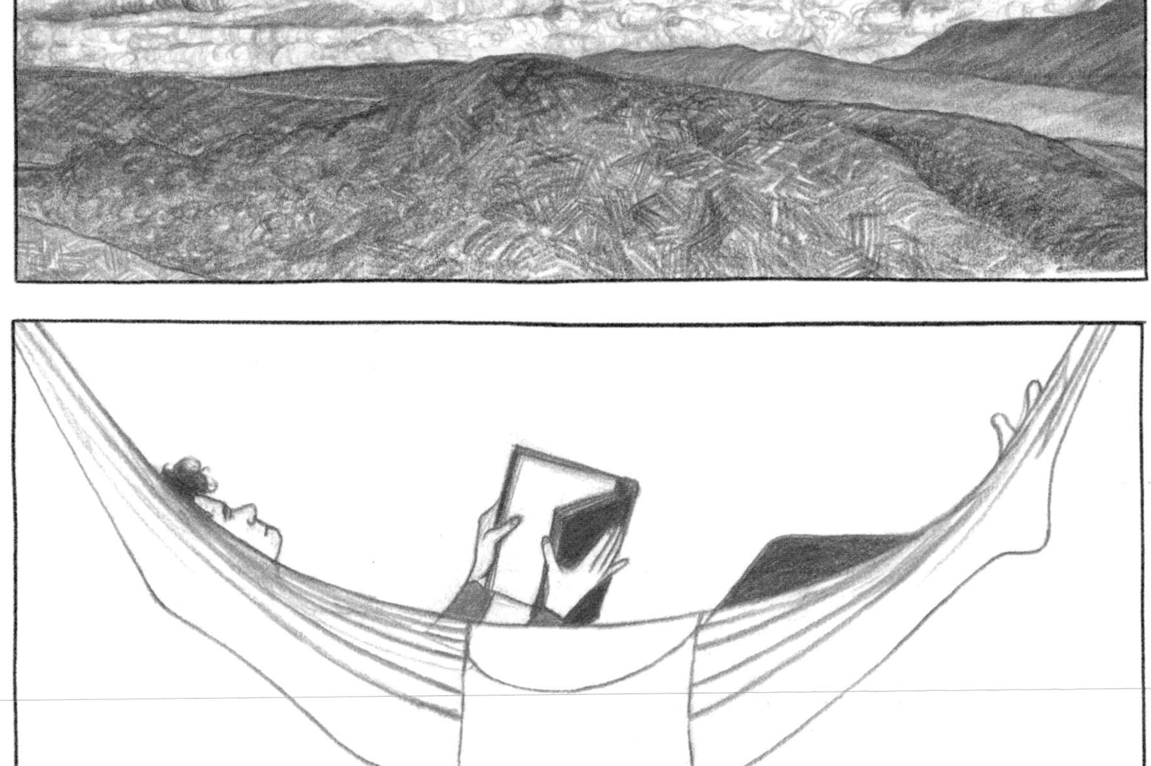

Saturday

Sigh is not coming back to school he joined the Might. I can't beleive it I'm so angry with him. What an idiot. Why does he think he is going to fit in with them? They are talking about making it compulsory. No way I'm doing it, they can't make me. Havn't shown Mum the 'anti-bullying policy' school sent home. It's supposed to stop people sending nasty stuff even when they are not at school!! Ha! They've no idea. Kids are horrible to each other and adults are not much beter. Mum and Dad have not stopped arguing since Dad lamped that bloke. They both think they are right. On and on!!

Wednesday

Whole school assembly this morning. Stuff about safety going straight home in groups if you're not stopping for Arcus Aim. Its Every night after school now! If you can't go straight home you have to wait in the gym with Steely for your parents to come. Steely will do 'alternative team activities'. Lucky I can come home but I've nobody to walk with. I'll have to sneak out. On the blob today PE tomorrow as well. Saturday lunch there's a demo my dad wants to go to. Gonna go with him I think. Never been on a demo before. Will borrow Dad's phone and take pictures.

Monday

Loads of homework this year. Free periods are not actually free so that's a bit dissapointing. History is good. English Lit bit boring all old stuff. Studying a film called Stepford Wives in Critical Thinking. Just seems like life round here to me. Stepford wives and their gammon boyfreinds. Can't possibly be so many blonde girls naturally. Boys with their stupid macho waddle. Saw Sigh outside Dixie Chicken in his Might colours with his mates. They don't have uniforms just blue, grey and white. But they can't wear jeans?! Jacko had red plastic trainers on (?) trackies and his dad's jacket. Ha! Jacko strutting about, Sigh didn't speak to me. I hate this town. And I'm angry all the time.

Friday finally!

Gonna get up tomorrow morning and have a run on the moor by myself. Need some air and get my eyes and my heart working again. I do like running on my own, but sometimes I get so lonely. I see other people out together and I think why havn't I got someone like that? I want someone to share things with someone like me why is there no one like me? It feels awful in my stomach. Deep and dull sort of. Maybe there's something wrong with me.

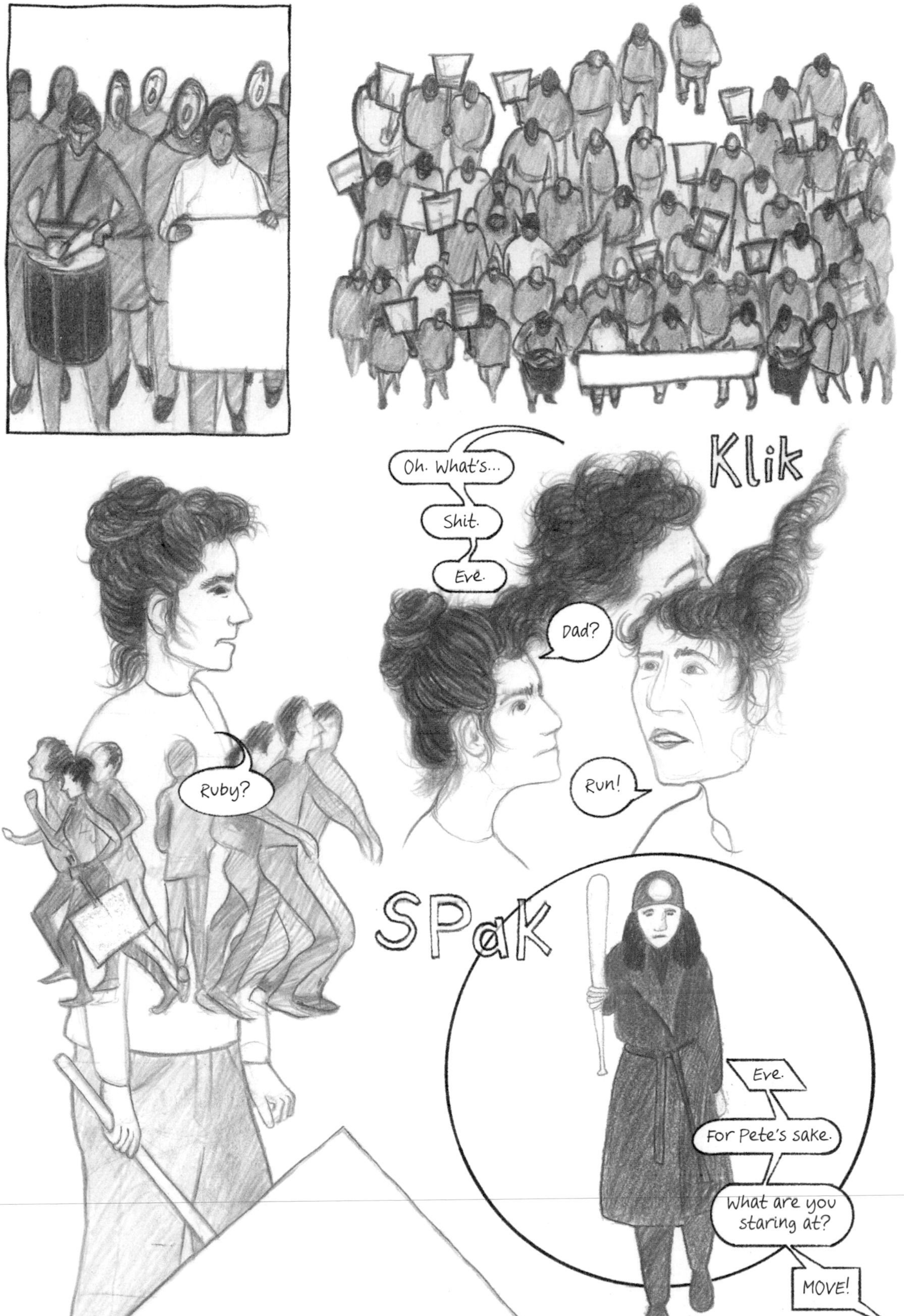

Oh. What's...
Shit.
Eve.
Klik
Dad?
Run!
Ruby?
SPaK
Eve.
For Pete's sake.
What are you staring at?
MOVE!

This weekend saw the first exercise of the government's new special powers to preserve public order, when continuous rounds of tear-gas and rubber bullets were fired to contain rioting when anti-government groups clashed. The Domestic Order Schedule allows the use of rubber bullets to contain rioting in the UK for the first time since the 1970s. This is a temporary measure, overseen by the Special Committee for Domestic Peace-Keeping. From today the right to protest peacefully is no longer in place and groups of more than six people can be dispersed by the combined forces.

The Home Secretary Sir Clifford Dormer appealed for calm, reiterated there has been intolerable behaviour *on all sides,* and stated that the Domestic Order Schedule would protect people and property. Sir Clifford reiterated decisions about policy *will* be made by parliament and will *not* be influenced by pressure from unruly mobs. He added that anyone thinking of engaging in civil disobedience would feel the full force of the law. At level 6 the schedule will allow for indefinite internment of any person behaving in a manner so as to be prejudicial to the preservation of the peace.

In other news, 10,000 new 'support officer' positions will be filled by unemployed young people, who have acquired the necessary skills as Arcus scouts. They will be equipped with defensive weapons and protective wear. On the line is Lucy Green of Arcus Aim. Ms Green, can you tell us about your plans with the civil defence service?

'Our movement is for a youth squeezed out of employment and the economy, bombarded by unnecessary competition in the jobs market, oppressed by the weight of exams and crushed by a lack of opportunity. Arcus Aim says let's see what they might do with a *real* education, lessons you can't learn in class, an aim, a university of life.'

Ms Green, you haven't answered my question.

'Arcus Aim will help defeat the scourge of violent extremism currently damaging our country; they will be the best scouts in the world, and of course, they will receive training.'

Thank you. Don't you think trained, professional officers would be better for our country? Isn't this exploitation of our jobless youth, doing the police and the army on the cheap?

'That's a cheap question! Our scouts are always eager to serve and it is for the government to decide how they will achieve that service.'

So you agree the future of the scouts is more complicated than you claim? ... OK, we seem to have lost Ms Green... now over to the weather. Charley, what's the forecast for today?

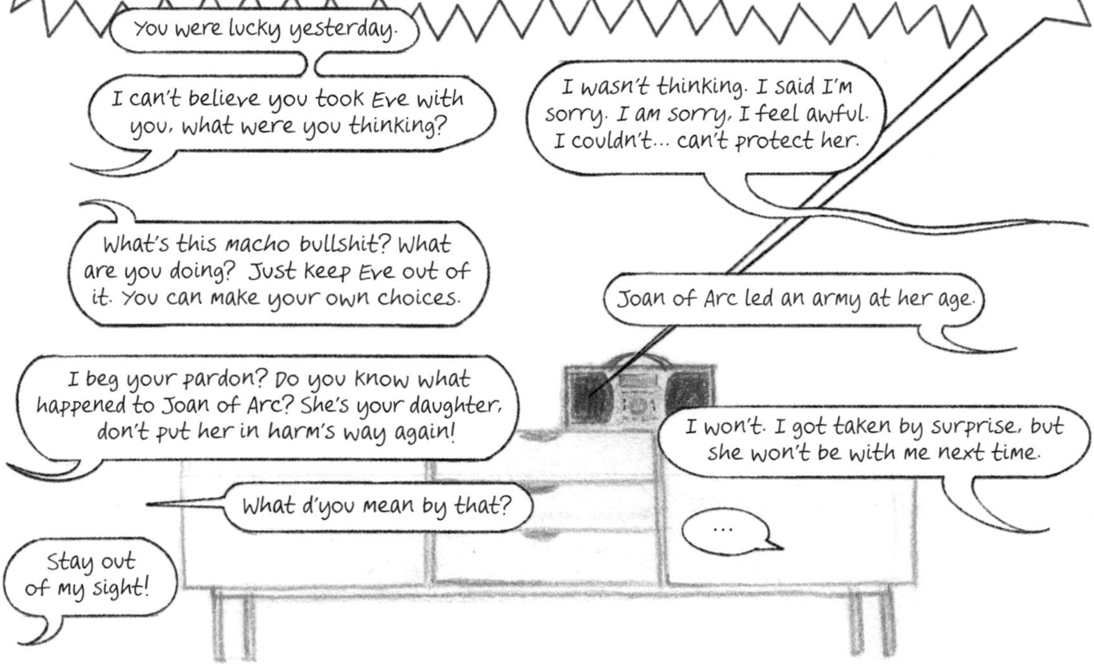
You were lucky yesterday.
I can't believe you took Eve with you, what were you thinking?
I wasn't thinking. I said I'm sorry. I am sorry, I feel awful. I couldn't... can't protect her.
What's this macho bullshit? What are you doing? Just keep Eve out of it. You can make your own choices.
Joan of Arc led an army at her age.
I beg your pardon? Do you know what happened to Joan of Arc? She's your daughter, don't put her in harm's way again!
I won't. I got taken by surprise, but she won't be with me next time.
What d'you mean by that?
...
Stay out of my sight!

Was this when it started? It was when something ended. When we knew for certain what was coming.

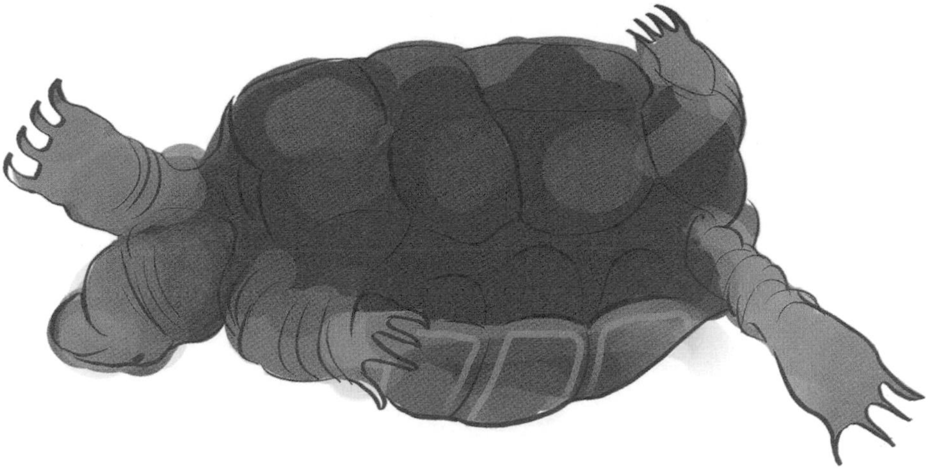

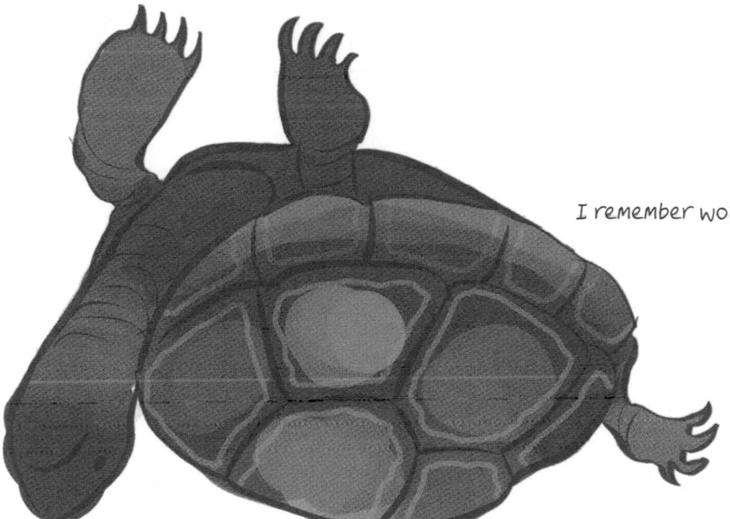

I remember wondering which way it would turn.

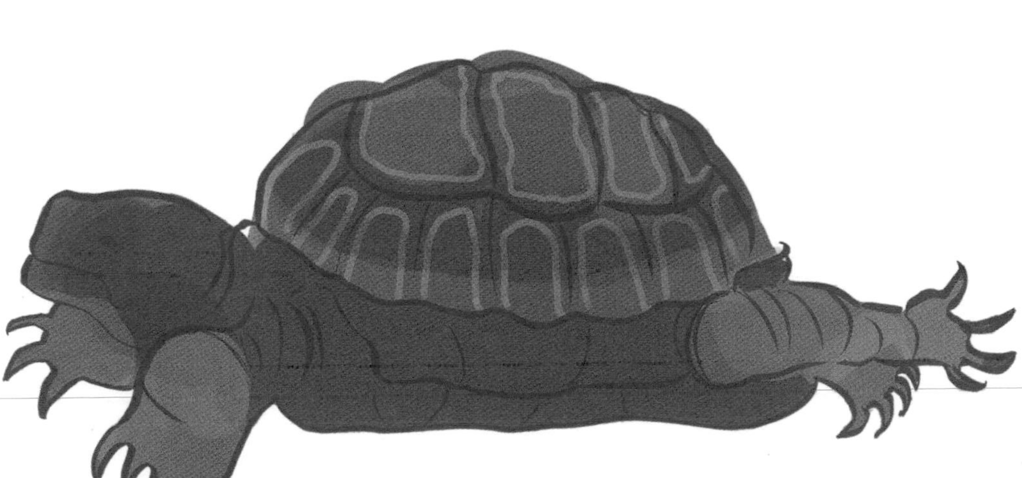

It turned the way it always turns. 'Til it was over.

A new dawning

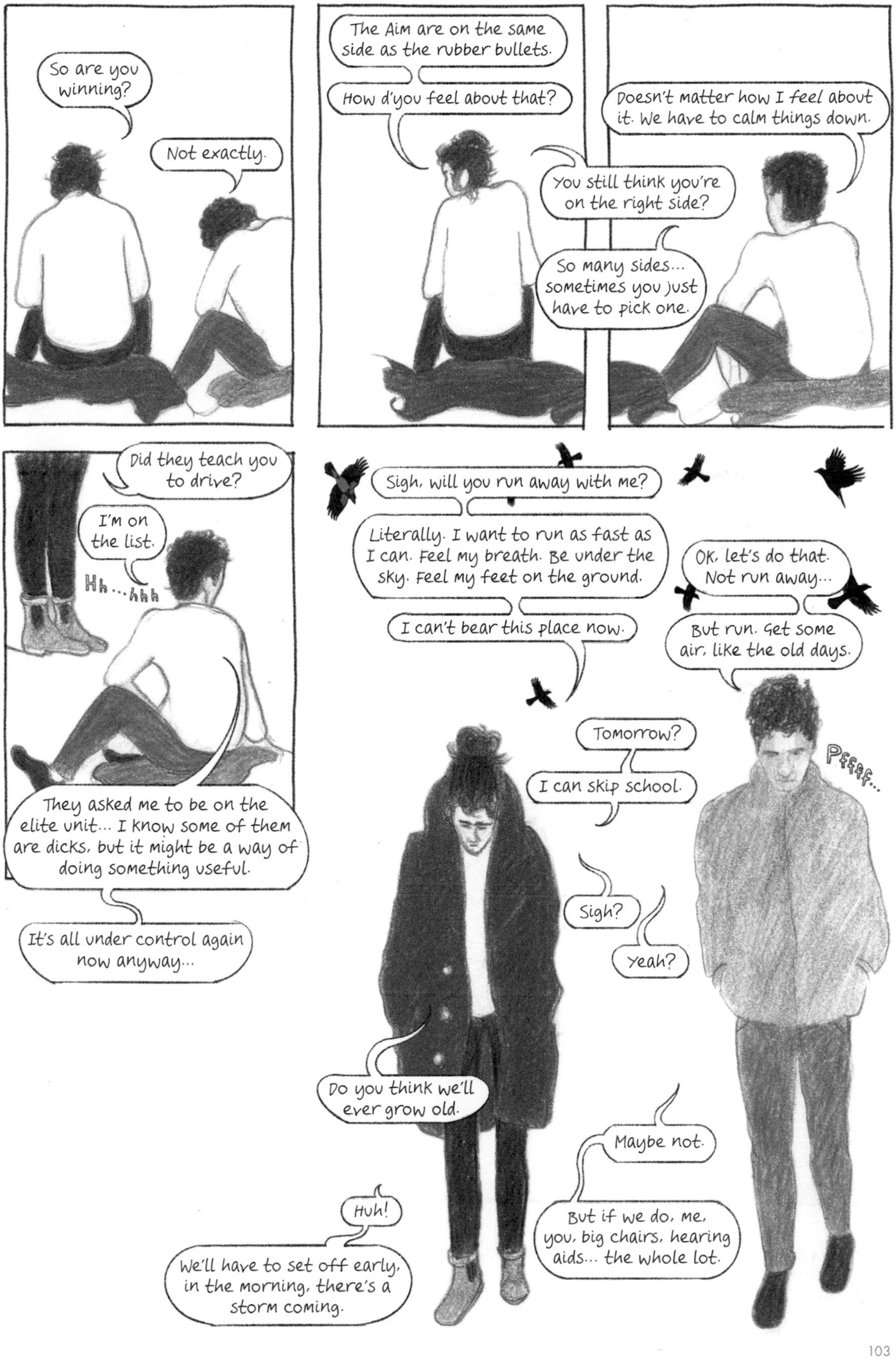
So are you winning?
Not exactly.
The Aim are on the same side as the rubber bullets.
How d'you feel about that?
You still think you're on the right side?
So many sides... sometimes you just have to pick one.
Doesn't matter how I feel about it. We have to calm things down.
Did they teach you to drive?
I'm on the list.
Hh...hhh
They asked me to be on the elite unit... I know some of them are dicks, but it might be a way of doing something useful.
It's all under control again now anyway...
Sigh, will you run away with me?
Literally. I want to run as fast as I can. Feel my breath. Be under the sky. Feel my feet on the ground.
I can't bear this place now.
OK, let's do that. Not run away...
But run. Get some air, like the old days.
Pffff...
Tomorrow?
I can skip school.
Sigh?
Yeah?
Do you think we'll ever grow old.
Maybe not.
But if we do, me, you, big chairs, hearing aids... the whole lot.
Huh!
We'll have to set off early, in the morning, there's a storm coming.

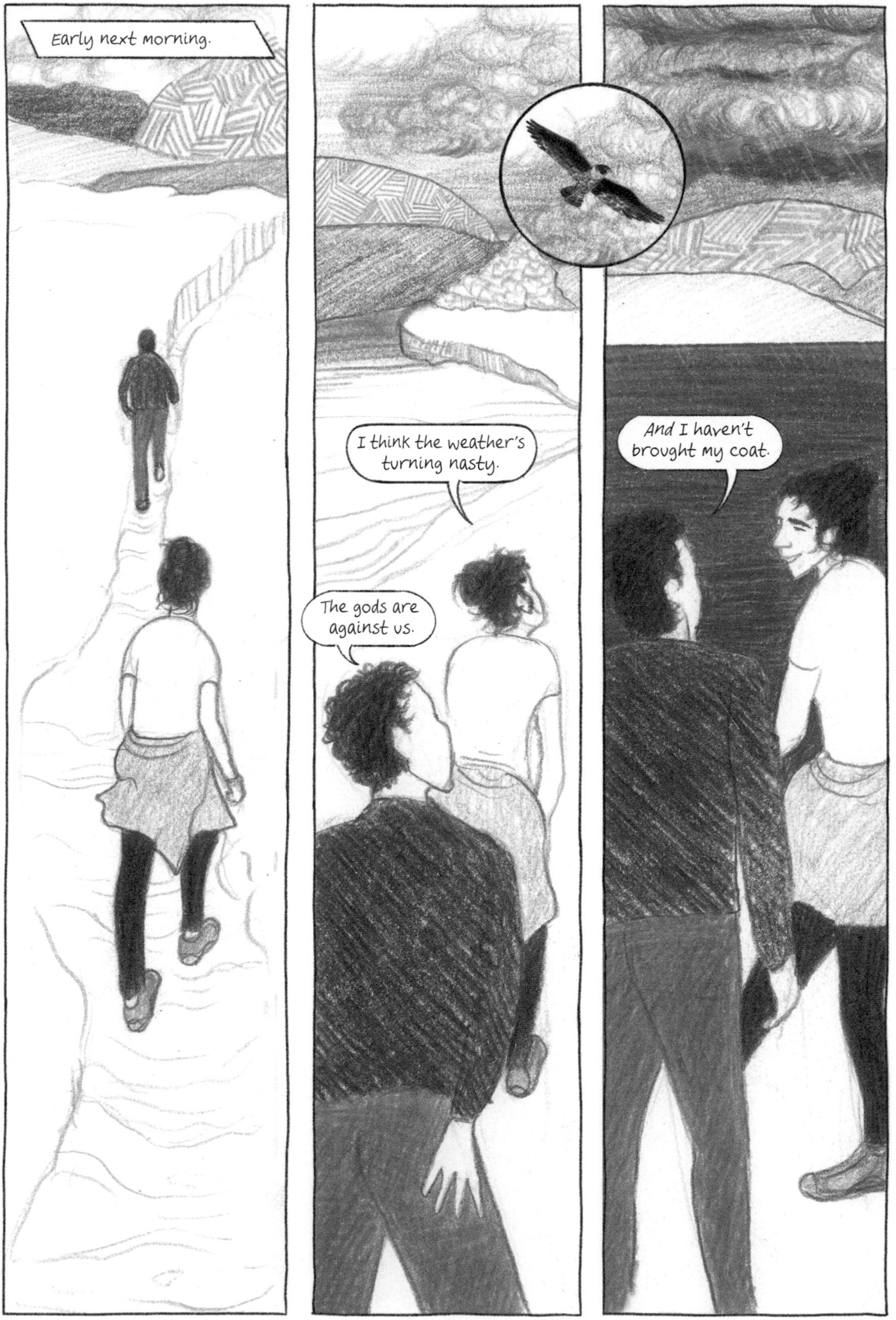
Early next morning.
I think the weather's turning nasty.
The gods are against us.
And I haven't brought my coat.

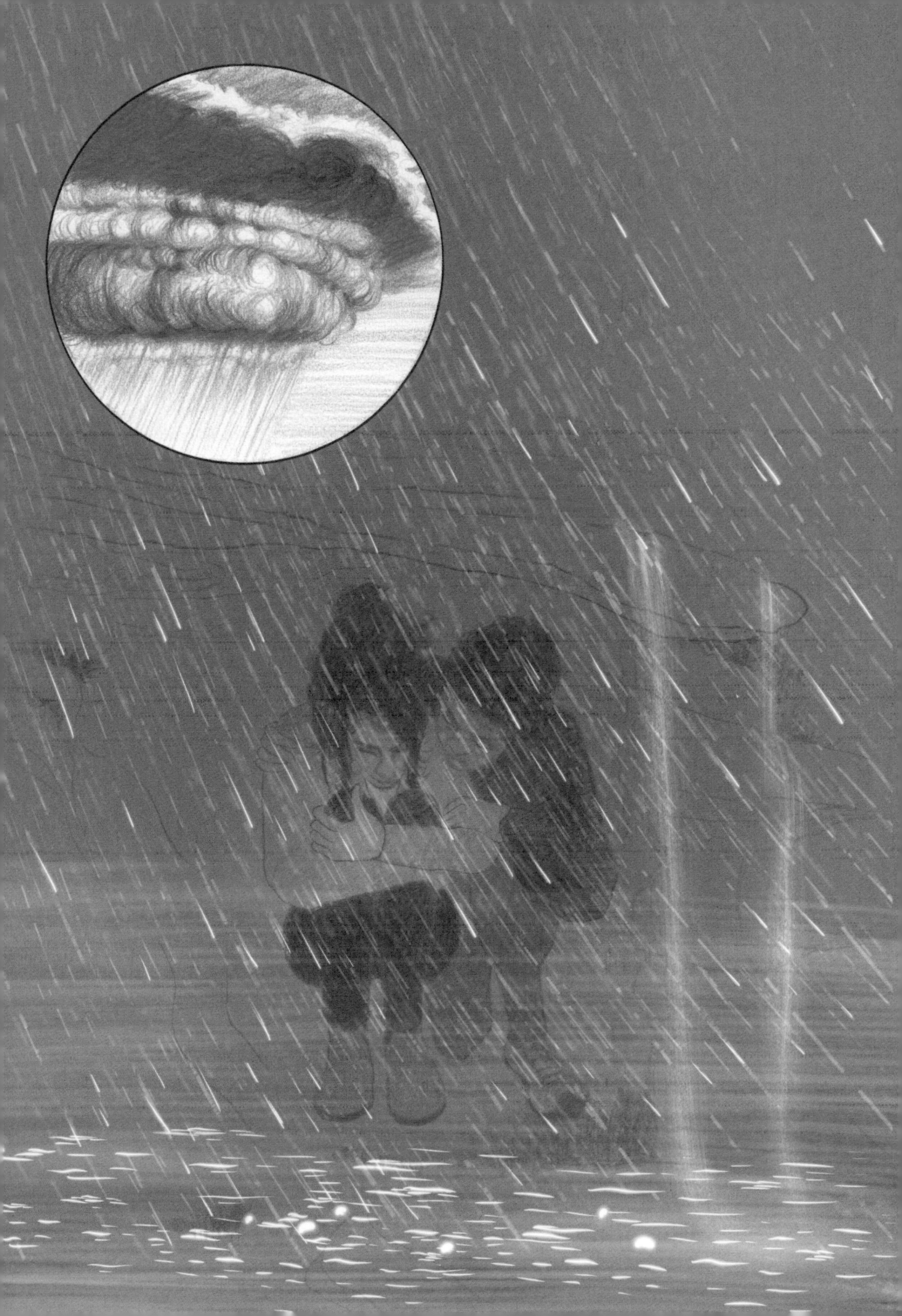

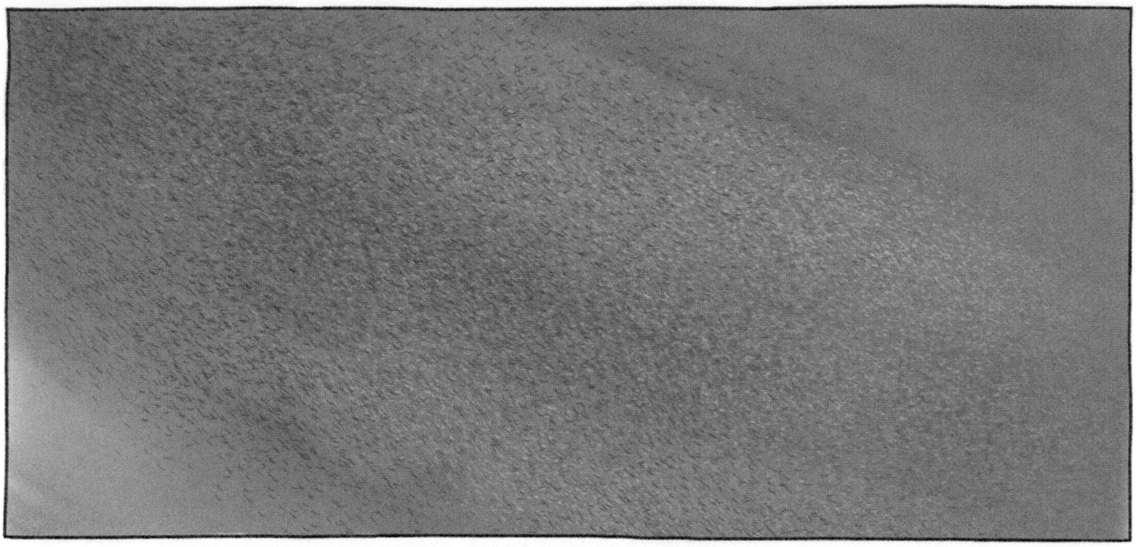

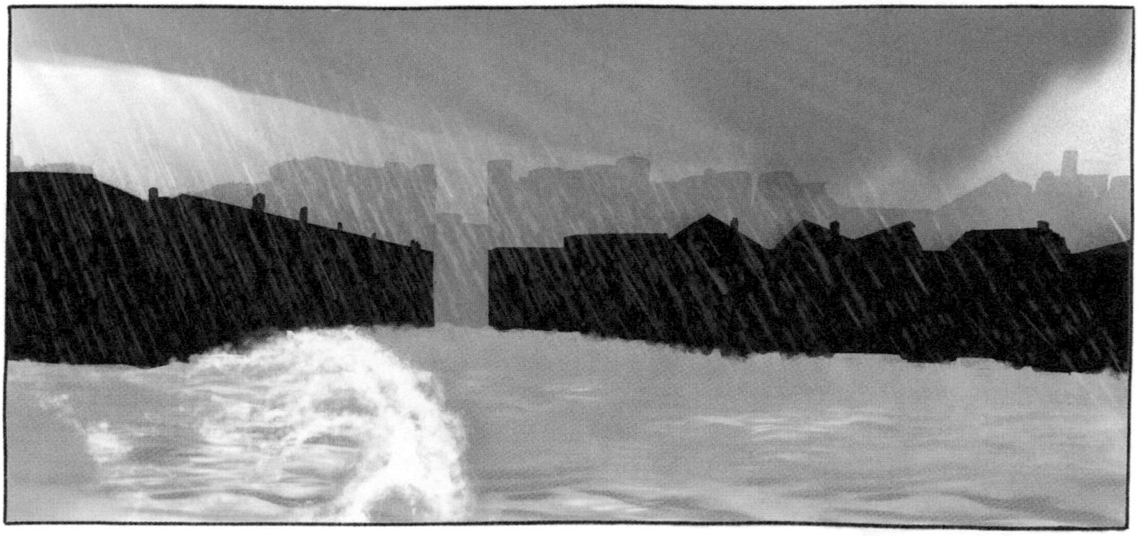

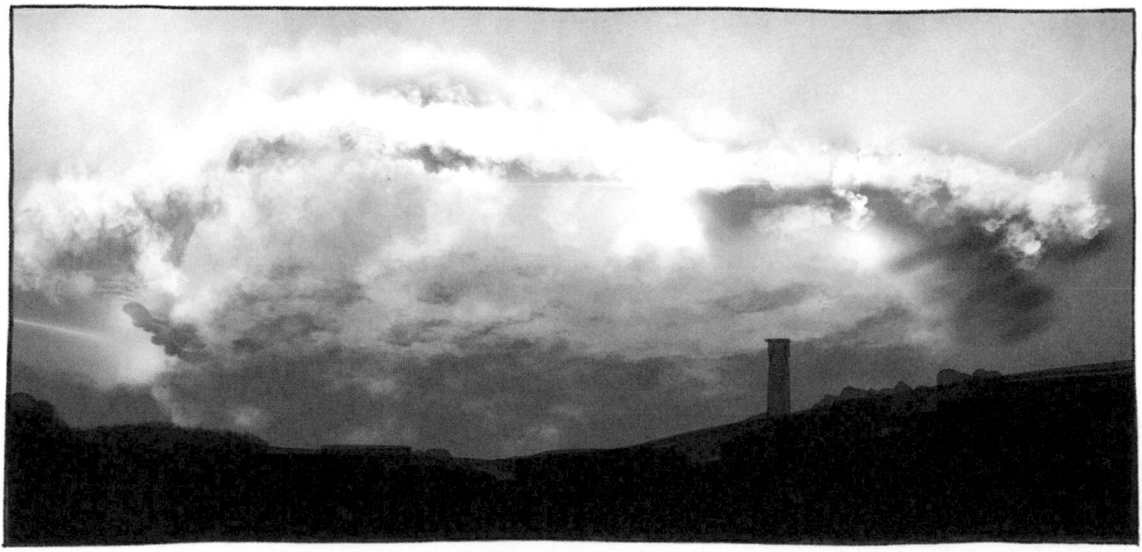

A storm that travelled the length of the British Isles on Friday has been described as an
explosive cyclogenesis by meteorologists. Some areas saw 120cm of rain fall in two days
leading to widespread flash flooding. Two hundred and seventy-one people are known to
have died and thousands have been left homeless or without power and clean drinking
water. These storms are sometimes called 'weather bombs' because of their rapid
development. Here's our weather correspondent to explain. Hi Nigel, where are you?
'I'm just south of Derby where almost 80% of land is under water. It's a terrible sight, Sally,
water and debris everywhere. Shops and houses flooded up to the second floor.'
Nigel, can you tell us more about these weather bombs?
'Yes, it's a type of extra-tropical cyclone that occurs after a rapid deepening of low
pressure, with hurricane-force winds and heavy rain. We've had them before but this is
the worst in British history.'
Should the area have been evacuated?
'There was no time to evacuate and I'm not sure where people would have gone. It's
controversial to say so but climate scientists think these events are no longer avoidable
and the best we can do is plan for emergencies, which the government clearly hasn't done
in this instance. There's a lot of anger about the government's slow response here and in
other affected areas. People have lost their lives, Sally. Environmentalists say the only way
to avert even bigger, extinction-level disasters in future is to curb all carbon emissions
immediately with a global ban on use of fossil fuels. So, no road traffic, no flights, no air
conditioning or refrigeration, no meat from farmed animals, no pet dogs and cats.'
That's hardly realistic, is it, Nigel?
'Perhaps not, but it's a whole new world now, Sally. The government is considering these
extreme measures but there's a lot of reluctance to act unilaterally. The Minister for
Energy and the Minister for Industry have called for further talks before any concrete
action is taken.'
Thank you, Nigel. Now back to the studio...

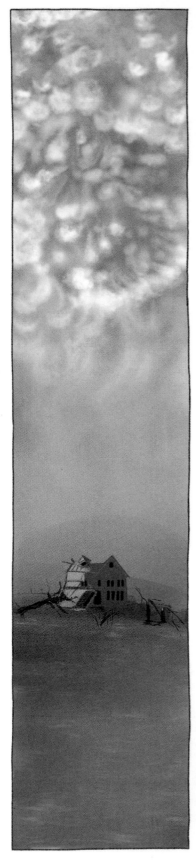

That old story about boiling frogs? It's not true. It's probably a nice metaphor but apart from the fact you'd hurt a frog quite badly by heating it slowly in water, it will jump out of the pot to safety before it boils. They say humans are like boiling frogs and don't notice when things are going bad, but we do. We notice.

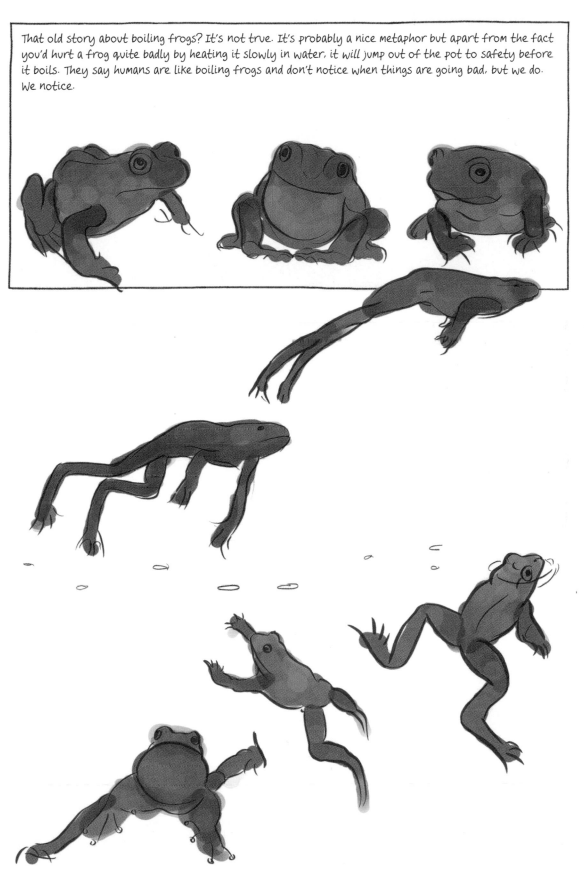

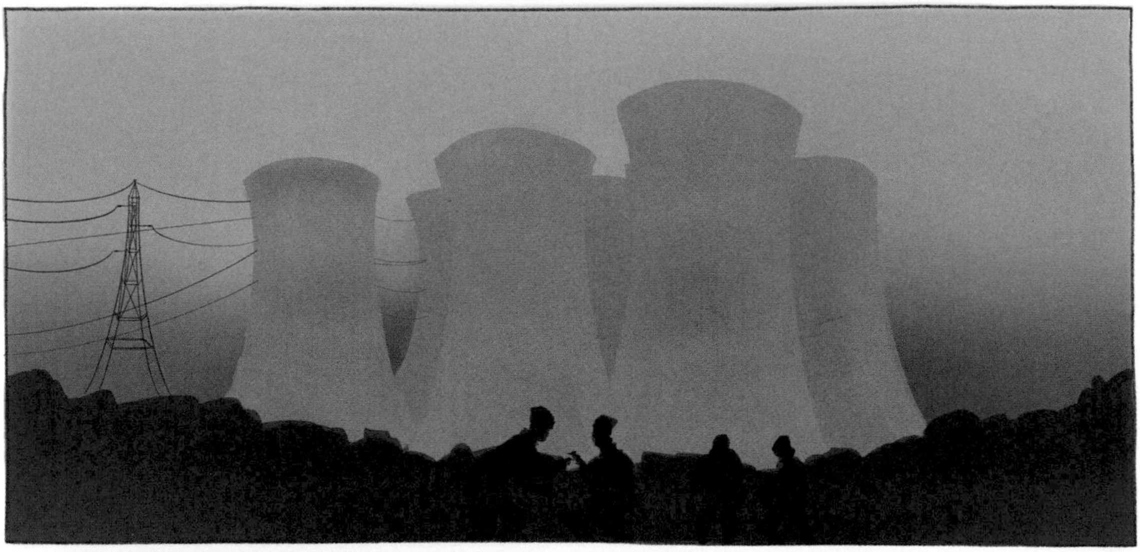

They say a watched pot never boils too, but it does...

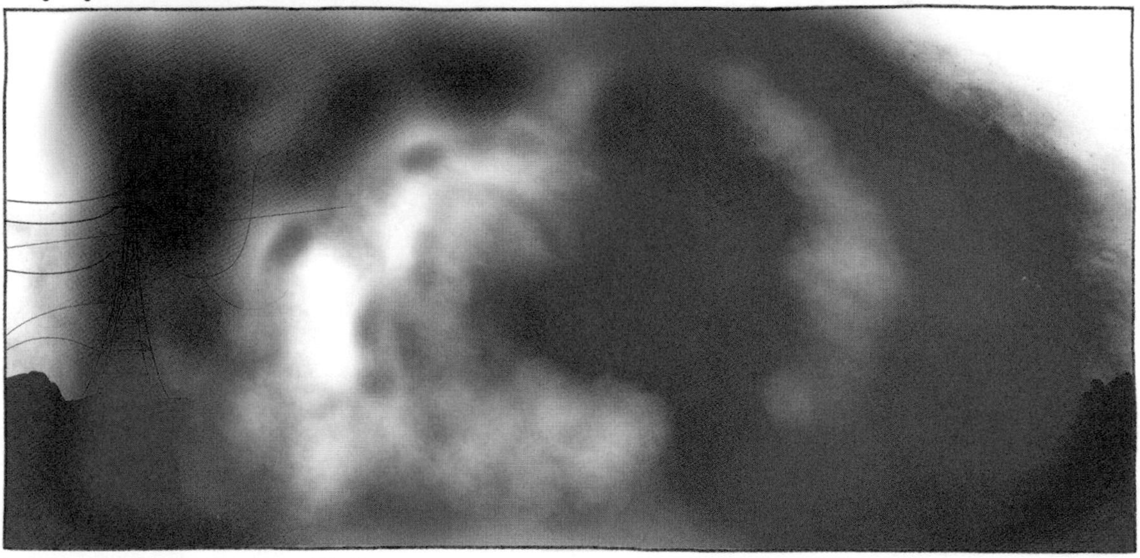

Because people like to play with fire.

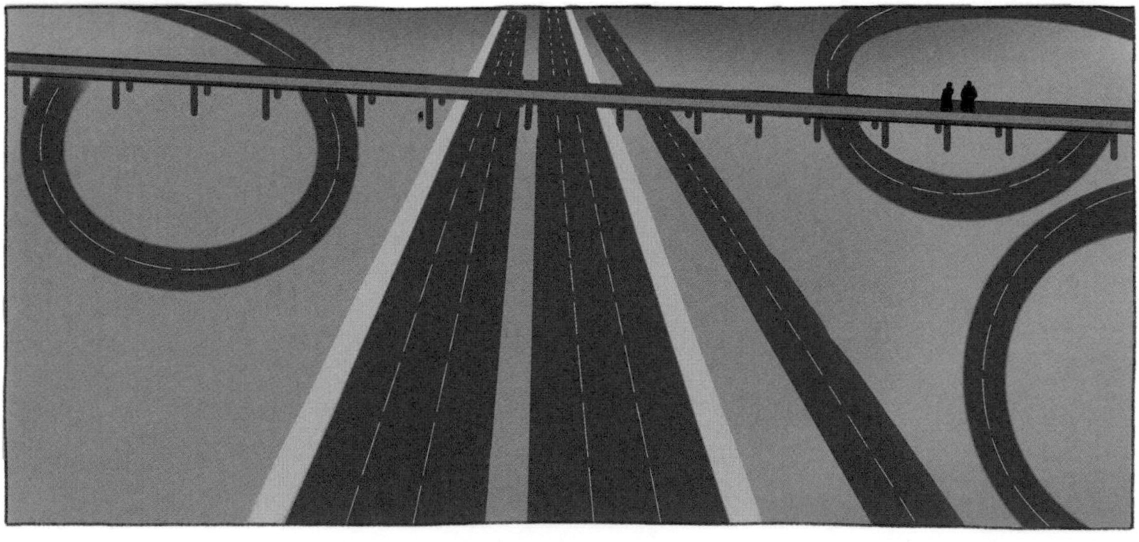

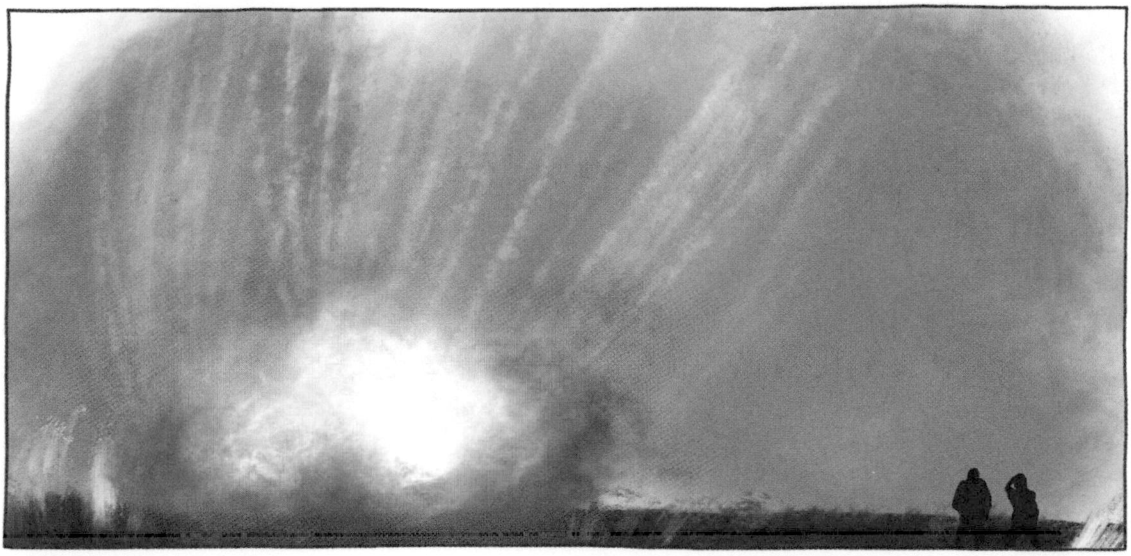

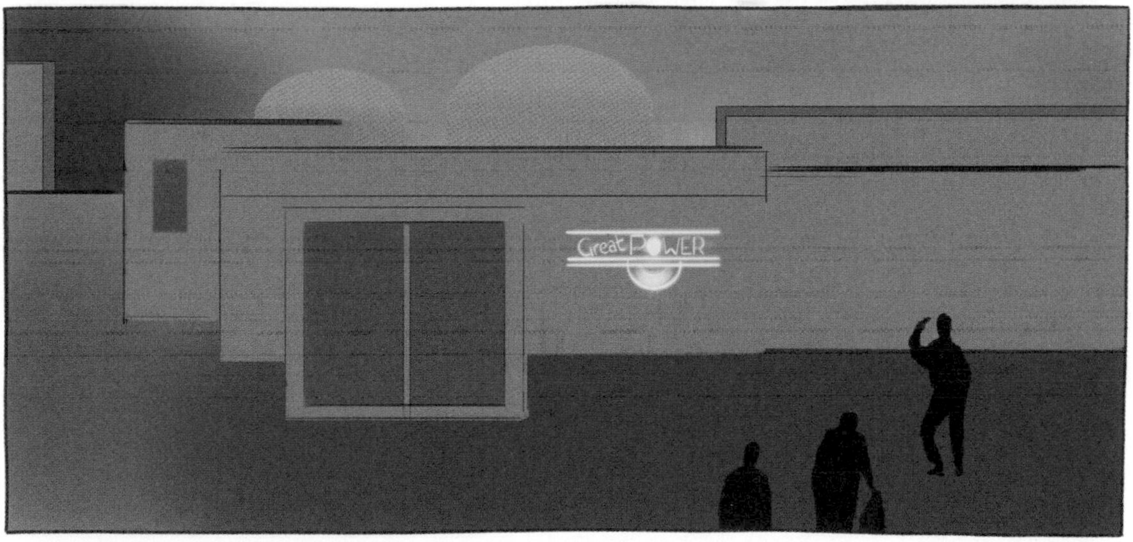
Great POWER

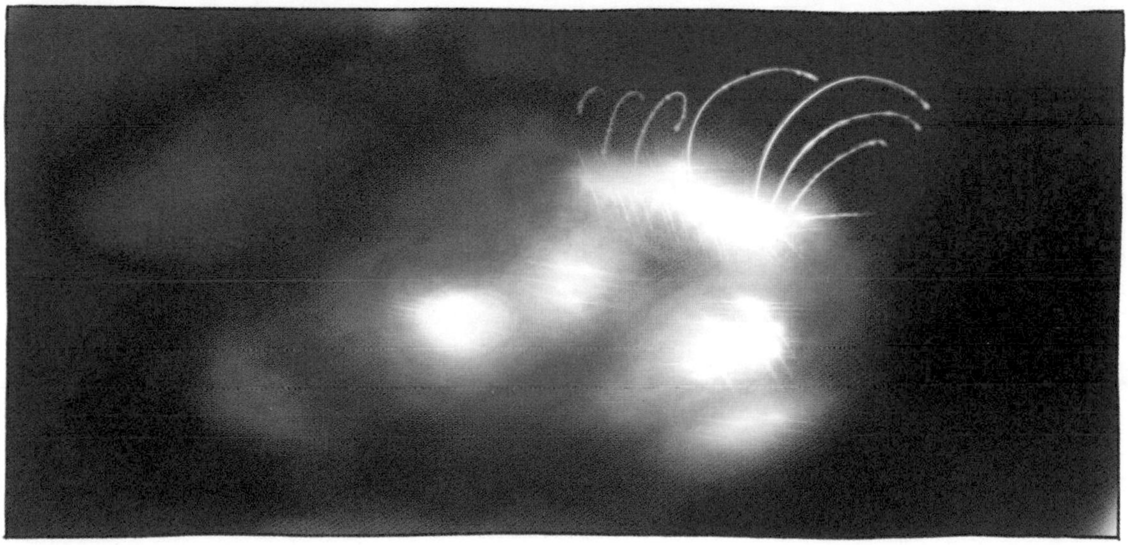

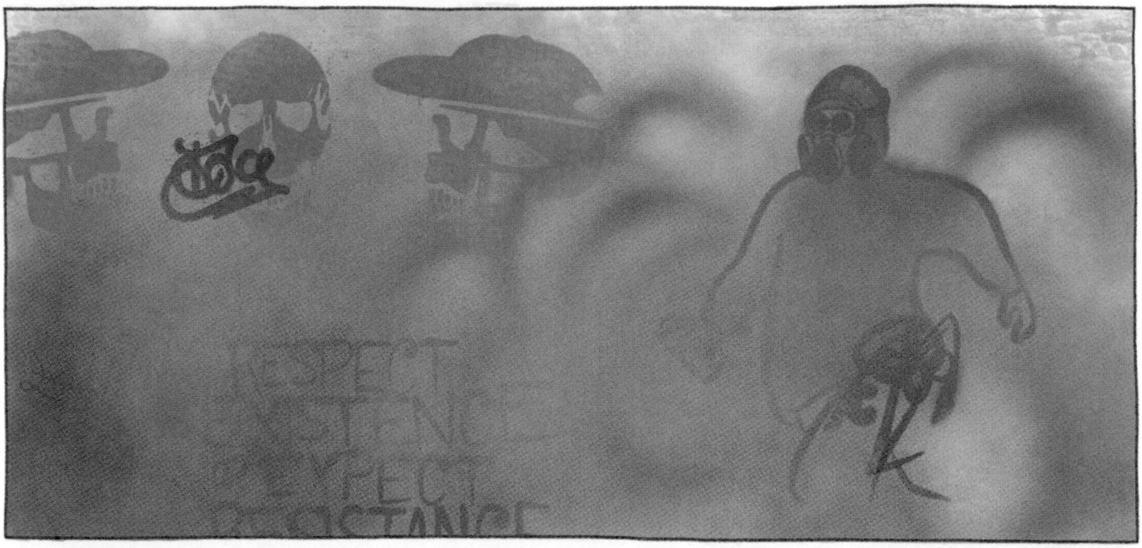
RESPECT

It simmered.

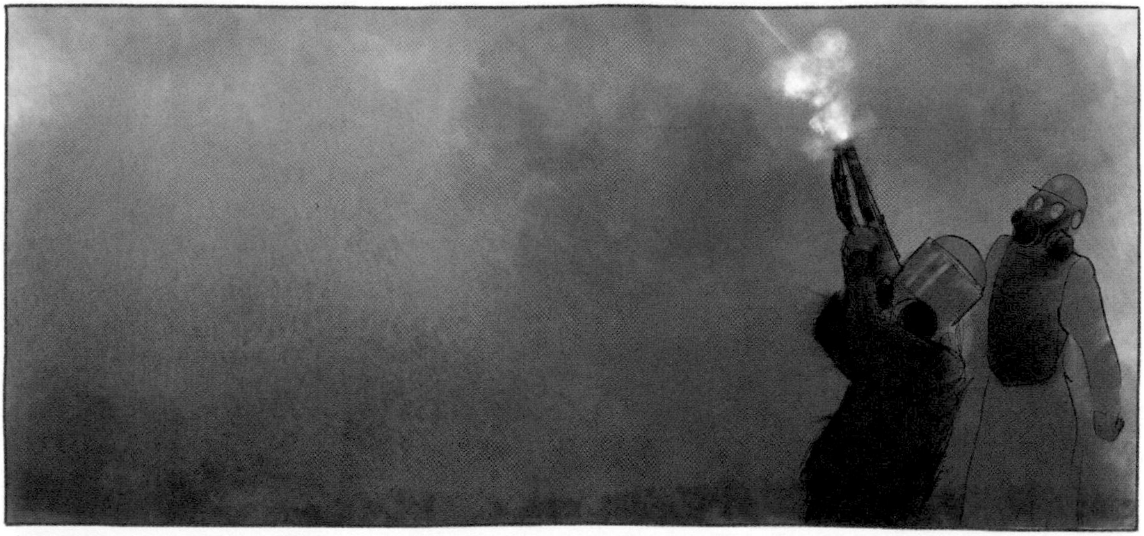

It boiled...

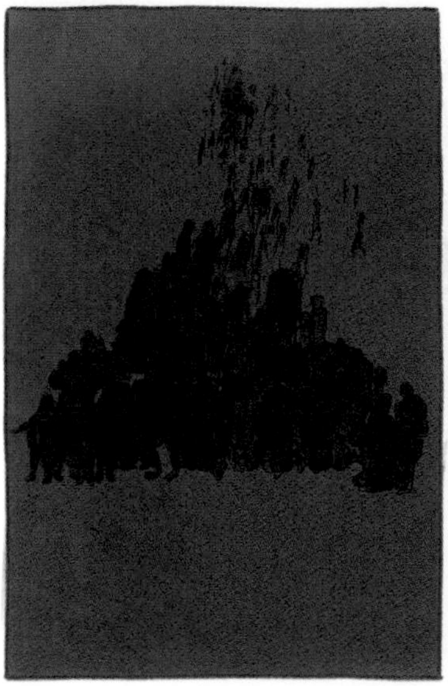

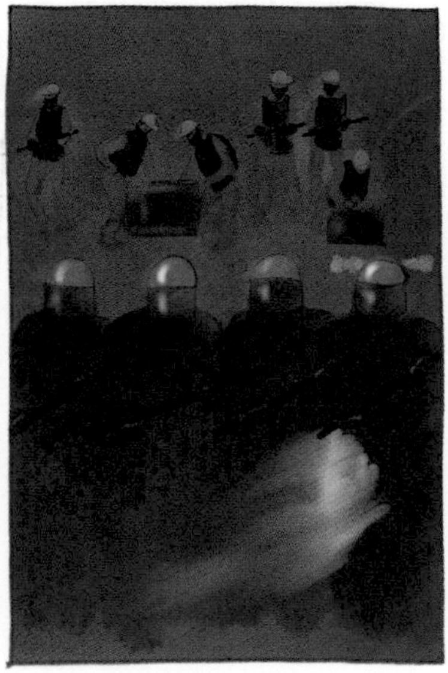

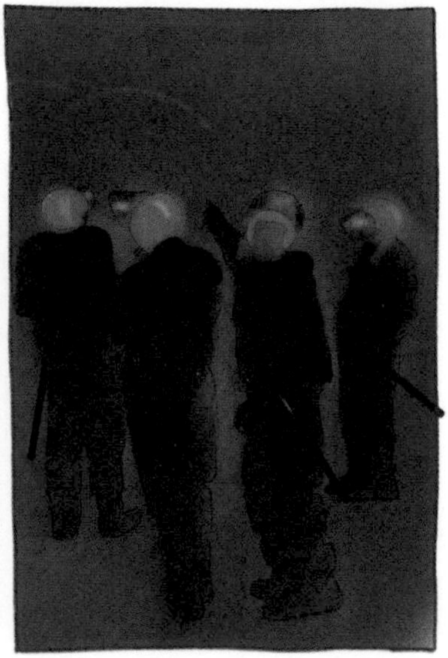

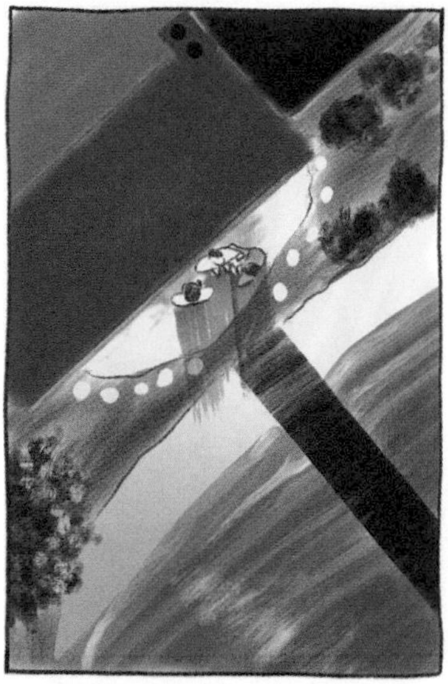
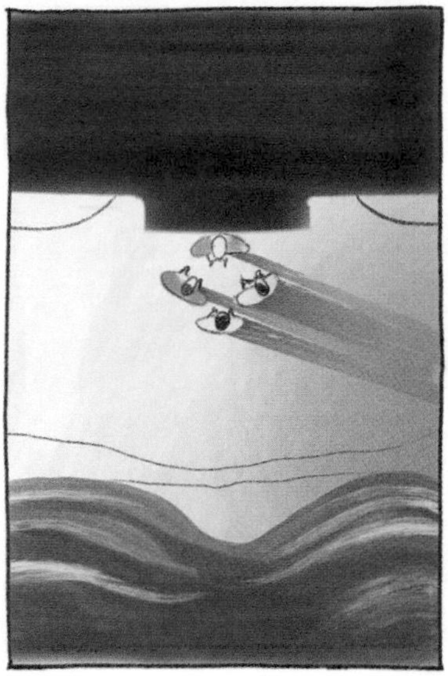
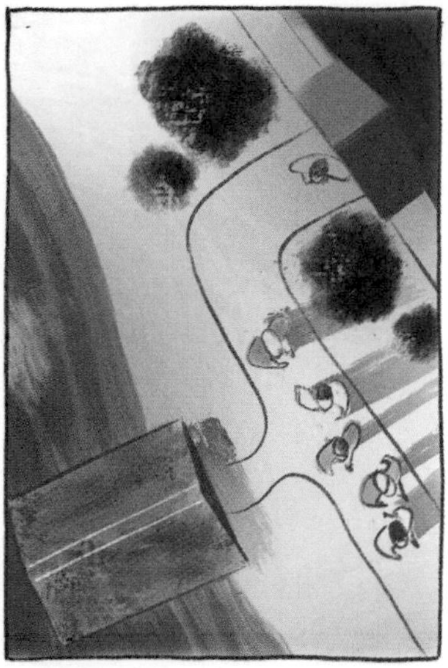
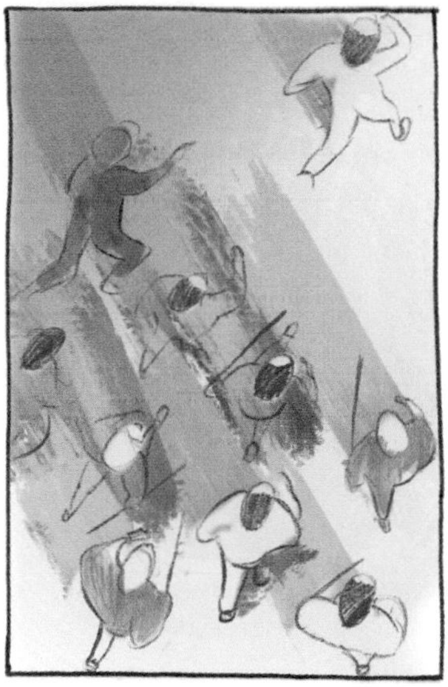

It bubbled up lakeside in Crakewick.

First, Adam came a-calling, then the residents came together with one purpose. Some were obliged to run for their lives, others joined the hunt and pursued.

The baggy circle of houses, the landings, the jetties, the pretty pebbled beaches looked different in this light.

And so, that bright, intoxicating spot that once seemed so distant drew closer with a jolt and we were all thrown towards it. Man, woman, child.

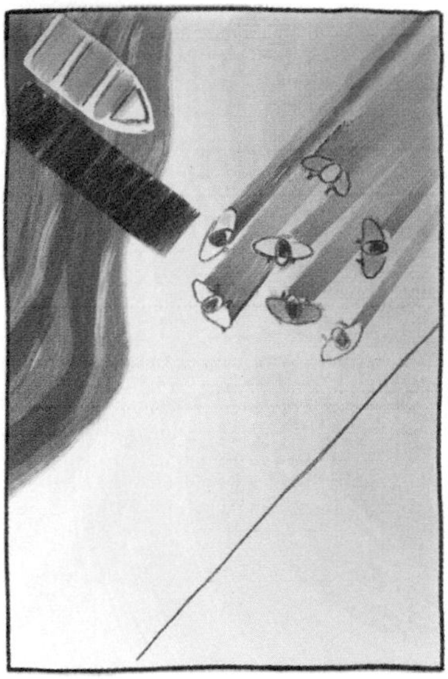
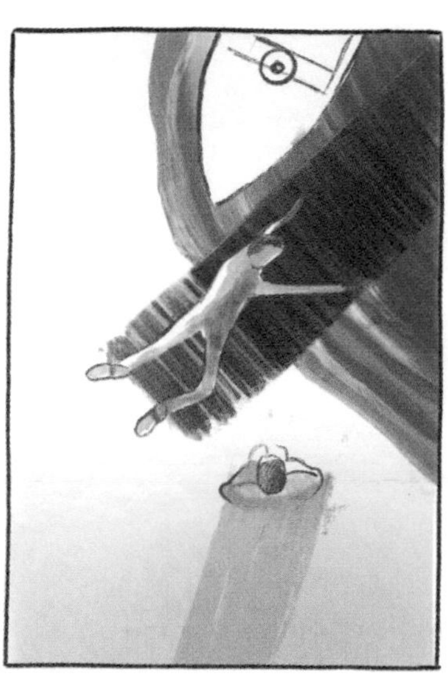
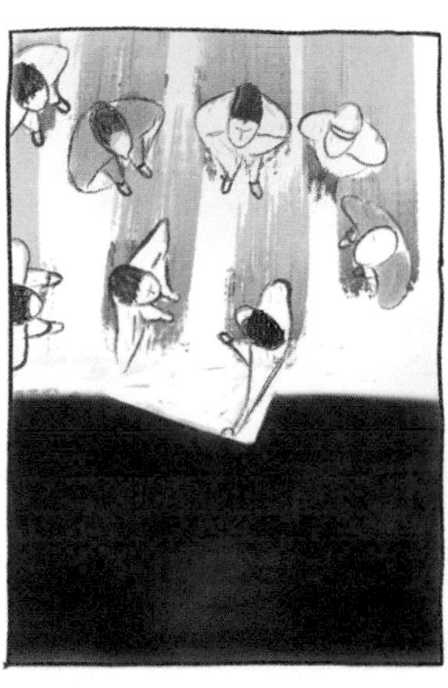
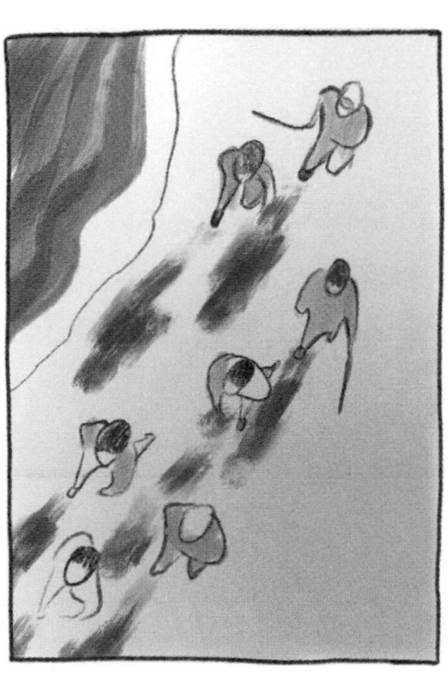

That some among us took to killing shouldn't be a surprise, because that's what they've always done.

We were a country with few guns, thankfully, but so much can be achieved with sharp objects, booted feet and a big, cold lake nearby.

What ingenuity man can muster when he lusts for blood.

Ktang

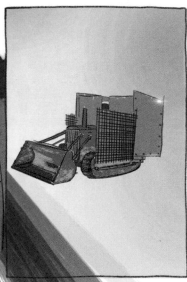

GAIN BOO

rRrrrRrr

RL UP & DYE

So I don't know when it started, but I know it started to end when all the sickened souls stormed towards death with a thrilling rage.

A cacophony of miserable, murderous bastards who'd long forgotten what it was they were angry at.

£ SAVER

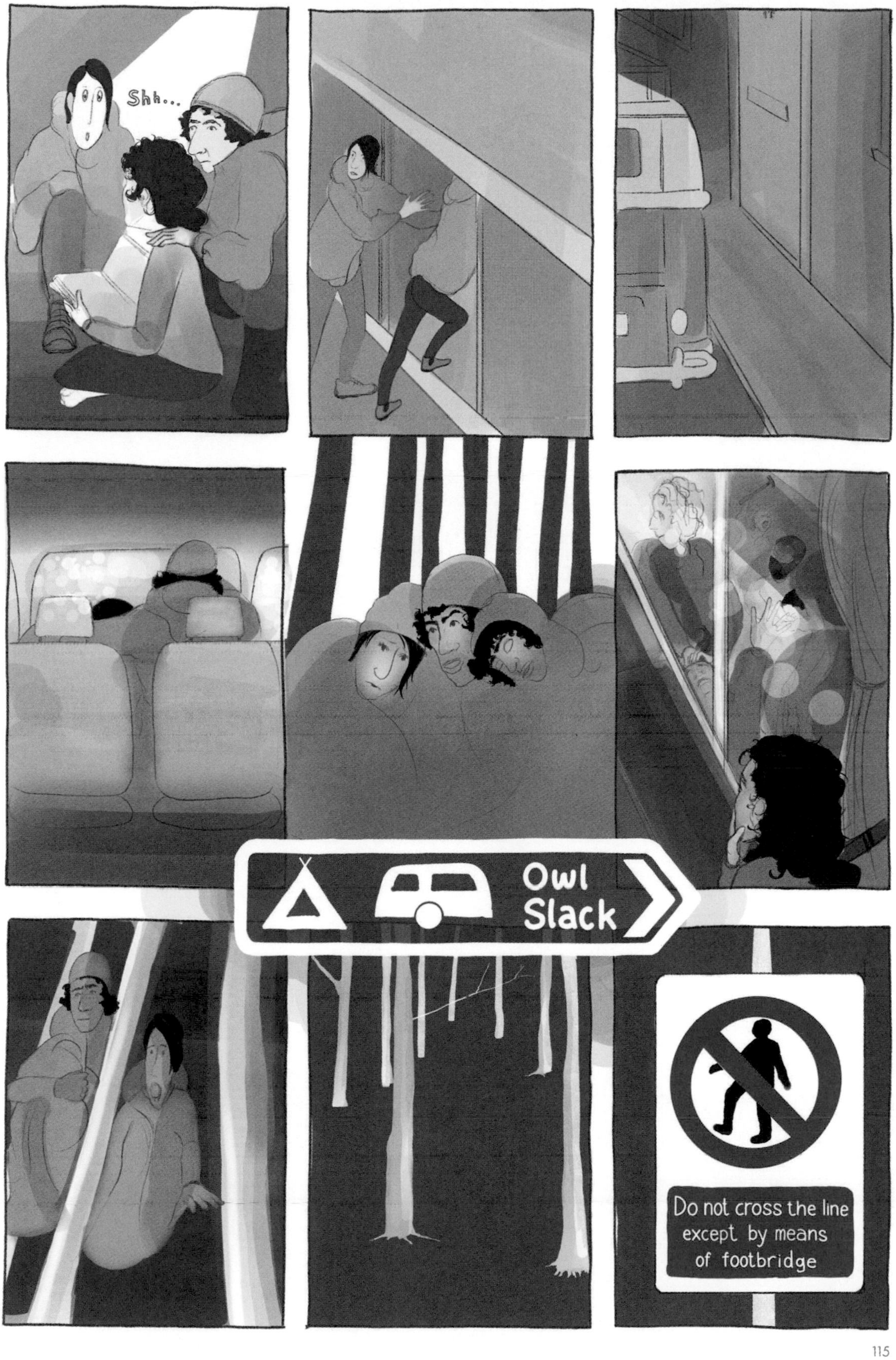
Shh...
Owl
Slack
Do not cross the line
except by means
of footbridge

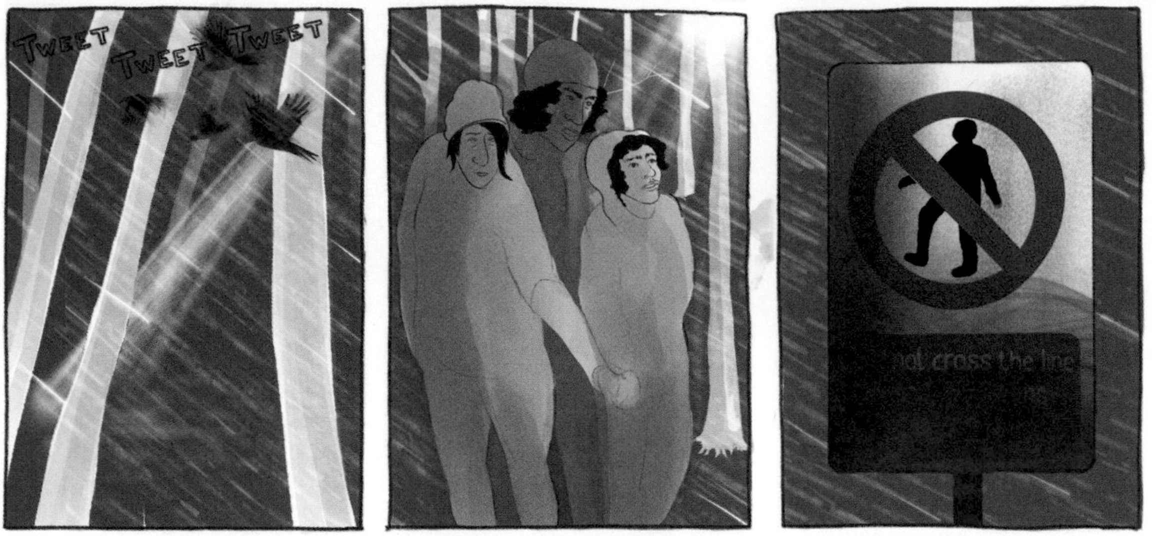
TWEET
TWEET
TWEET
cross the line

The killing stopped as suddenly as it had started, mostly, and an uneasy quiet fell over Crakewick.

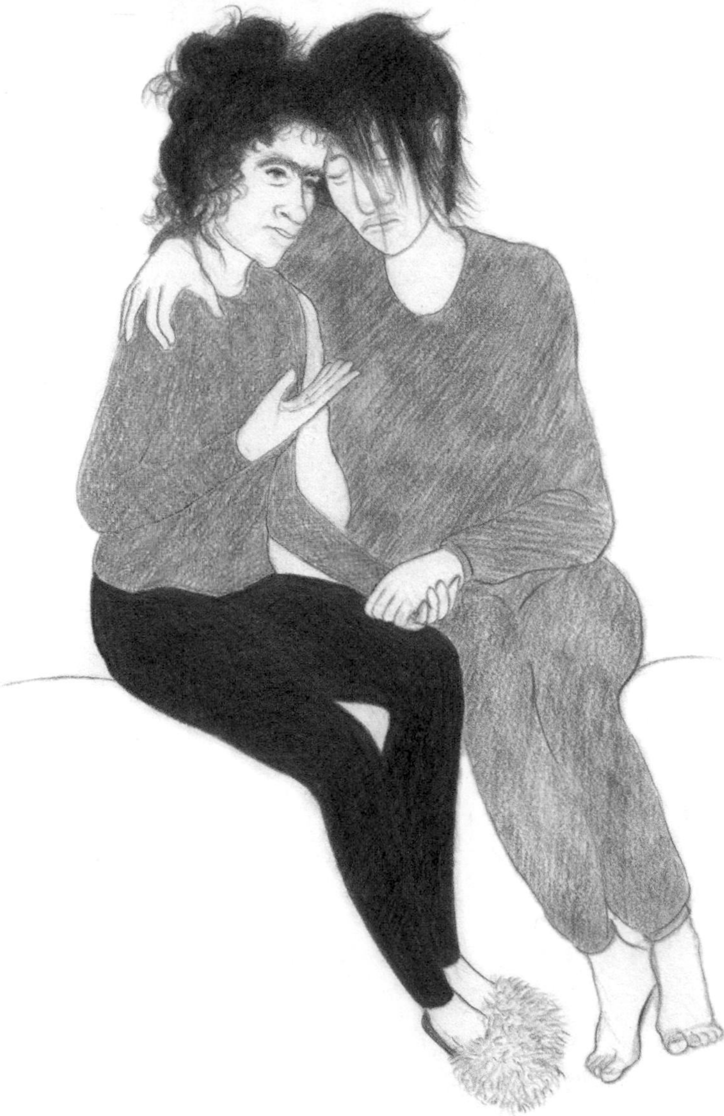

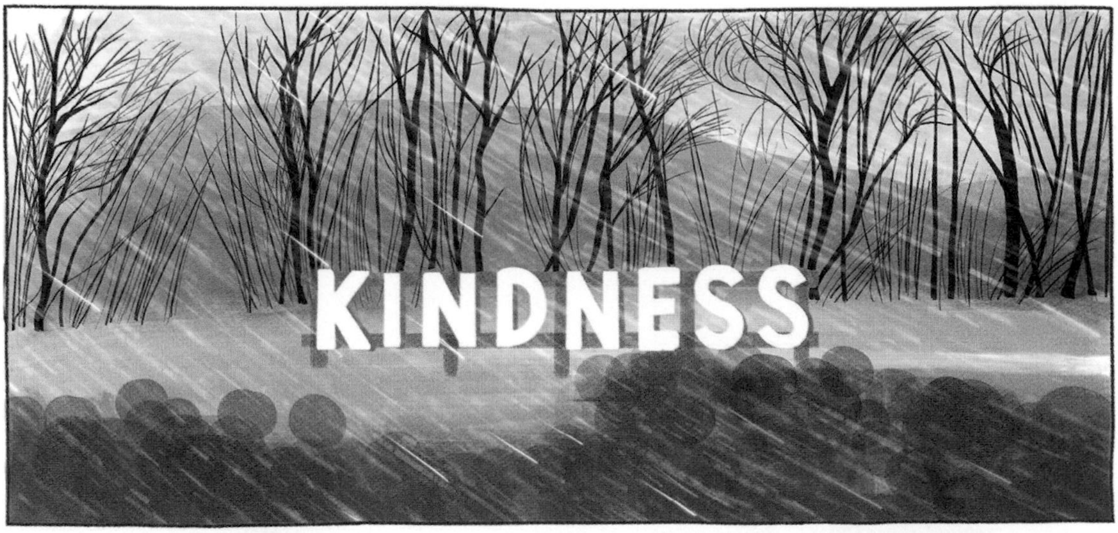
KINDNESS

The shame was foetid, like the weather. Someone, somewhere, with the power to do it, shut down the internet.

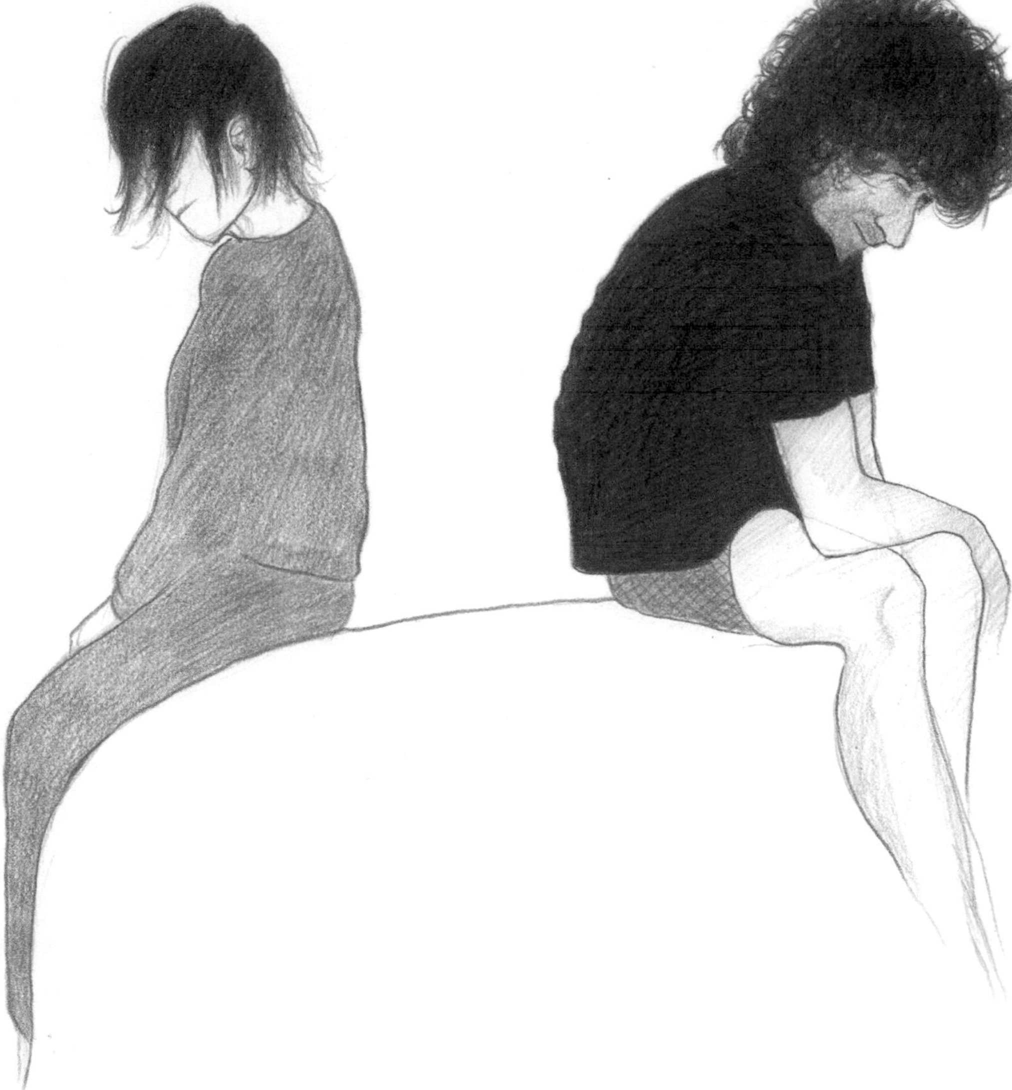

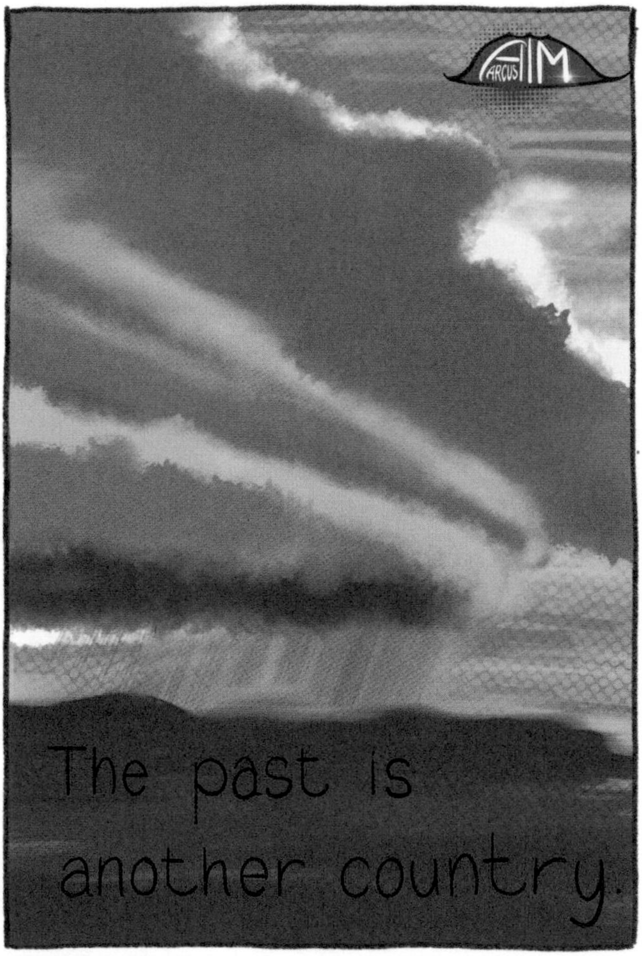
The past is
another country.

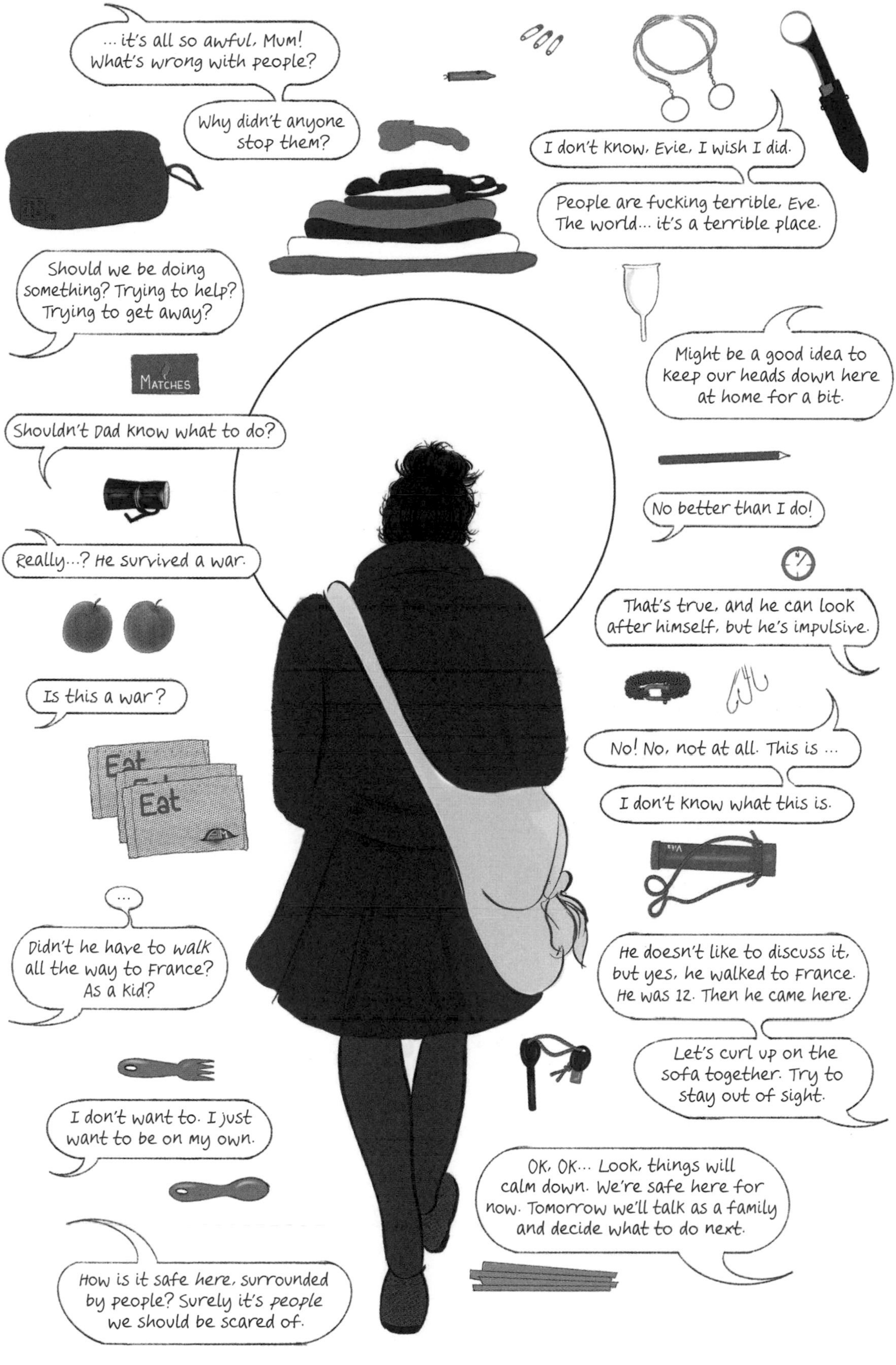

... it's all so awful, Mum! What's wrong with people?
Why didn't anyone stop them?
I don't know, Evie, I wish I did.
People are fucking terrible, Eve. The world... it's a terrible place.
Should we be doing something? Trying to help? Trying to get away?
Might be a good idea to keep our heads down here at home for a bit.
MATCHES
Shouldn't Dad know what to do?
No better than I do!
Really...? He survived a war.
That's true, and he can look after himself, but he's impulsive.
Is this a war?
No! No, not at all. This is ...
I don't know what this is.
Eat
...
Didn't he have to *walk* all the way to France? As a kid?
He doesn't like to discuss it, but yes, he walked to France. He was 12. Then he came here.
Let's curl up on the sofa together. Try to stay out of sight.
I don't want to. I just want to be on my own.
OK, OK... Look, things will calm down. We're safe here for now. Tomorrow we'll talk as a family and decide what to do next.
How is it safe *here*, surrounded by people? Surely it's *people* we should be scared of.

I don't know the day Might be Friday.

Yesterday we walked over Hunger Hills and down the river to see what was happening because Dad said we should try not to be seen. No one was out in the village all the doors and windows were closed all the blinds down, no sound in the street But we could hear fighting and glass breaking in the distance, so we came away.

I didn't see much when it started we drove off in the camper as fast as we could, parked near the railway line and hid in the woods all night But I saw some ~~fighti~~ stuff out of the windows. A man digging into another man really quickly outside Home Bargains. He had a knife I think. A woman pointing and laughing. I wanted to sleep in the van but Mum said it was too dangerous and she was right because when we went down in the morning it had been torched. Dad cried. Mum shouted at him. Dad shouted back. Now they are not talking. Im staying out of the way. Dad looks so little and old. Mum is mostly furious about everything. Lights are back on tonight. Dad's phone is blocked, Mum's still works, sometimes the radio still works a bit. The storm and floods seem ages ago but it's only been a week or so. The garden is still ruined but at least our house is okay because we are quite high

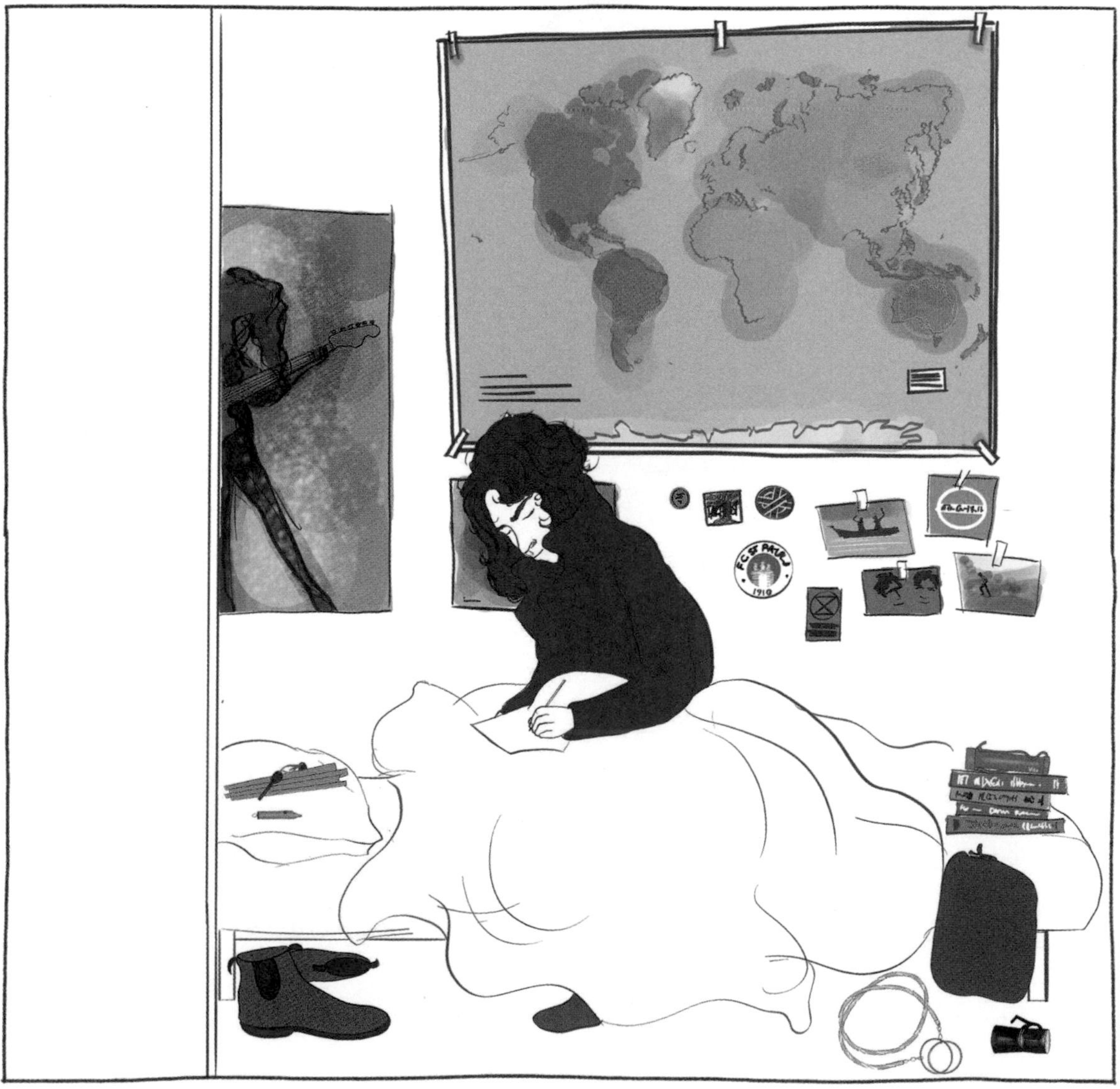

Another horrible day. Stuck in the house. Apparently loads of people with no water so we are lucky we've got water butts. You have to boil it though. I wanted to suck it up through my life straw but Mum won't let me. There were little worms in it so I'm glad now I didn't. Water in the hills is perfect. Clear and cold. We should go up there.

Down the hill everthing is still flooded. You can't drive out of Crakewick because all the bridges were washed away in the storm. People keep coming up our street trying to drive up the fell asking how to get out of the town. I want to help them but Mum said to stay out of their way. Well I want to get out of the town too! Nothing wrong with that. I feel so ~~sad~~ ~~awful~~ like I won't ever enjoy anything again. Like I'm dead, or numb. I can't stop seeing that man Not the one with the knife the one that was dying. It's like I've lost my balance. Where is my inner smile? I only have this void. What is the point of the human race? I hate all this. Everthing. Everyone. What are we supposed to do? What am I supposed to do? I wish someone could tell me what to do. Such a weird quiet in our house. <u>They</u> don't know what to do so whats the point in them? Weird atmosphere in our house everyone not quite looking at each other. Maybe tomorrow I'll just go.

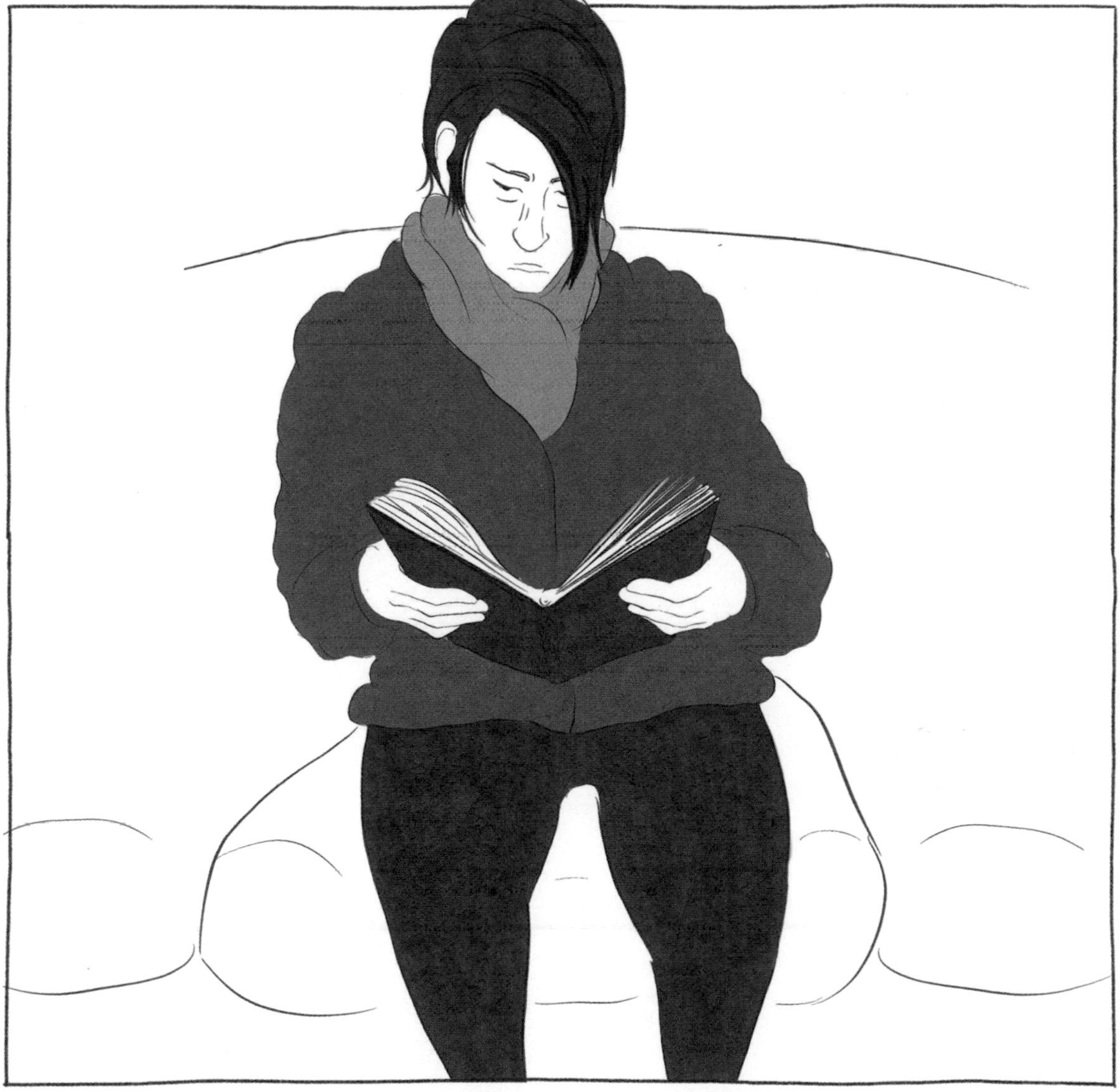

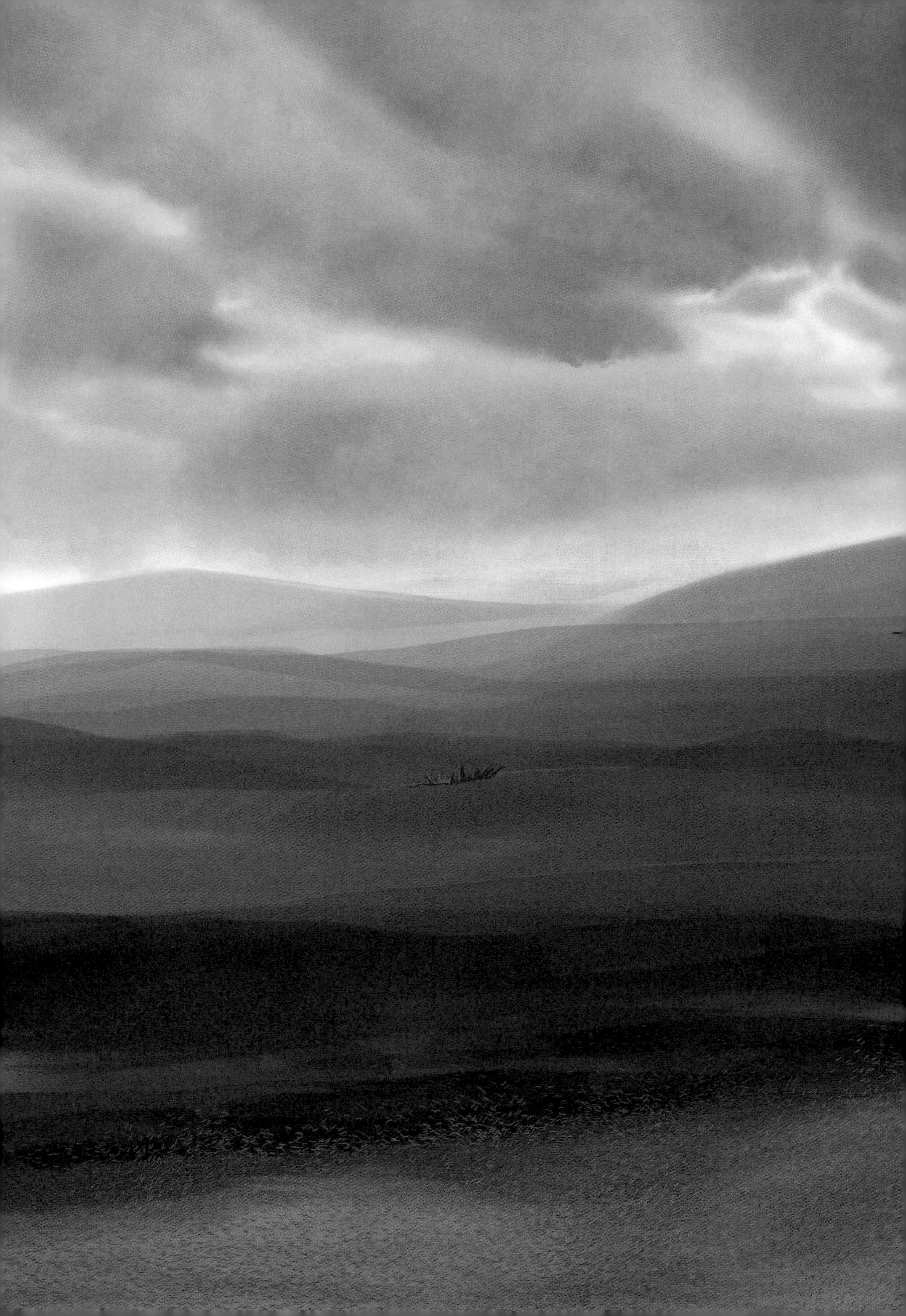

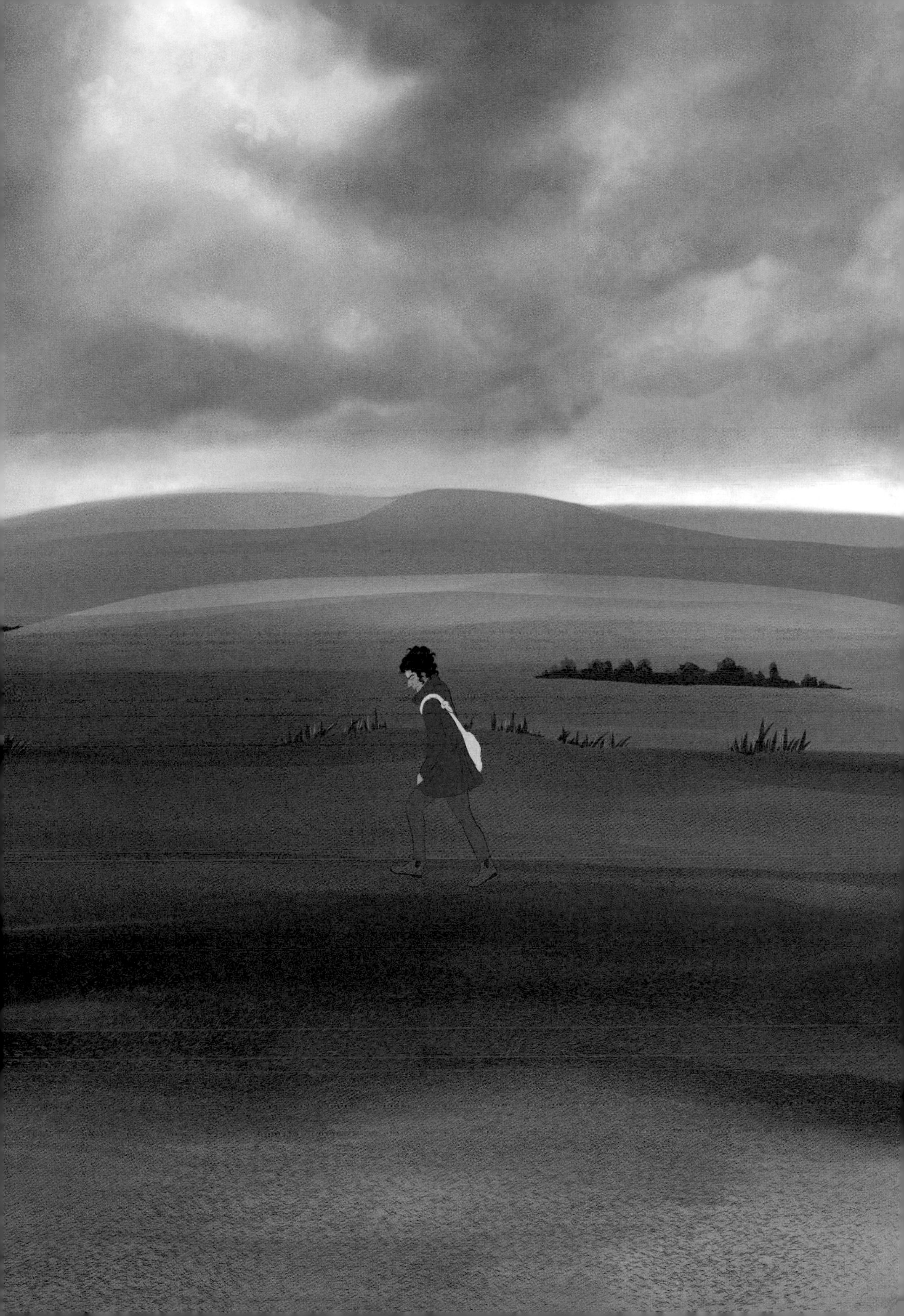

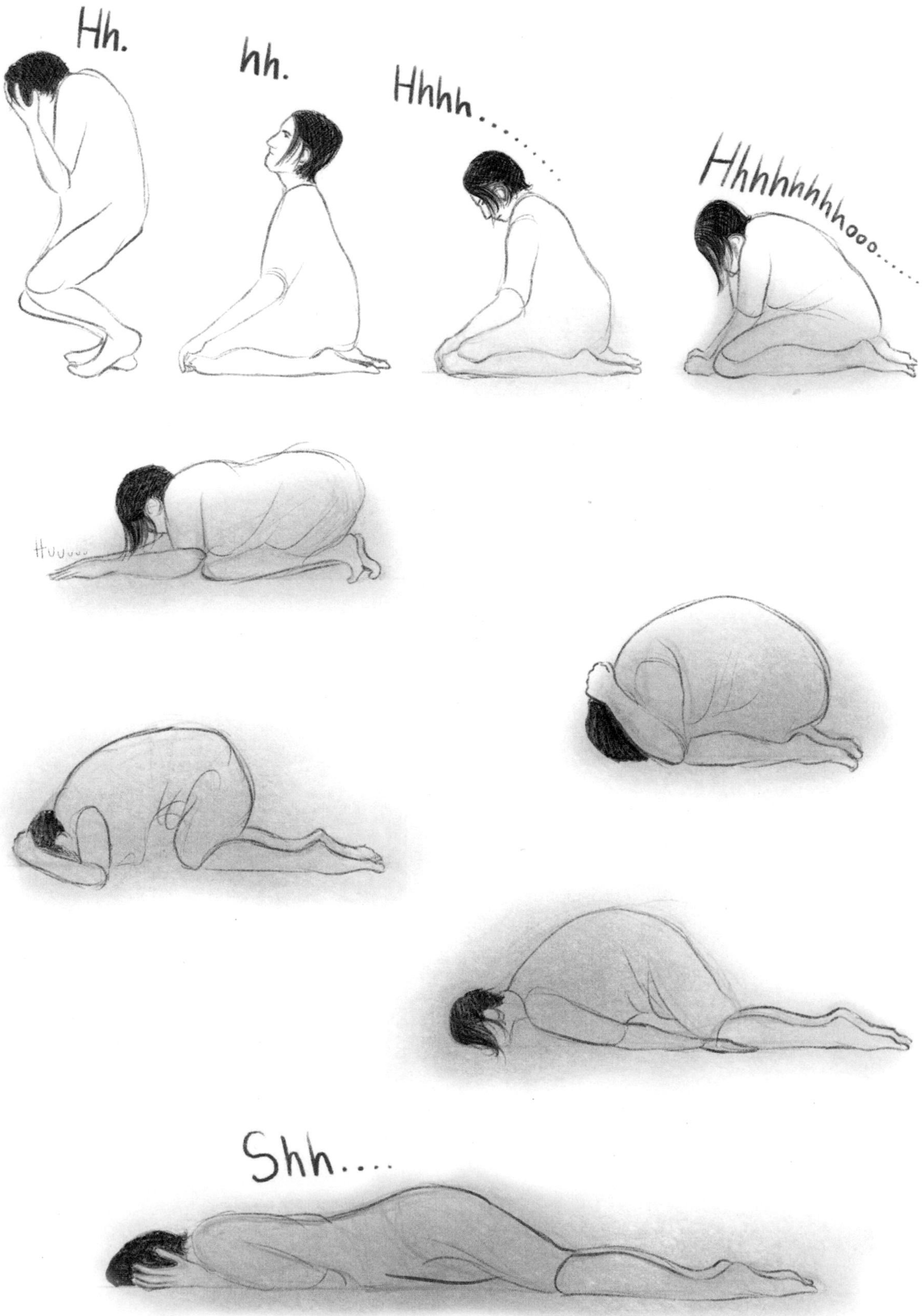
Hh.
hh.
Hhhh.......
Hhhhhhhhhooo......
Shh....

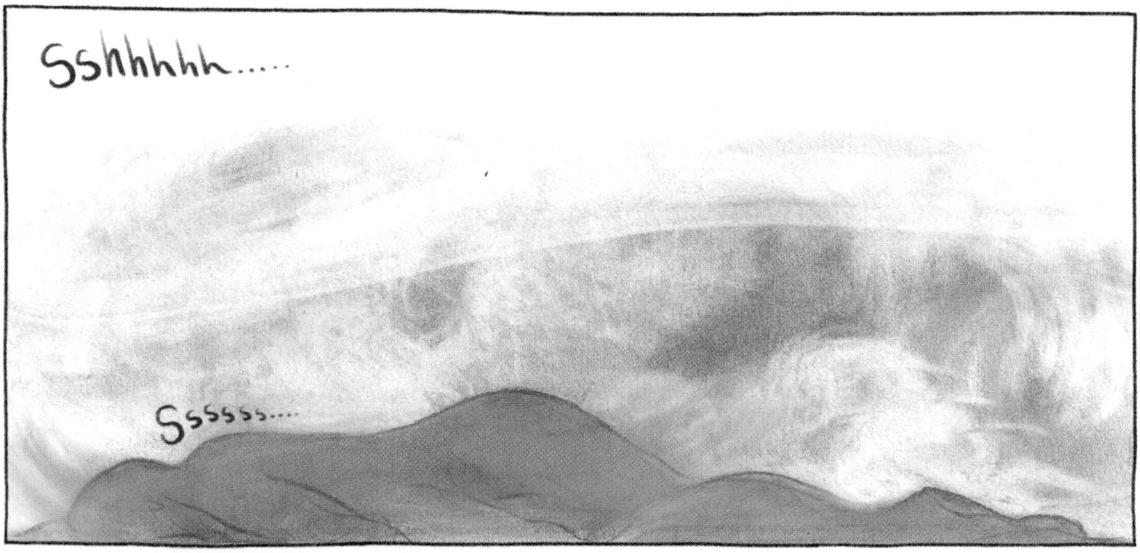
Sshhhhh.....
Ssssss....

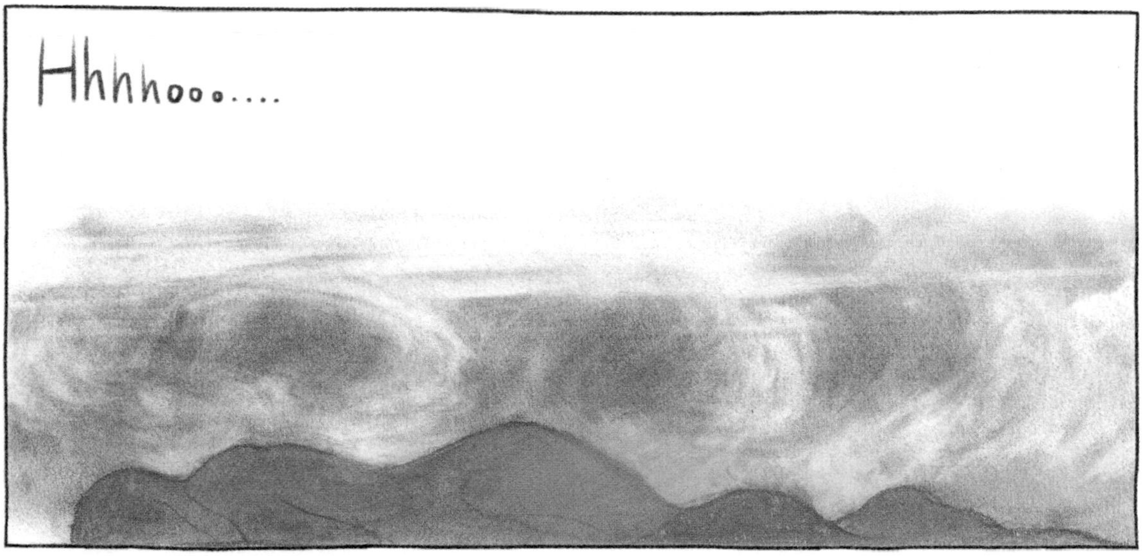
Hhhhooo....

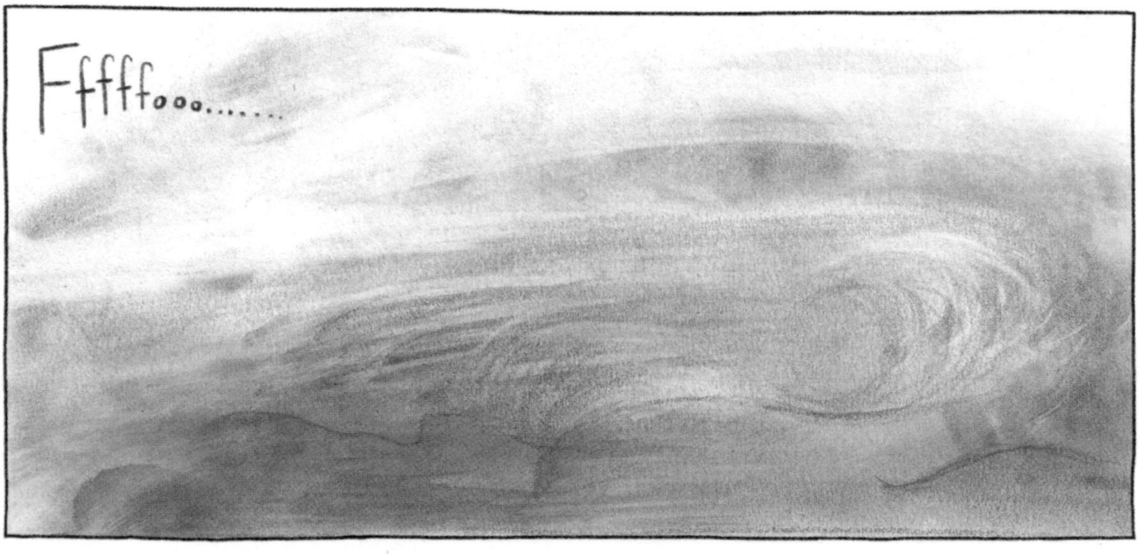
Fffffooo.......

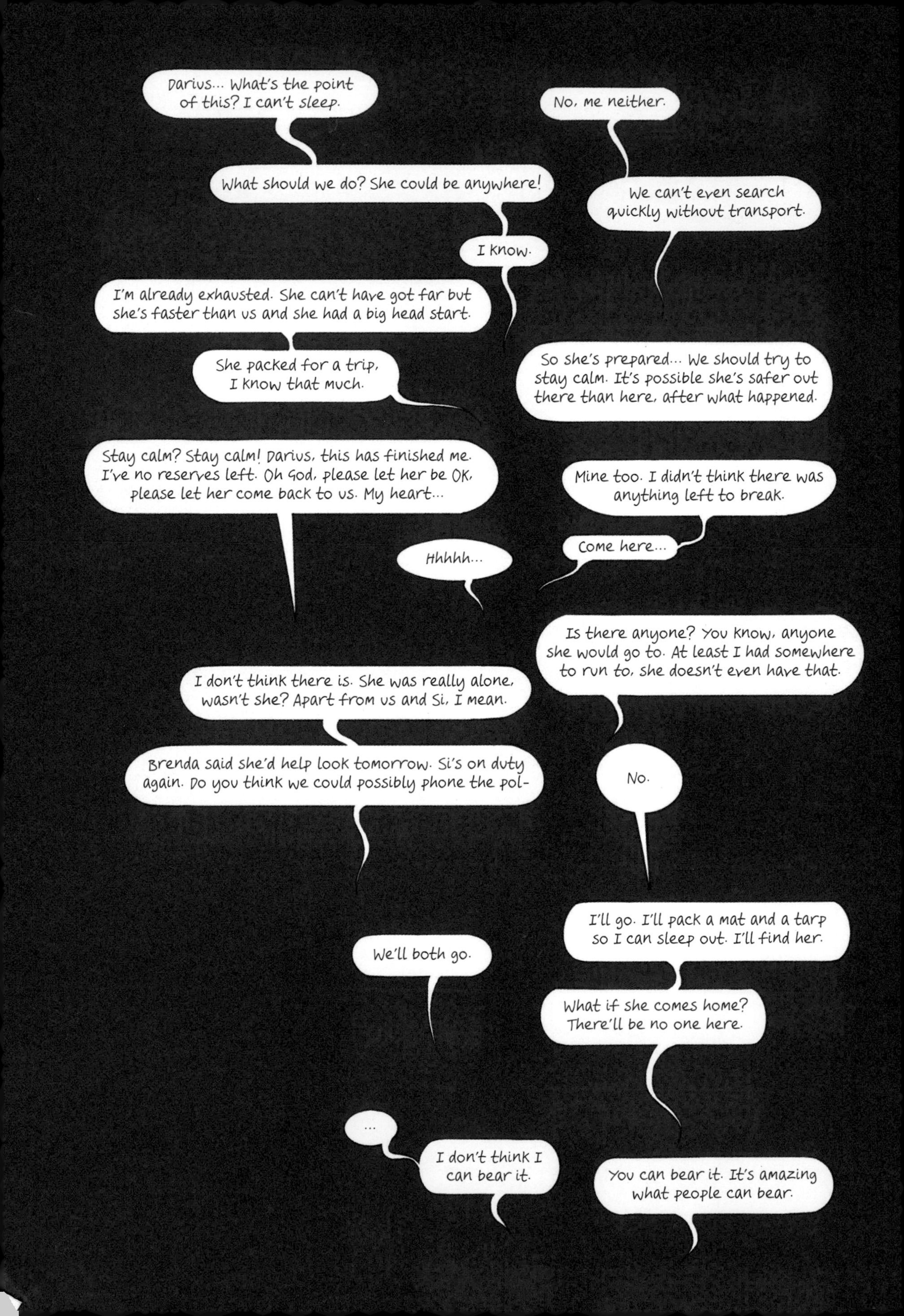
Darius... What's the point of this? I can't sleep.
No, me neither.
What should we do? She could be anywhere!
We can't even search quickly without transport.
I know.
I'm already exhausted. She can't have got far but she's faster than us and she had a big head start.
She packed for a trip, I know that much.
So she's prepared... We should try to stay calm. It's possible she's safer out there than here, after what happened.
Stay calm? Stay calm! Darius, this has finished me. I've no reserves left. Oh God, please let her be OK, please let her come back to us. My heart...
Mine too. I didn't think there was anything left to break.
Come here...
Hhhhh...
Is there anyone? You know, anyone she would go to. At least I had somewhere to run to, she doesn't even have that.
I don't think there is. She was really alone, wasn't she? Apart from us and Si, I mean.
Brenda said she'd help look tomorrow. Si's on duty again. Do you think we could possibly phone the pol-
No.
I'll go. I'll pack a mat and a tarp so I can sleep out. I'll find her.
We'll both go.
What if she comes home? There'll be no one here.
...
I don't think I can bear it.
You can bear it. It's amazing what people can bear.

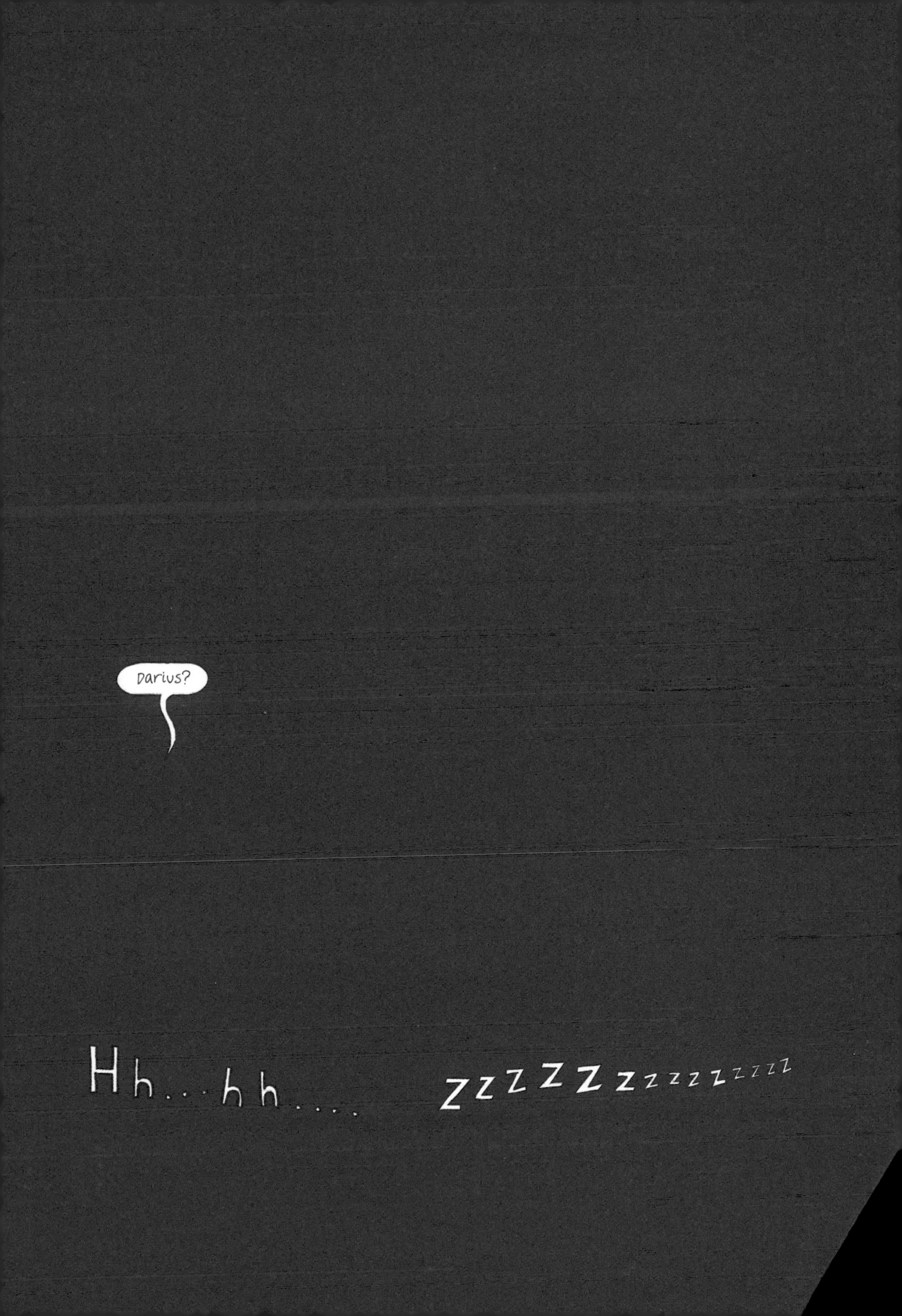
Darius?
Hh...hh....
ZZZZZZZZZZZZZZ

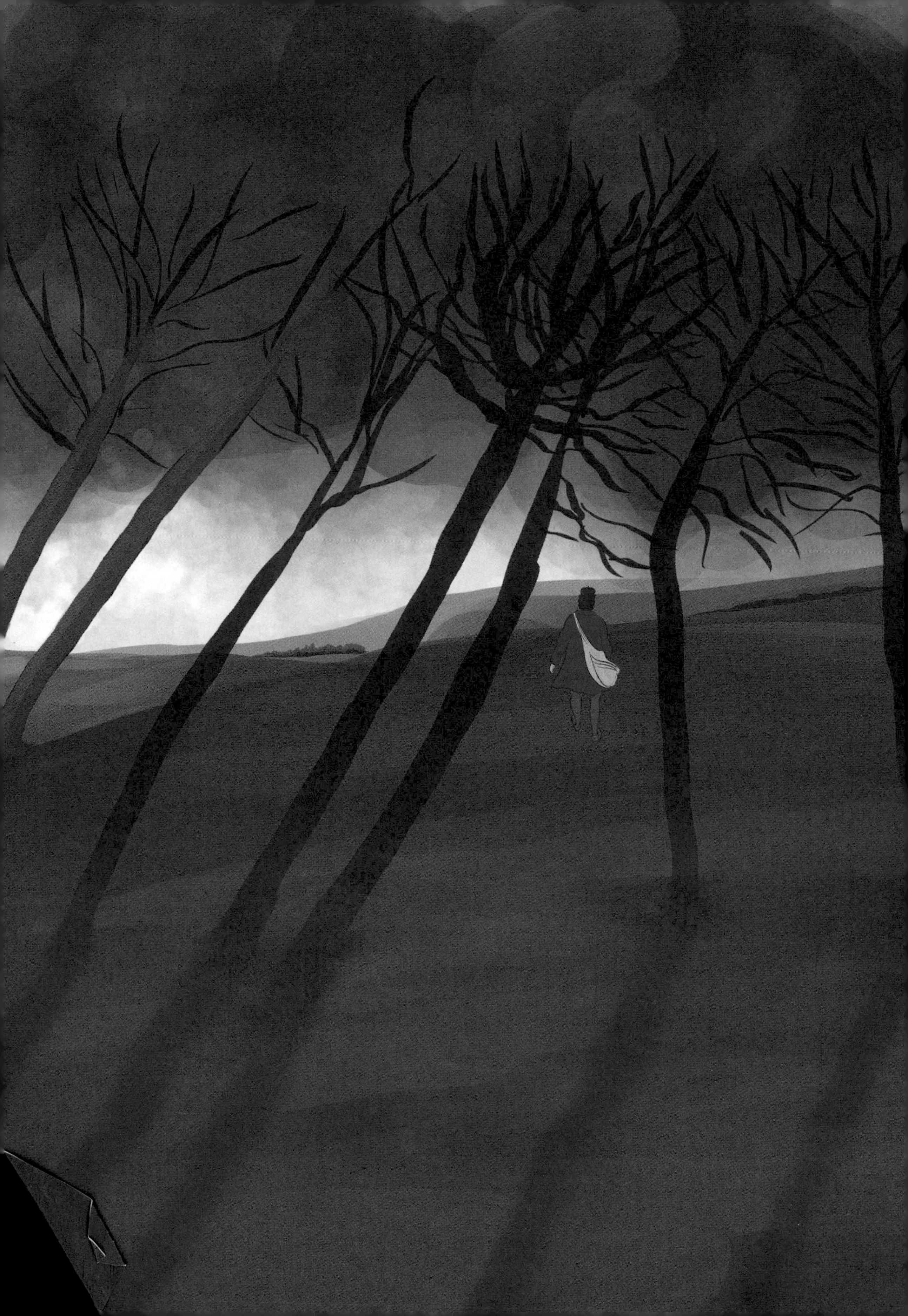

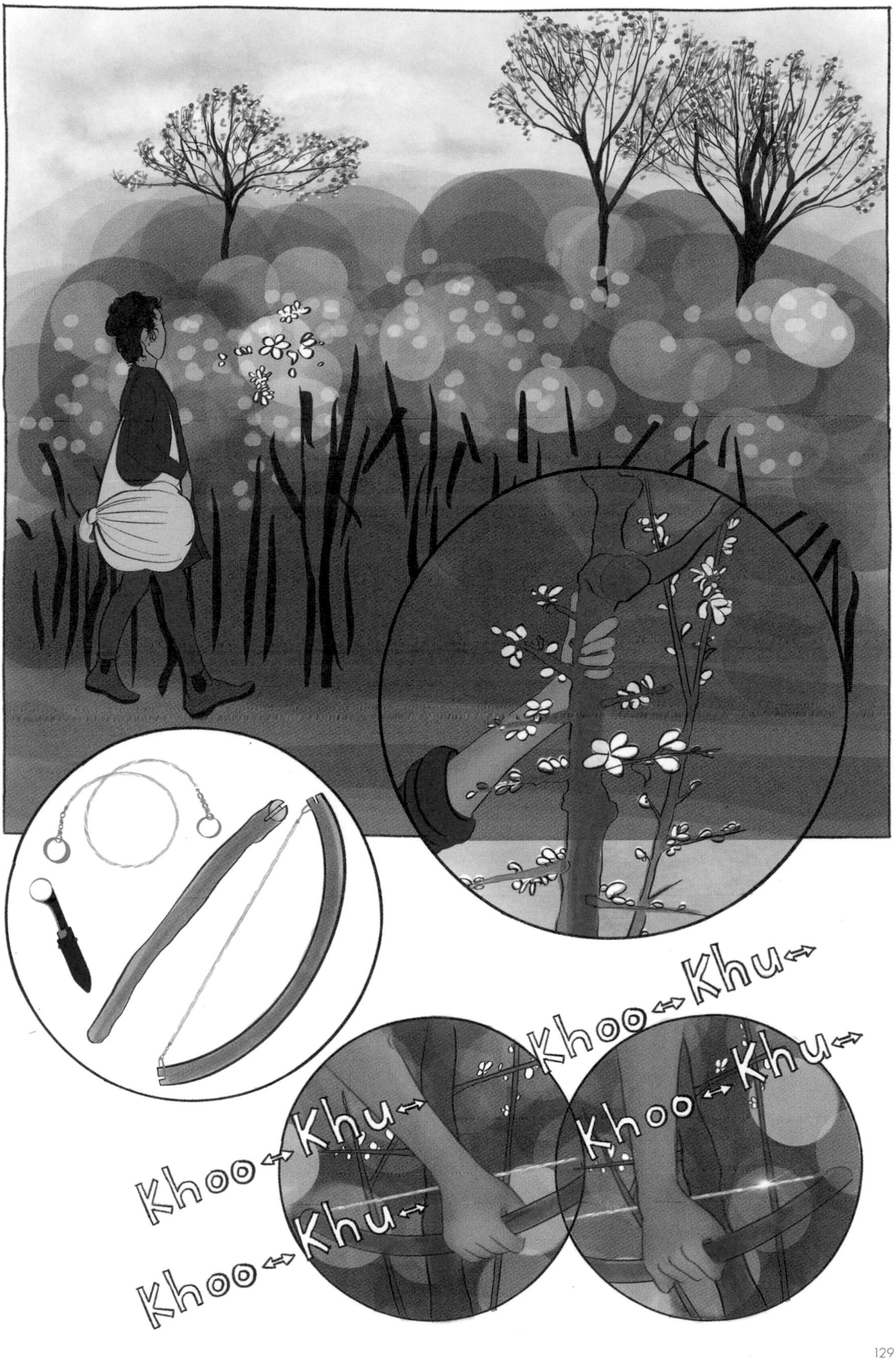
Khoo↔ Khu↔
Khoo↔ Khu↔
Khoo↔ Khu↔
Khoo↔ Khu↔

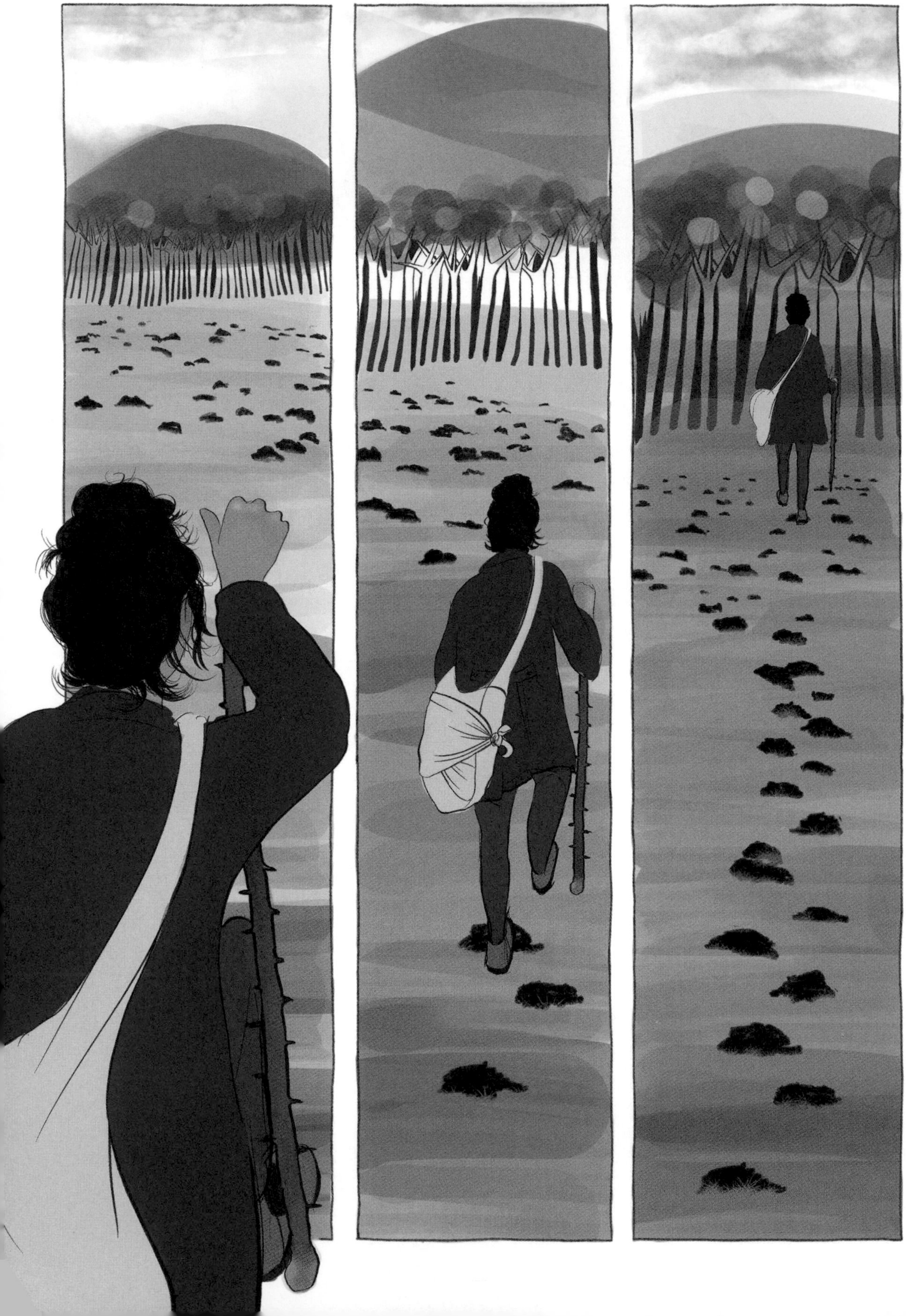

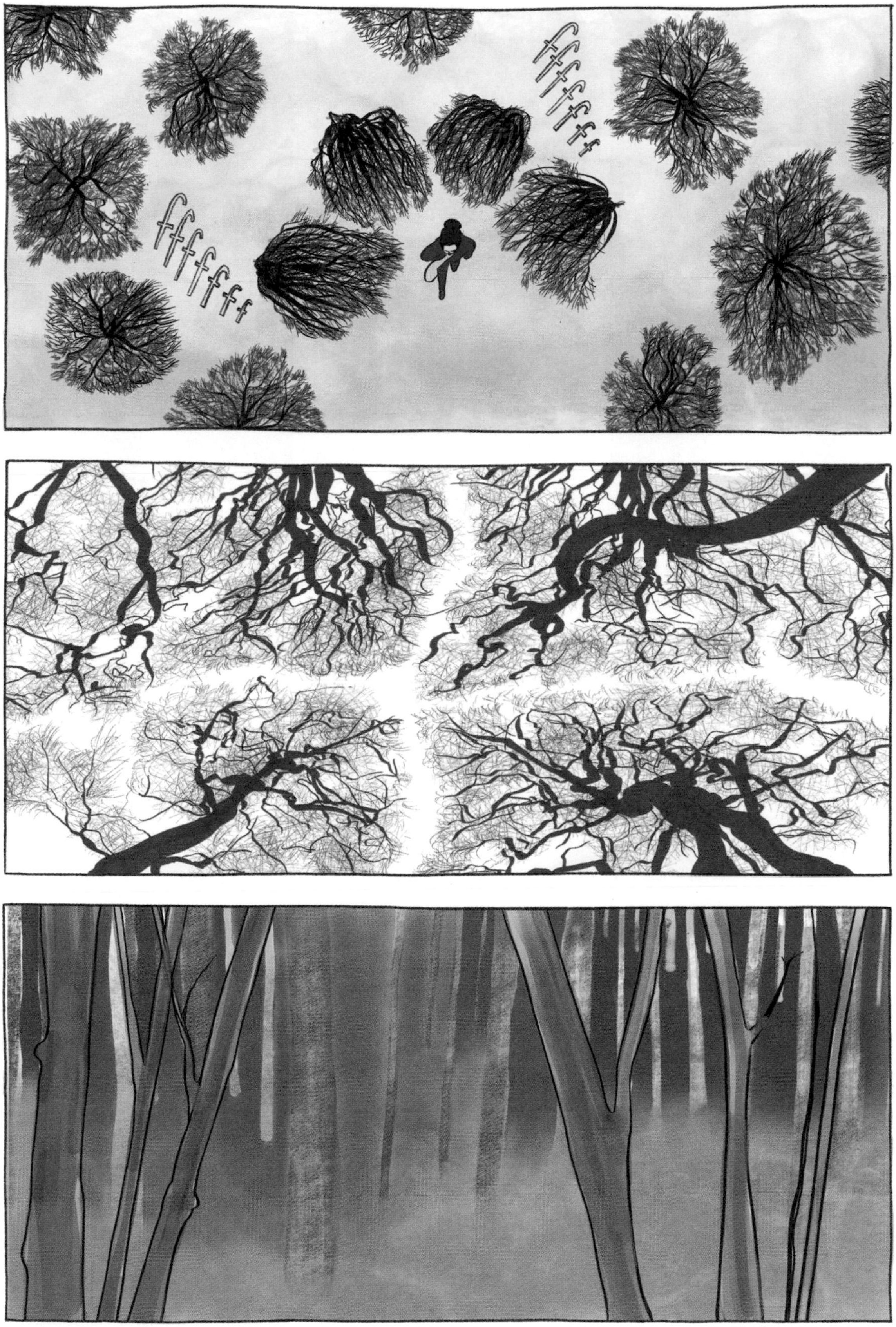
fffffff
fffffff

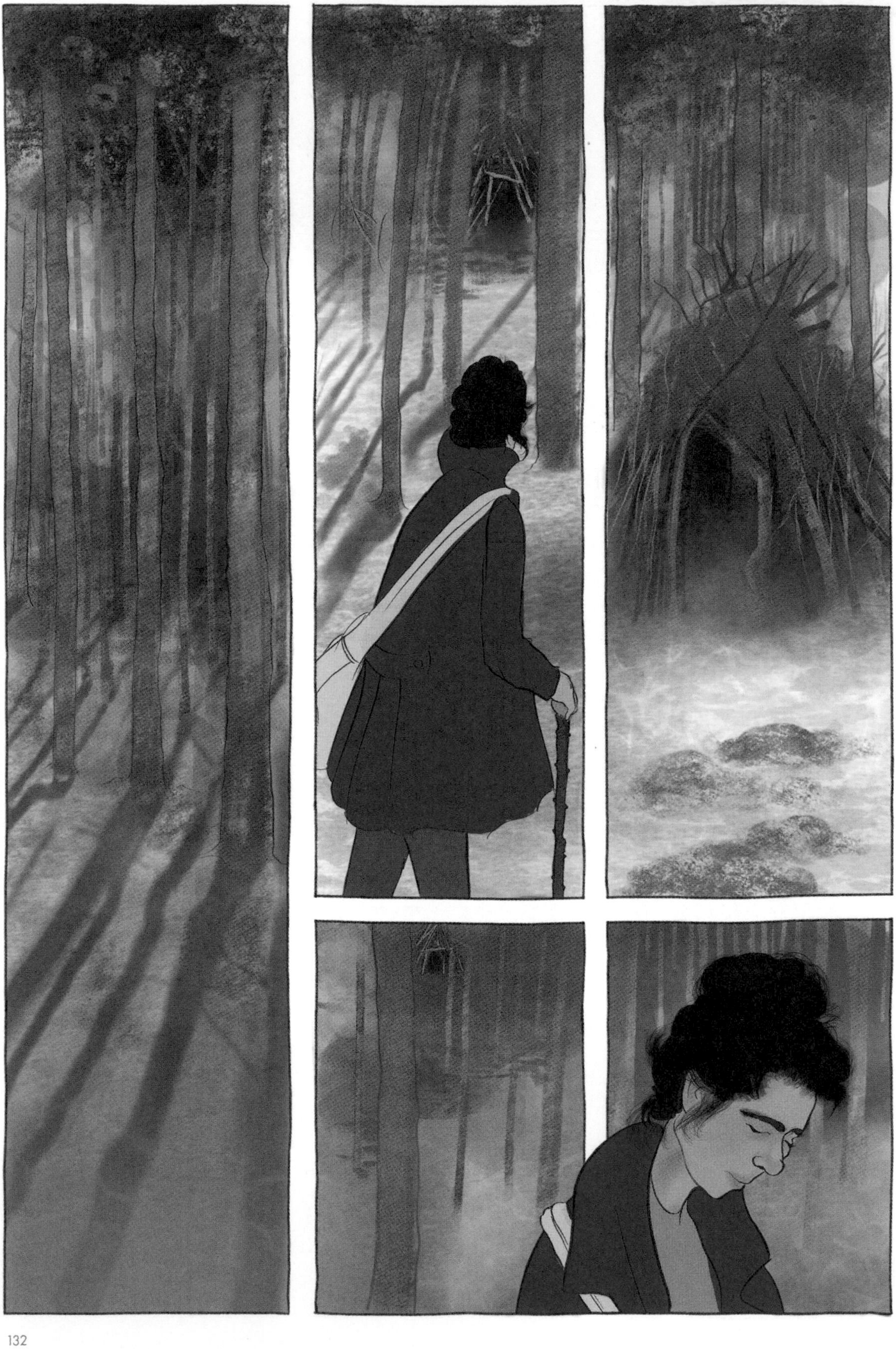

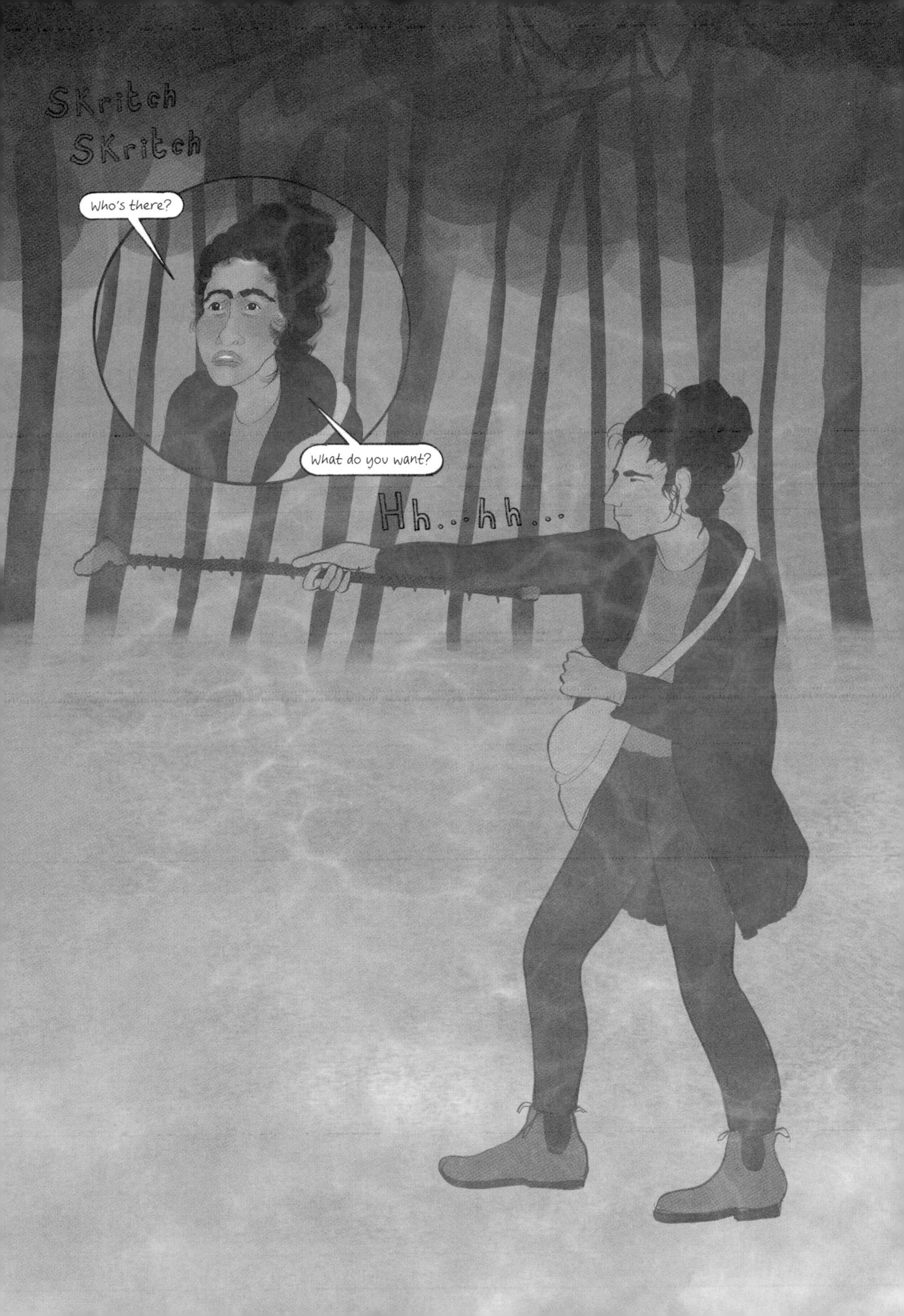
SKritch
SKritch
Who's there?
What do you want?
Hh...hh...

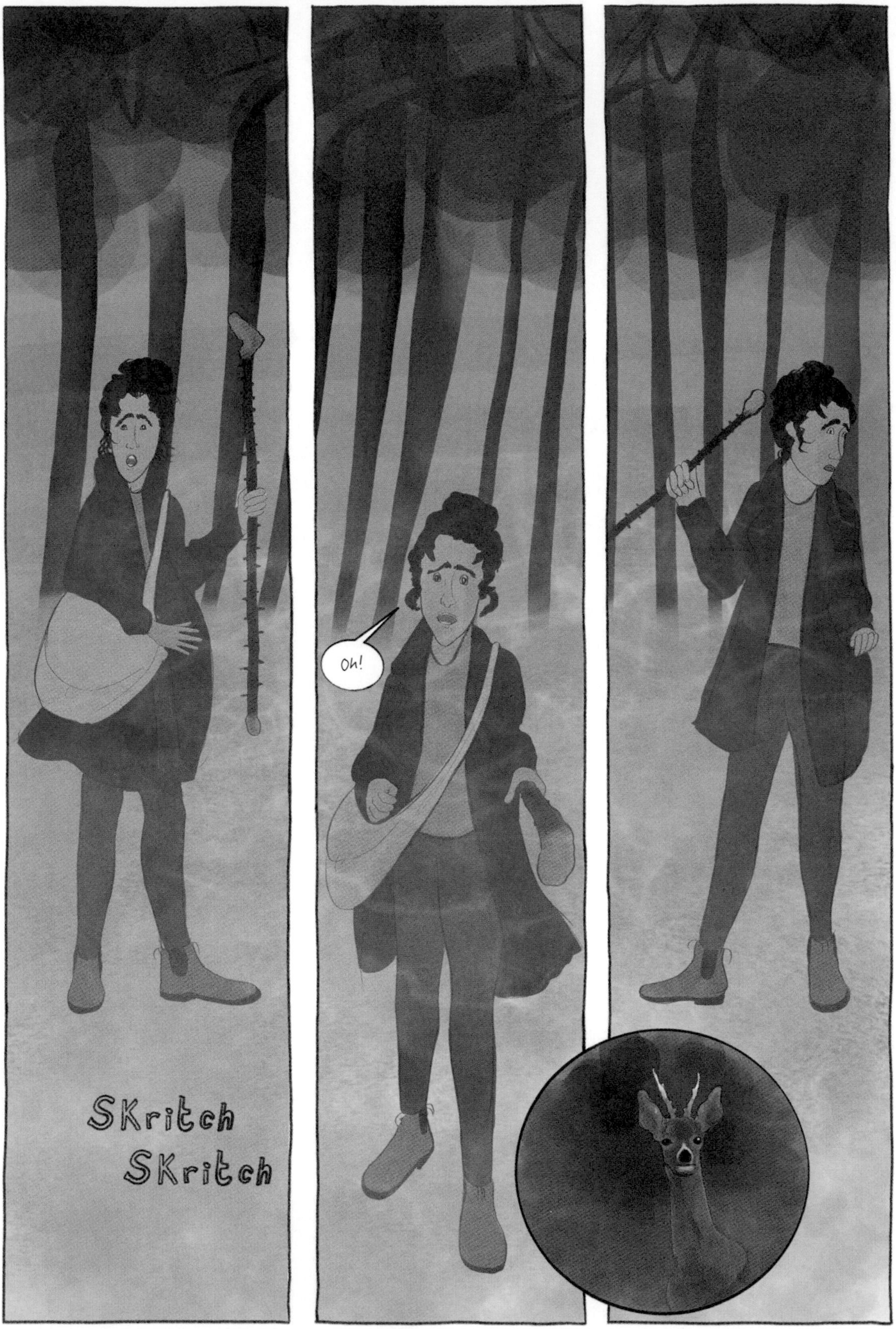
SKritch
SKritch
Oh!

Come on, get a grip, Eve.

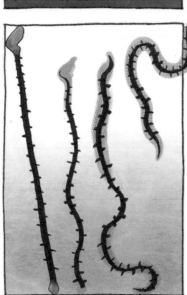

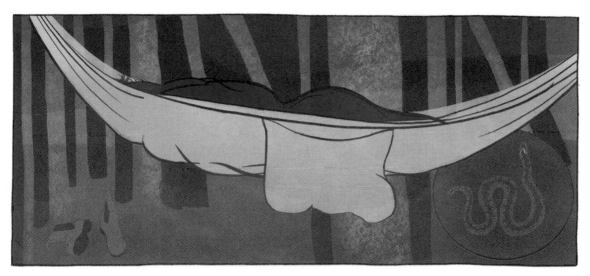

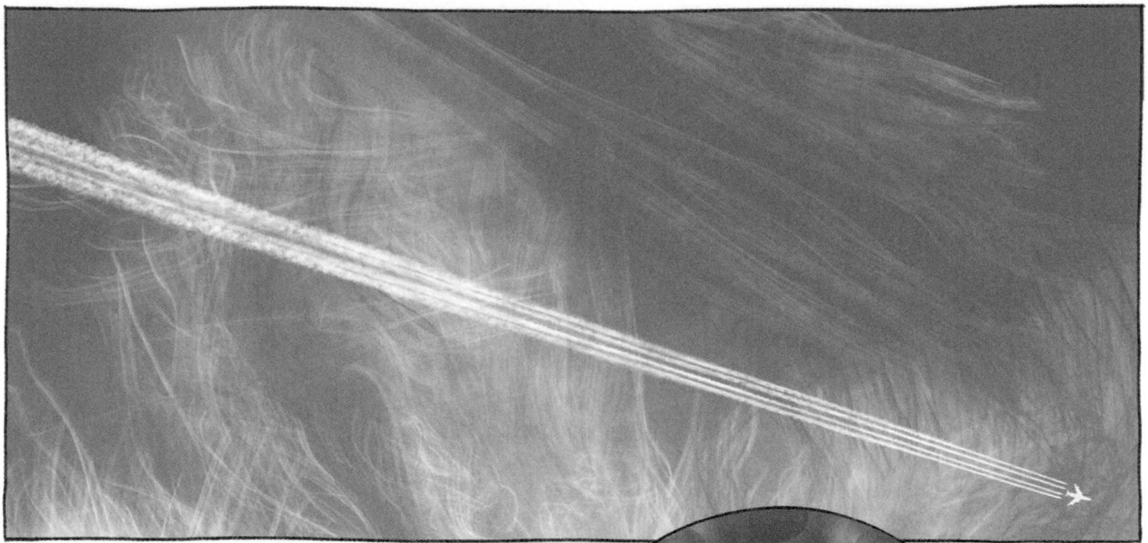

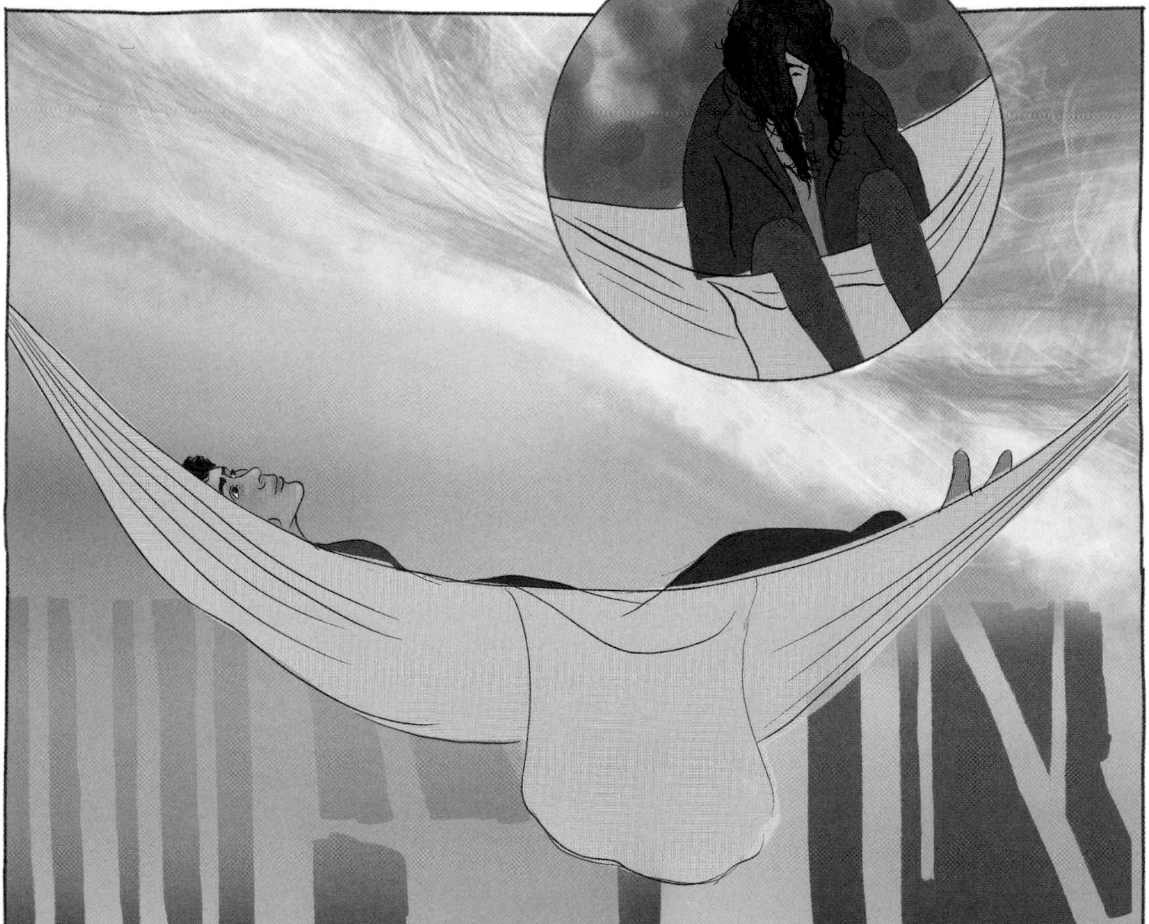

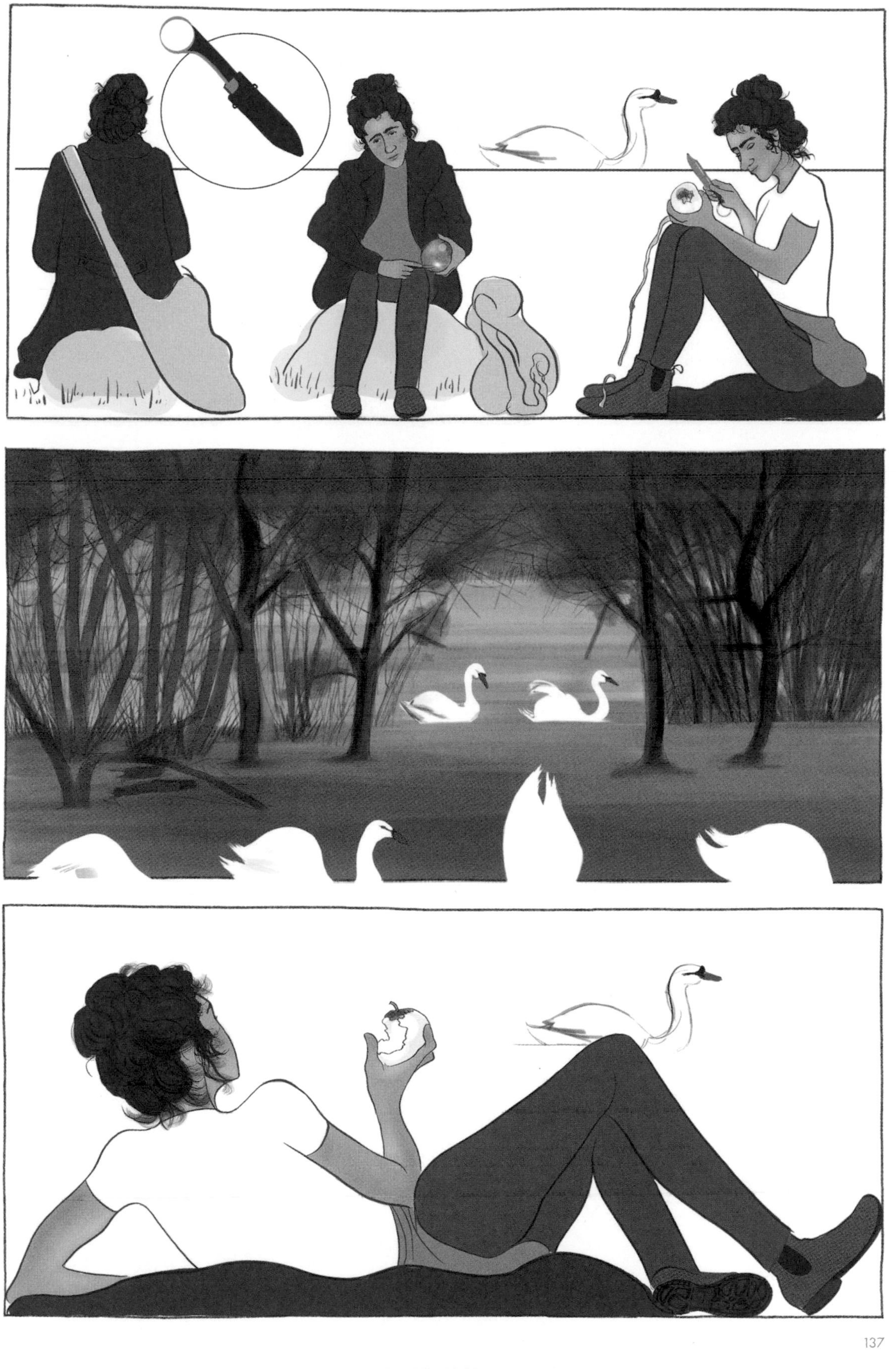

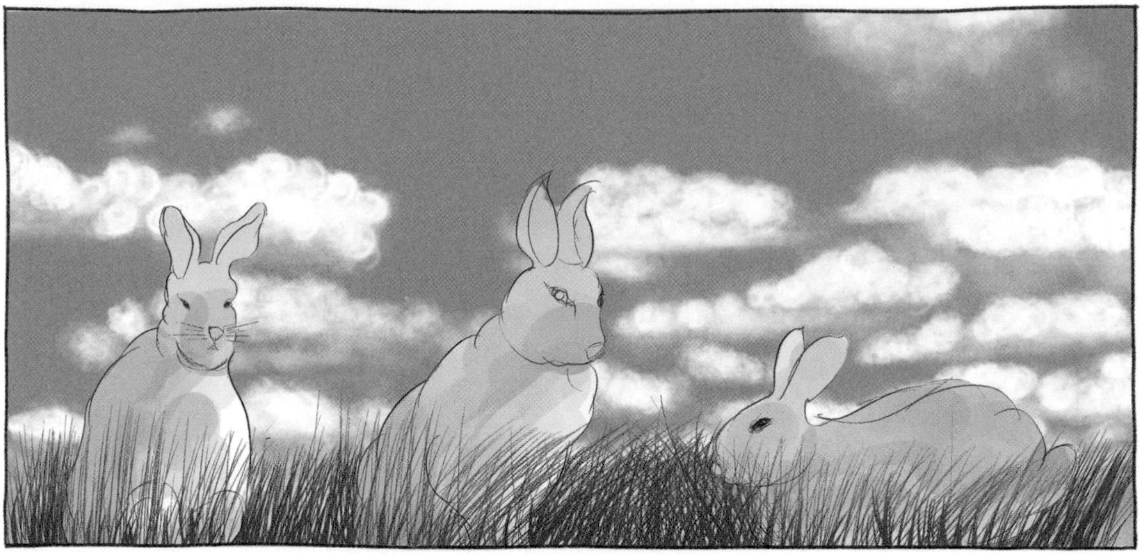

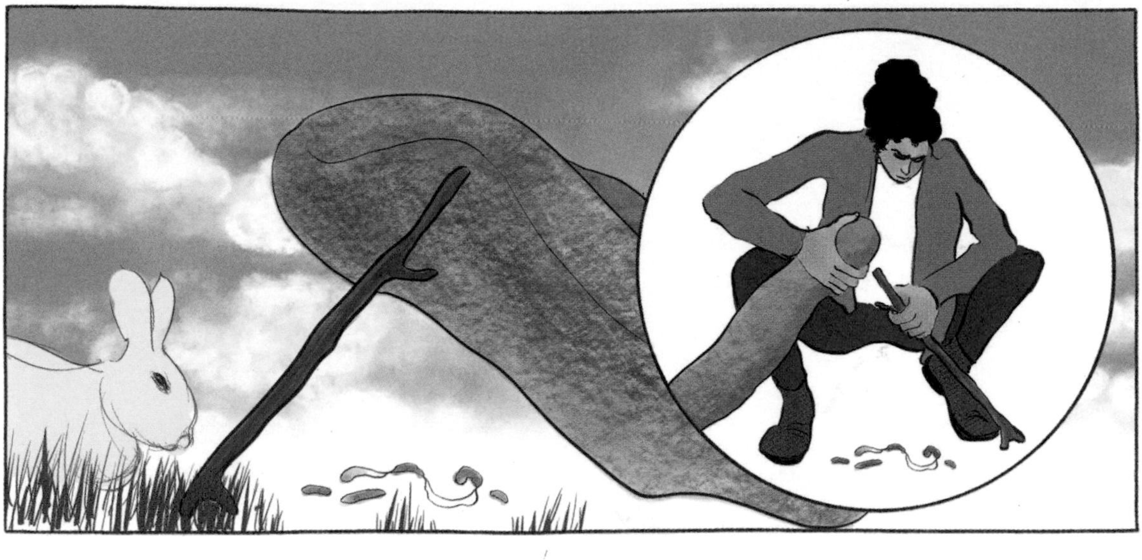

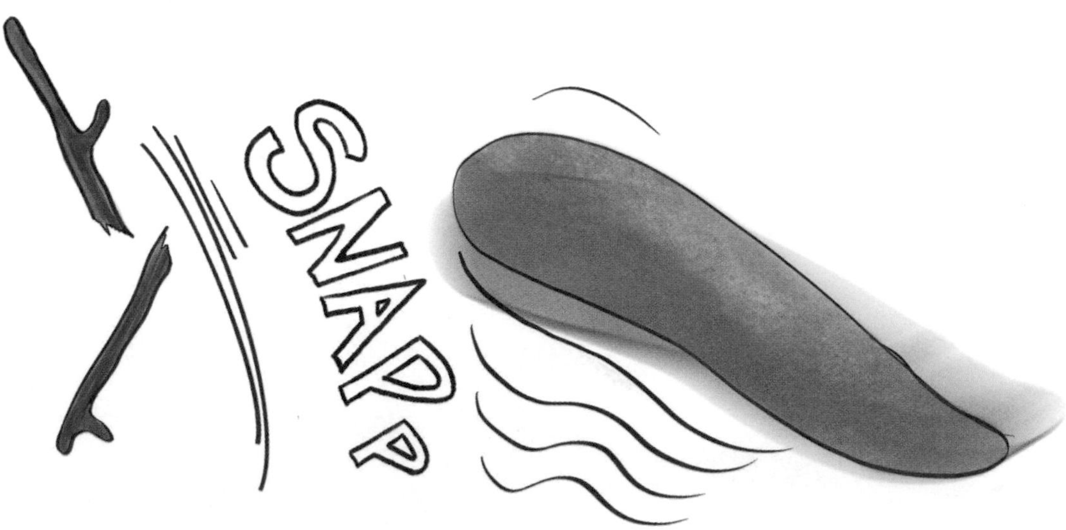
SNAPP

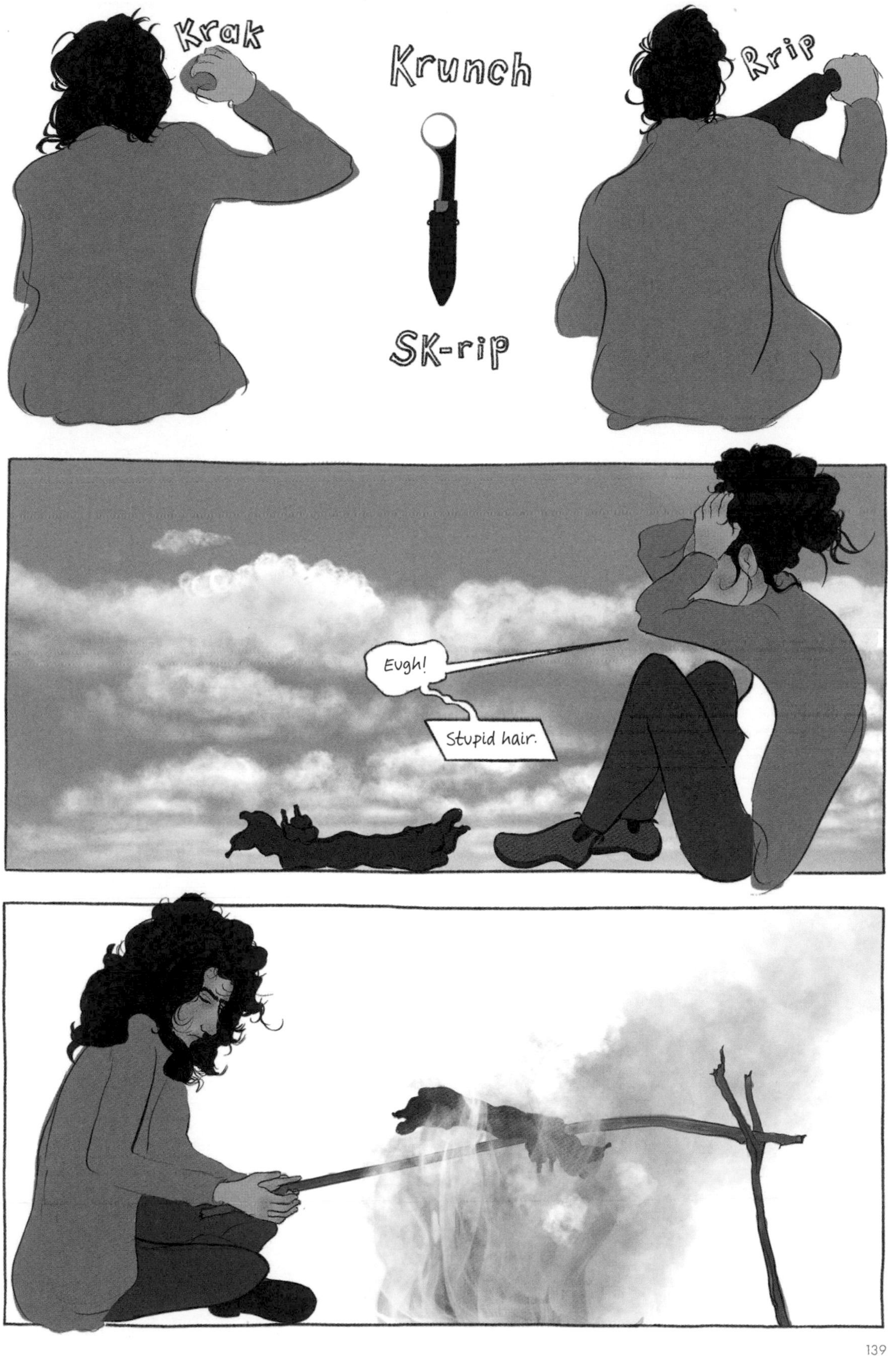
Krak
Krunch
SK-rip
Rrip
Eugh!
Stupid hair.

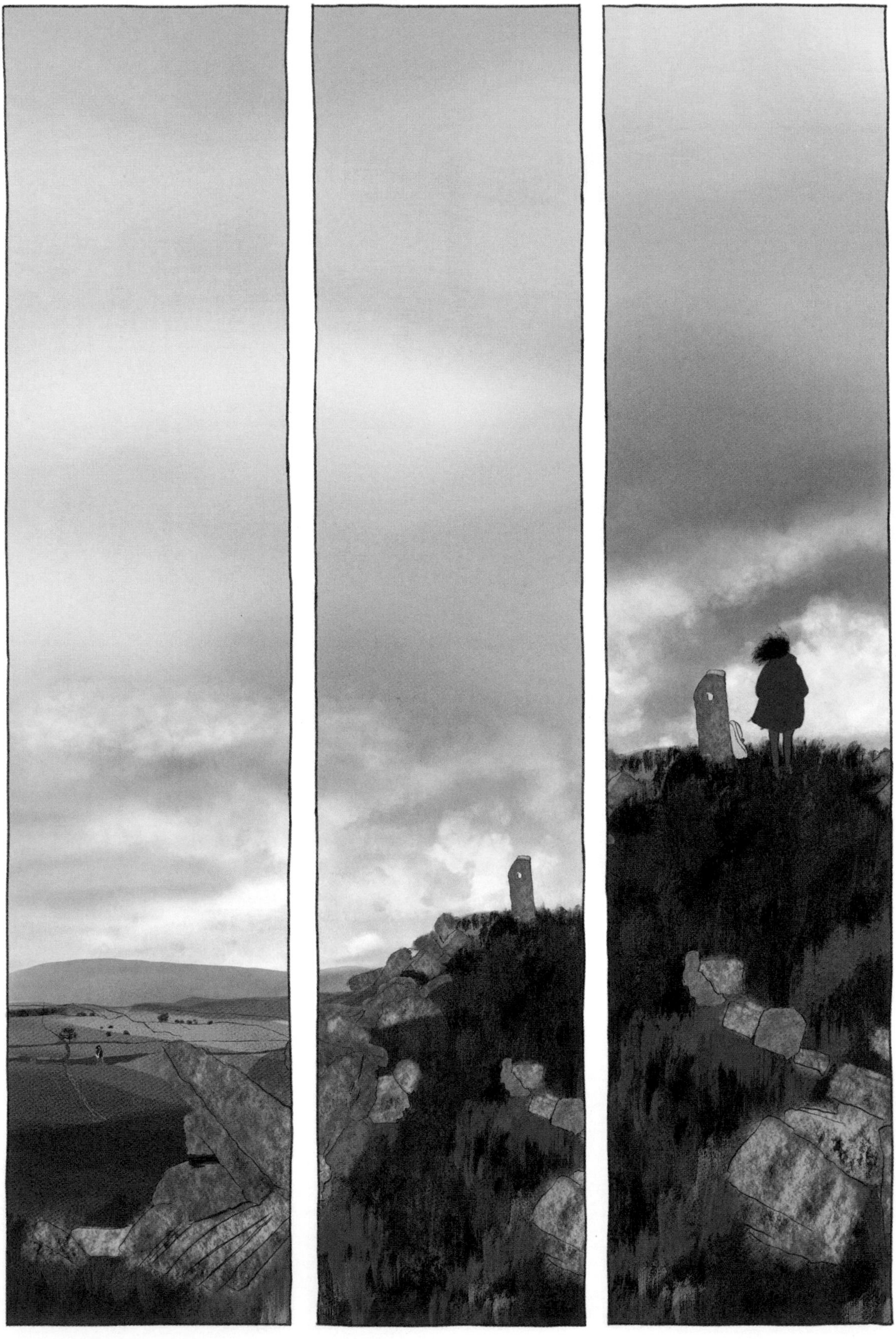

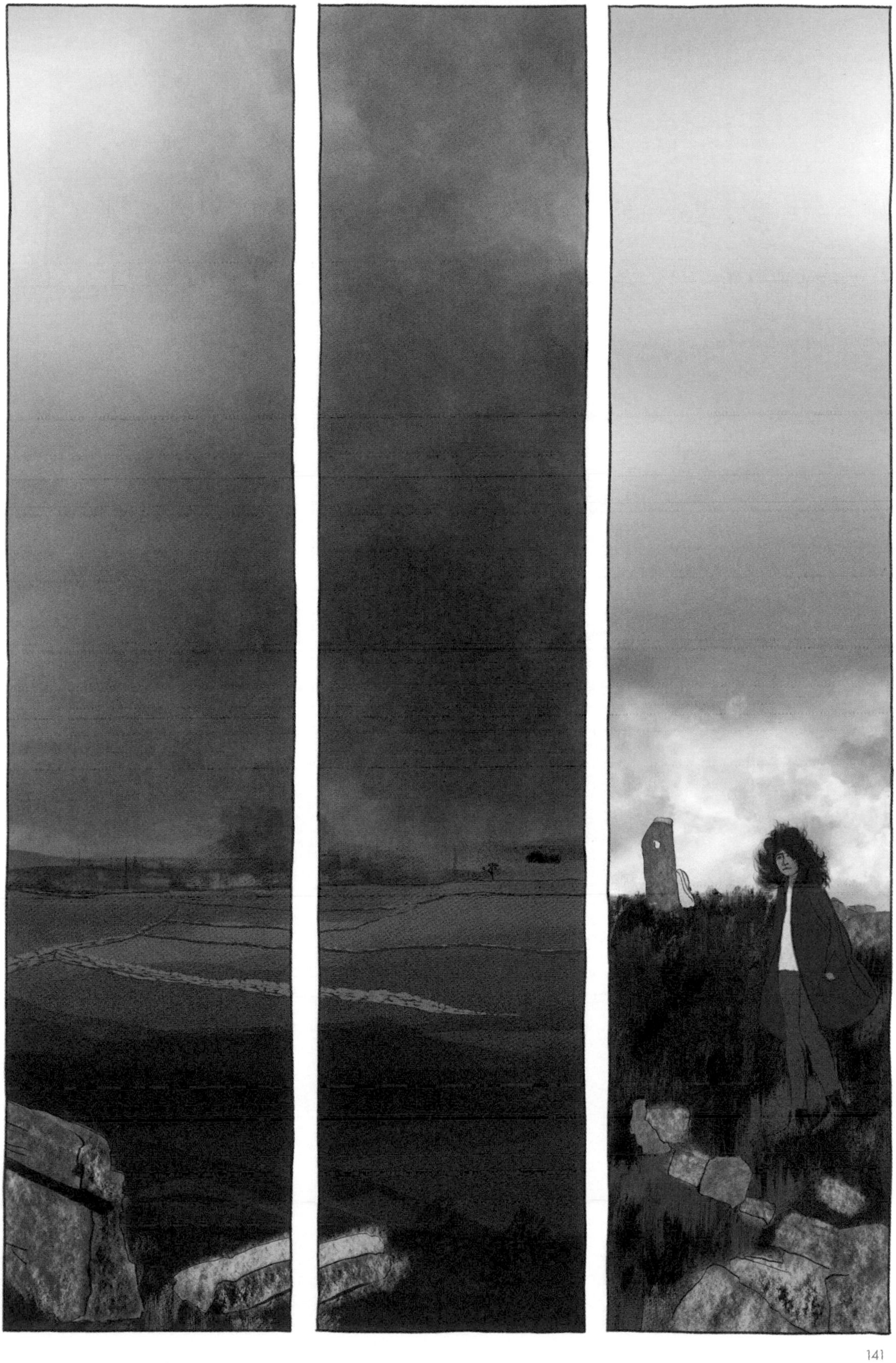

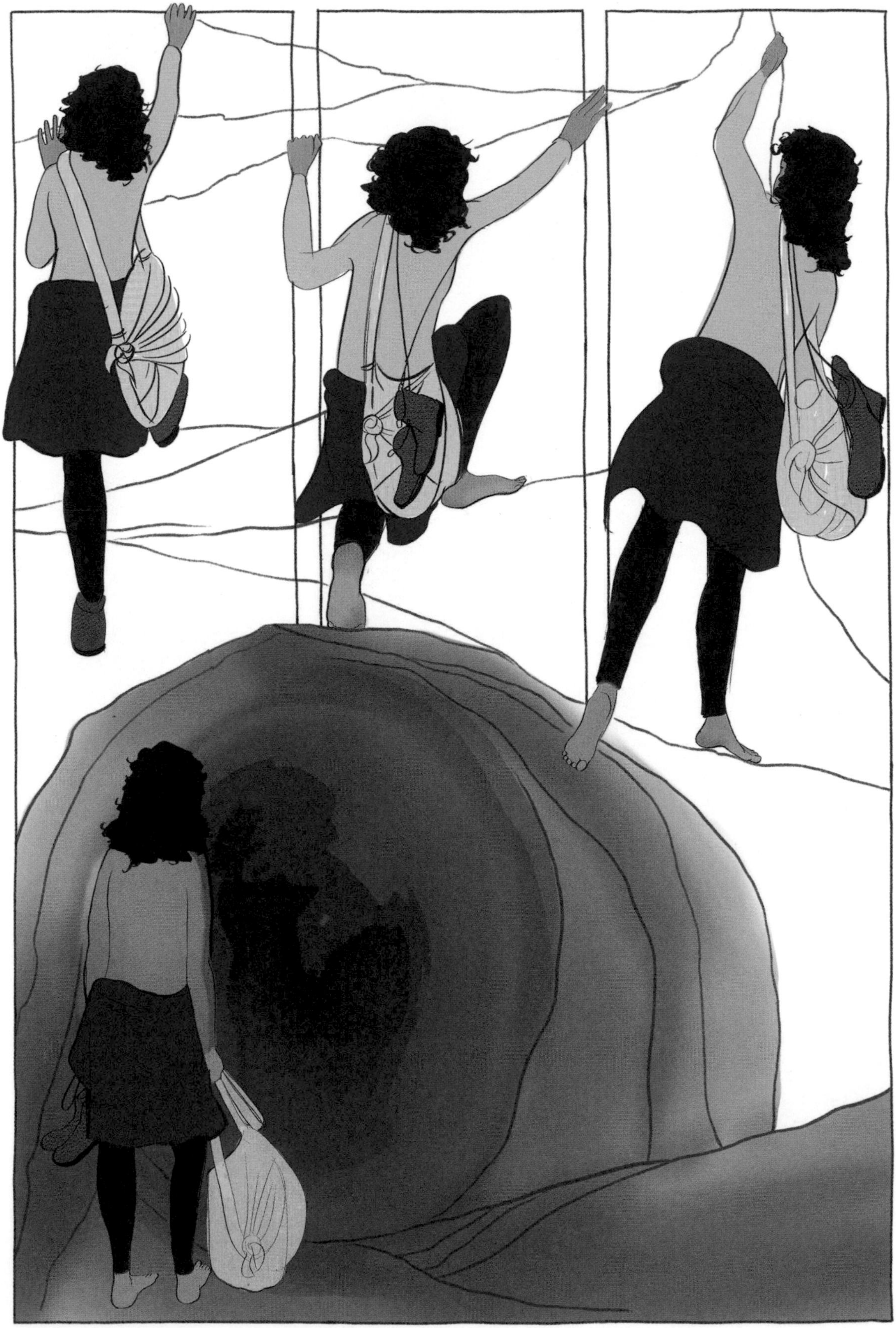

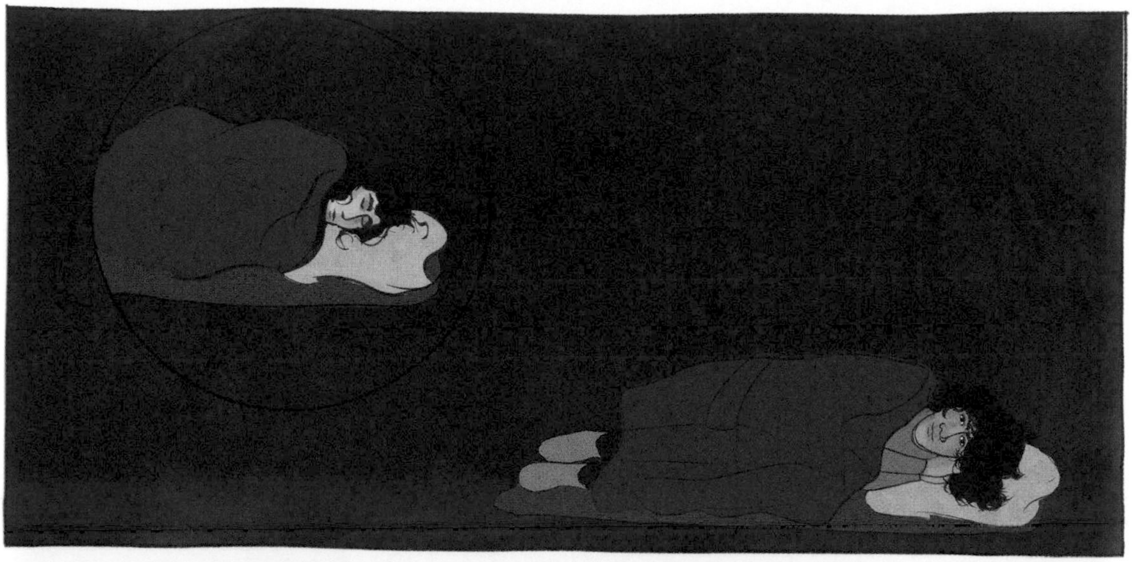

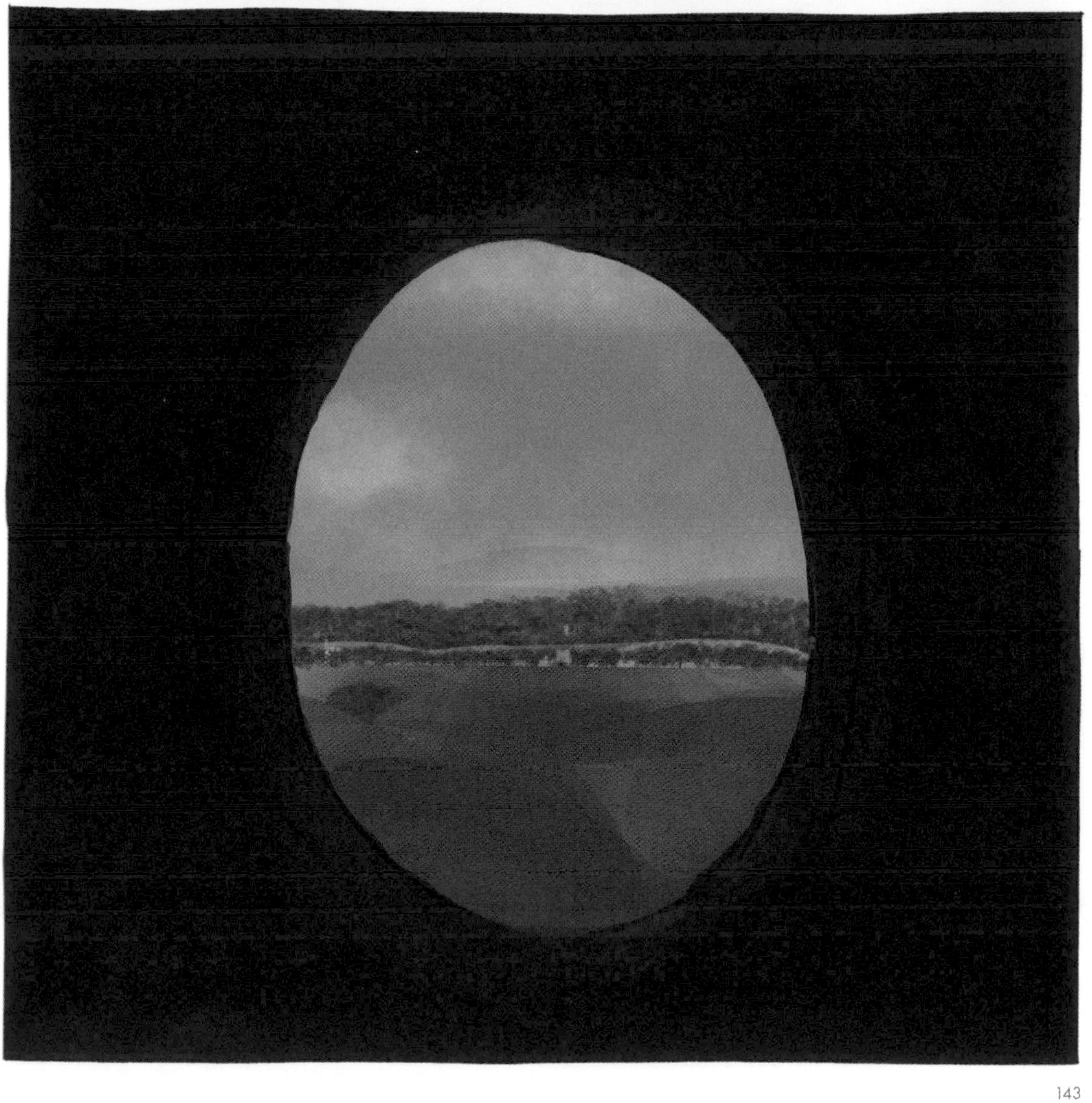

IF THE CAP
FITS

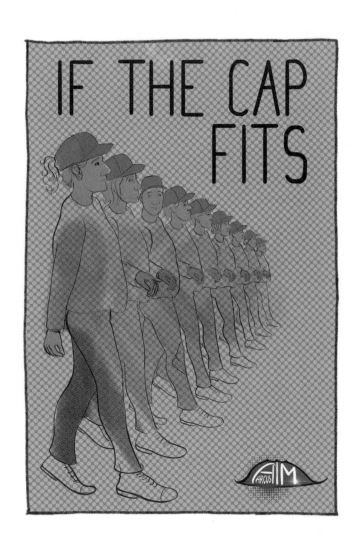

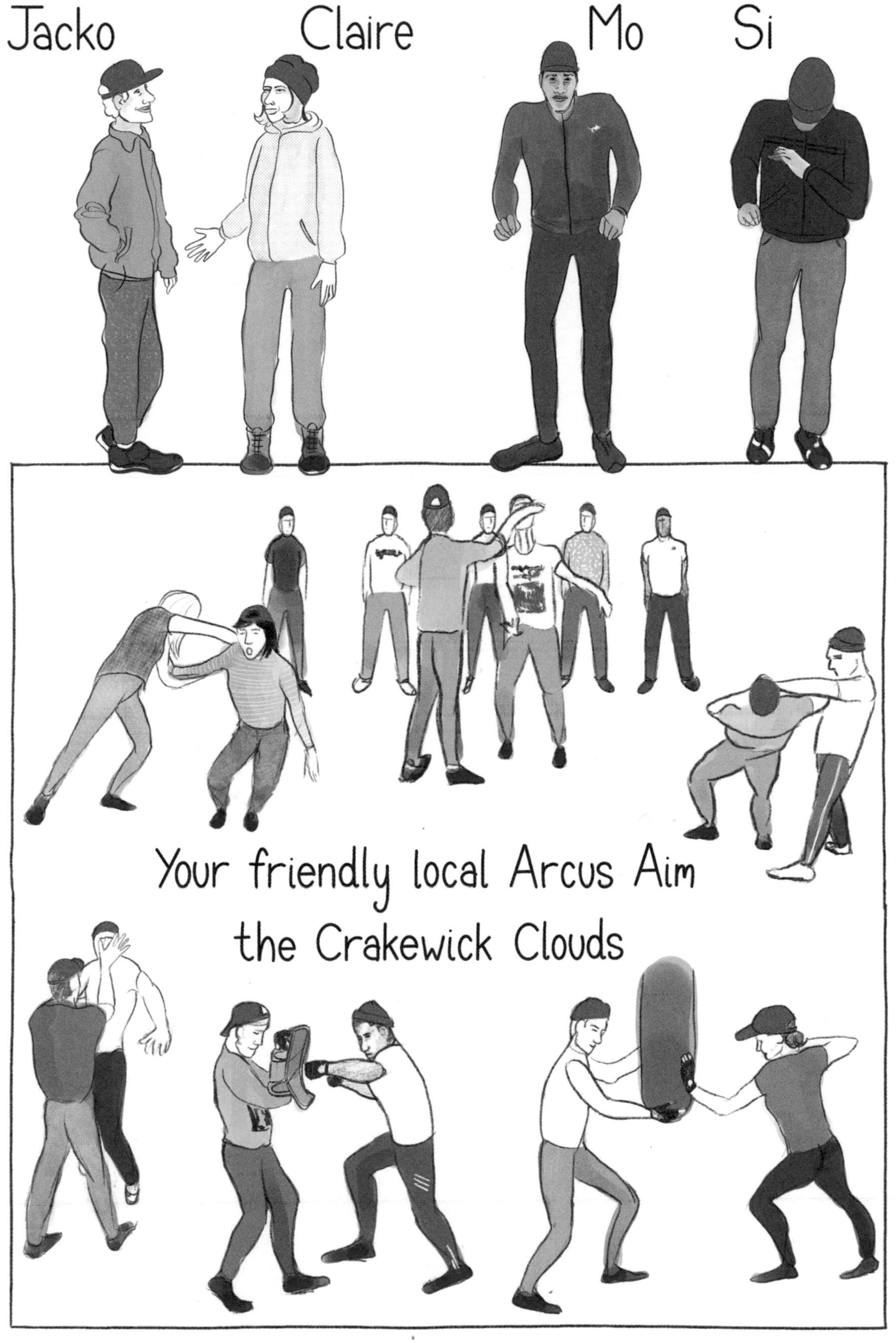
Jacko
Claire
Mo
Si
Your friendly local Arcus Aim
the Crakewick Clouds

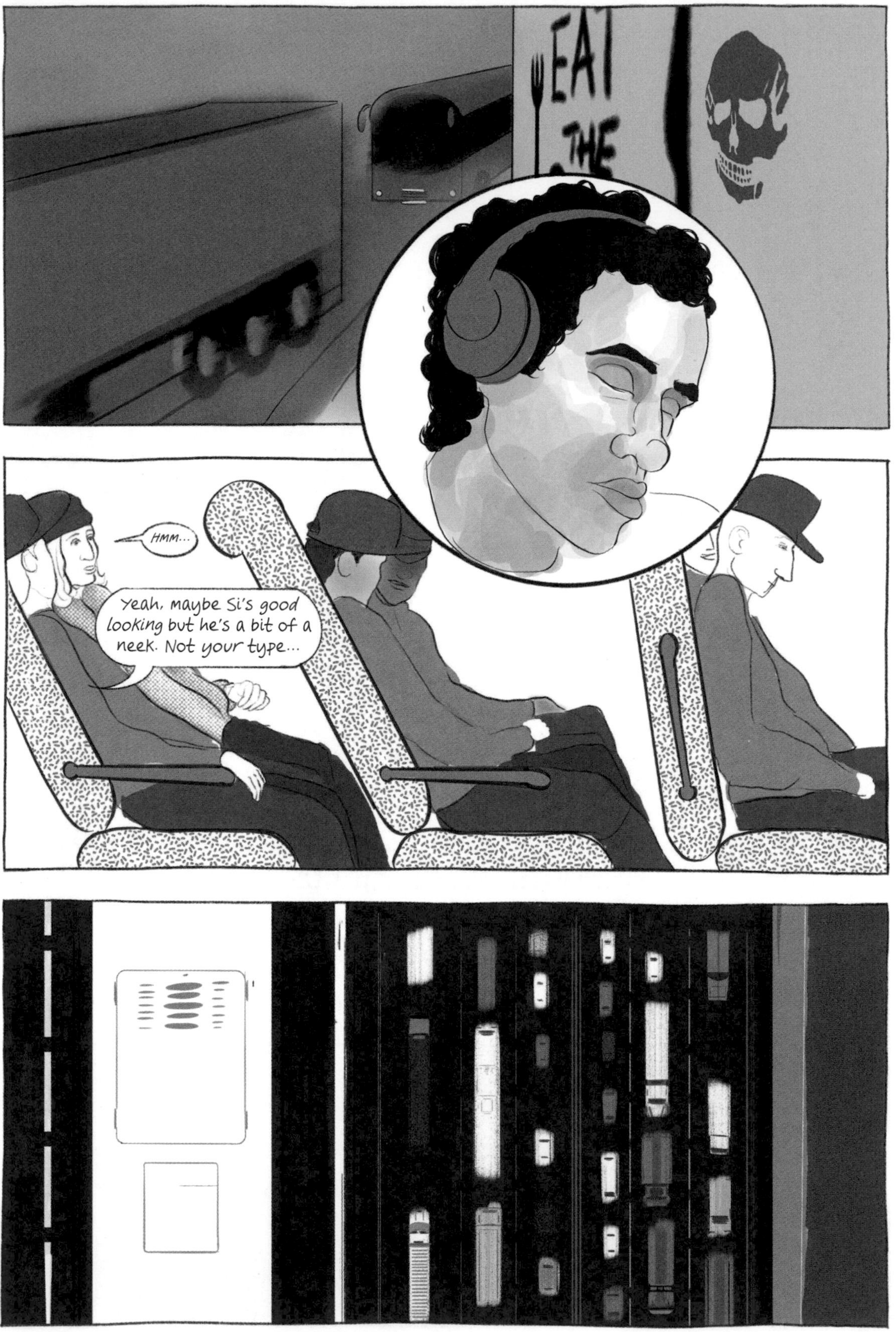
EAT
THE
HMM...
Yeah, maybe Si's good looking but he's a bit of a neek. Not your type...

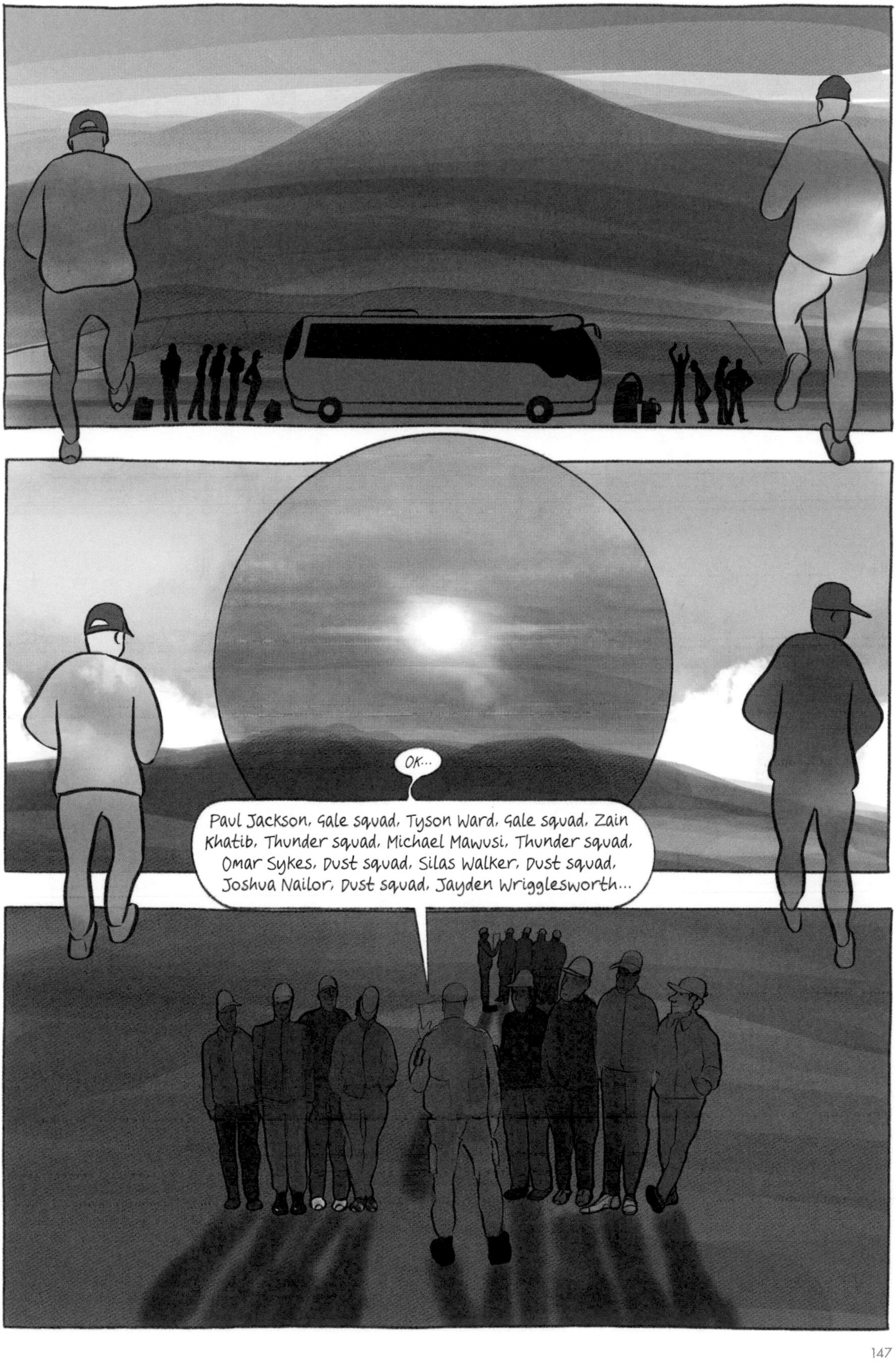
OK...
Paul Jackson, Gale squad, Tyson Ward, Gale squad, Zain Khatib, Thunder squad, Michael Mawusi, Thunder squad, Omar Sykes, Dust squad, Silas Walker, Dust squad, Joshua Nailor, Dust squad, Jayden Wrigglesworth...

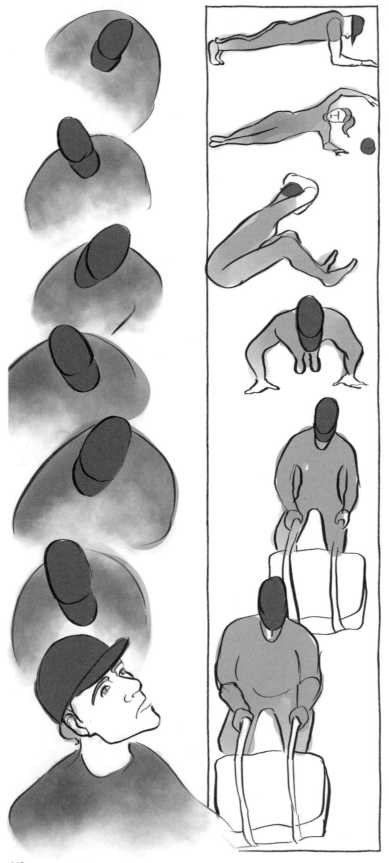

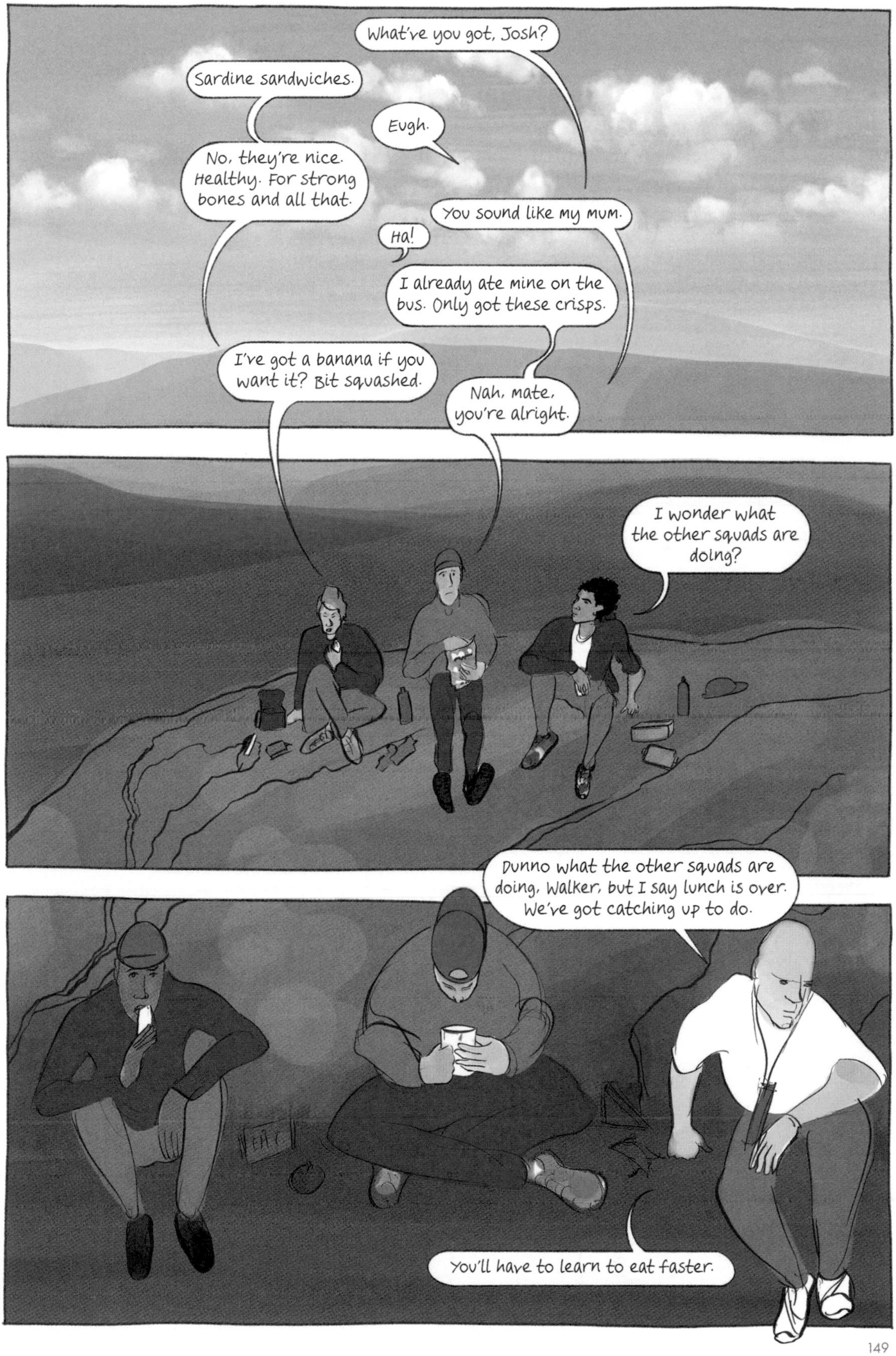
What've you got, Josh?
Sardine sandwiches.
Eugh.
No, they're nice. Healthy. For strong bones and all that.
You sound like my mum.
Ha!
I already ate mine on the bus. Only got these crisps.
I've got a banana if you want it? Bit squashed.
Nah, mate, you're alright.
I wonder what the other squads are doing?
Dunno what the other squads are doing, Walker, but I say lunch is over. We've got catching up to do.
You'll have to learn to eat faster.

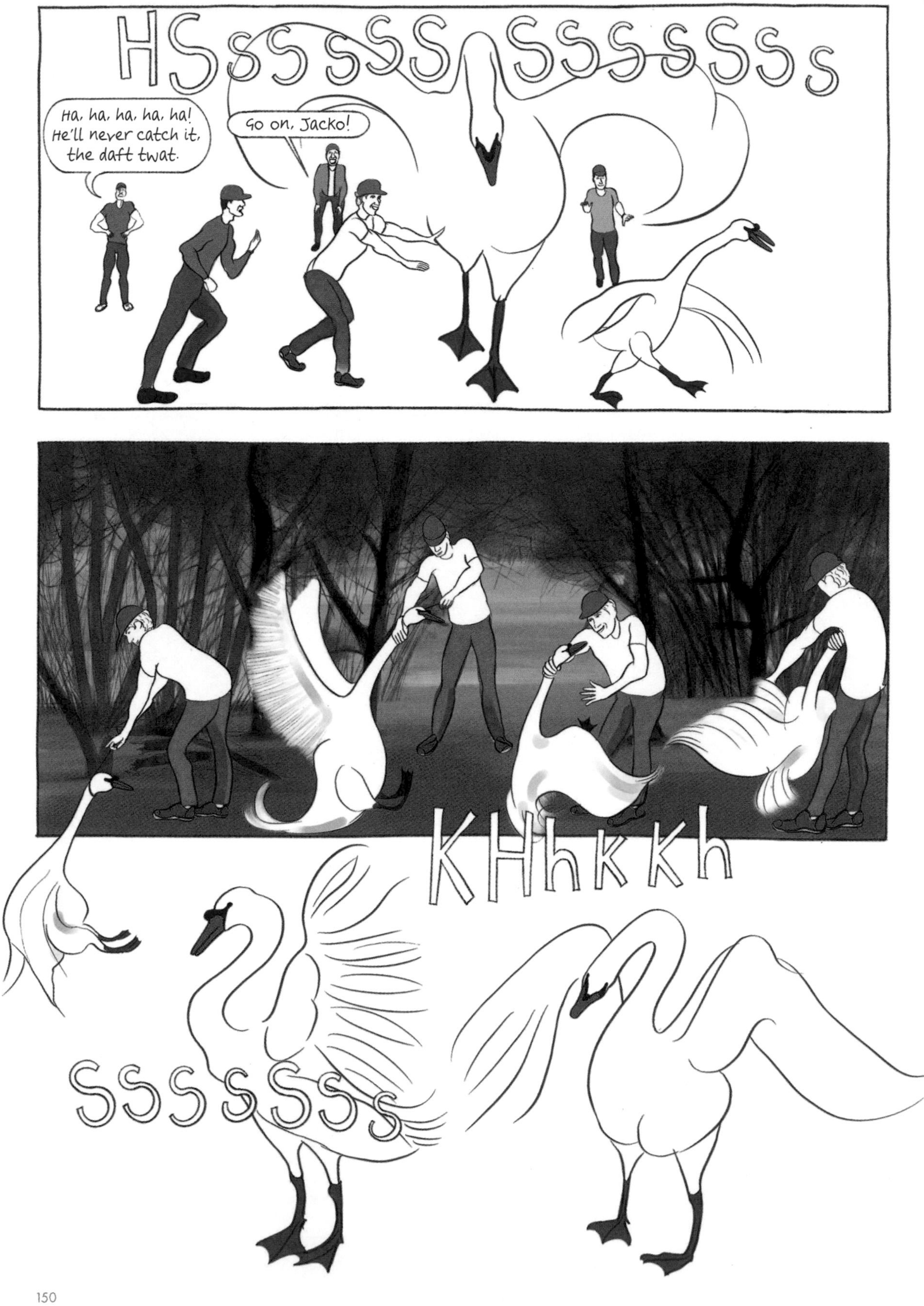
HSssssS SSSSSSSs
Ha, ha, ha, ha, ha! He'll never catch it, the daft twat.
Go on, Jacko!
KHhkkh
SSSSSSSS

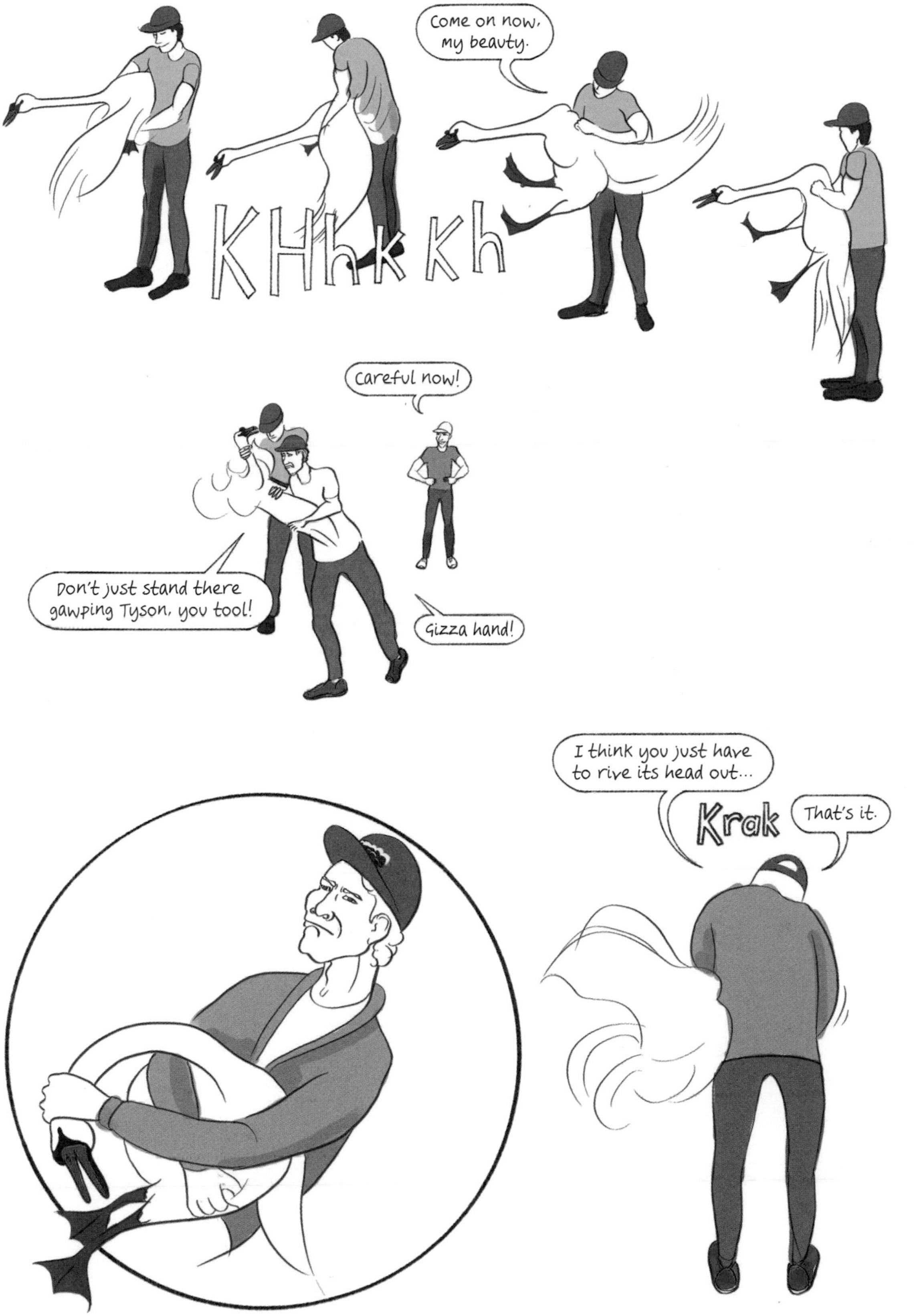

KHhk kh
Come on now, my beauty.
Careful now!
Don't just stand there gawping Tyson, you tool!
Gizza hand!
I think you just have to rive its head out...
Krak
That's it.

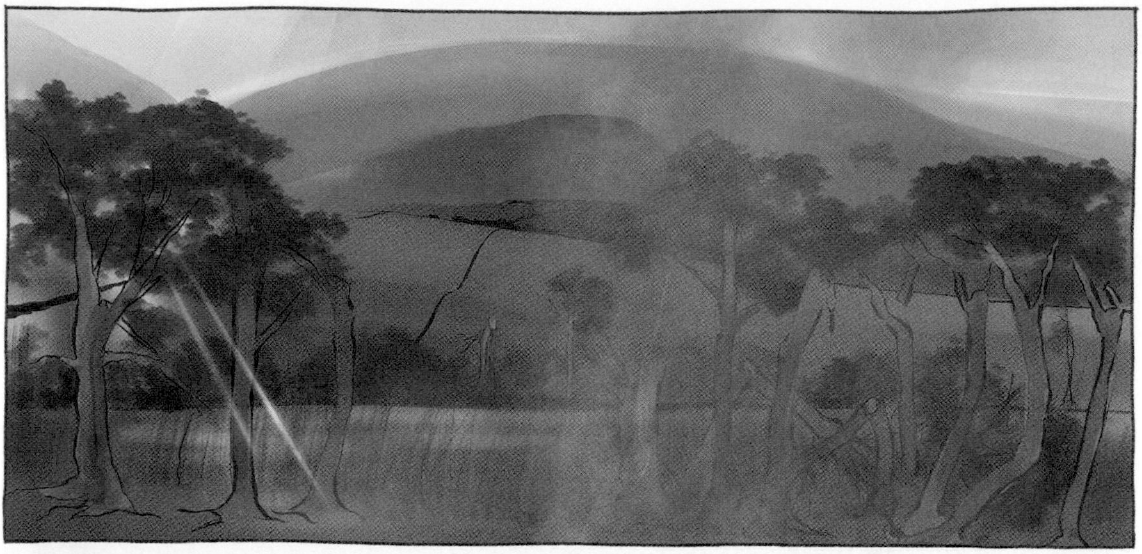

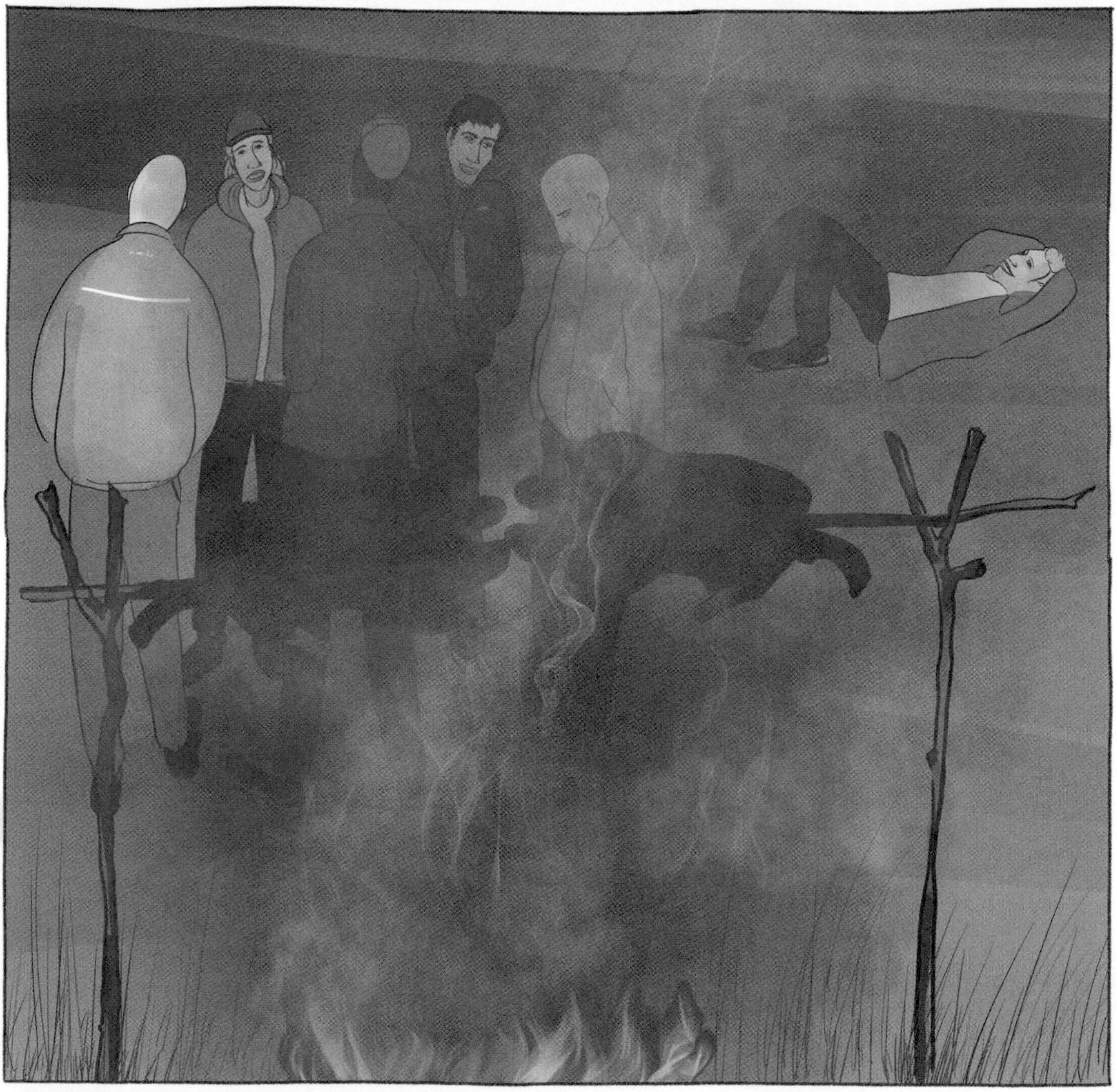

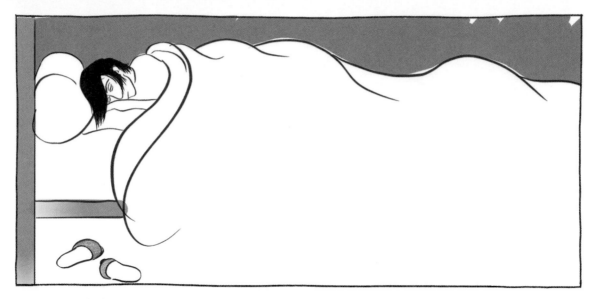

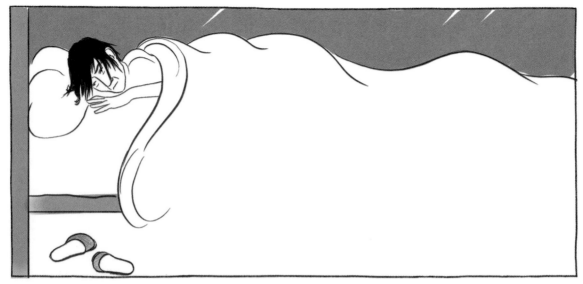

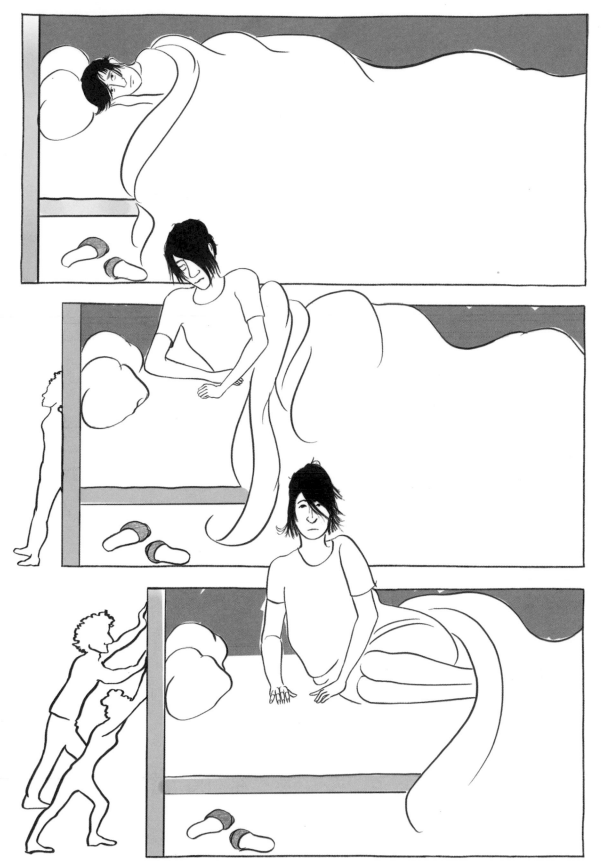

155

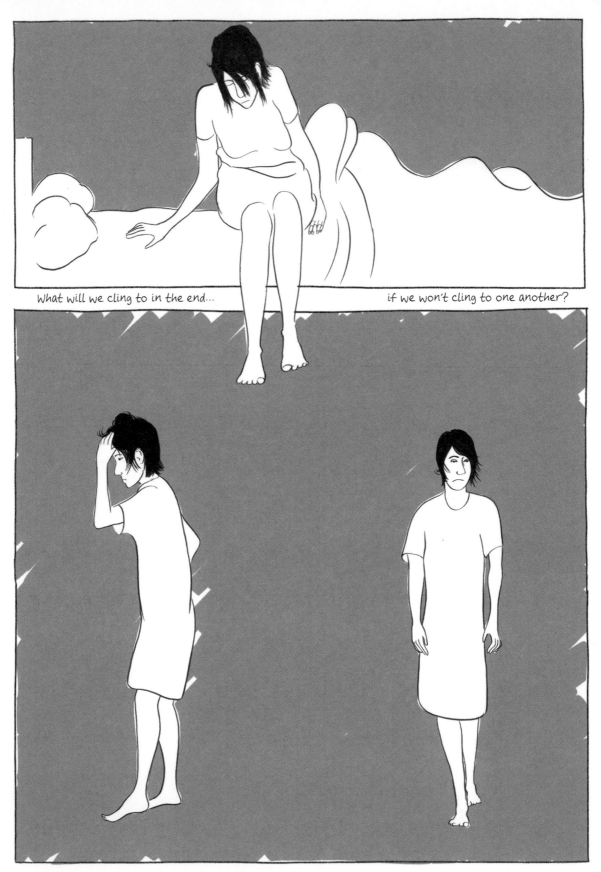

What will we cling to in the end...   if we won't cling to one another?

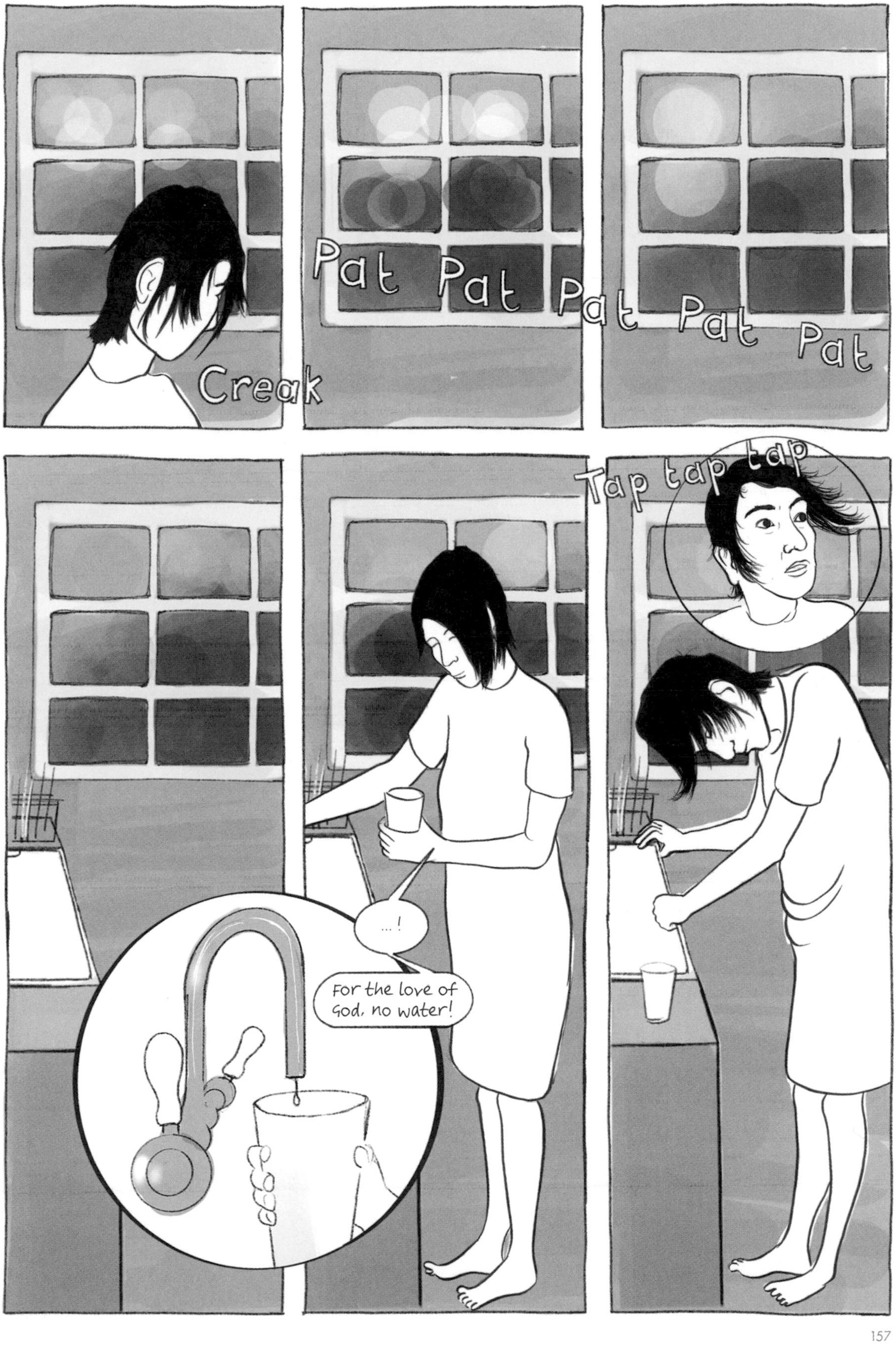
Creak
Pat Pat Pat Pat Pat
...!
For the love of God, no water!
Tap tap tap

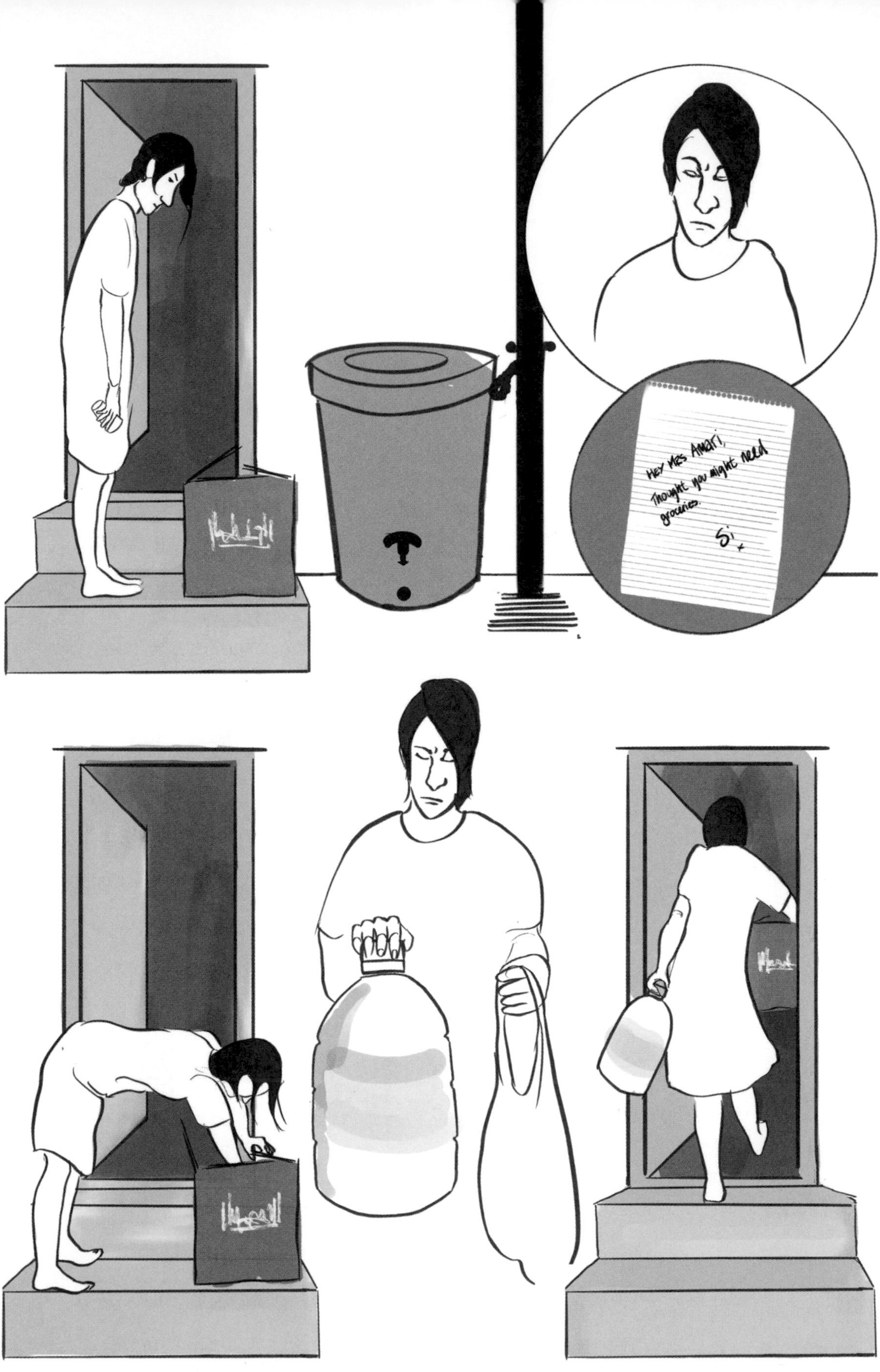
Hey Mrs Amari,
Thought you might need groceries.
Si x

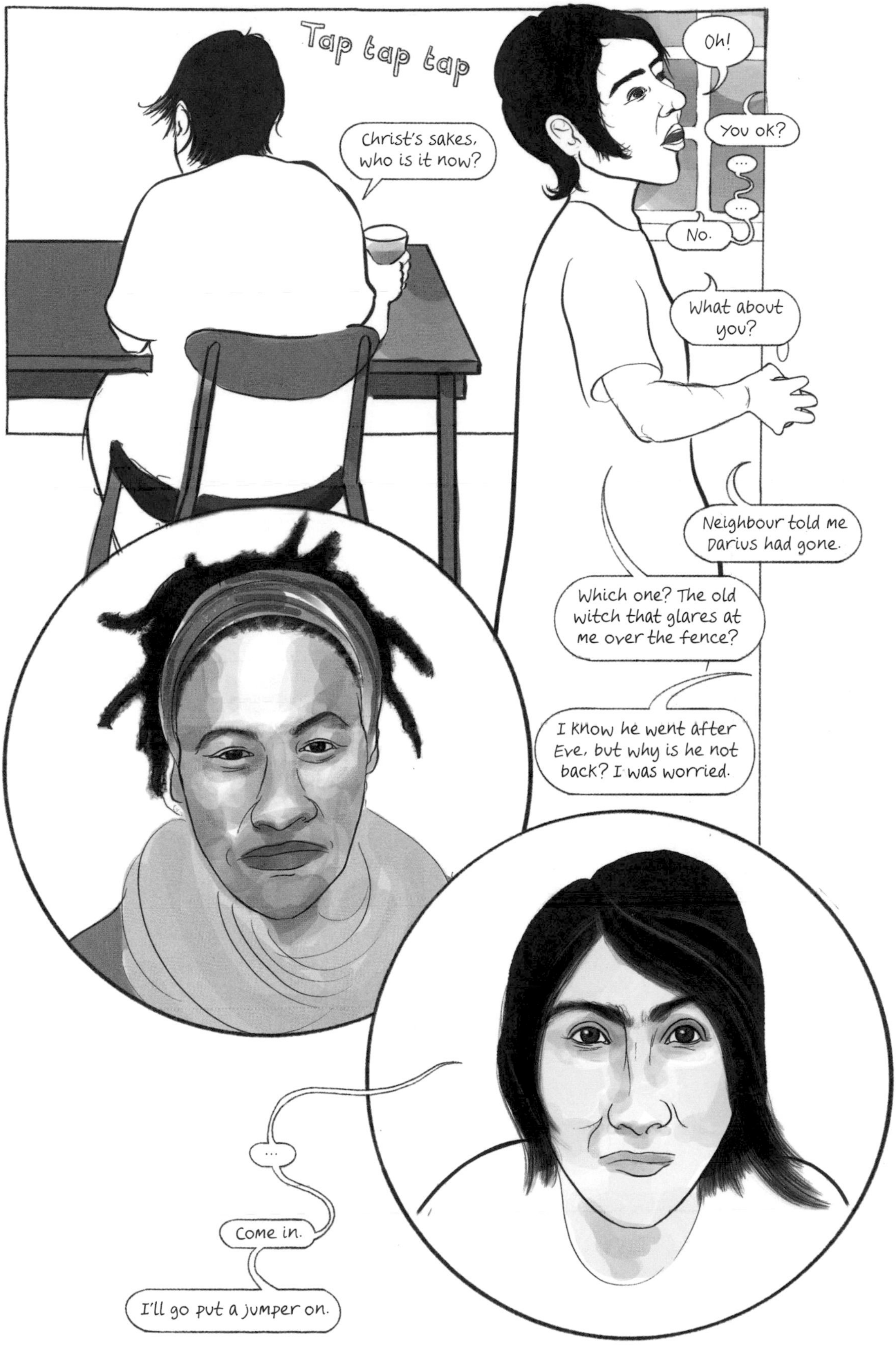
Tap tap tap
Christ's sakes, who is it now?
Oh!
You ok?
...
...
No.
What about you?
Neighbour told me Darius had gone.
Which one? The old witch that glares at me over the fence?
I know he went after Eve, but why is he not back? I was worried.
...
Come in.
I'll go put a jumper on.

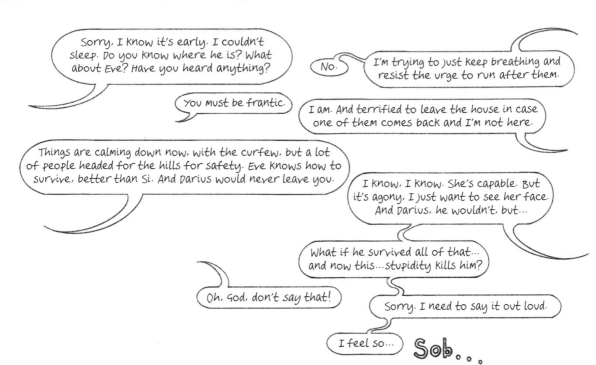

Sorry, I know it's early. I couldn't sleep. Do you know where he is? What about Eve? Have you heard anything?

No.

I'm trying to just keep breathing and resist the urge to run after them.

You must be frantic.

I am. And terrified to leave the house in case one of them comes back and I'm not here.

Things are calming down now, with the curfew, but a lot of people headed for the hills for safety. Eve knows how to survive, better than Si. And Darius would never leave you.

I know, I know. She's capable. But it's agony, I just want to see her face. And Darius, he wouldn't, but...

What if he survived all of that... and now this...stupidity kills him?

Oh, God, don't say that!

Sorry. I need to say it out loud.

I feel so...

Sob...

Hhhhh....

I don't know.

How's Si doing?

He left me a box with some groceries.

I know.

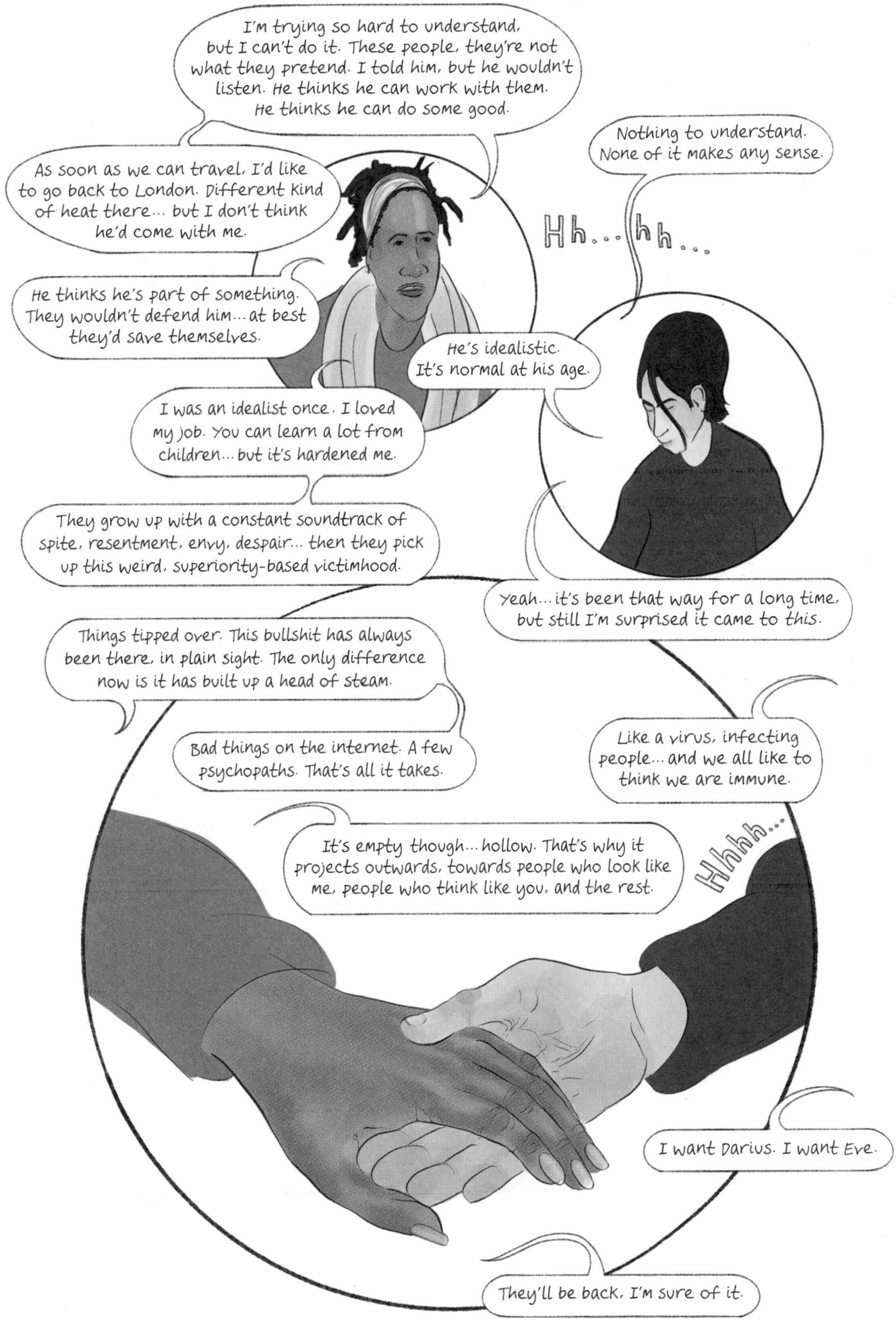
I'm trying so hard to understand, but I can't do it. These people, they're not what they pretend. I told him, but he wouldn't listen. He thinks he can work with them. He thinks he can do some good.
As soon as we can travel, I'd like to go back to London. Different kind of heat there... but I don't think he'd come with me.
Nothing to understand. None of it makes any sense.
Hh... hh...
He thinks he's part of something. They wouldn't defend him... at best they'd save themselves.
He's idealistic. It's normal at his age.
I was an idealist once. I loved my job. You can learn a lot from children... but it's hardened me.
They grow up with a constant soundtrack of spite, resentment, envy, despair... then they pick up this weird, superiority-based victimhood.
Yeah... it's been that way for a long time, but still I'm surprised it came to this.
Things tipped over. This bullshit has always been there, in plain sight. The only difference now is it has built up a head of steam.
Bad things on the internet. A few psychopaths. That's all it takes.
Like a virus, infecting people... and we all like to think we are immune.
It's empty though... hollow. That's why it projects outwards, towards people who look like me, people who think like you, and the rest.
Hhhh...
I want Darius. I want Eve.
They'll be back, I'm sure of it.

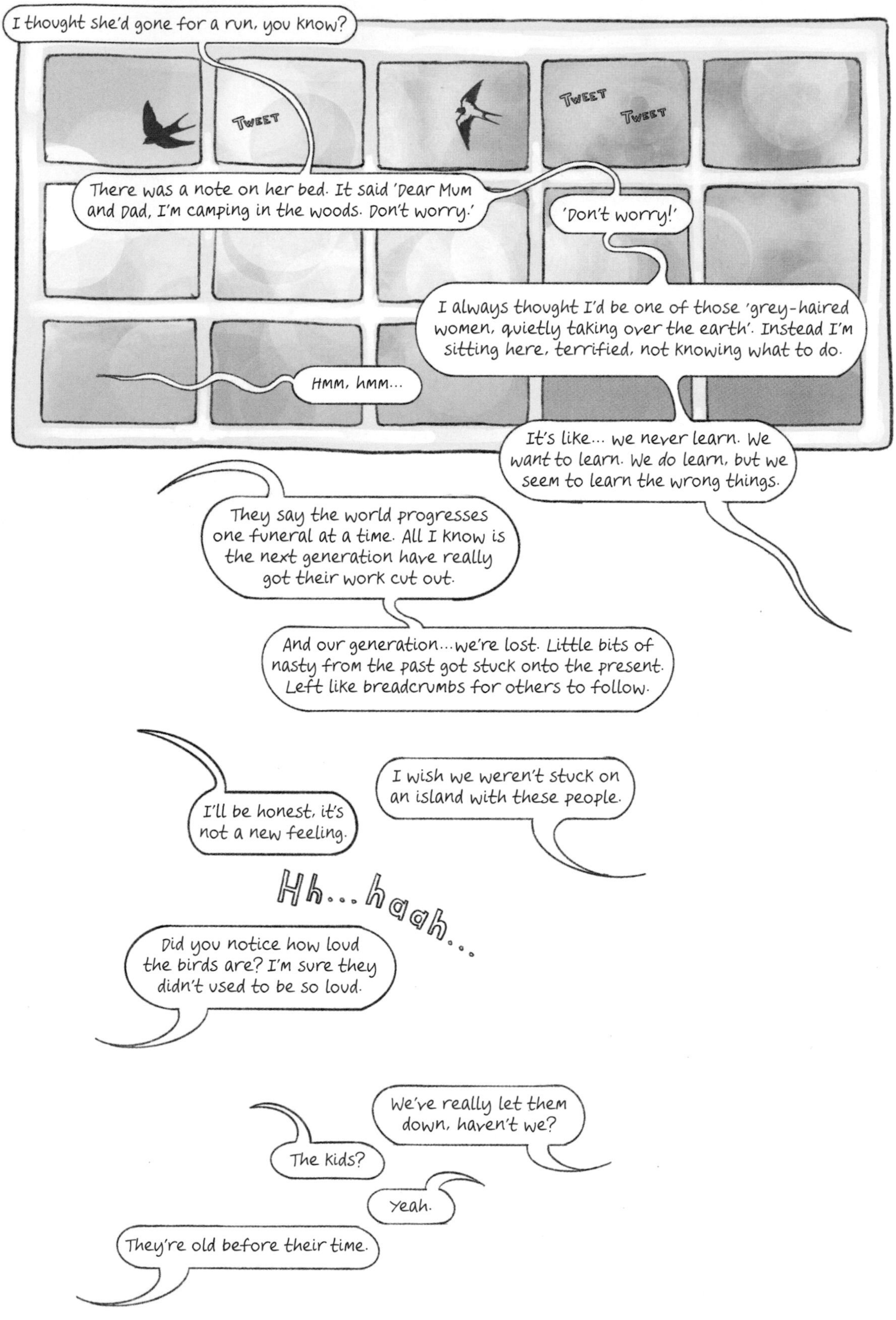
I thought she'd gone for a run, you know?
TWEET
TWEET
TWEET
There was a note on her bed. It said 'Dear Mum and Dad, I'm camping in the woods. Don't worry.'
'Don't worry!'
I always thought I'd be one of those 'grey-haired women, quietly taking over the earth'. Instead I'm sitting here, terrified, not knowing what to do.
Hmm, hmm...
It's like... we never learn. We want to learn. We do learn, but we seem to learn the wrong things.
They say the world progresses one funeral at a time. All I know is the next generation have really got their work cut out.
And our generation...we're lost. Little bits of nasty from the past got stuck onto the present. Left like breadcrumbs for others to follow.
I'll be honest, it's not a new feeling.
I wish we weren't stuck on an island with these people.
Hh...haah...
Did you notice how loud the birds are? I'm sure they didn't used to be so loud.
We've really let them down, haven't we?
The kids?
Yeah.
They're old before their time.

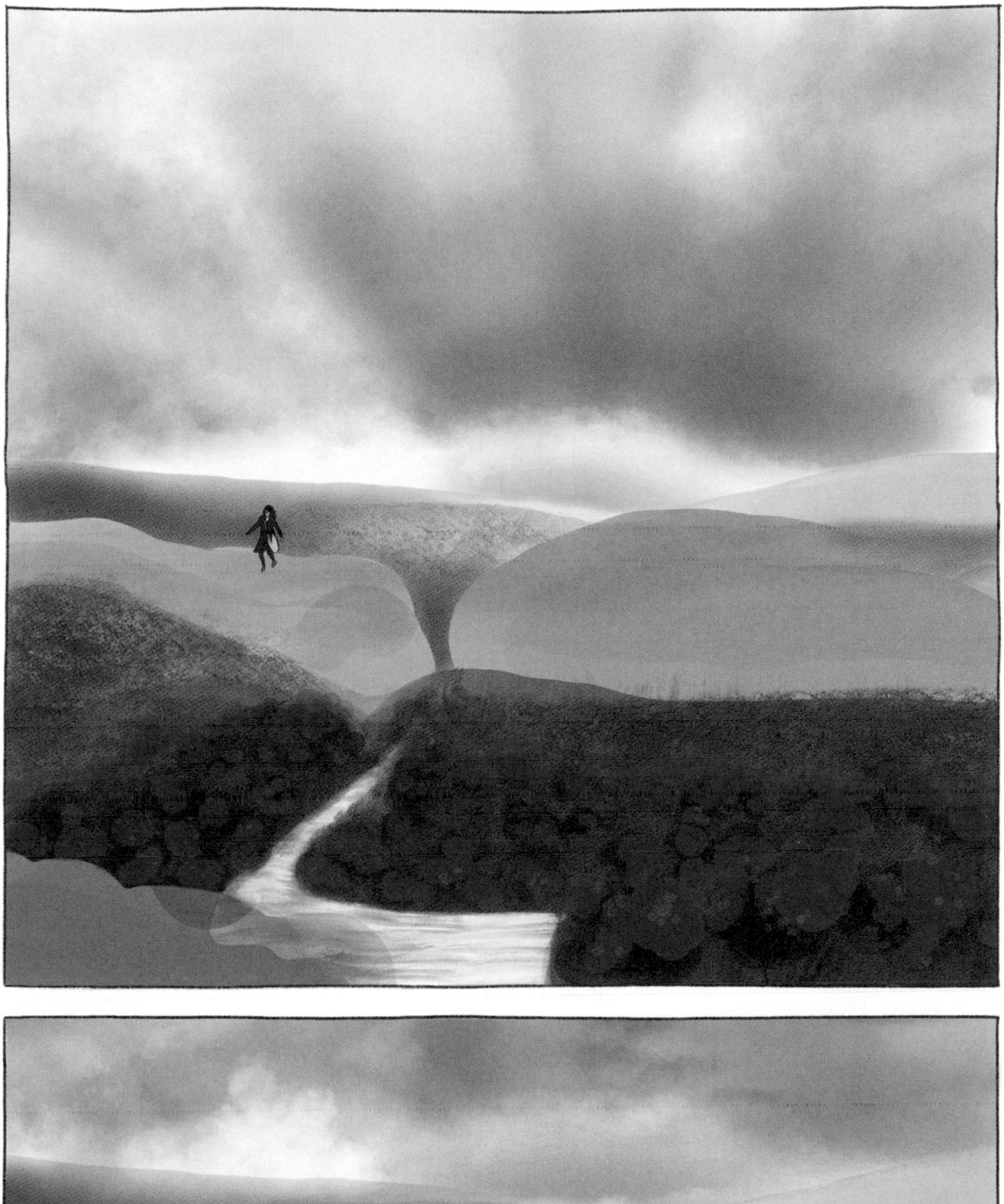

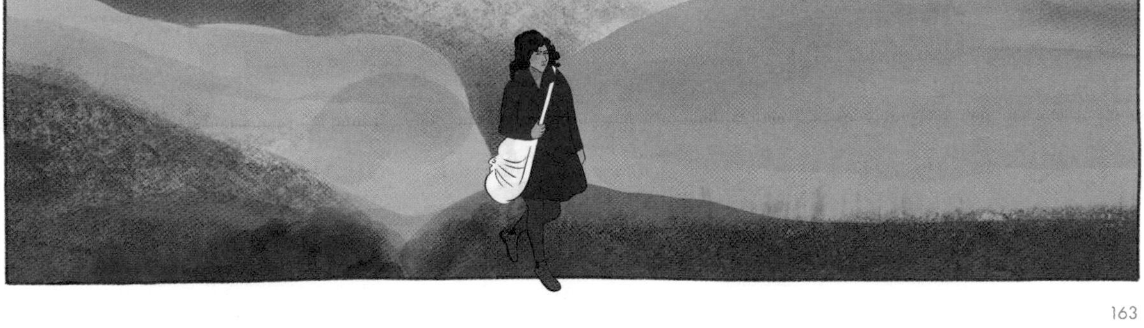

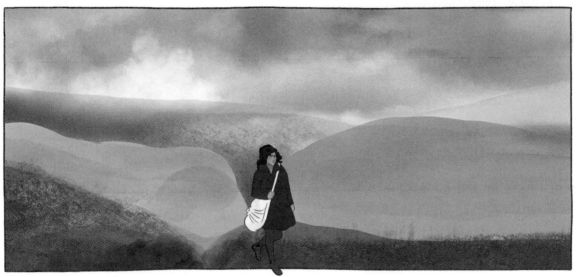

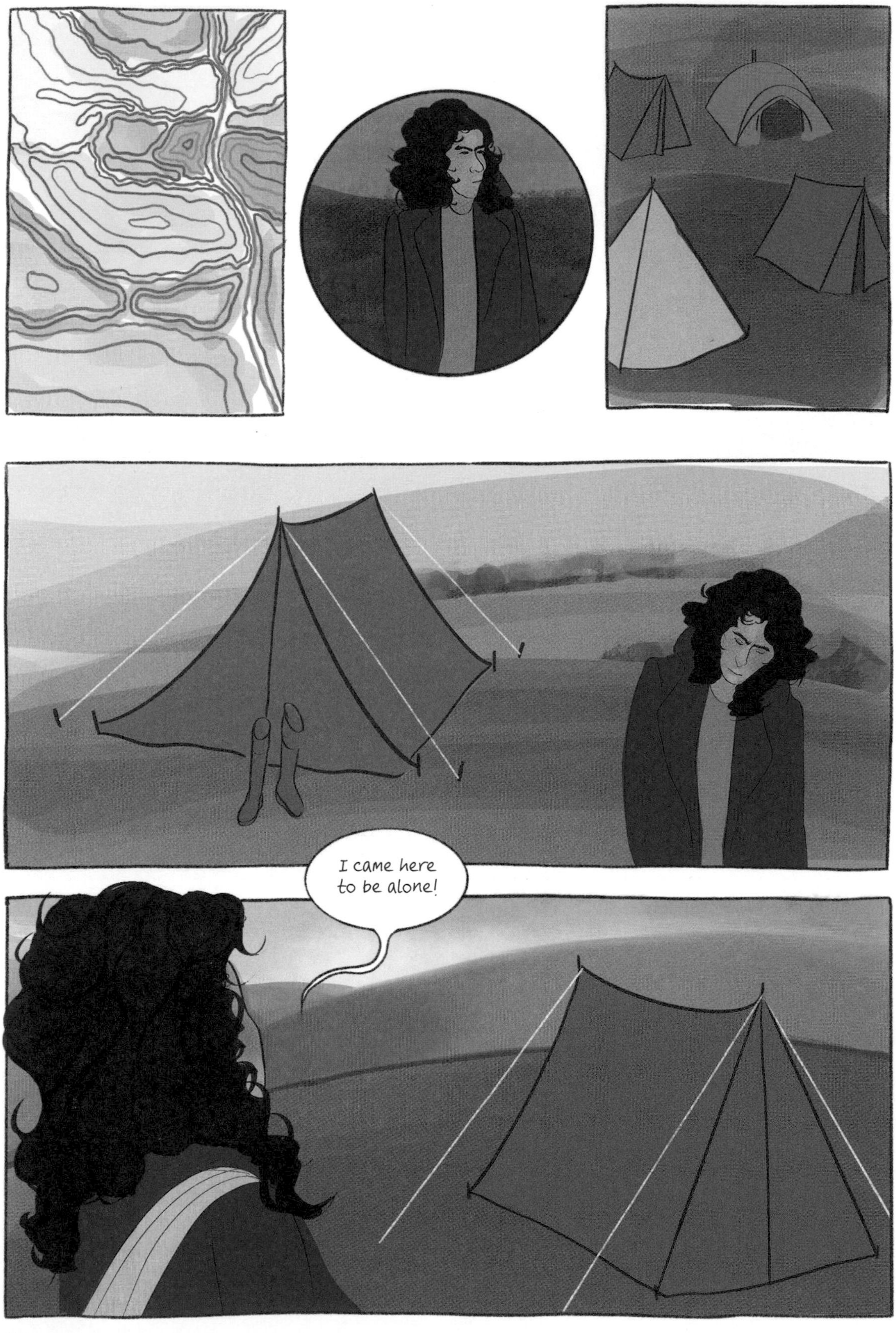
I came here to be alone!

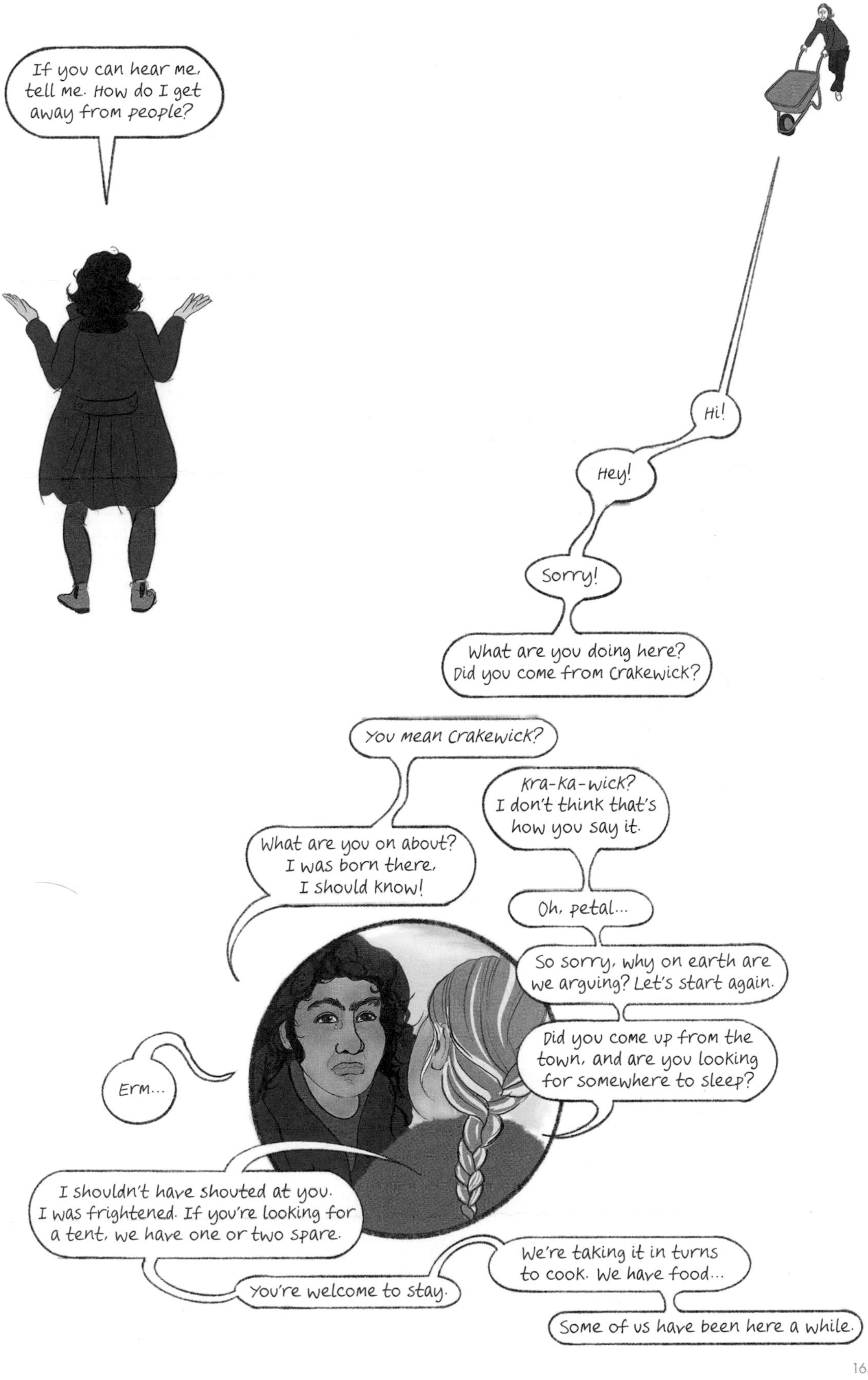
If you can hear me, tell me. How do I get away from people?
Hi!
Hey!
Sorry!
What are you doing here? Did you come from Crakewick?
You mean Crakewick?
Kra-ka-wick? I don't think that's how you say it.
What are you on about? I was born there, I should know!
Oh, petal...
So sorry, why on earth are we arguing? Let's start again.
Did you come up from the town, and are you looking for somewhere to sleep?
Erm...
I shouldn't have shouted at you. I was frightened. If you're looking for a tent, we have one or two spare.
You're welcome to stay.
We're taking it in turns to cook. We have food...
Some of us have been here a while.

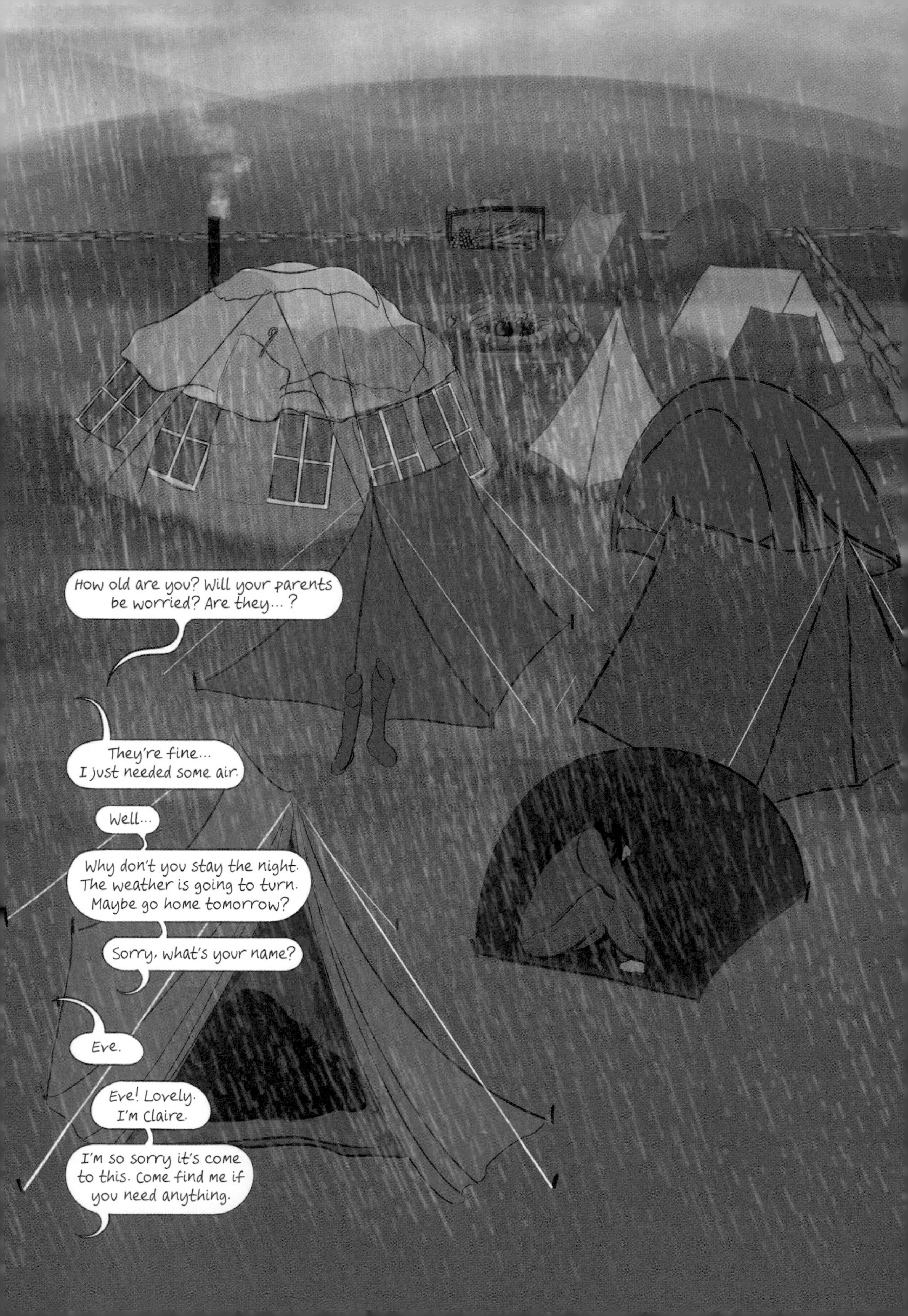
How old are you? Will your parents be worried? Are they... ?
They're fine... I just needed some air.
Well...
Why don't you stay the night. The weather is going to turn. Maybe go home tomorrow?
Sorry, what's your name?
Eve.
Eve! Lovely. I'm Claire.
I'm so sorry it's come to this. Come find me if you need anything.

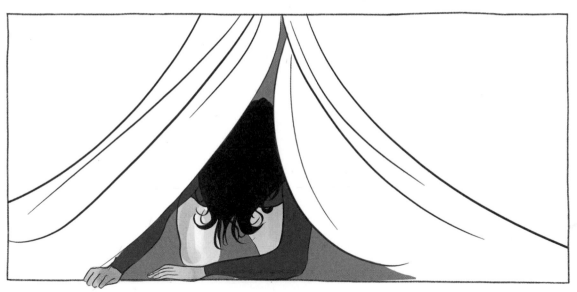

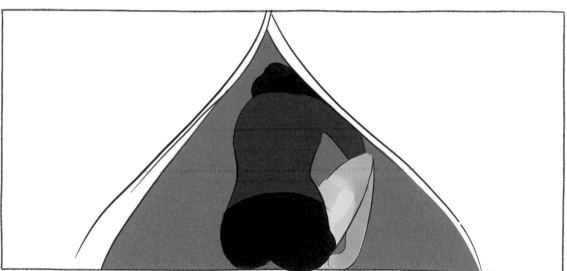

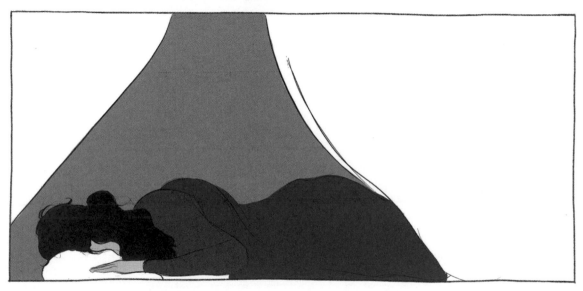

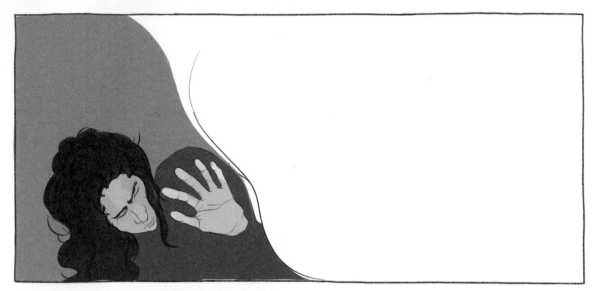

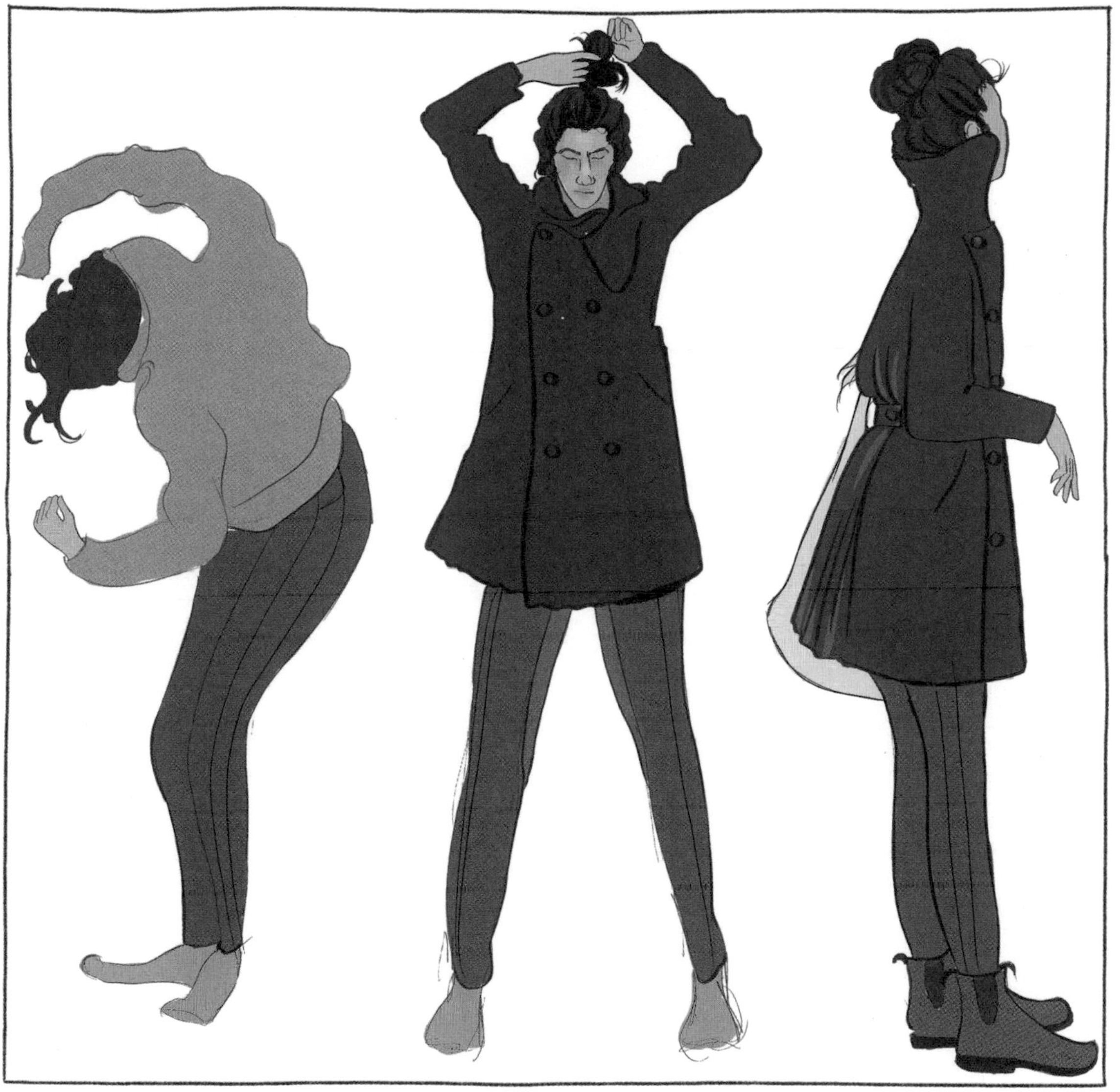

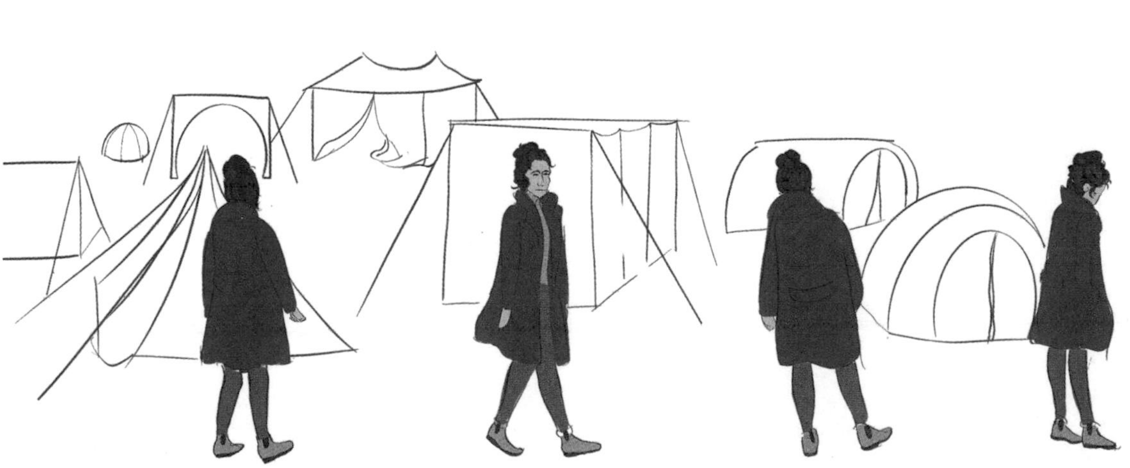

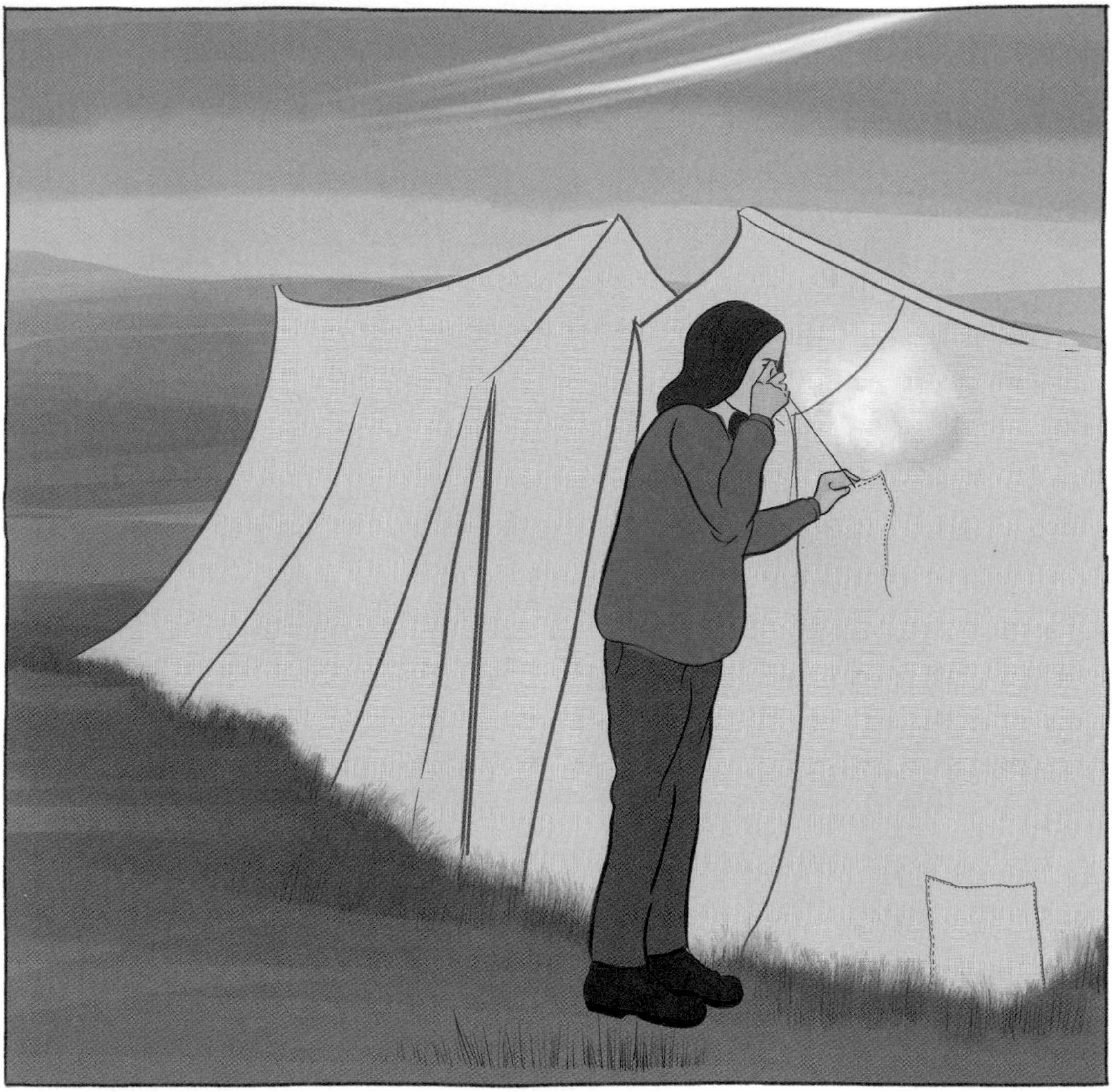

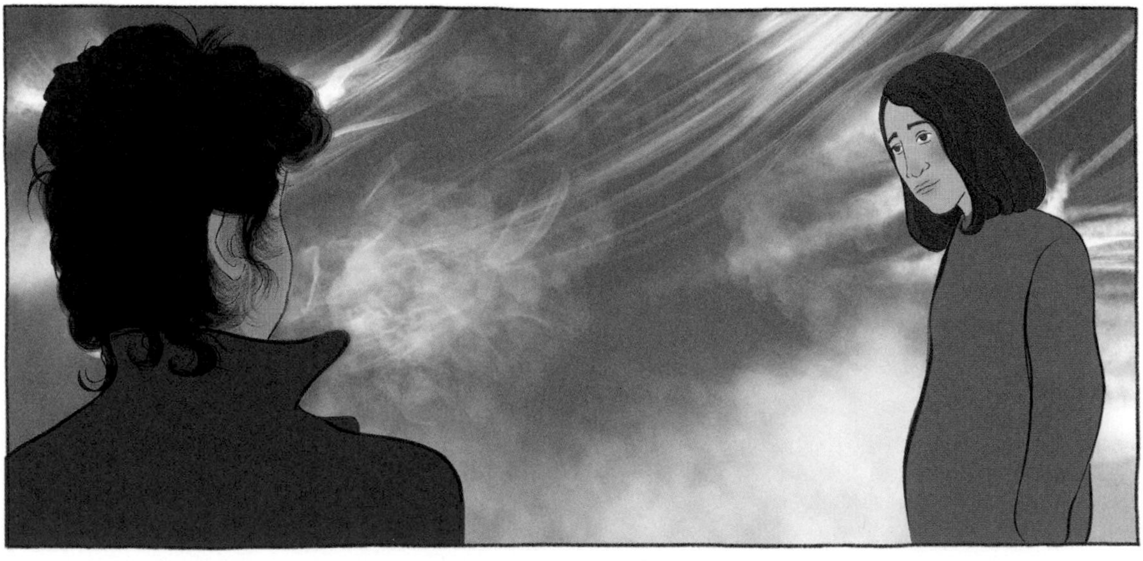

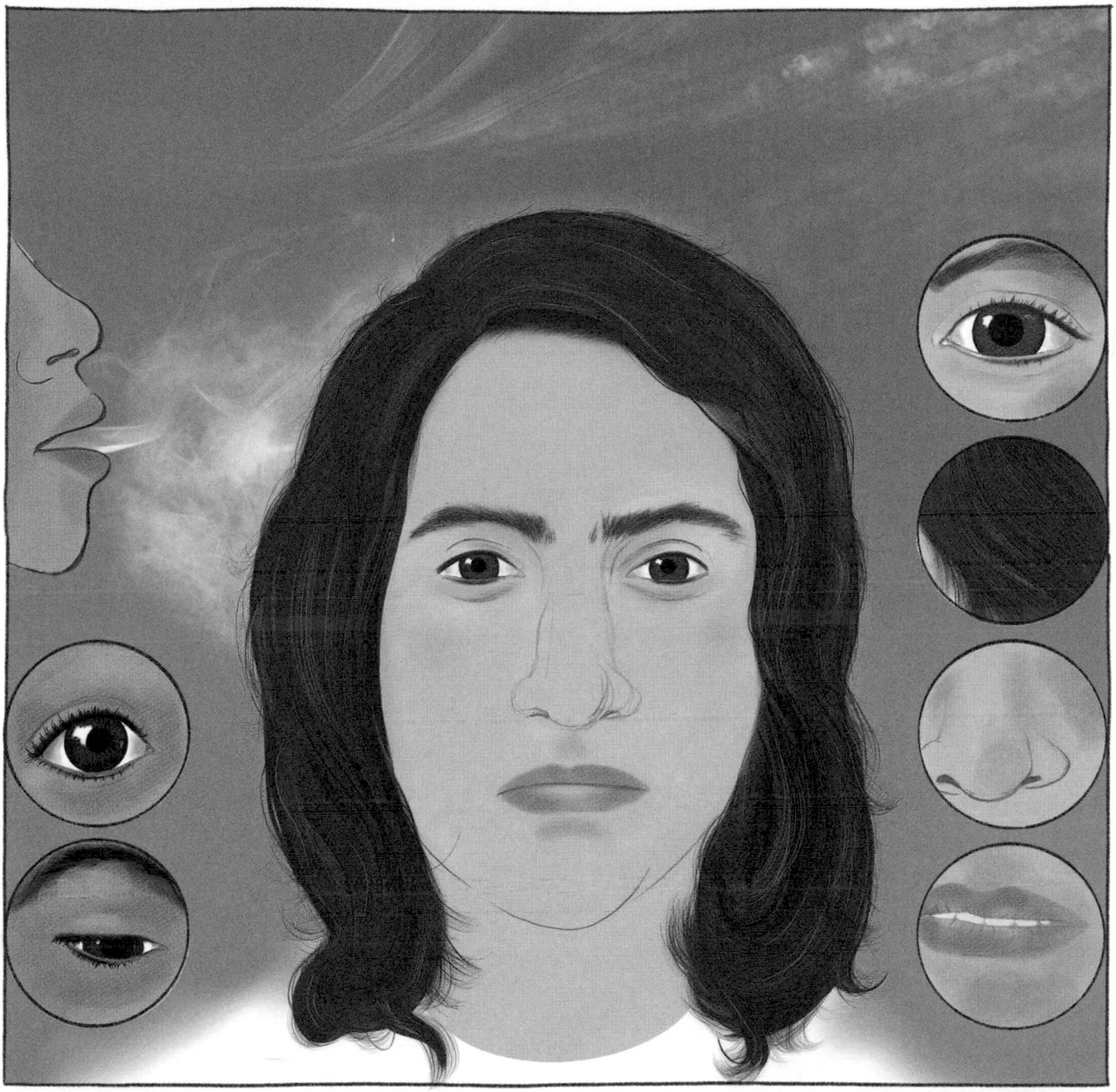

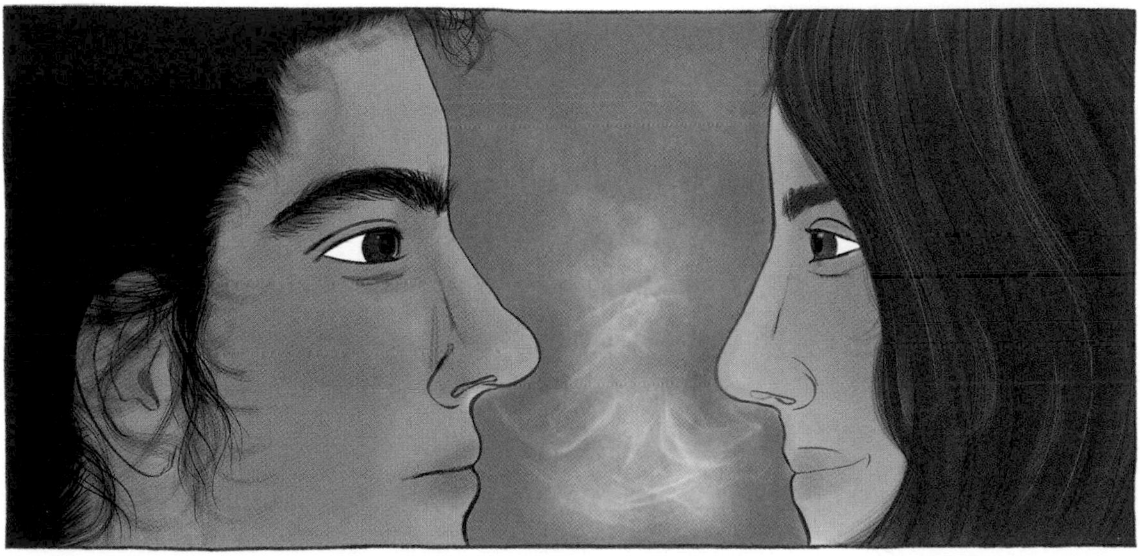

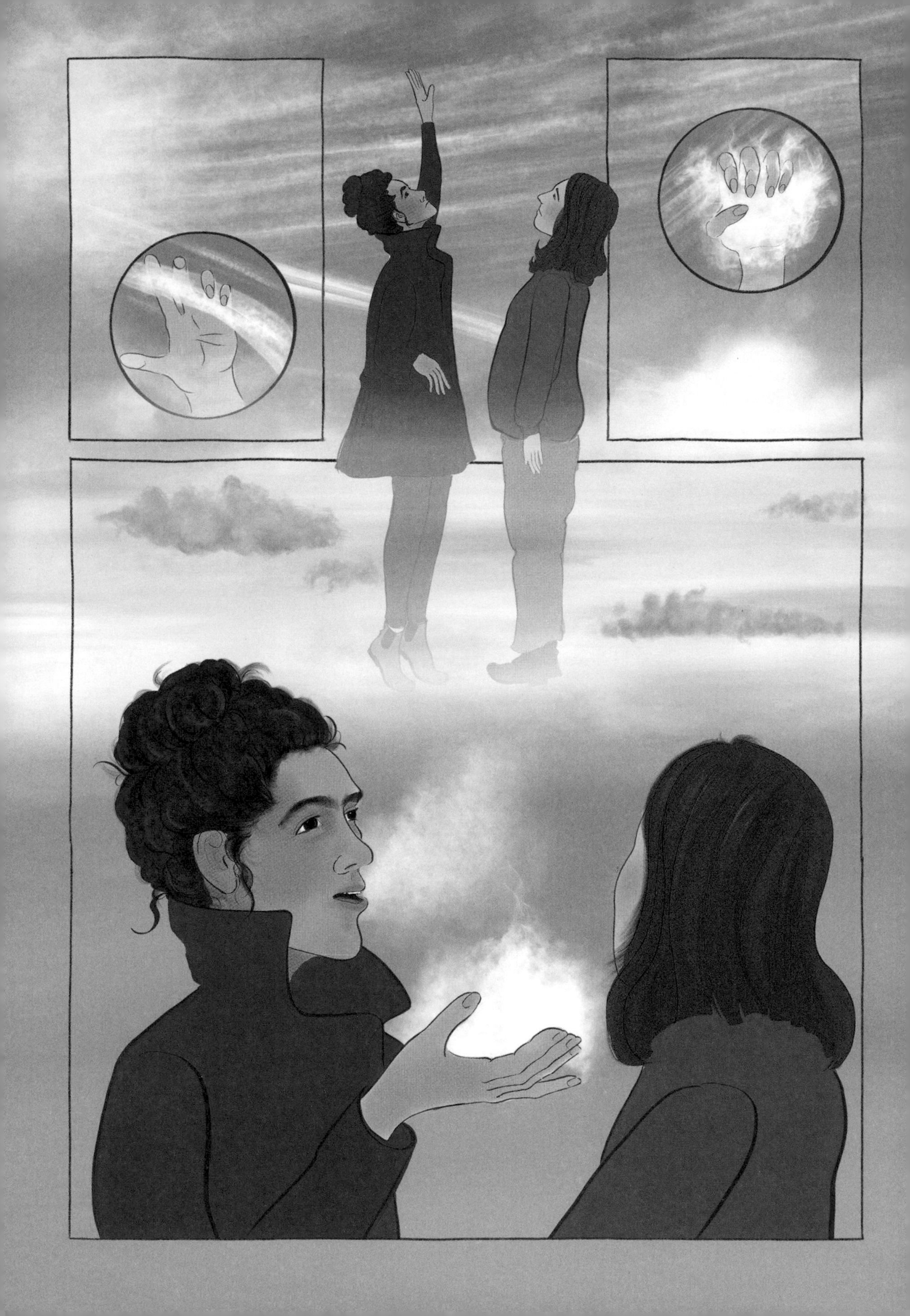

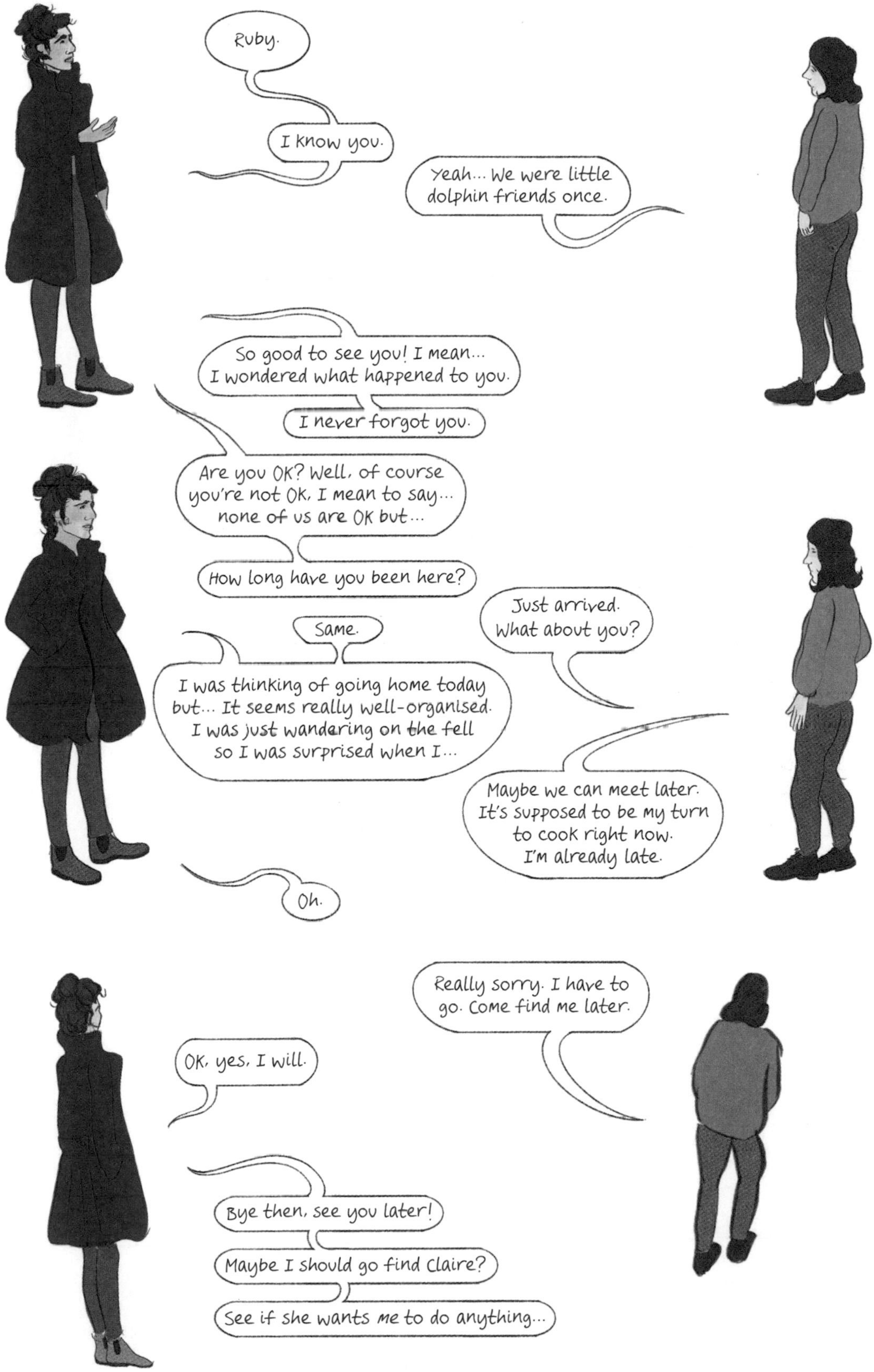
Ruby.
I know you.
Yeah... We were little dolphin friends once.
So good to see you! I mean... I wondered what happened to you.
I never forgot you.
Are you OK? Well, of course you're not OK, I mean to say... none of us are OK but...
How long have you been here?
Just arrived. What about you?
Same.
I was thinking of going home today but... It seems really well-organised. I was just wandering on the fell so I was surprised when I...
Maybe we can meet later. It's supposed to be my turn to cook right now. I'm already late.
Oh.
Really sorry. I have to go. Come find me later.
OK, yes, I will.
Bye then, see you later!
Maybe I should go find Claire?
See if she wants me to do anything...

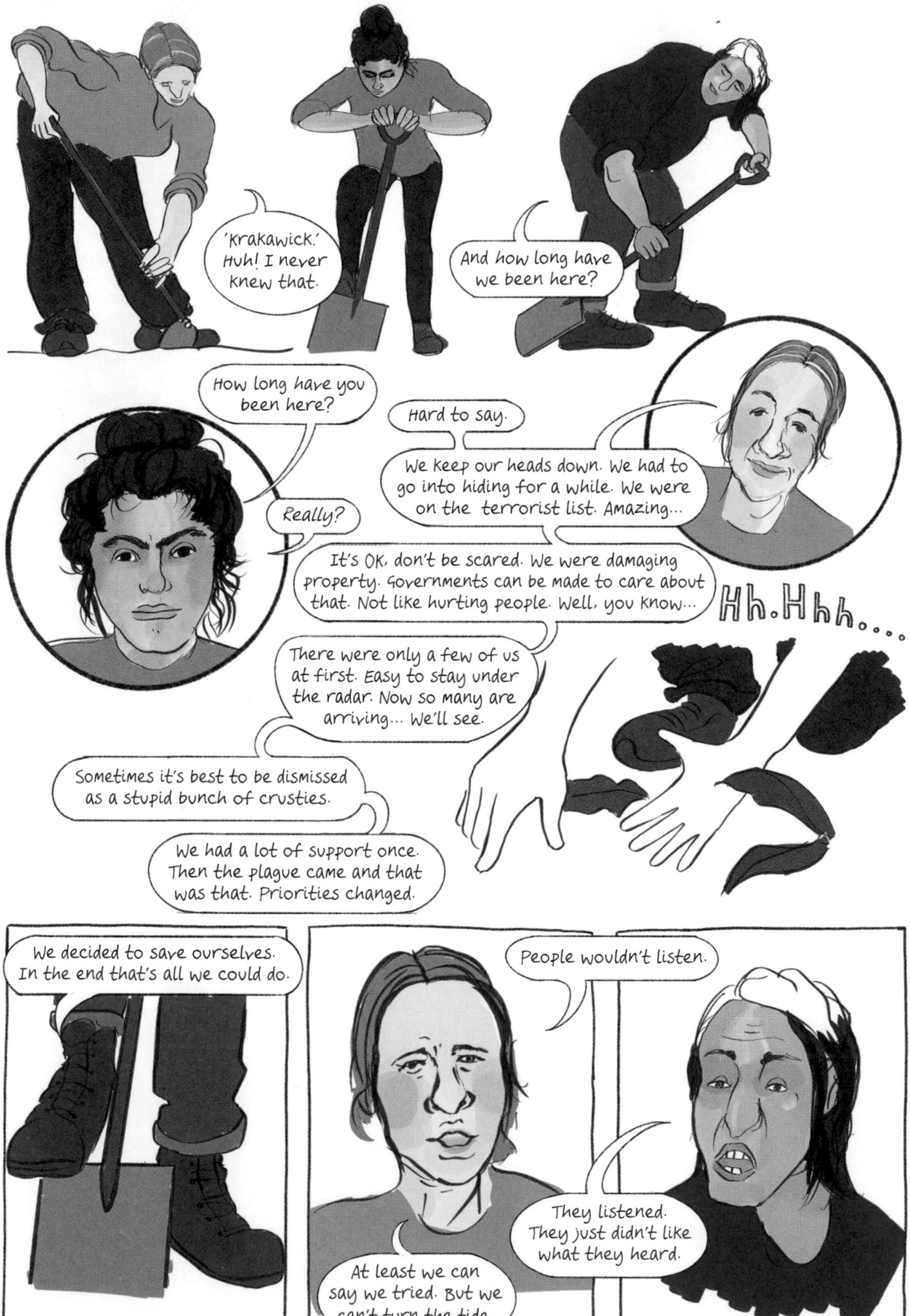
'Krakawick.' Huh! I never knew that.
And how long have we been here?
How long have you been here?
Hard to say.
We keep our heads down. We had to go into hiding for a while. We were on the terrorist list. Amazing...
Really?
It's OK, don't be scared. We were damaging property. Governments can be made to care about that. Not like hurting people. Well, you know...
Hh.Hhh....
There were only a few of us at first. Easy to stay under the radar. Now so many are arriving... We'll see.
Sometimes it's best to be dismissed as a stupid bunch of crusties.
We had a lot of support once. Then the plague came and that was that. Priorities changed.
We decided to save ourselves. In the end that's all we could do.
People wouldn't listen.
At least we can say we tried. But we can't turn the tide.
They listened. They just didn't like what they heard.

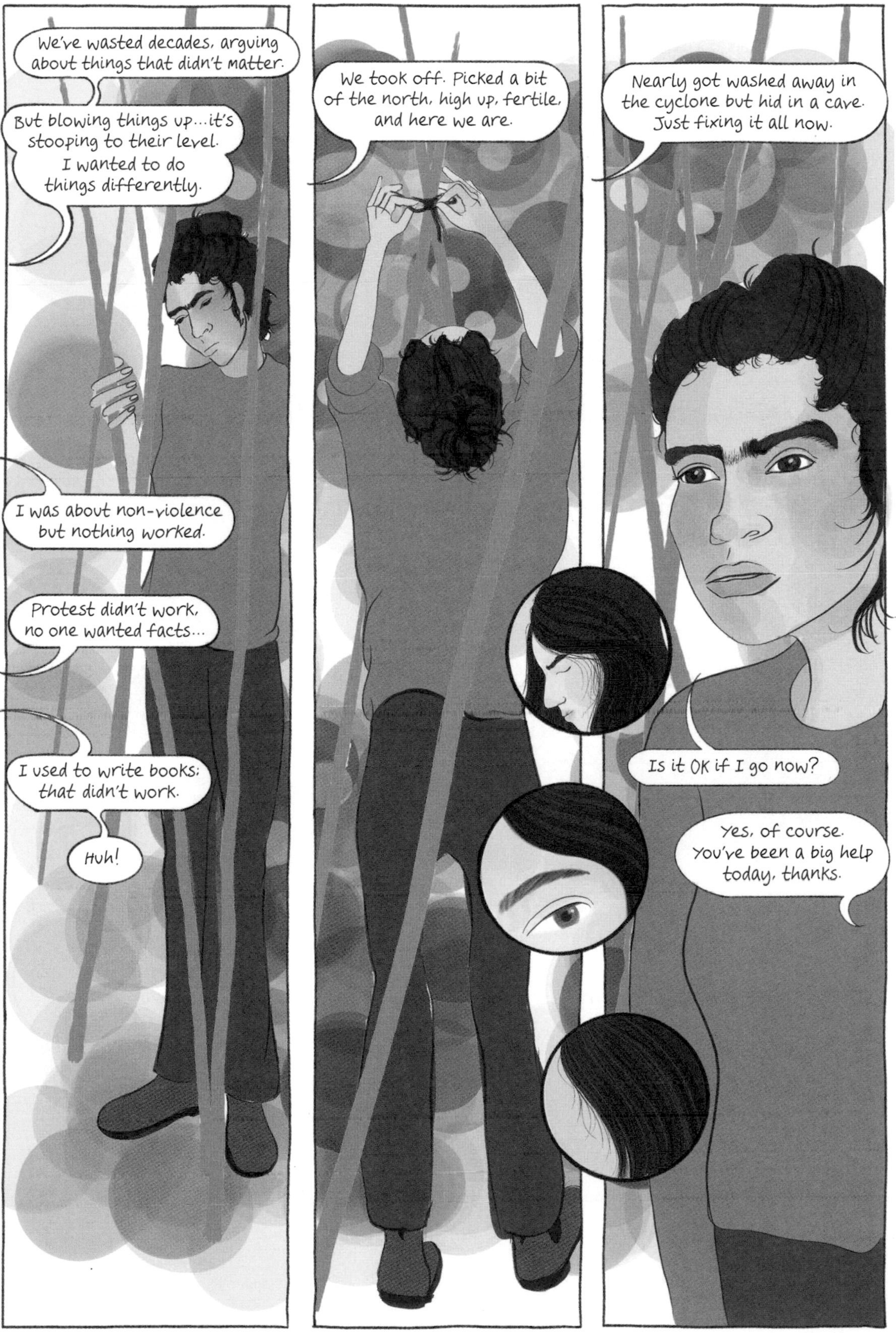
We've wasted decades, arguing about things that didn't matter.
But blowing things up...it's stooping to their level. I wanted to do things differently.
I was about non-violence but nothing worked.
Protest didn't work, no one wanted facts...
I used to write books; that didn't work.
Huh!
We took off. Picked a bit of the north, high up, fertile, and here we are.
Nearly got washed away in the cyclone but hid in a cave. Just fixing it all now.
Is it OK if I go now?
Yes, of course. You've been a big help today, thanks.

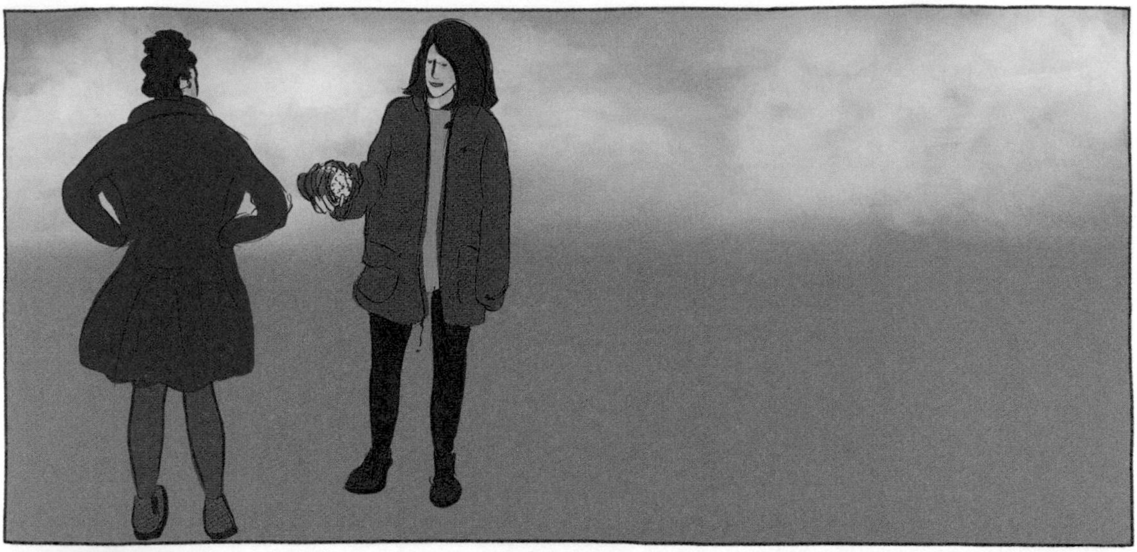

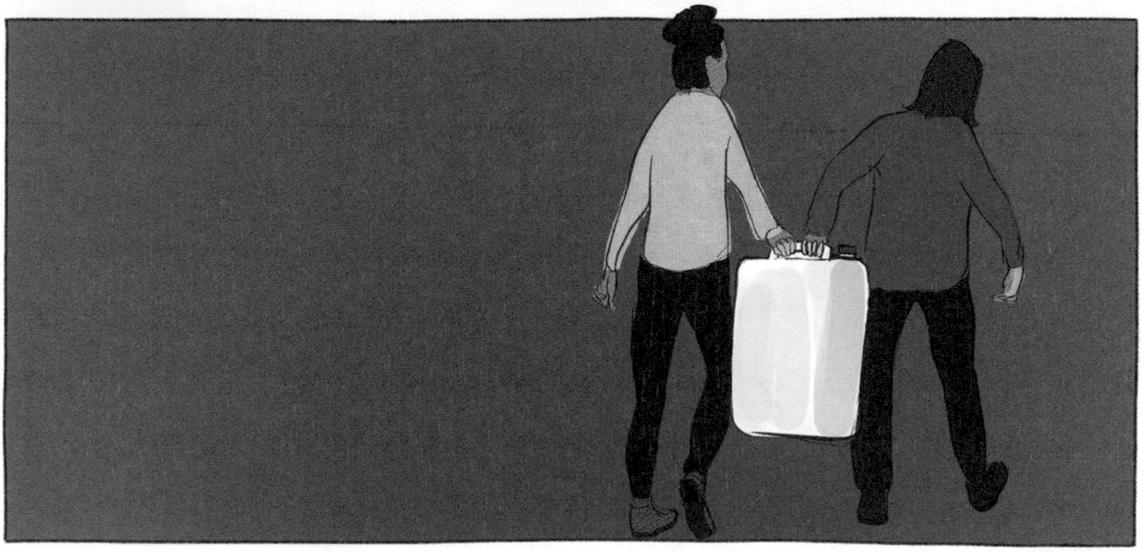

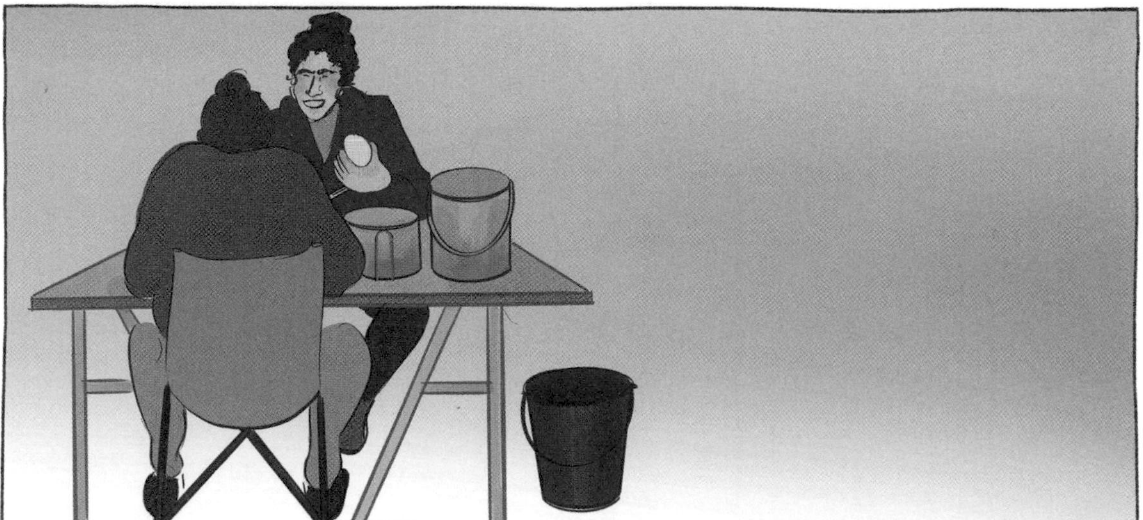

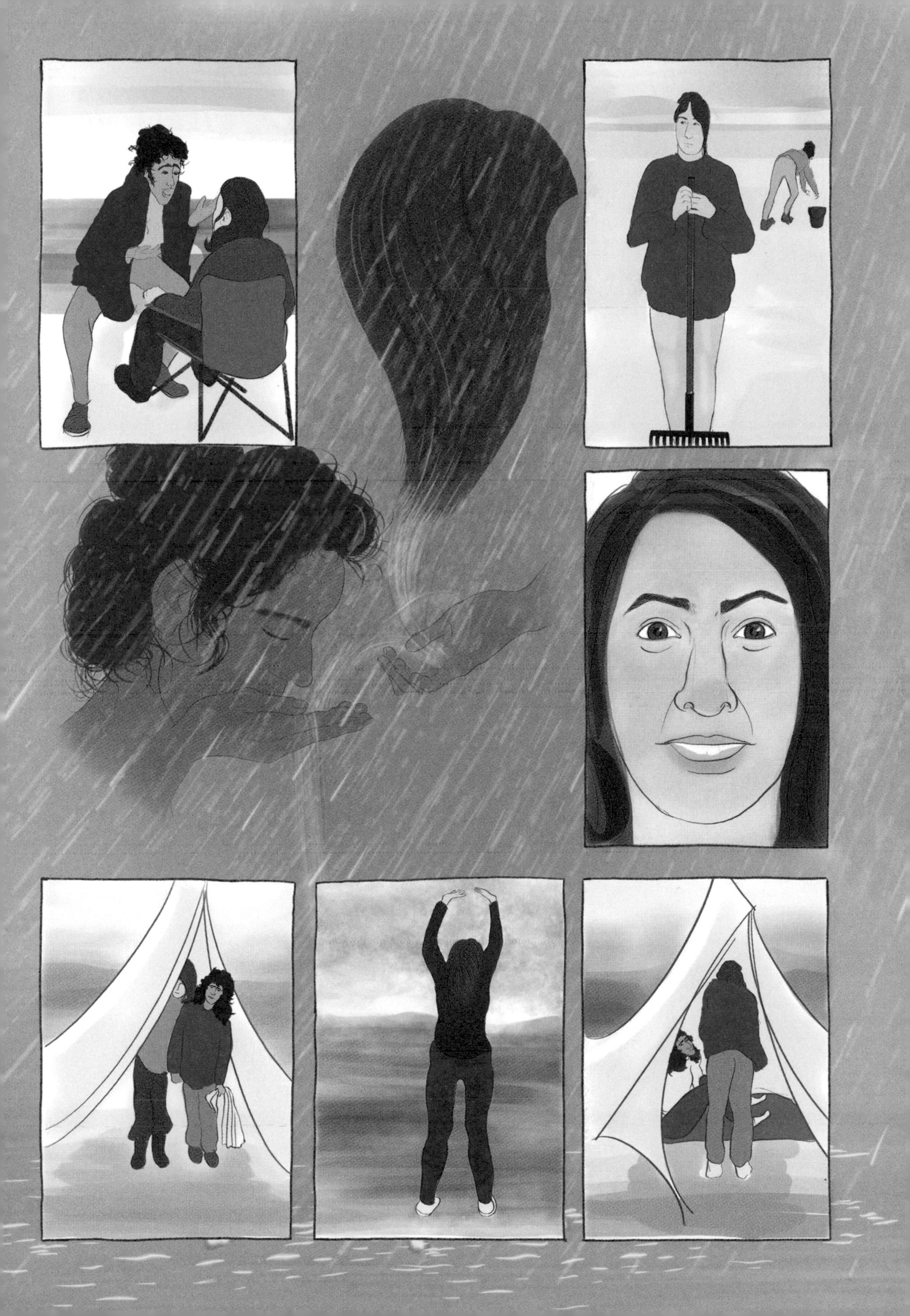

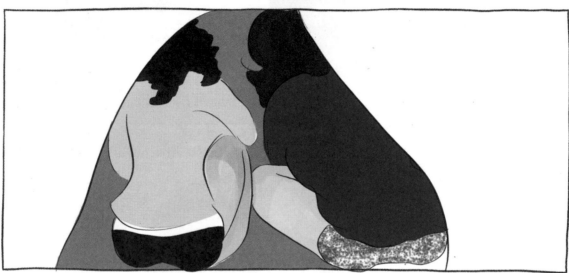

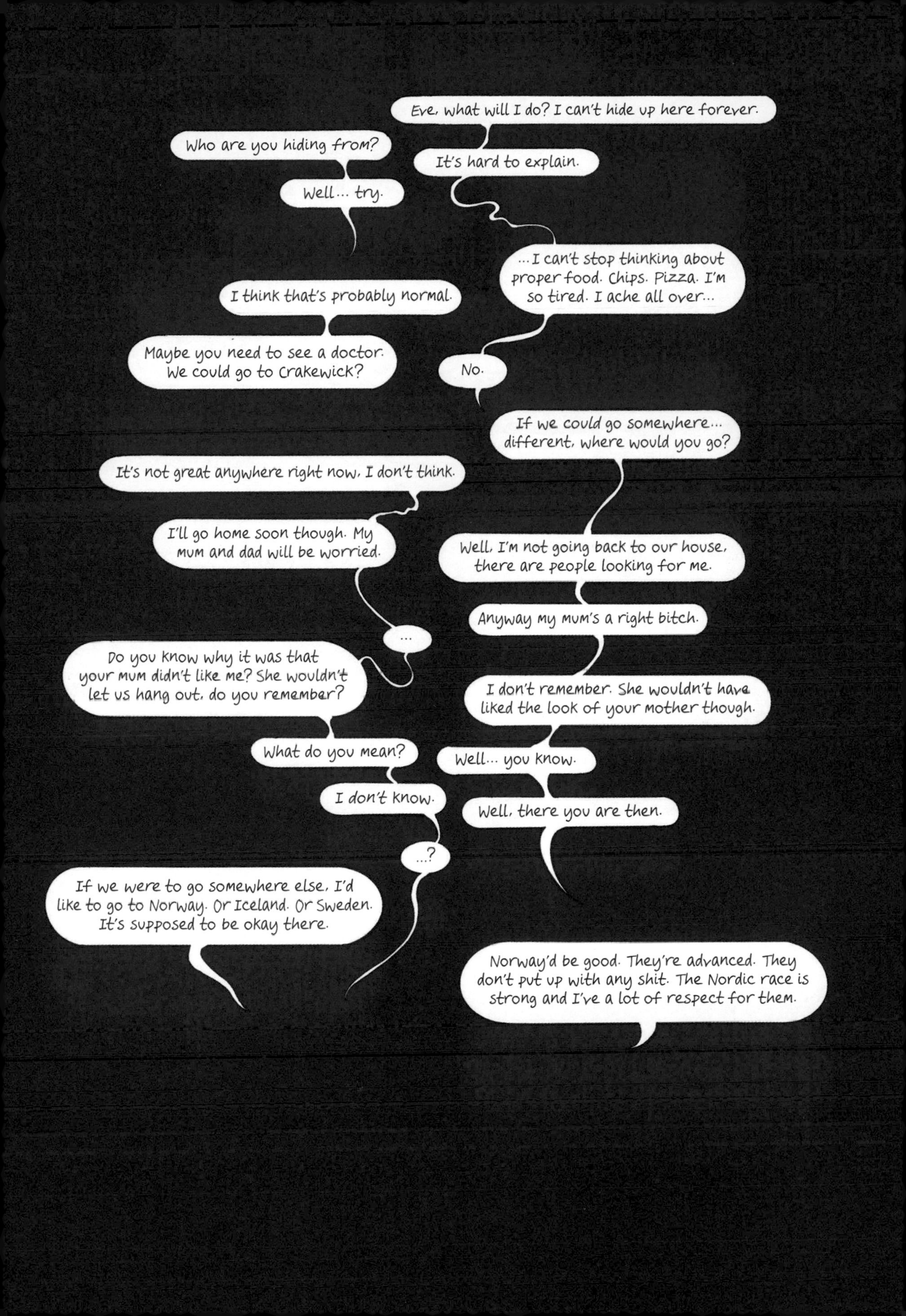
Eve, what will I do? I can't hide up here forever.
Who are you hiding from?
It's hard to explain.
Well... try.
...I can't stop thinking about proper food. Chips. Pizza. I'm so tired. I ache all over...
I think that's probably normal.
Maybe you need to see a doctor. We could go to Crakewick?
No.
If we could go somewhere... different, where would you go?
It's not great anywhere right now, I don't think.
I'll go home soon though. My mum and dad will be worried.
Well, I'm not going back to our house, there are people looking for me.
Anyway my mum's a right bitch.
...
Do you know why it was that your mum didn't like me? She wouldn't let us hang out, do you remember?
I don't remember. She wouldn't have liked the look of your mother though.
What do you mean?
Well... you know.
I don't know.
Well, there you are then.
...?
If we were to go somewhere else, I'd like to go to Norway. Or Iceland. Or Sweden. It's supposed to be okay there.
Norway'd be good. They're advanced. They don't put up with any shit. The Nordic race is strong and I've a lot of respect for them.

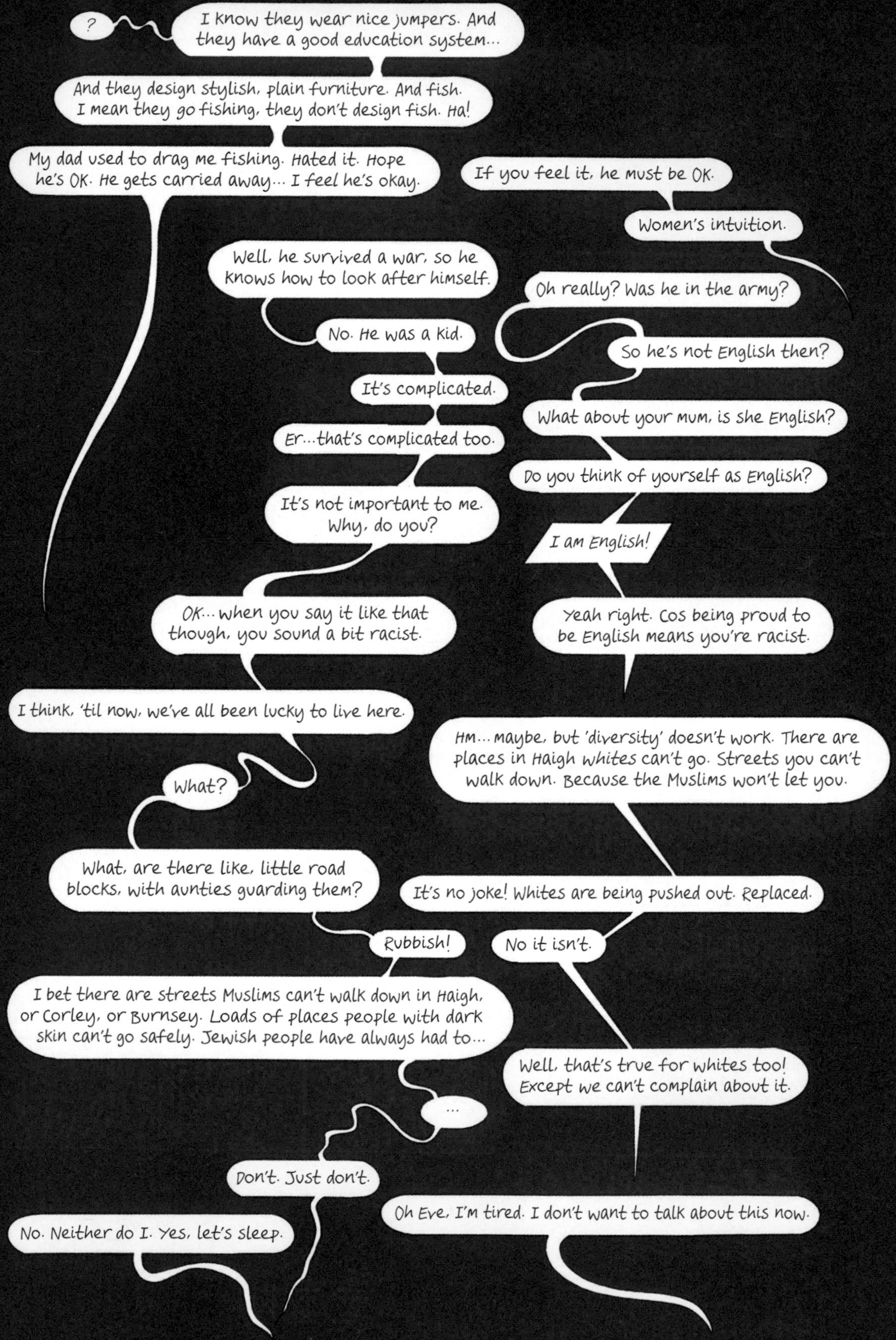
?
I know they wear nice jumpers. And they have a good education system...
And they design stylish, plain furniture. And fish. I mean they go fishing, they don't design fish. Ha!
My dad used to drag me fishing. Hated it. Hope he's OK. He gets carried away... I feel he's okay.
If you feel it, he must be OK.
Women's intuition.
Well, he survived a war, so he knows how to look after himself.
Oh really? Was he in the army?
No. He was a kid.
So he's not English then?
It's complicated.
What about your mum, is she English?
Er...that's complicated too.
Do you think of yourself as English?
It's not important to me. Why, do you?
I am English!
OK... when you say it like that though, you sound a bit racist.
Yeah right. Cos being proud to be English means you're racist.
I think, 'til now, we've all been lucky to live here.
Hm... maybe, but 'diversity' doesn't work. There are places in Haigh whites can't go. Streets you can't walk down. Because the Muslims won't let you.
What?
What, are there like, little road blocks, with aunties guarding them?
It's no joke! Whites are being pushed out. Replaced.
Rubbish!
No it isn't.
I bet there are streets Muslims can't walk down in Haigh, or Corley, or Burnsey. Loads of places people with dark skin can't go safely. Jewish people have always had to...
Well, that's true for whites too! Except we can't complain about it.
...
Don't. Just don't.
Oh Eve, I'm tired. I don't want to talk about this now.
No. Neither do I. Yes, let's sleep.

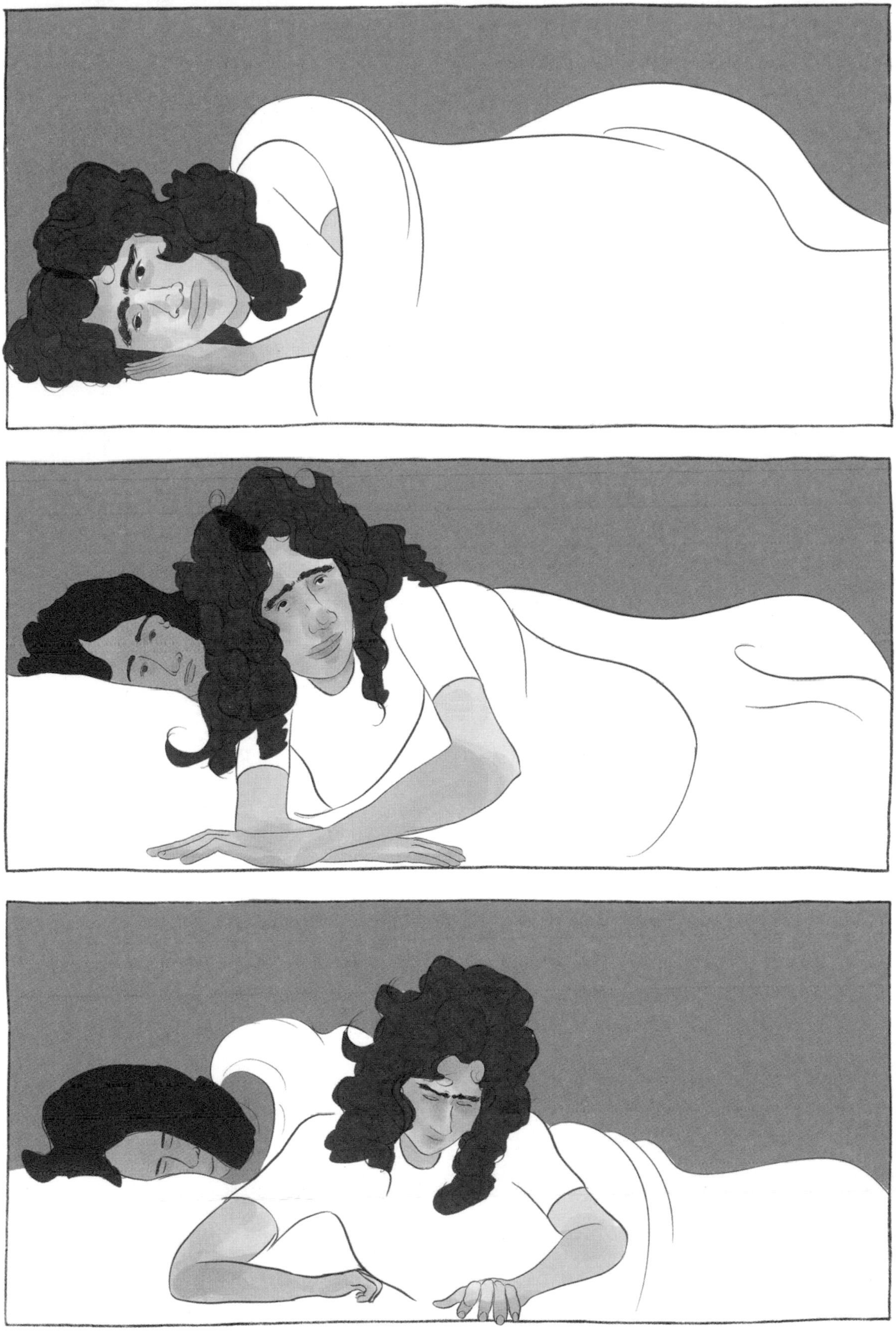

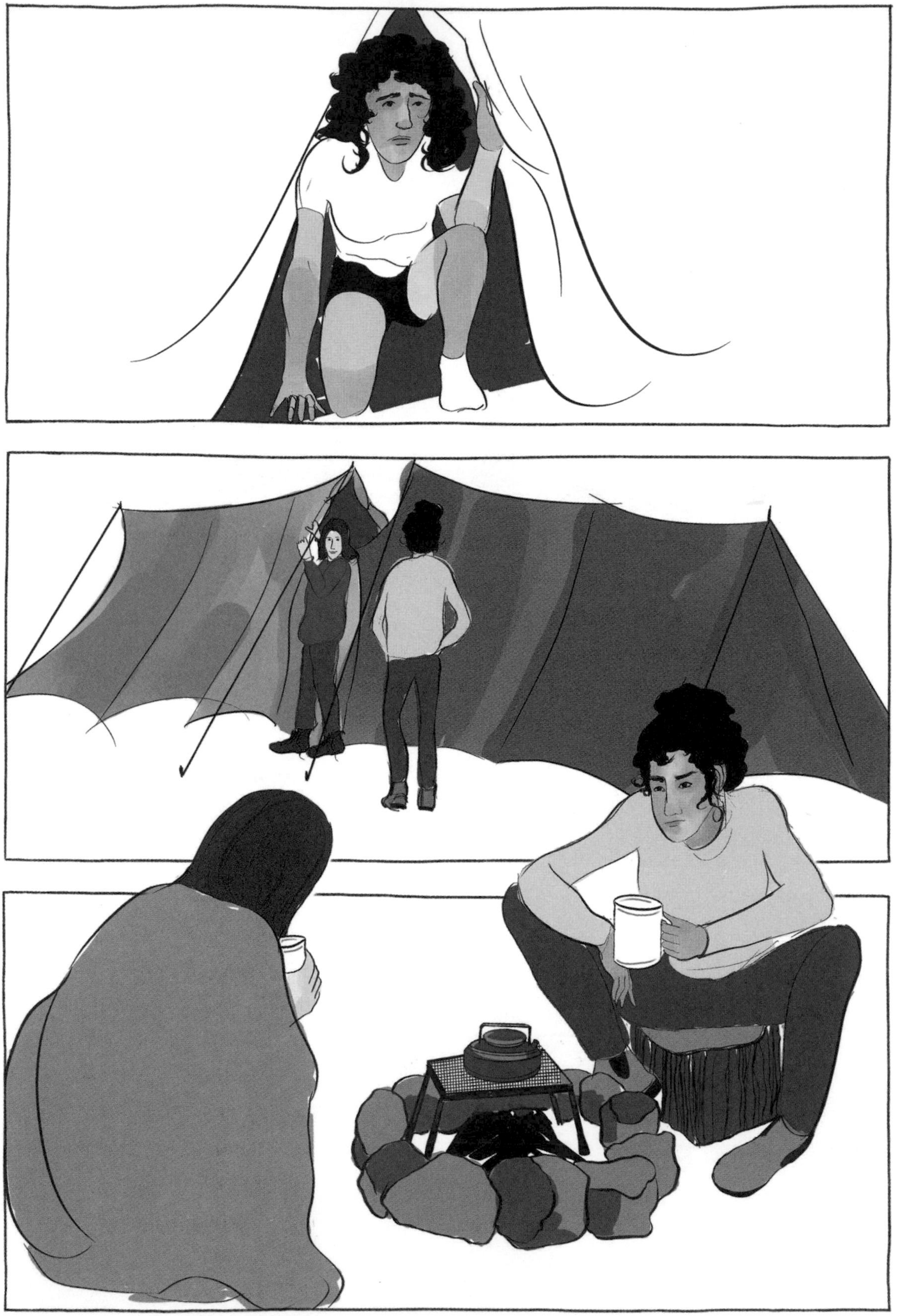

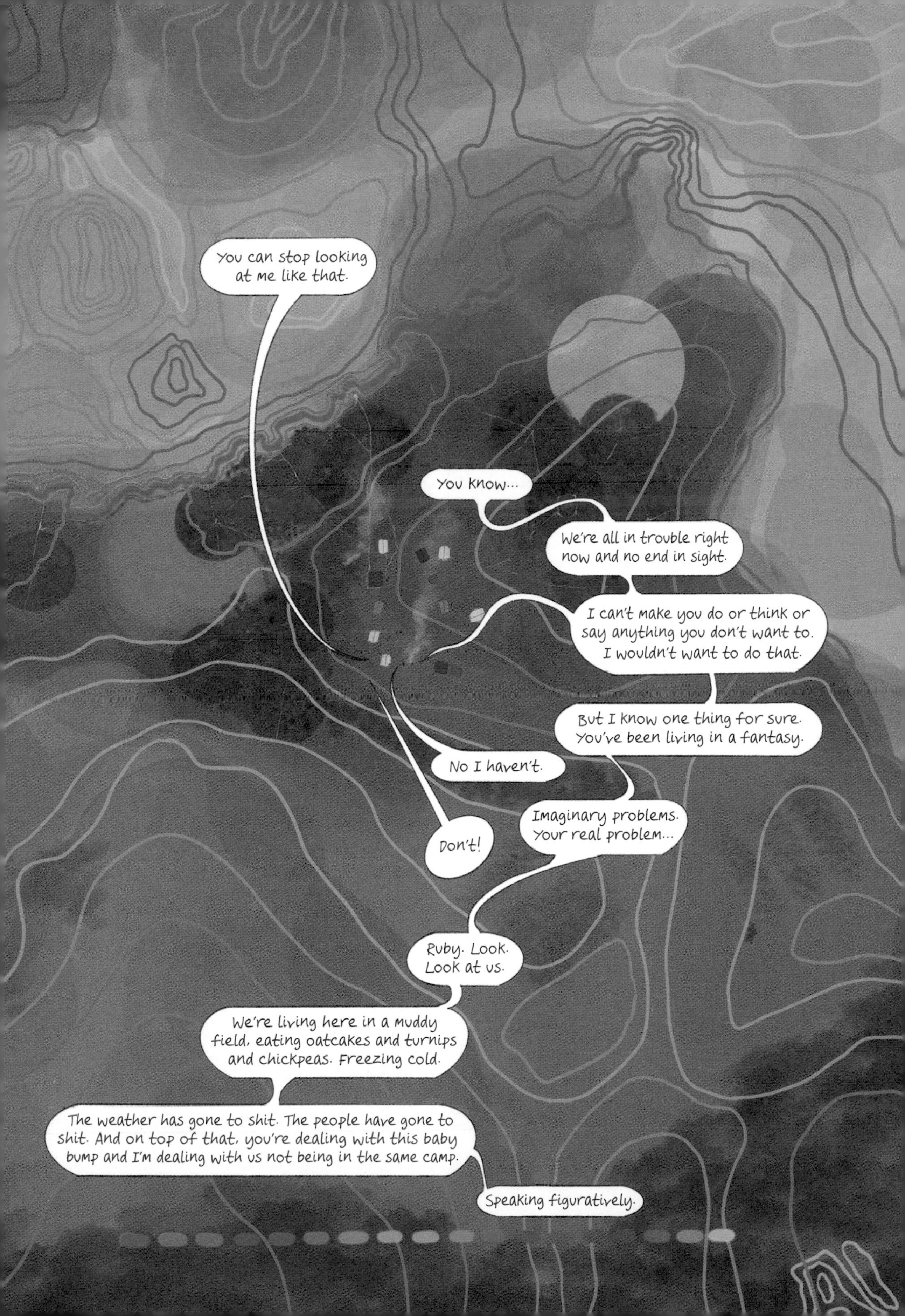
You can stop looking at me like that.
You know...
We're all in trouble right now and no end in sight.
I can't make you do or think or say anything you don't want to. I wouldn't want to do that.
But I know one thing for sure. You've been living in a fantasy.
No I haven't.
Imaginary problems. Your real problem...
Don't!
Ruby. Look. Look at us.
We're living here in a muddy field, eating oatcakes and turnips and chickpeas. Freezing cold.
The weather has gone to shit. The people have gone to shit. And on top of that, you're dealing with this baby bump and I'm dealing with us not being in the same camp.
Speaking figuratively.

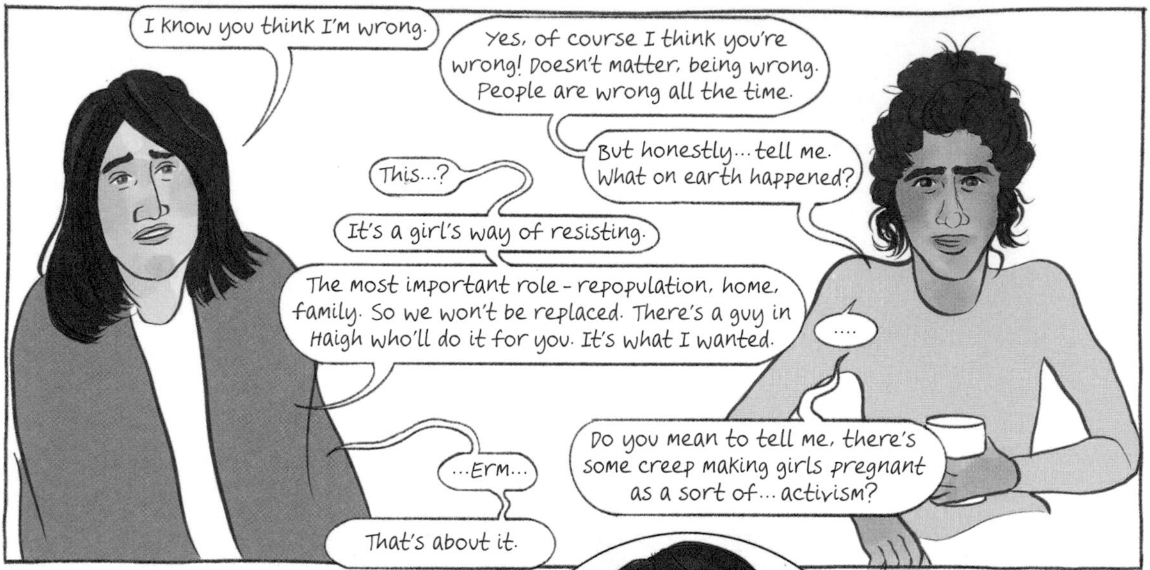
I know you think I'm wrong.
Yes, of course I think you're wrong! Doesn't matter, being wrong. People are wrong all the time.
But honestly... tell me. What on earth happened?
This...?
It's a girl's way of resisting.
The most important role - repopulation, home, family. So we won't be replaced. There's a guy in Haigh who'll do it for you. It's what I wanted.
....
Do you mean to tell me, there's some creep making girls pregnant as a sort of... activism?
...Erm...
That's about it.

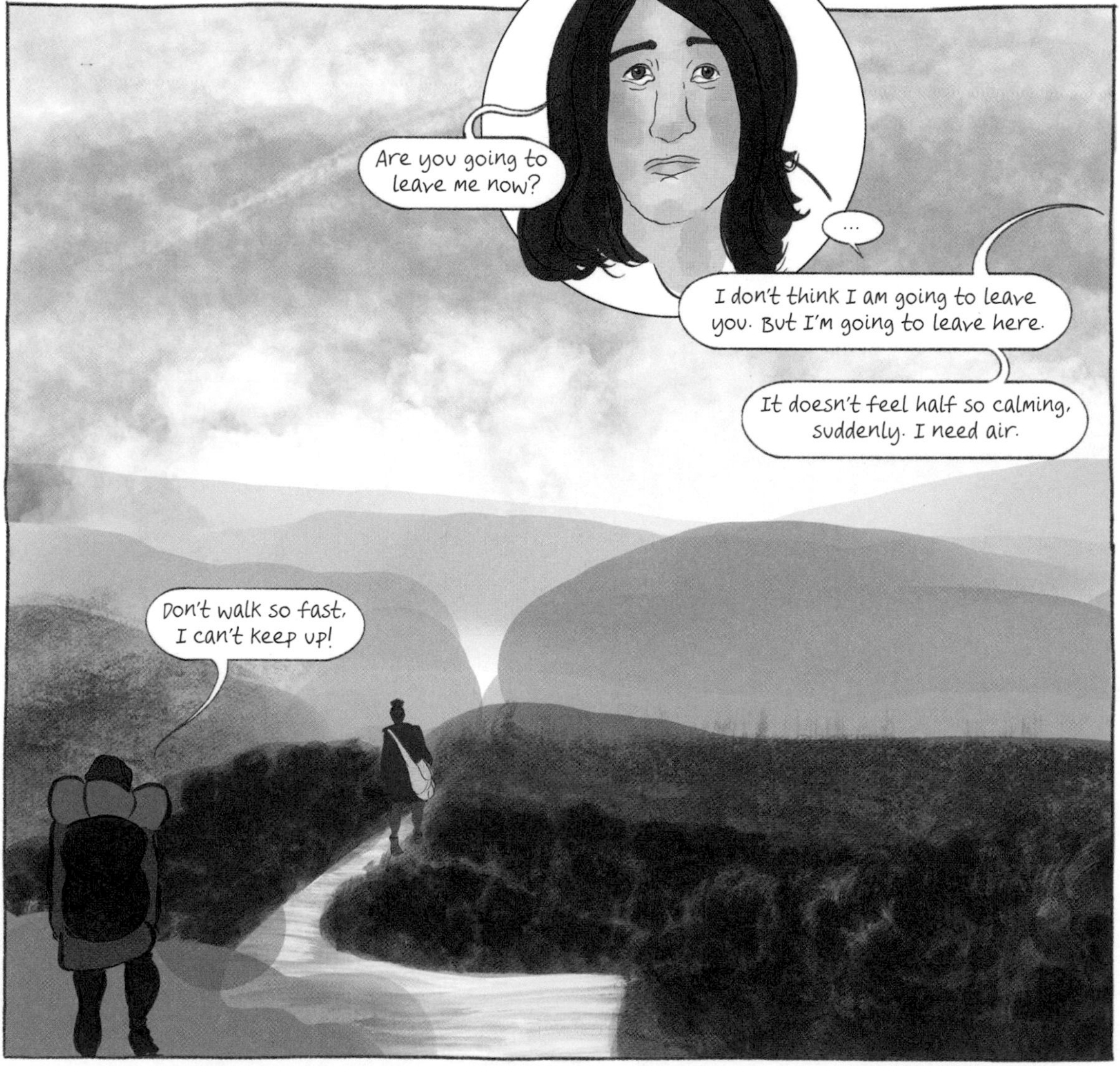
Are you going to leave me now?
...
I don't think I am going to leave you. But I'm going to leave here.
It doesn't feel half so calming, suddenly. I need air.
Don't walk so fast, I can't keep up!

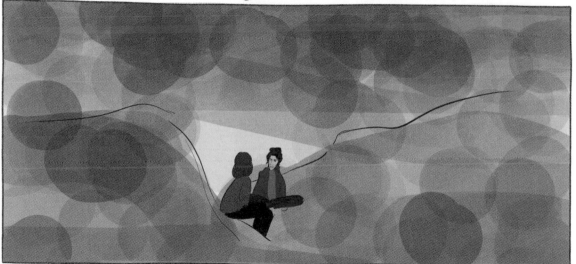

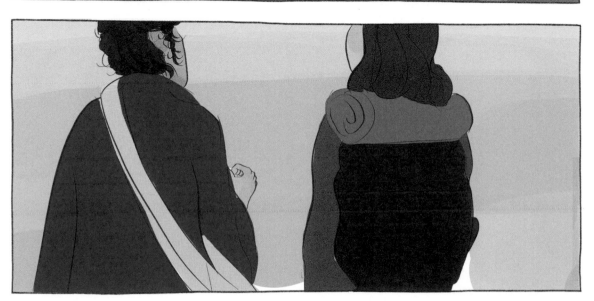

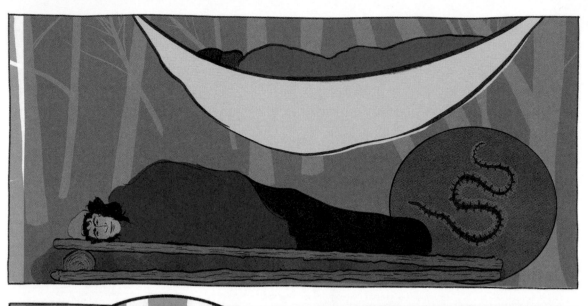

Eve? Where are you going? Eve?

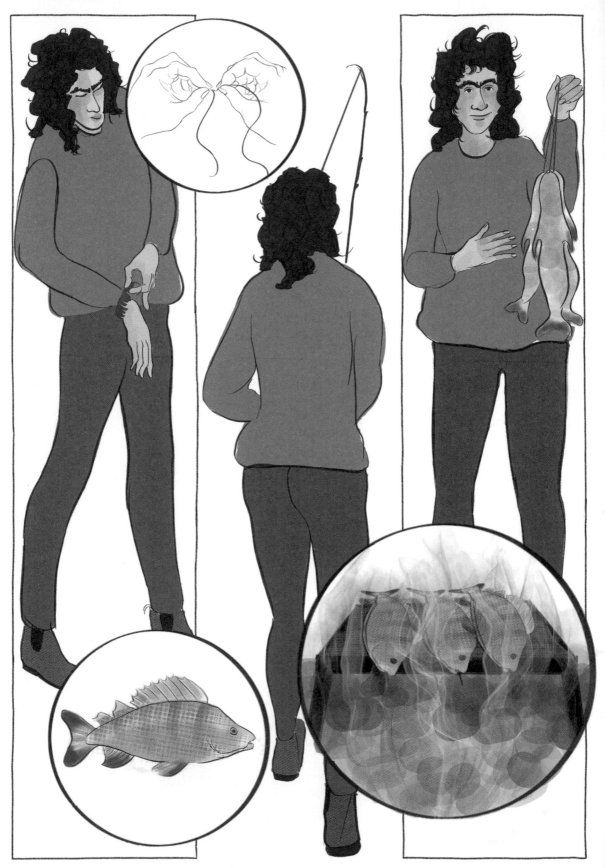

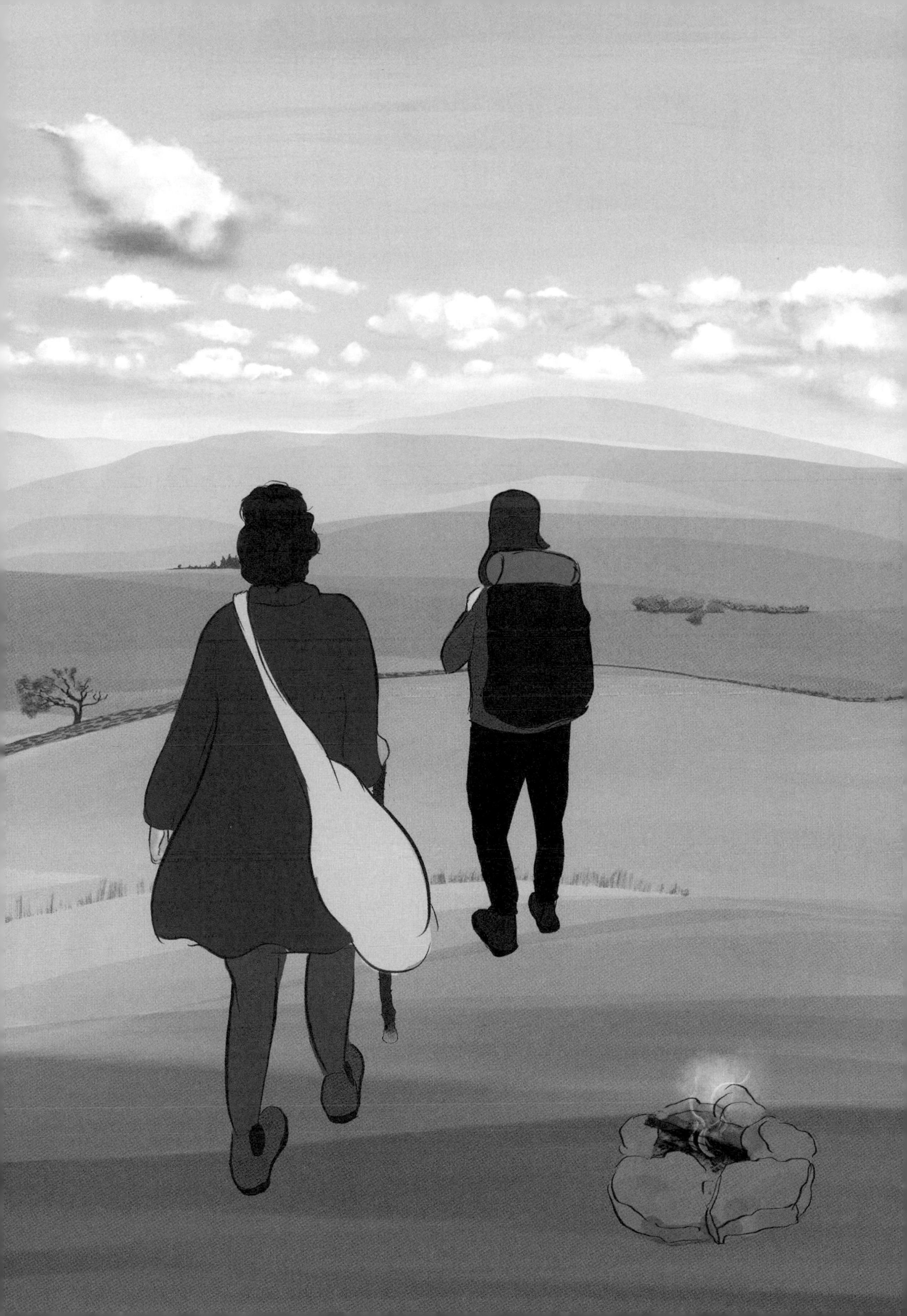

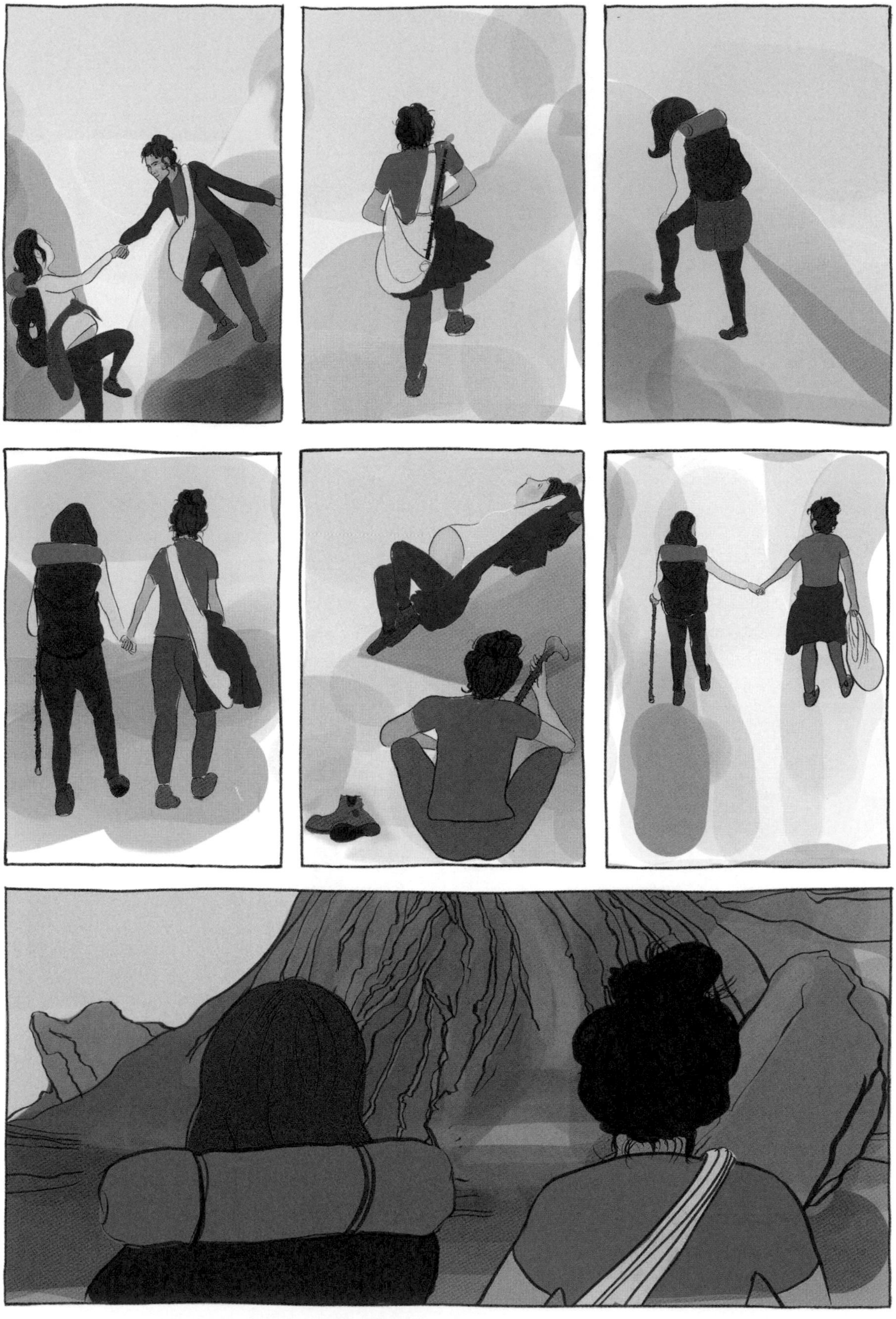

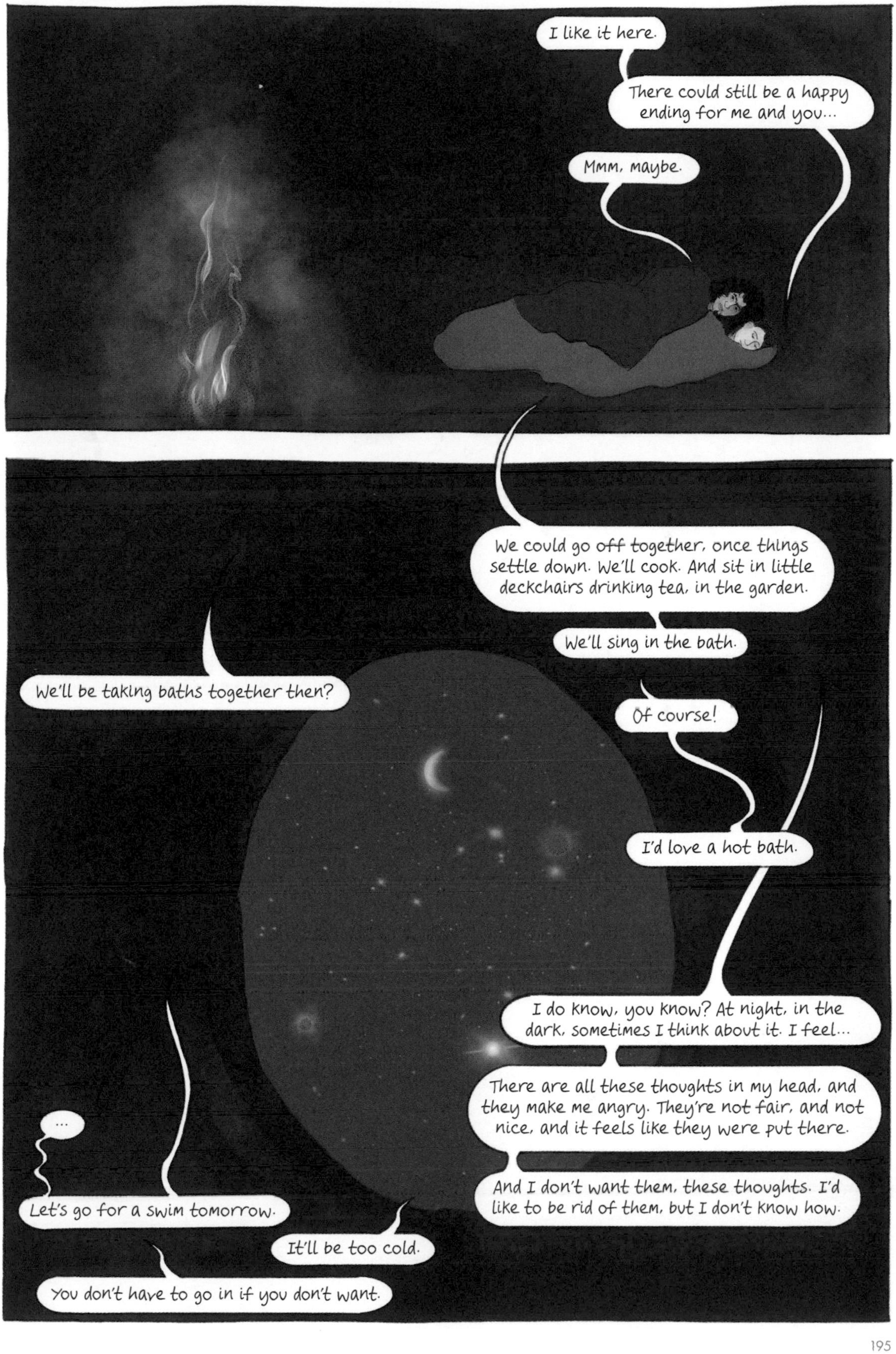
I like it here.
There could still be a happy ending for me and you...
Mmm, maybe.
We could go off together, once things settle down. We'll cook. And sit in little deckchairs drinking tea, in the garden.
We'll sing in the bath.
We'll be taking baths together then?
Of course!
I'd love a hot bath.
I do know, you know? At night, in the dark, sometimes I think about it. I feel...
There are all these thoughts in my head, and they make me angry. They're not fair, and not nice, and it feels like they were put there.
And I don't want them, these thoughts. I'd like to be rid of them, but I don't know how.
...
Let's go for a swim tomorrow.
It'll be too cold.
You don't have to go in if you don't want.

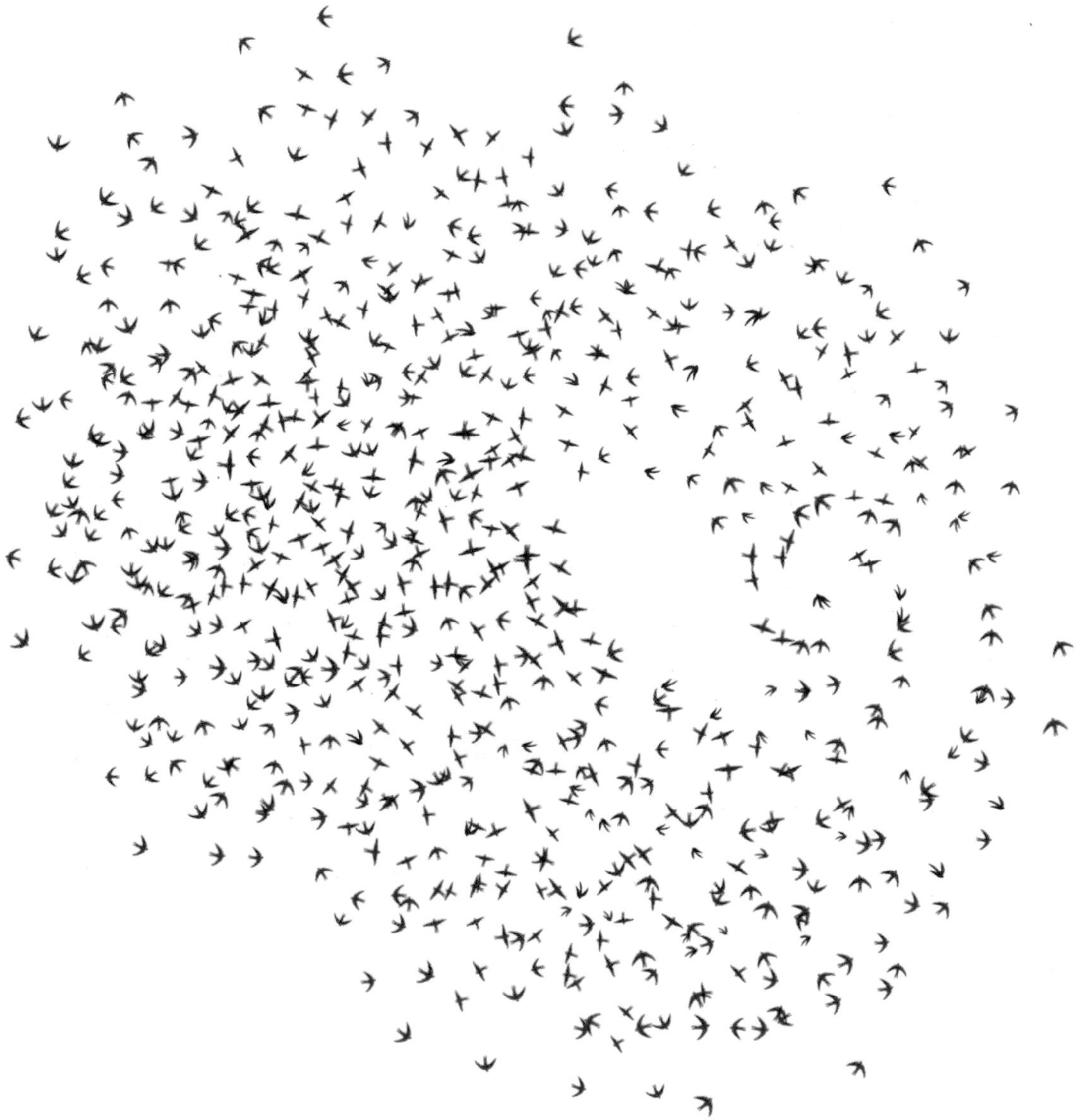

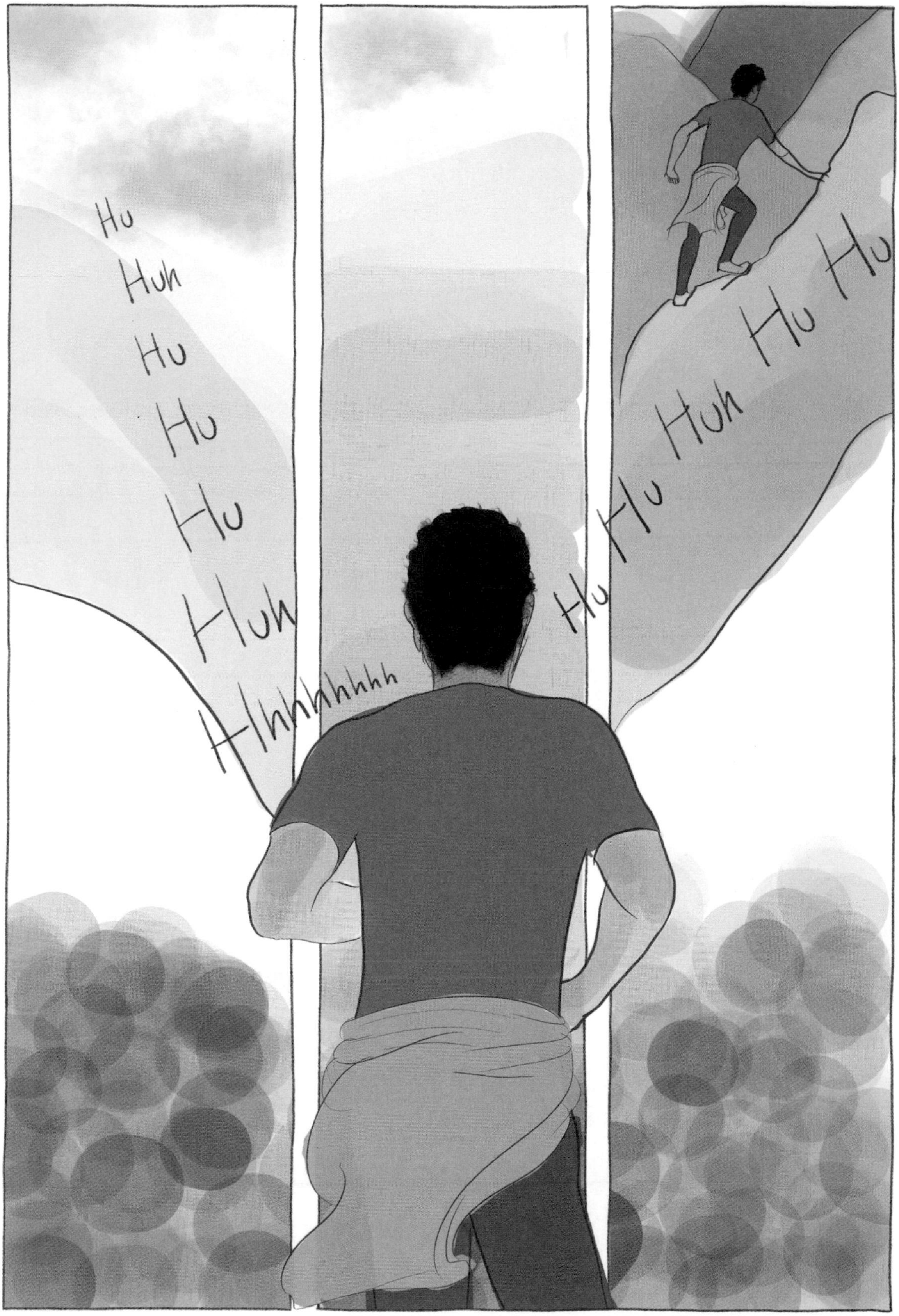
Hu
Huh
Hu
Hu
Hu
Huh
Hhhhhhhh
Hu
Hu
Huh
Hu
Hu

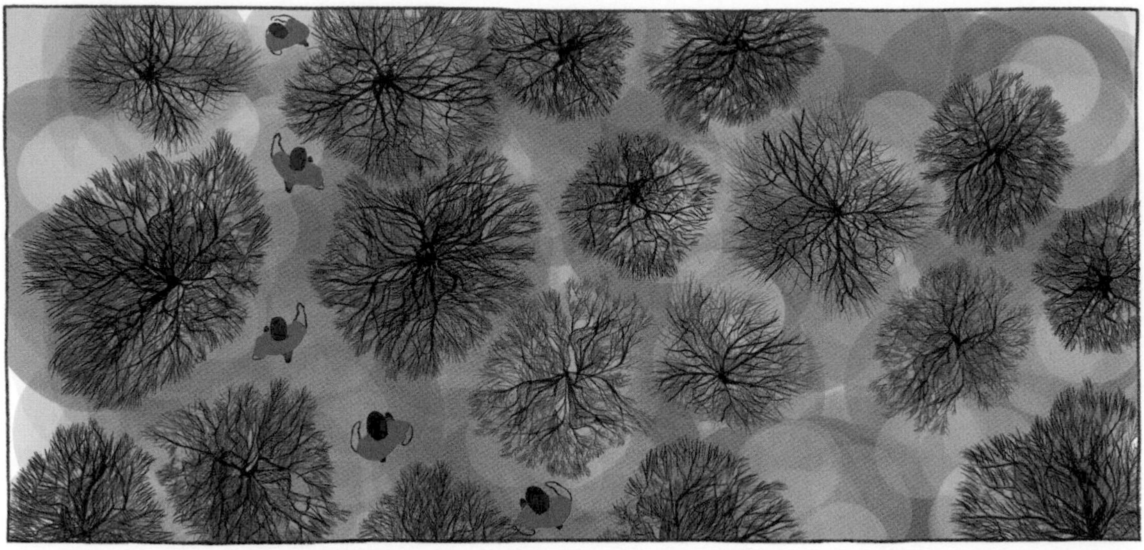

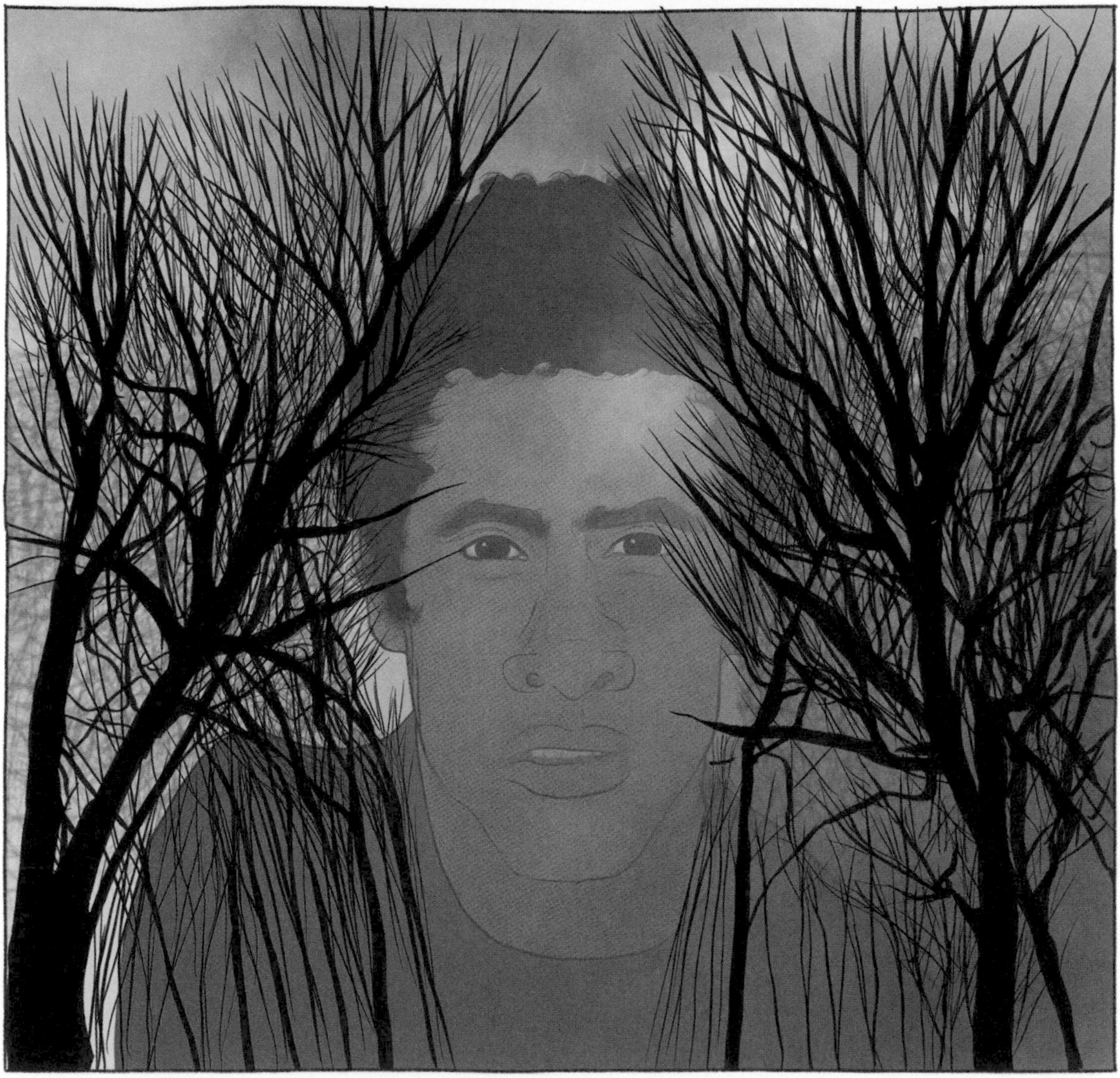

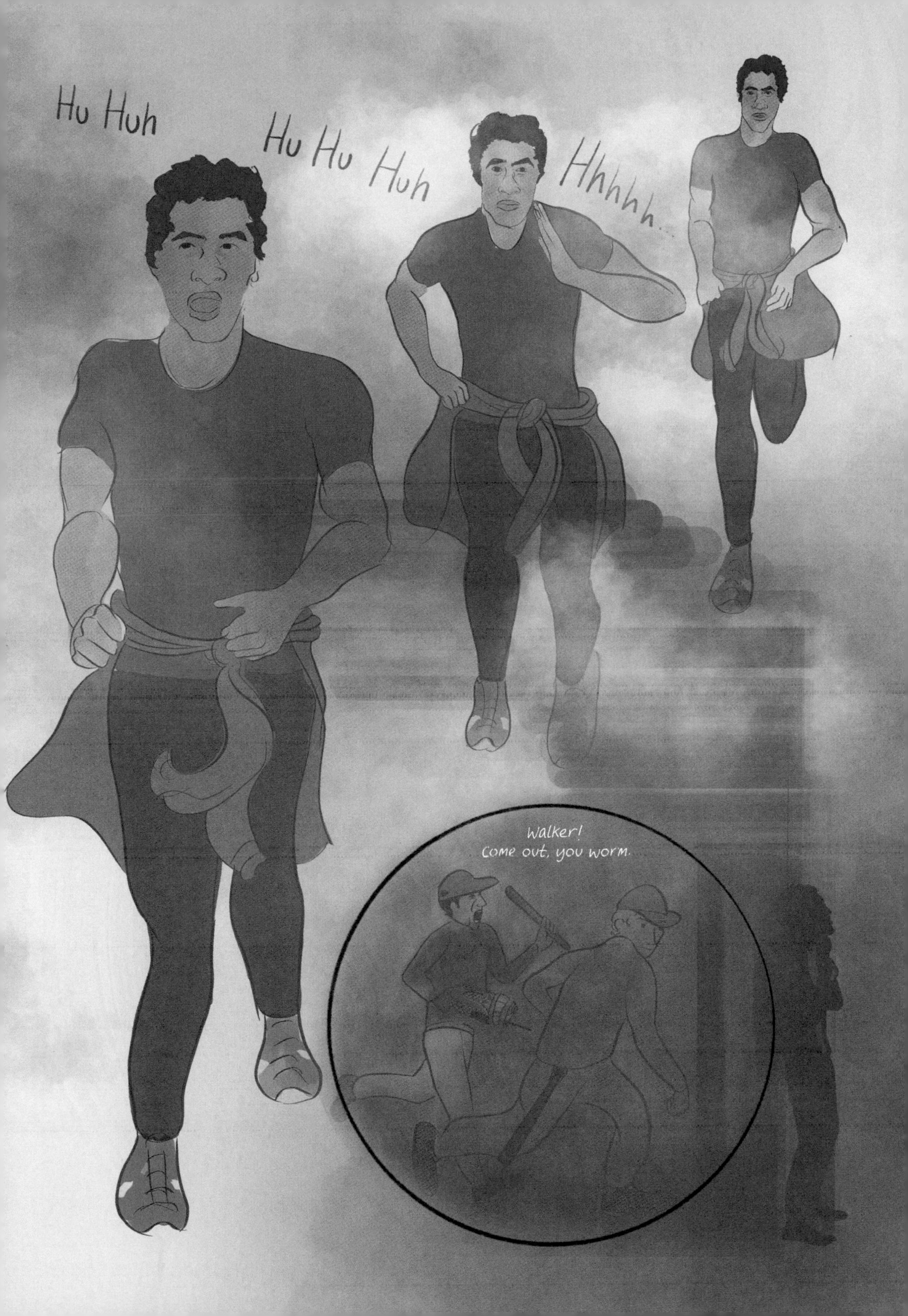
Hu Huh
Hu Hu Huh
Hhhhh...
Walker!
Come out, you worm.

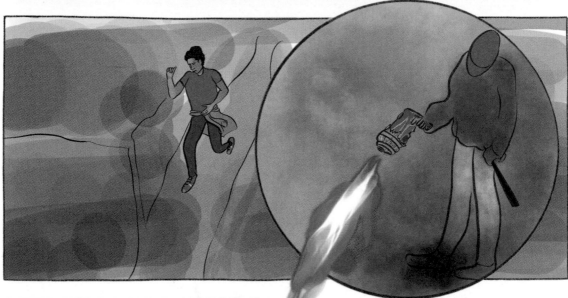

Hu Huh Hu Hu Huh

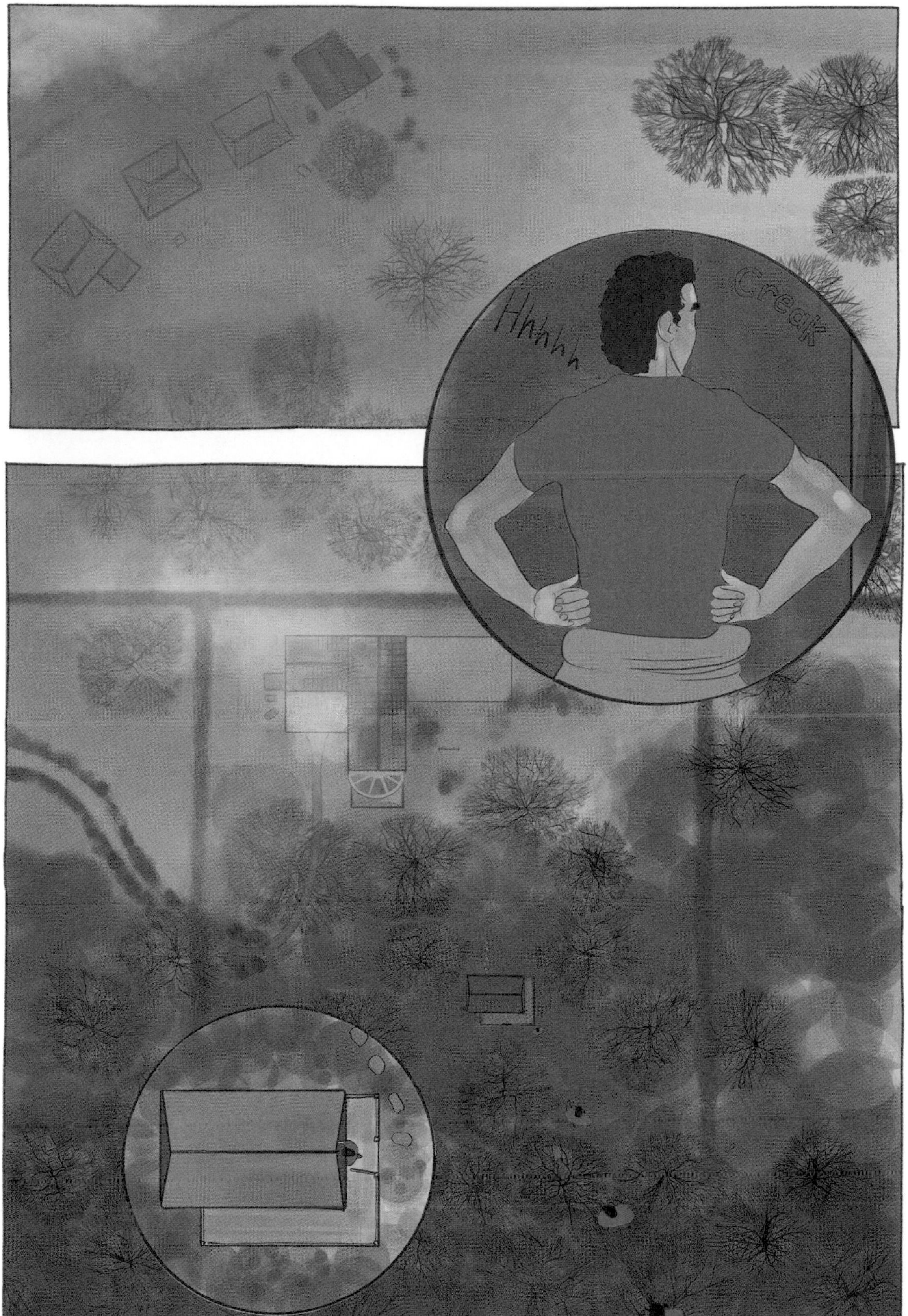
Hhhhh
Creak

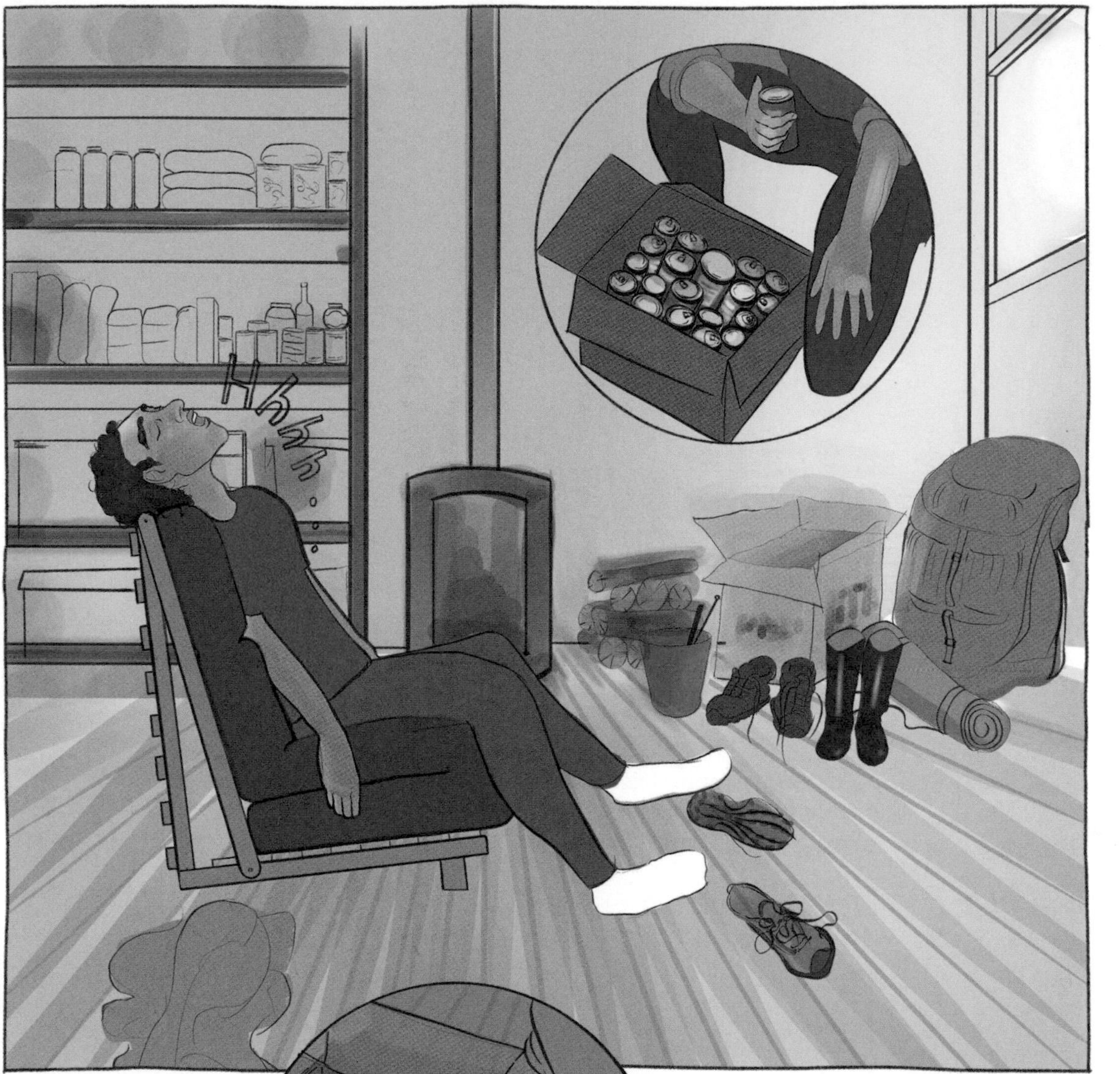
Hhhh...

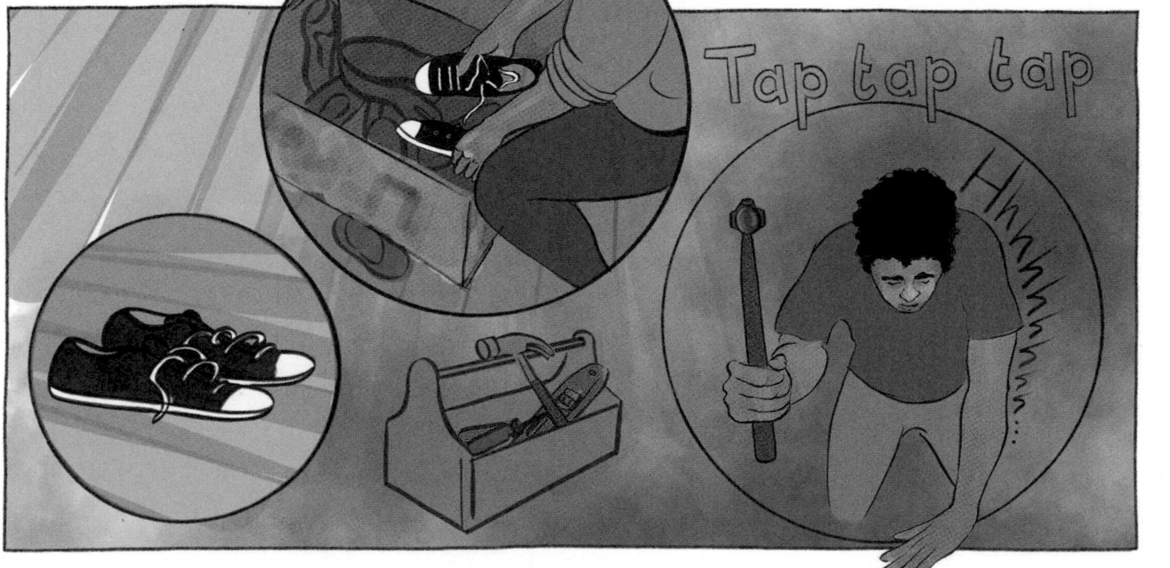
Tap tap tap
Hhhhhhhh...

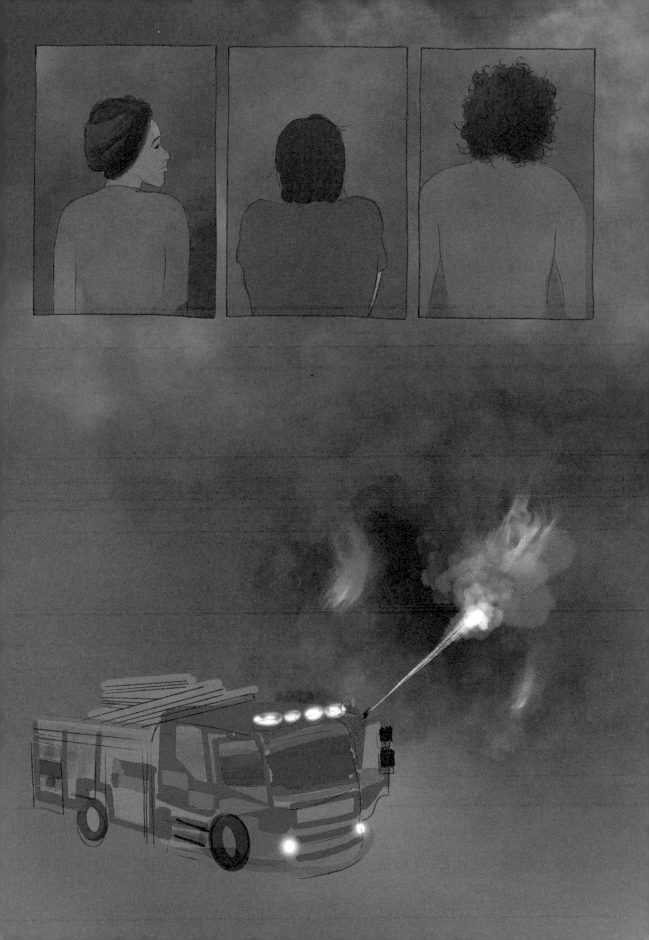

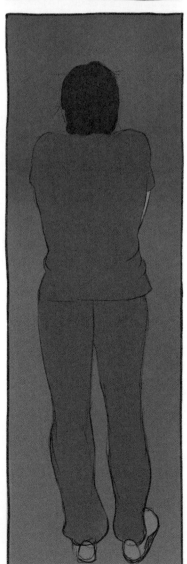

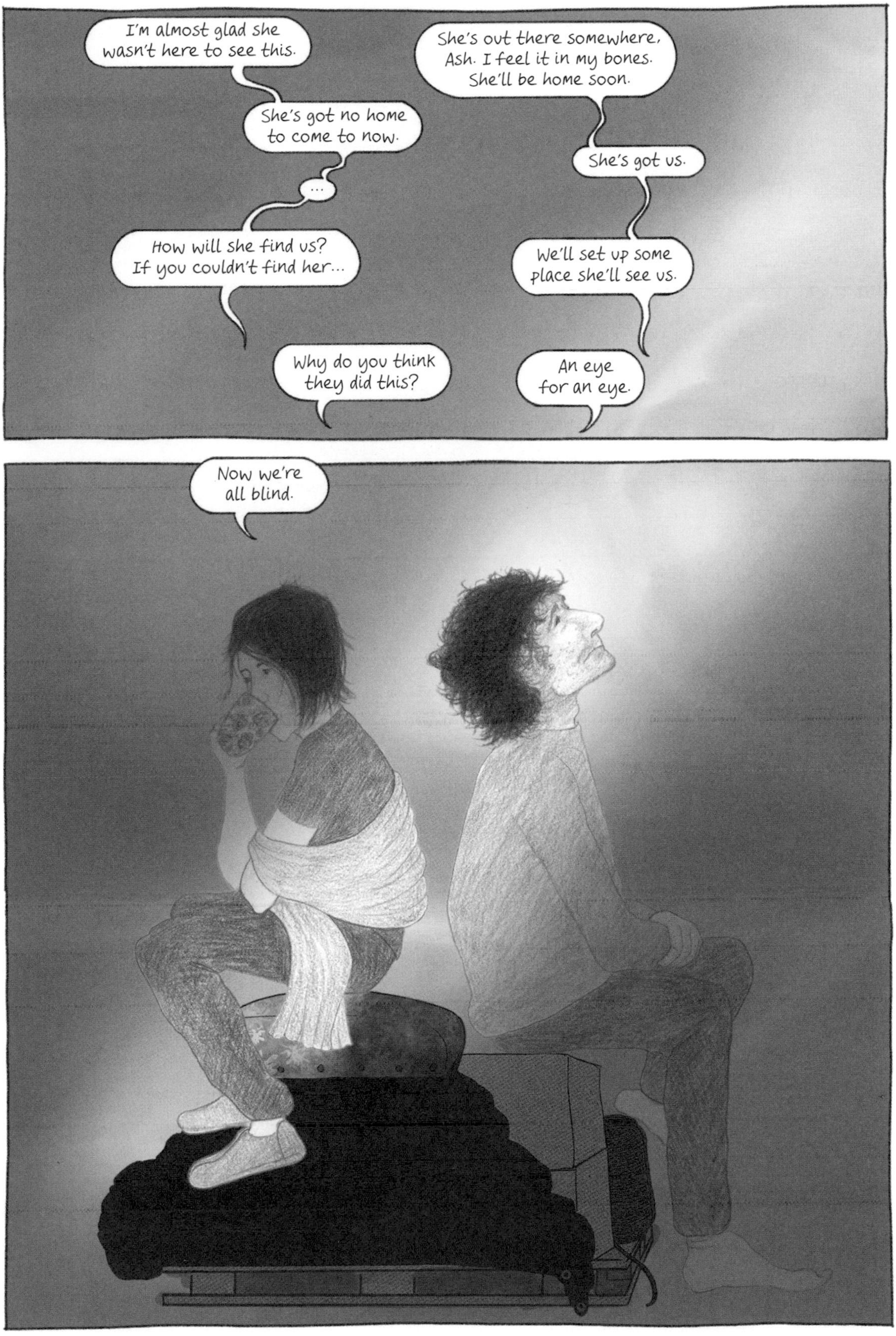
I'm almost glad she wasn't here to see this.
She's got no home to come to now.
...
How will she find us? If you couldn't find her...
She's out there somewhere, Ash. I feel it in my bones. She'll be home soon.
She's got us.
We'll set up some place she'll see us.
Why do you think they did this?
An eye for an eye.
Now we're all blind.

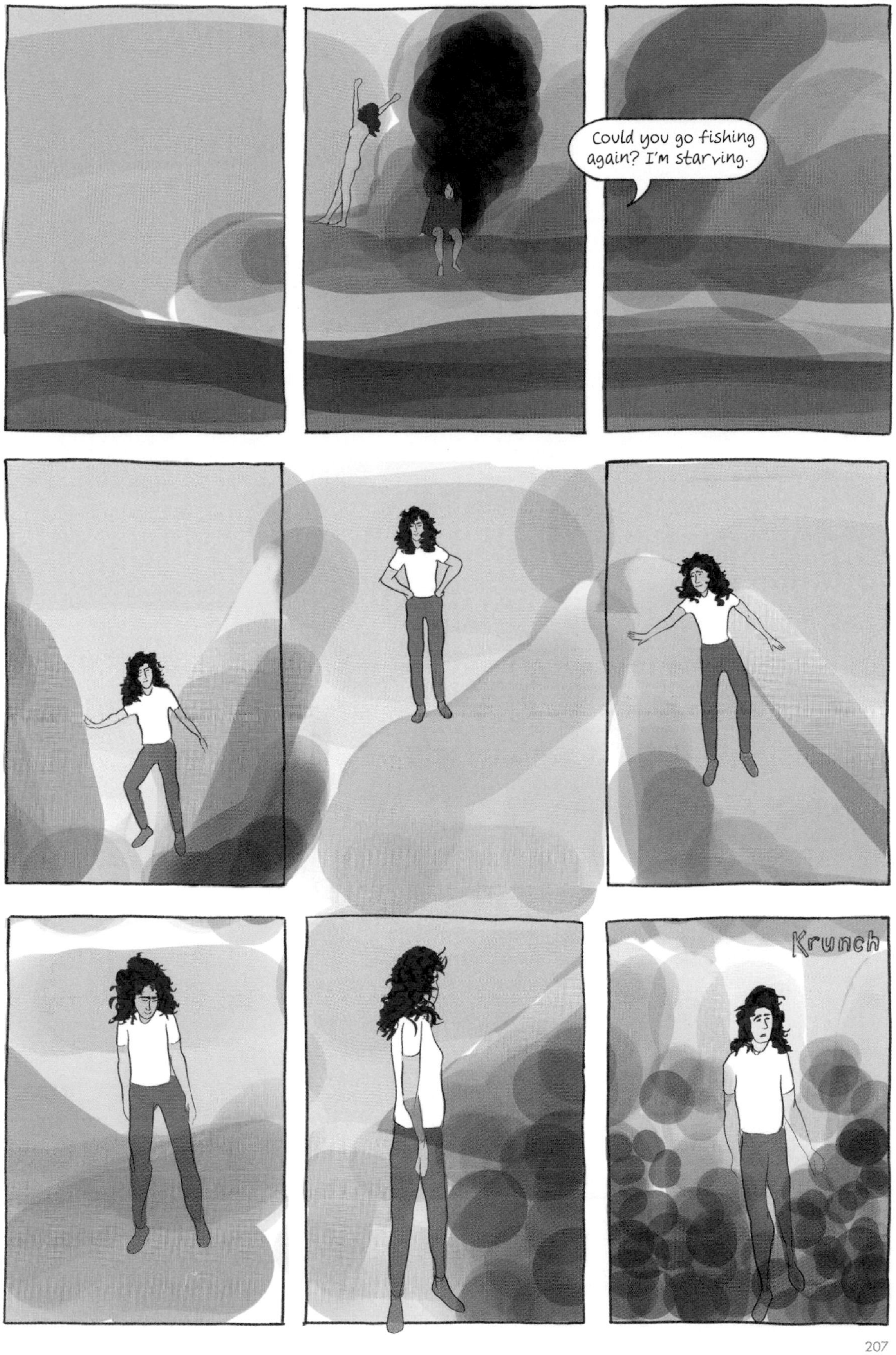
Could you go fishing again? I'm starving.
Krunch

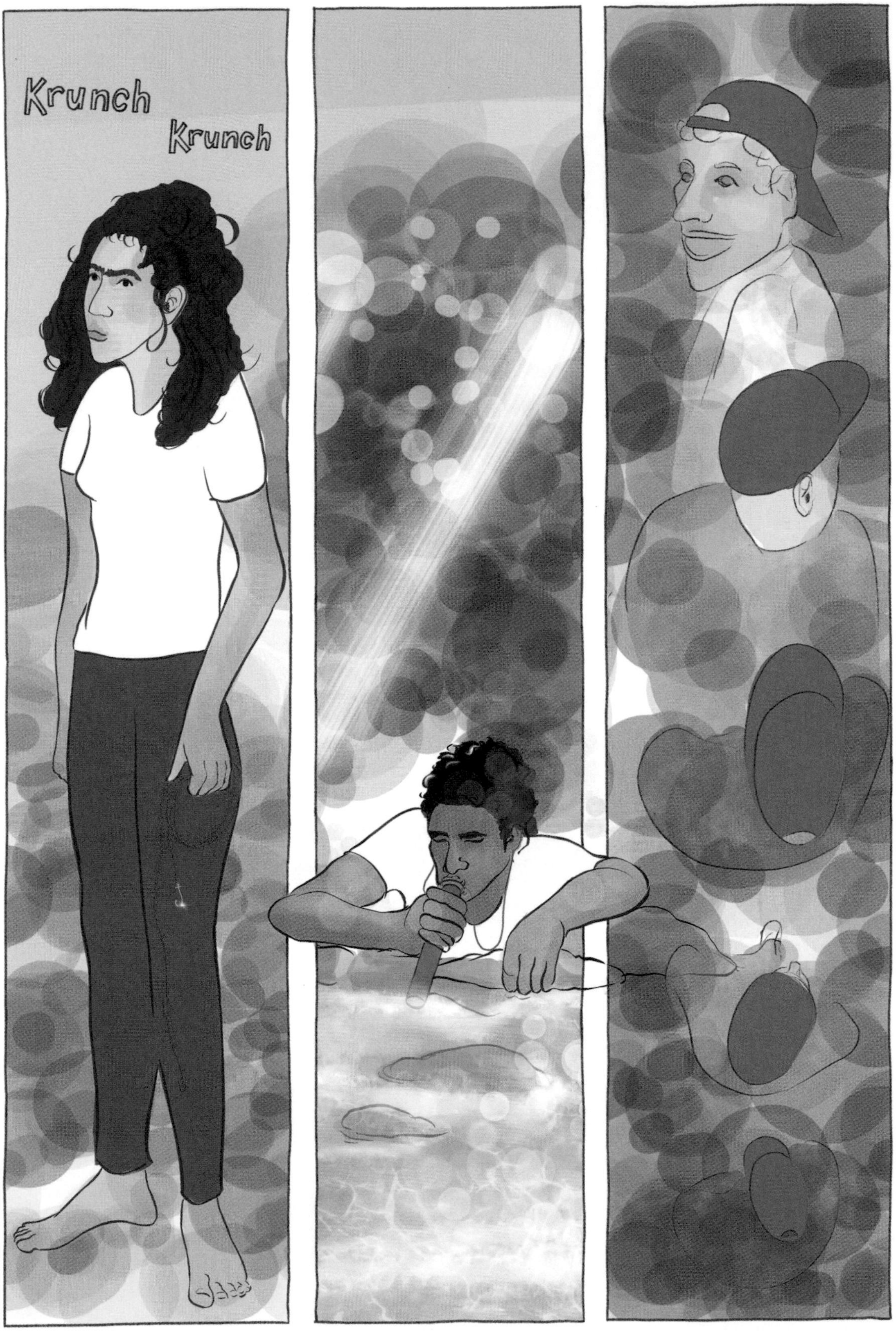
Krunch
Krunch

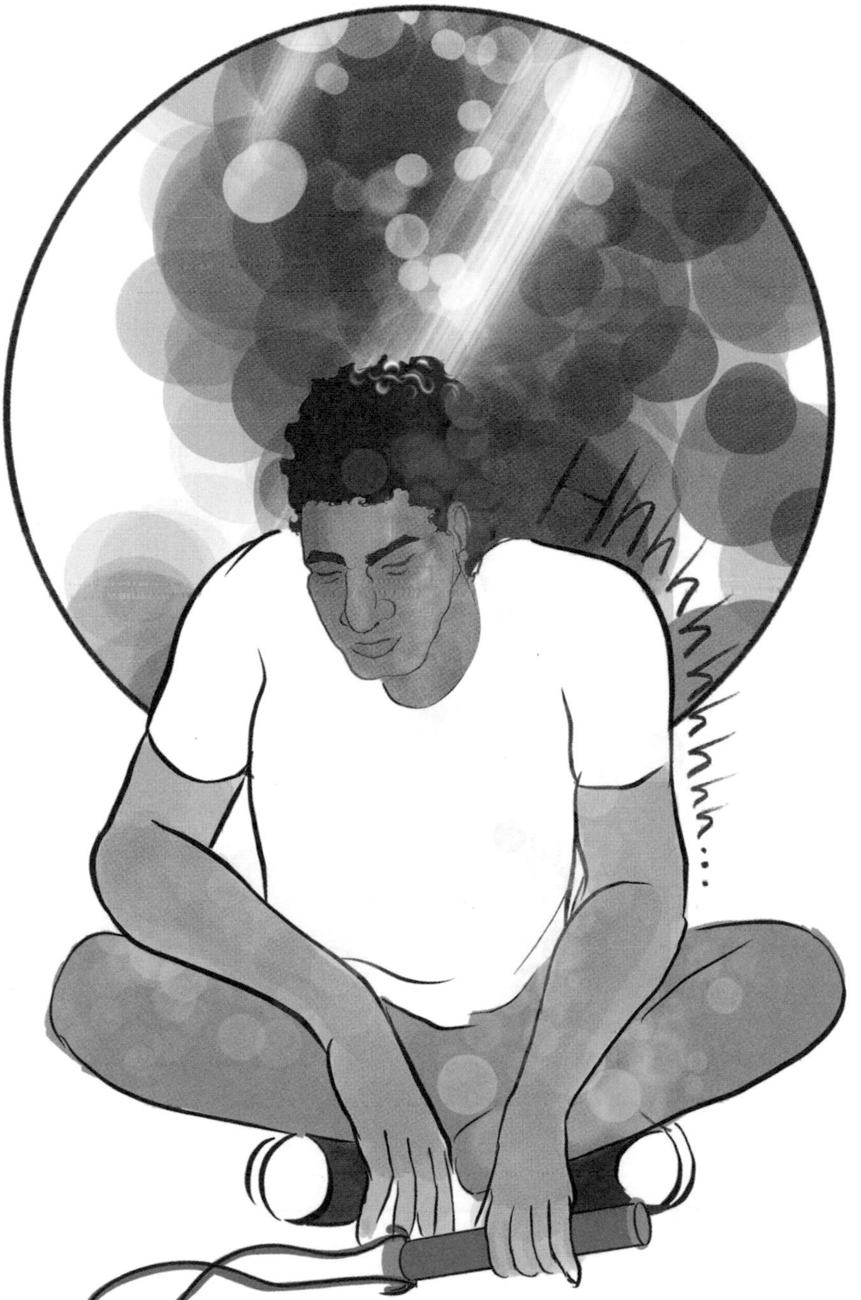
Hhhhhhhhhhhhhh...

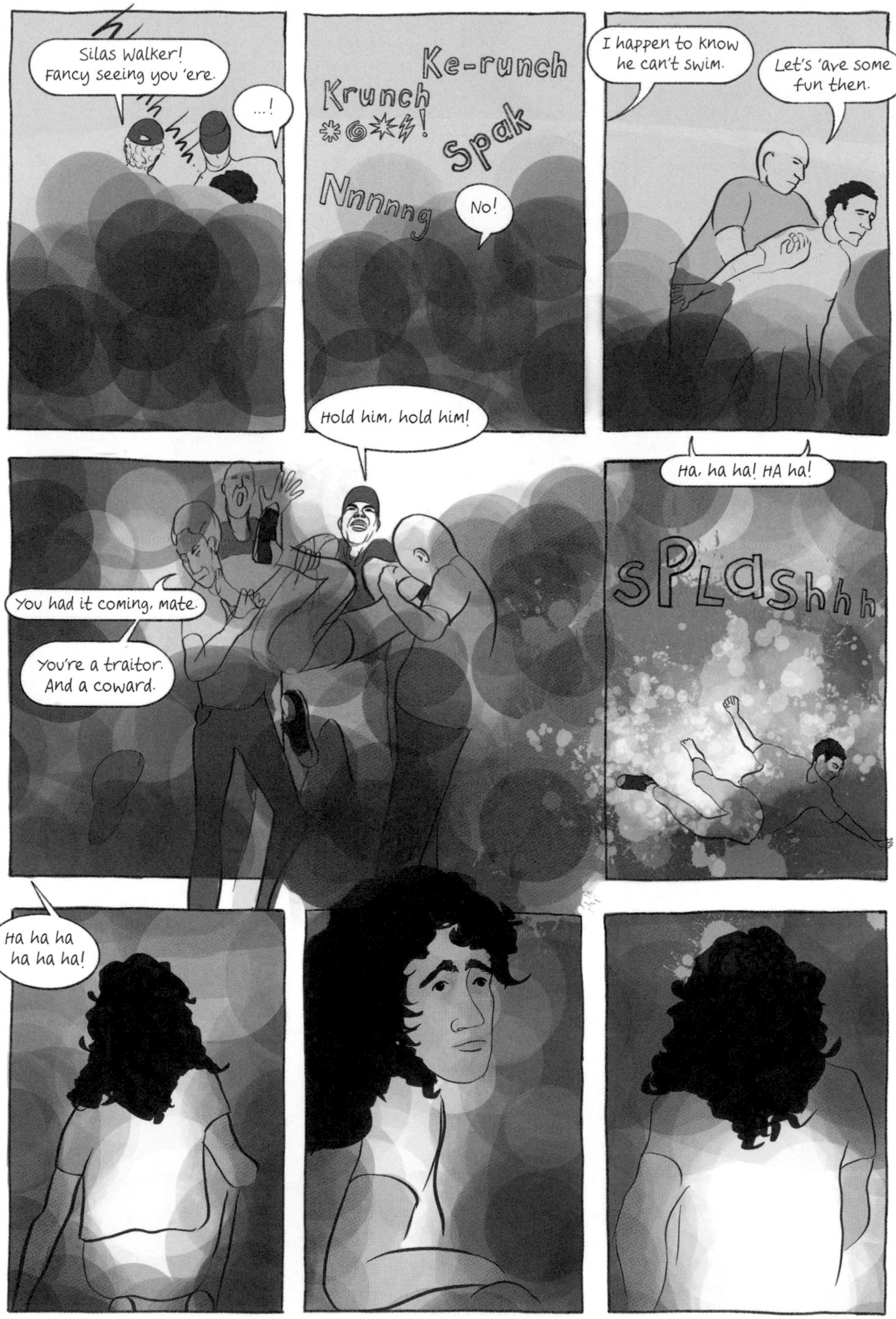
Silas Walker! Fancy seeing you 'ere.
...!
Ke-runch
Krunch
Spak
Nnnnng
No!
I happen to know he can't swim.
Let's 'ave some fun then.
Hold him, hold him!
You had it coming, mate.
You're a traitor. And a coward.
Ha, ha ha! HA ha!
sPLashhh
Ha ha ha ha ha ha!

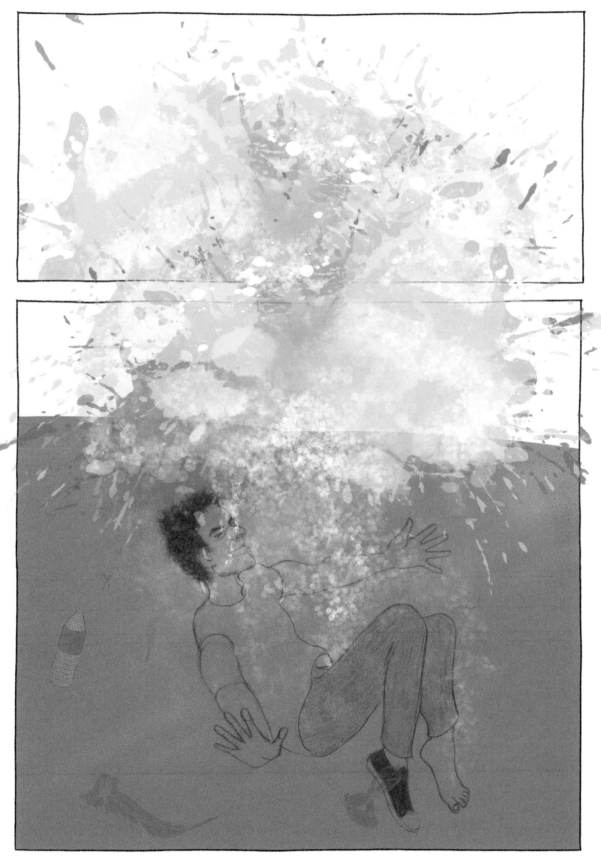

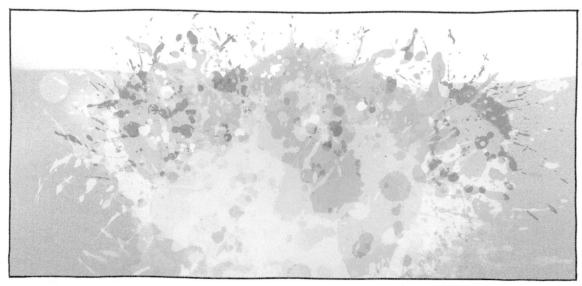

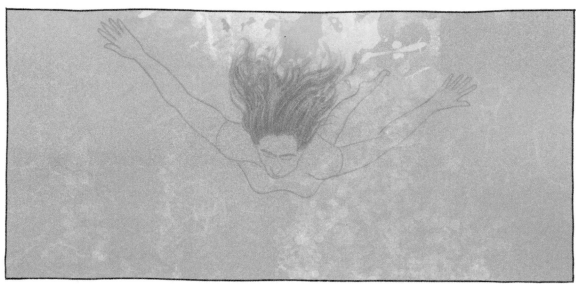

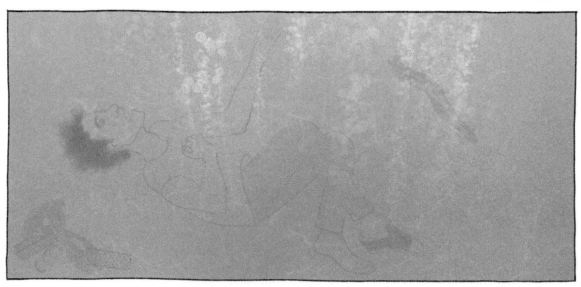

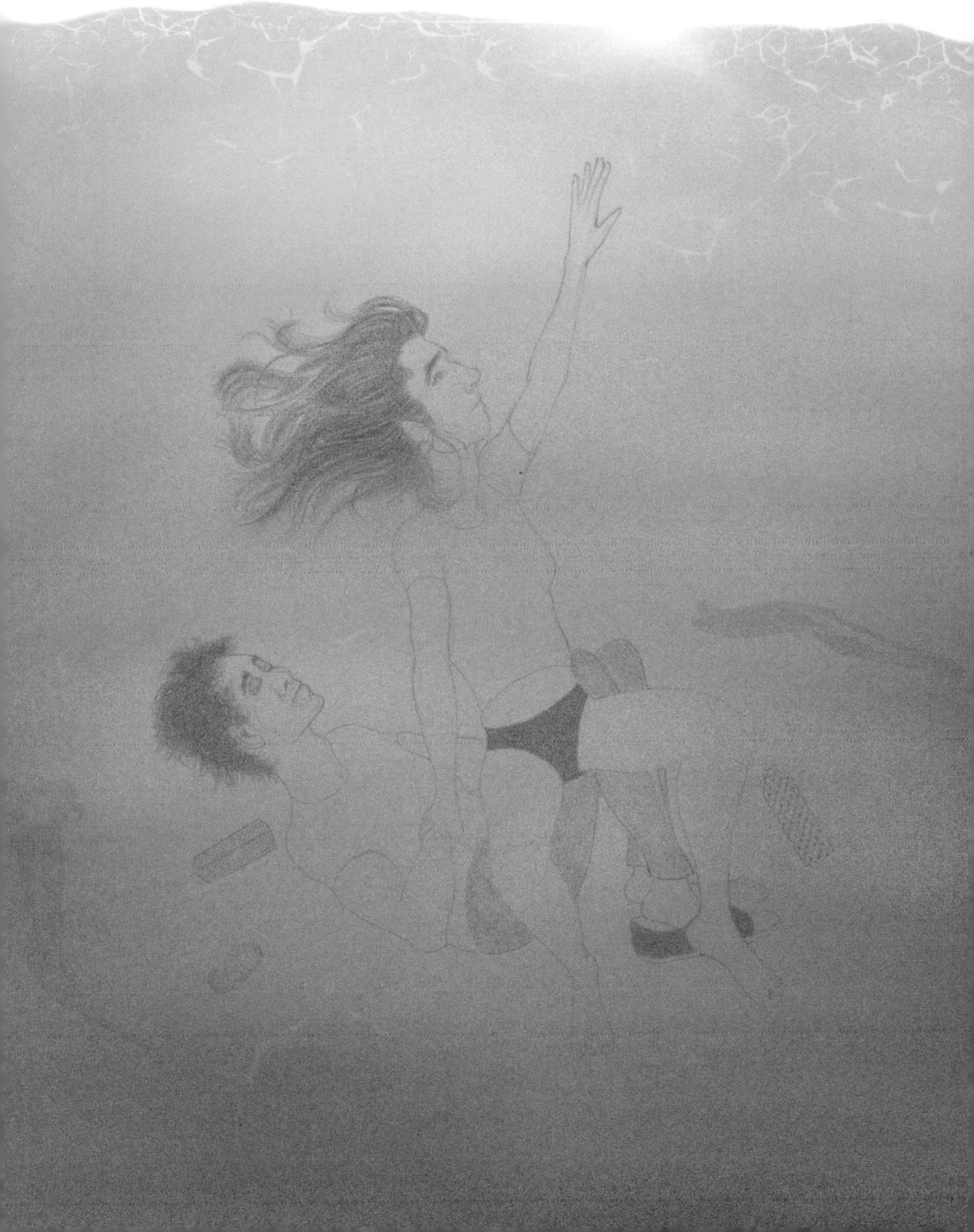

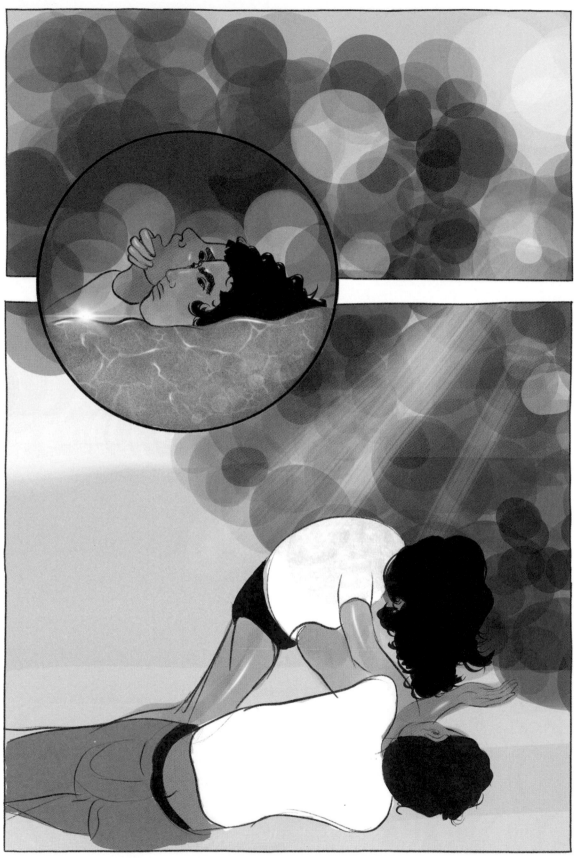

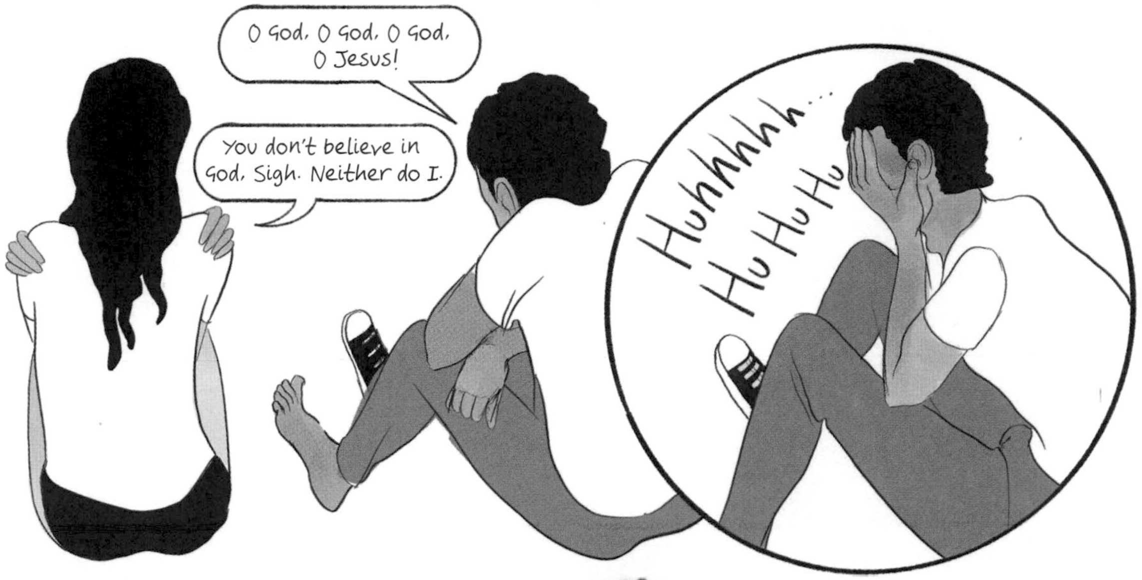
O God, O God, O God, O Jesus!
You don't believe in God, Sigh. Neither do I.
Huhhhhh... HuHuHu

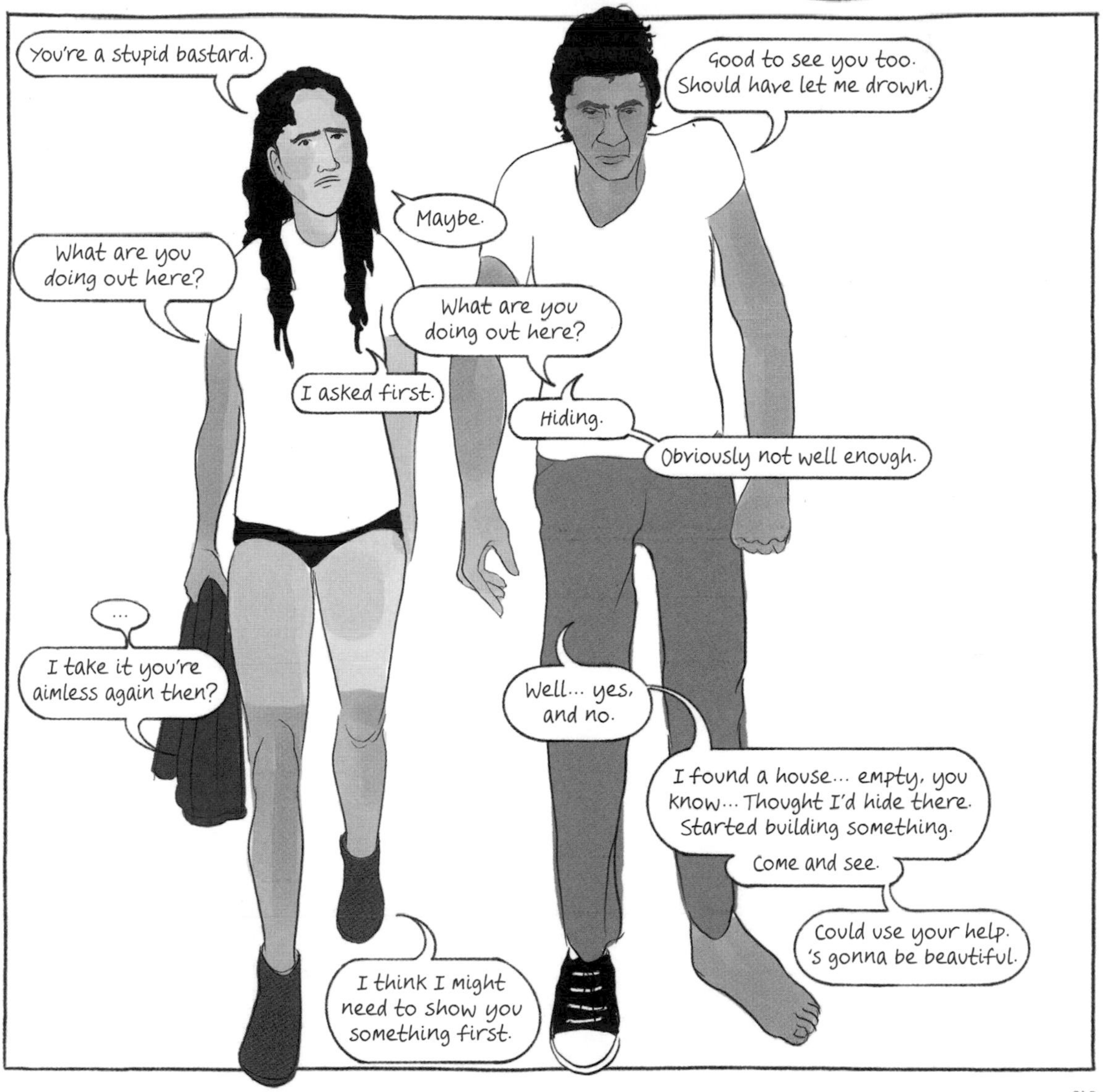
You're a stupid bastard.
Good to see you too. Should have let me drown.
Maybe.
What are you doing out here?
What are you doing out here?
I asked first.
Hiding.
Obviously not well enough.
...
I take it you're aimless again then?
Well... yes, and no.
I found a house... empty, you know... Thought I'd hide there. Started building something.
Come and see.
Could use your help. 's gonna be beautiful.
I think I might need to show you something first.

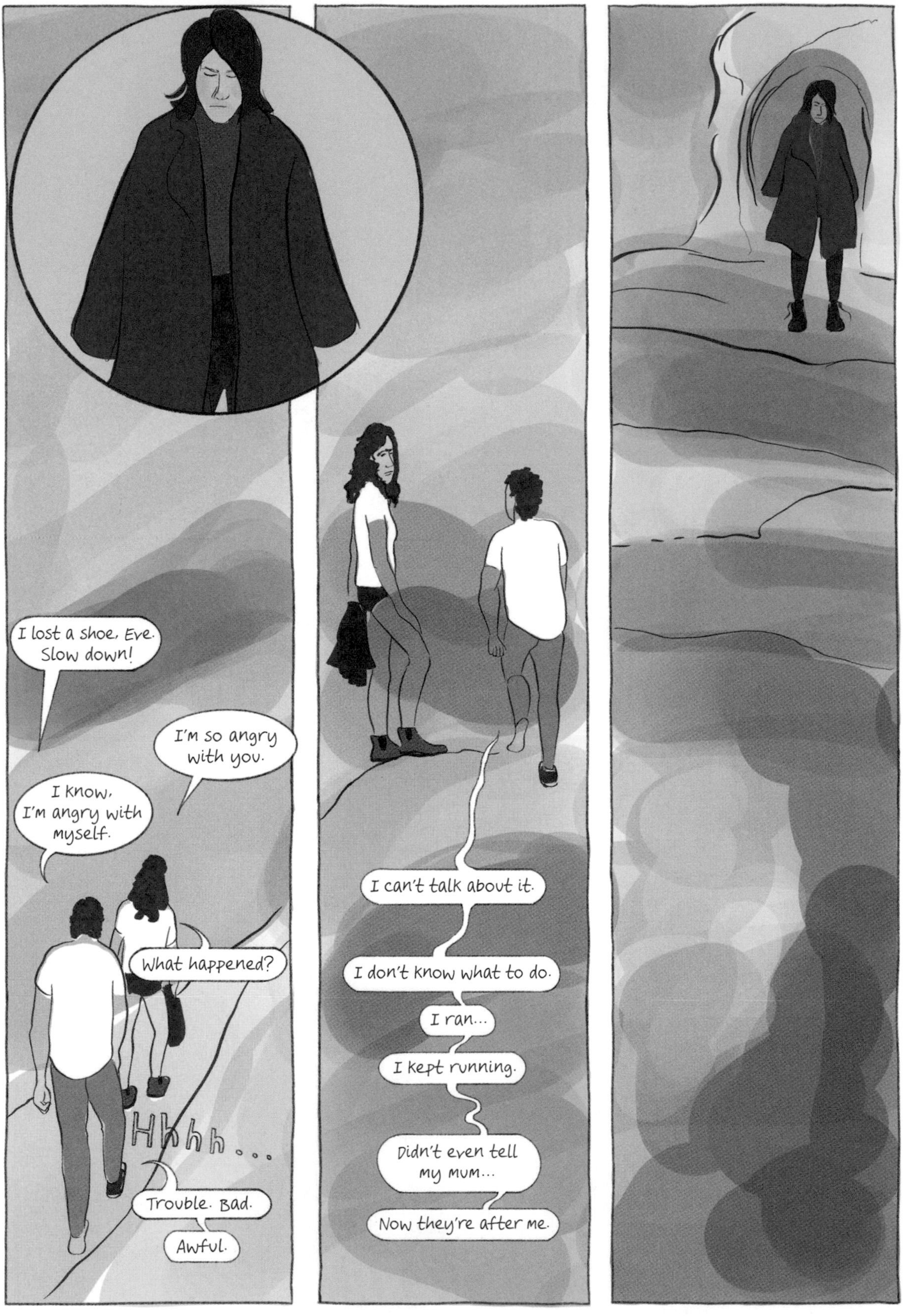
I lost a shoe, Eve. Slow down!
I'm so angry with you.
I know, I'm angry with myself.
What happened?
Hhhh...
Trouble. Bad.
Awful.
I can't talk about it.
I don't know what to do.
I ran...
I kept running.
Didn't even tell my mum...
Now they're after me.

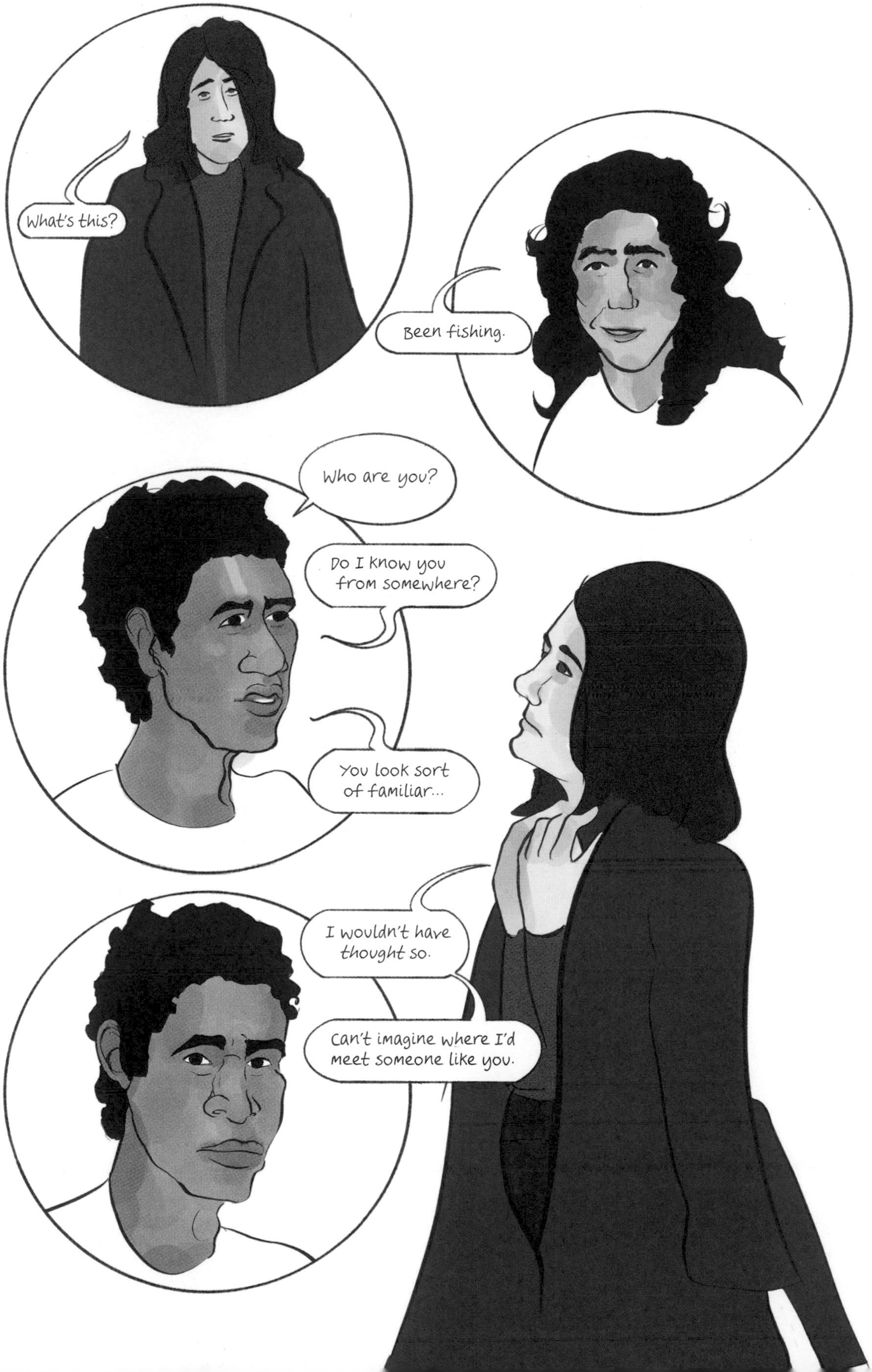
What's this?
Been fishing.
Who are you?
Do I know you from somewhere?
You look sort of familiar...
I wouldn't have thought so.
Can't imagine where I'd meet someone like you.

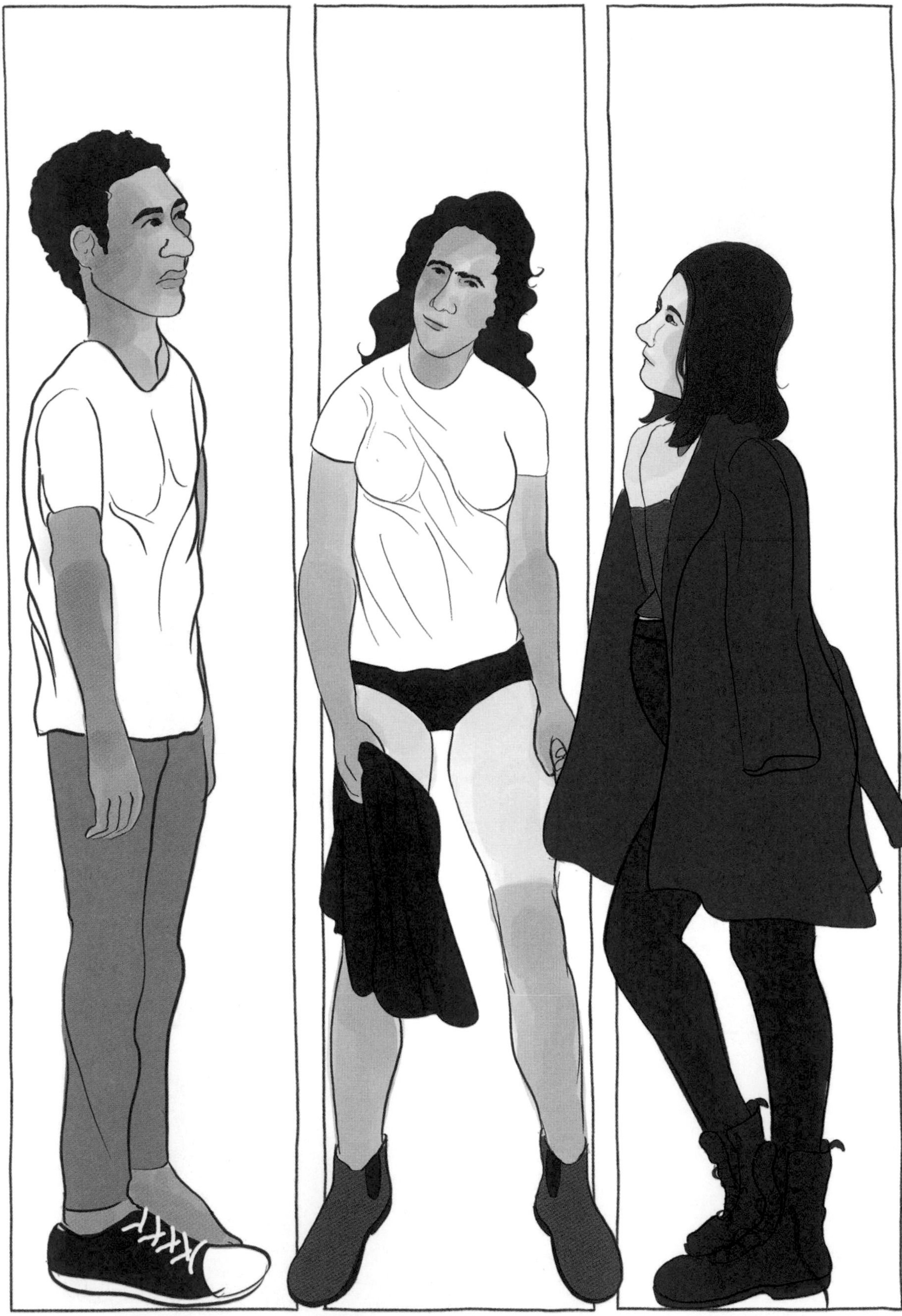

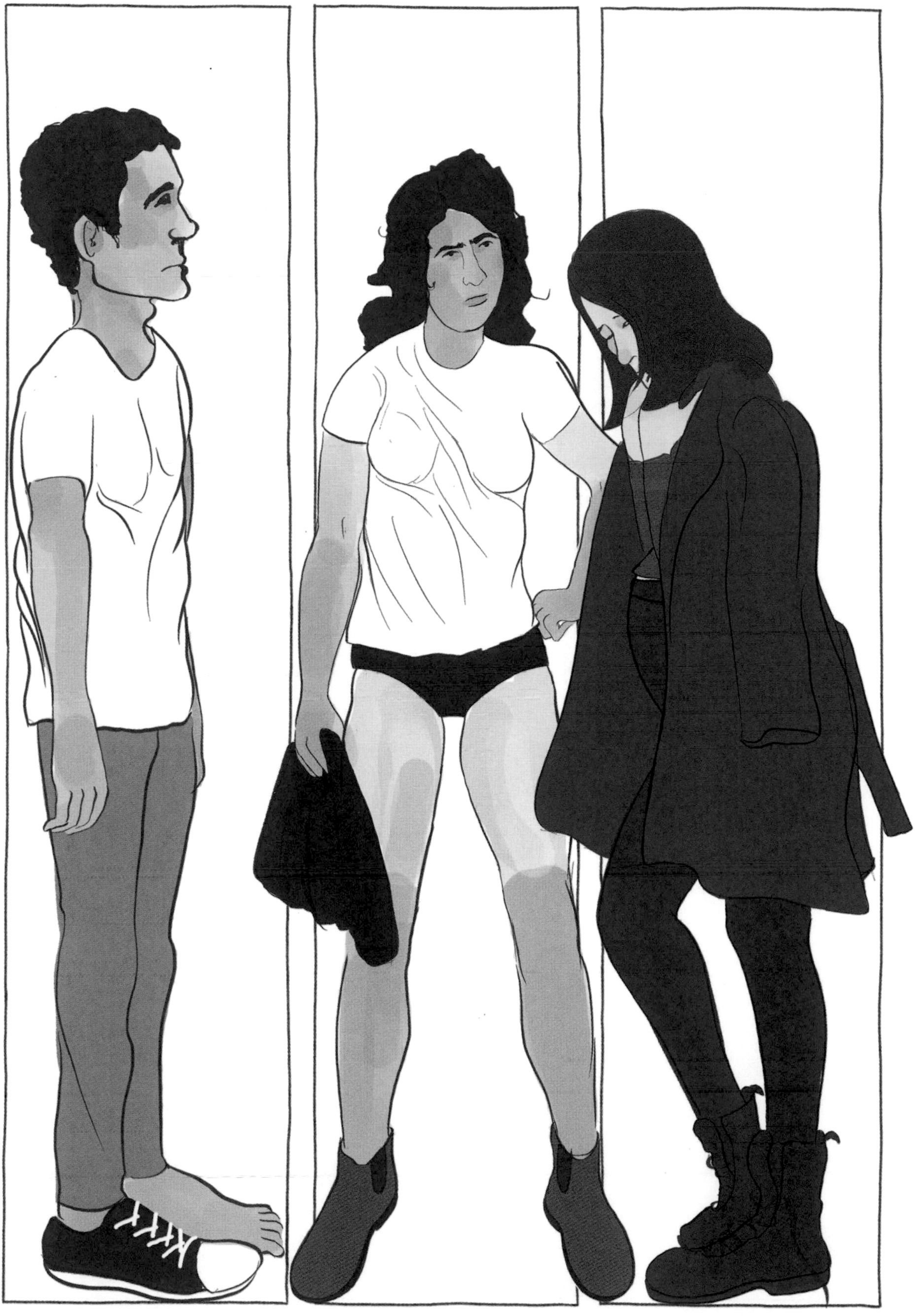

Coda

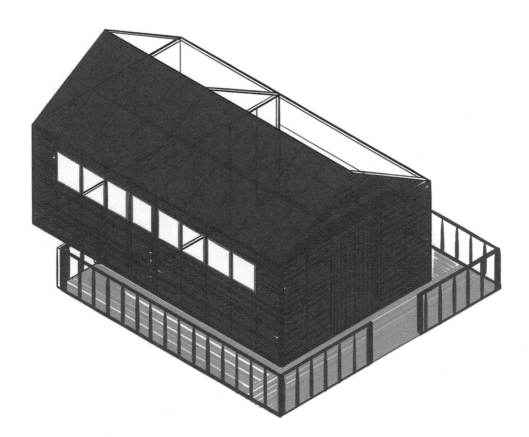

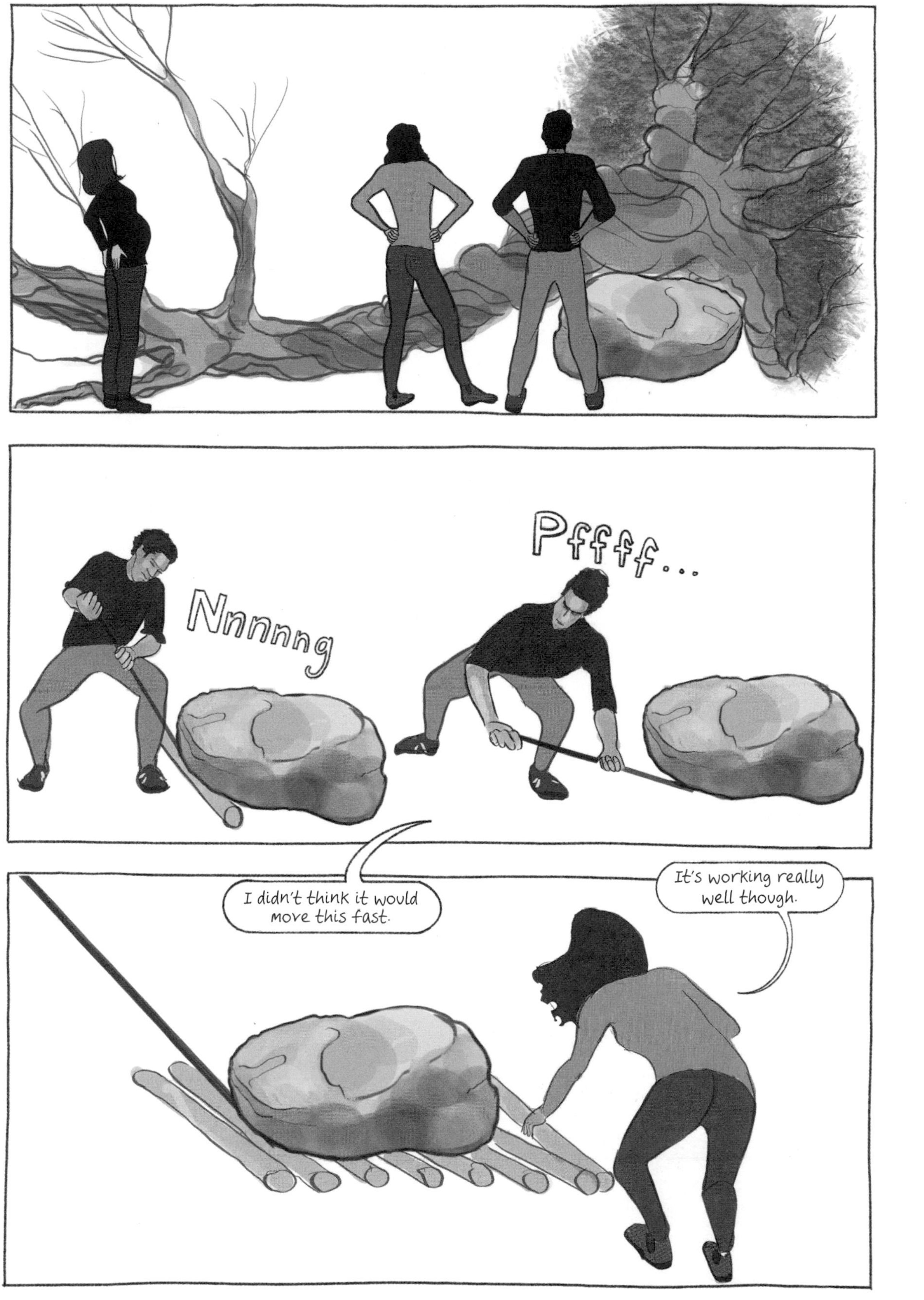
Nnnnng
Pffff...
I didn't think it would move this fast.
It's working really well though.

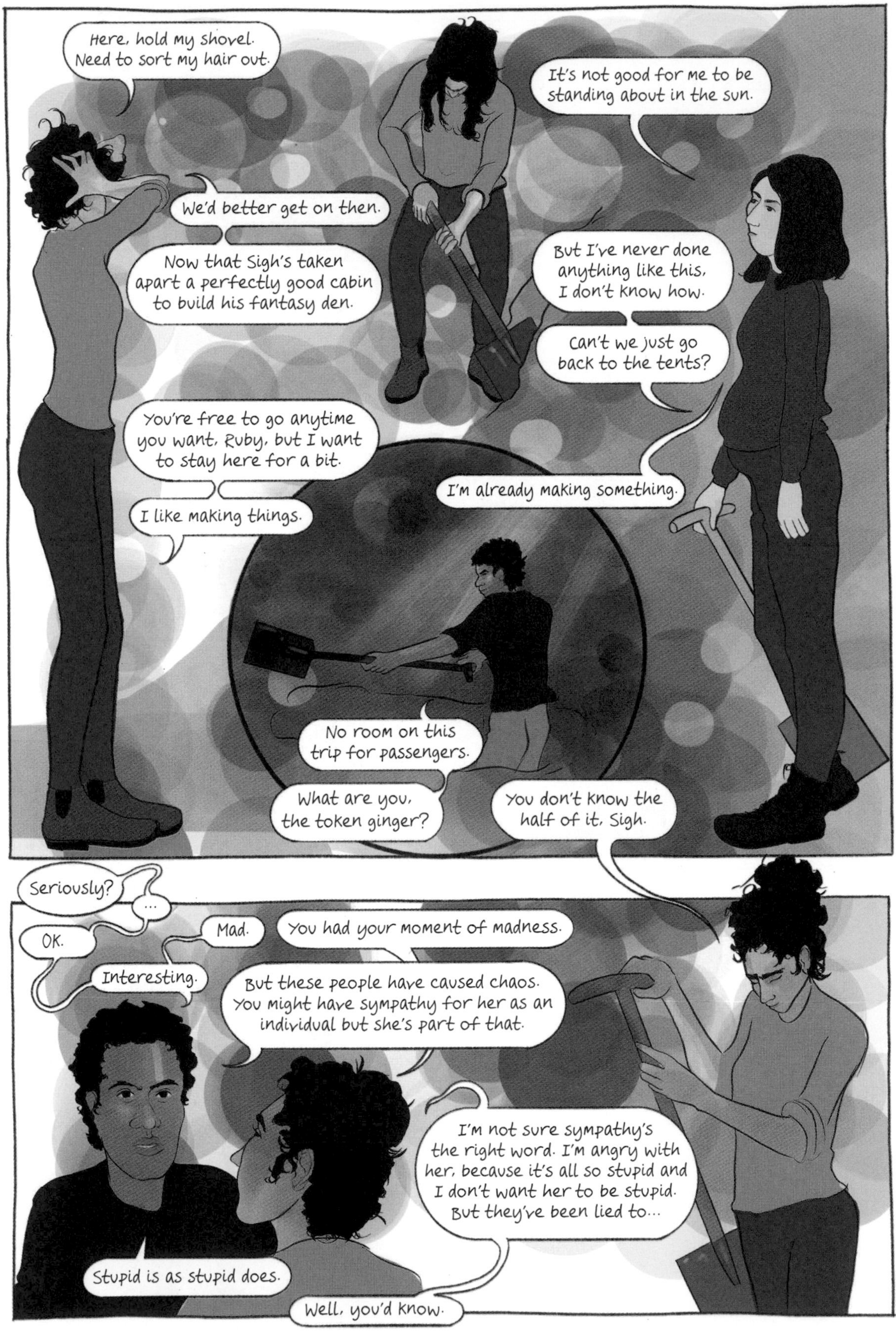
Here, hold my shovel. Need to sort my hair out.
It's not good for me to be standing about in the sun.
We'd better get on then.
Now that Sigh's taken apart a perfectly good cabin to build his fantasy den.
But I've never done anything like this, I don't know how.
Can't we just go back to the tents?
You're free to go anytime you want, Ruby, but I want to stay here for a bit.
I like making things.
I'm already making something.
No room on this trip for passengers.
What are you, the token ginger?
You don't know the half of it, Sigh.
Seriously?
...
OK.
Mad.
Interesting.
You had your moment of madness.
But these people have caused chaos. You might have sympathy for her as an individual but she's part of that.
I'm not sure sympathy's the right word. I'm angry with her, because it's all so stupid and I don't want her to be stupid. But they've been lied to...
Stupid is as stupid does.
Well, you'd know.

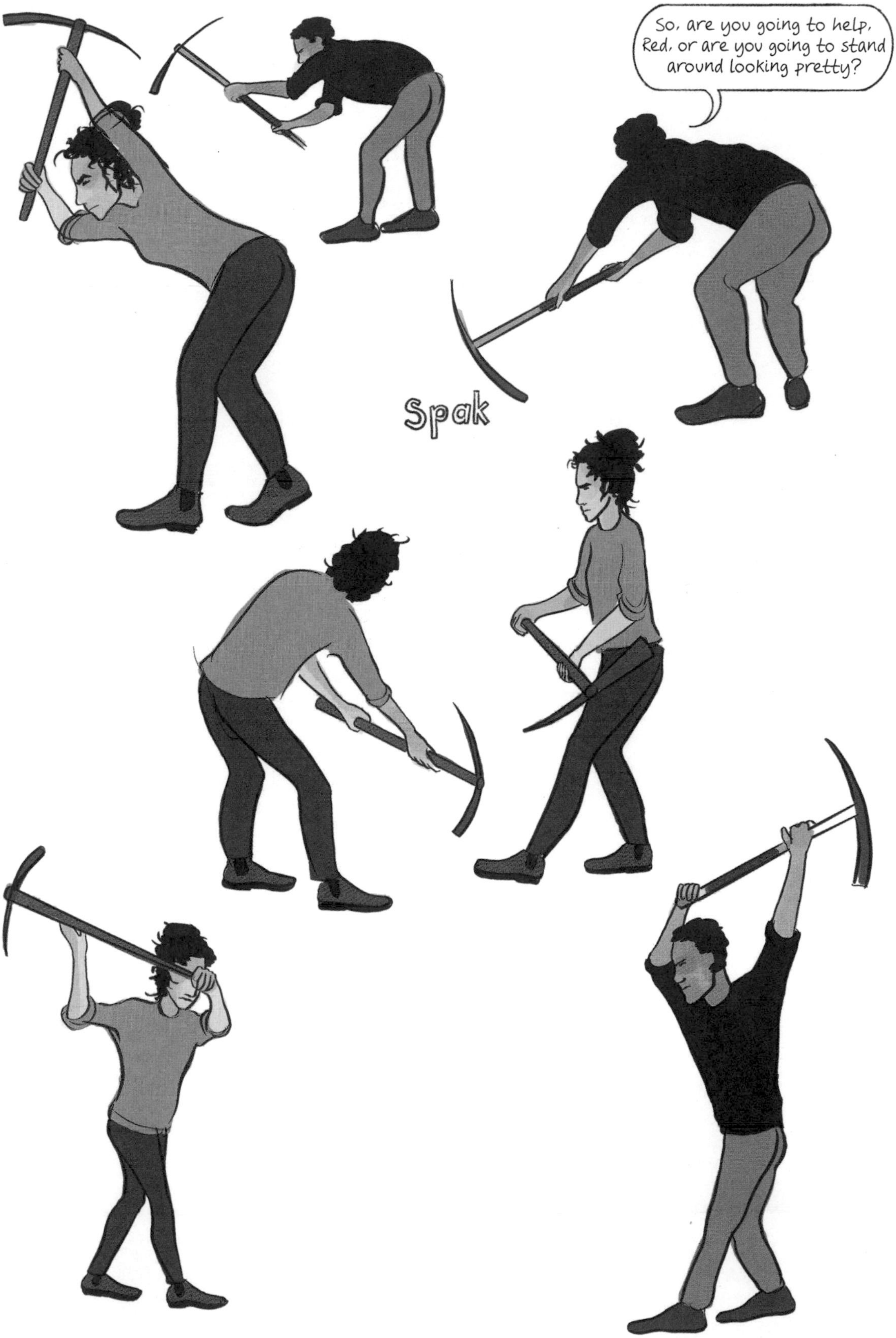

So, are you going to help, Red, or are you going to stand around looking pretty?
Spak

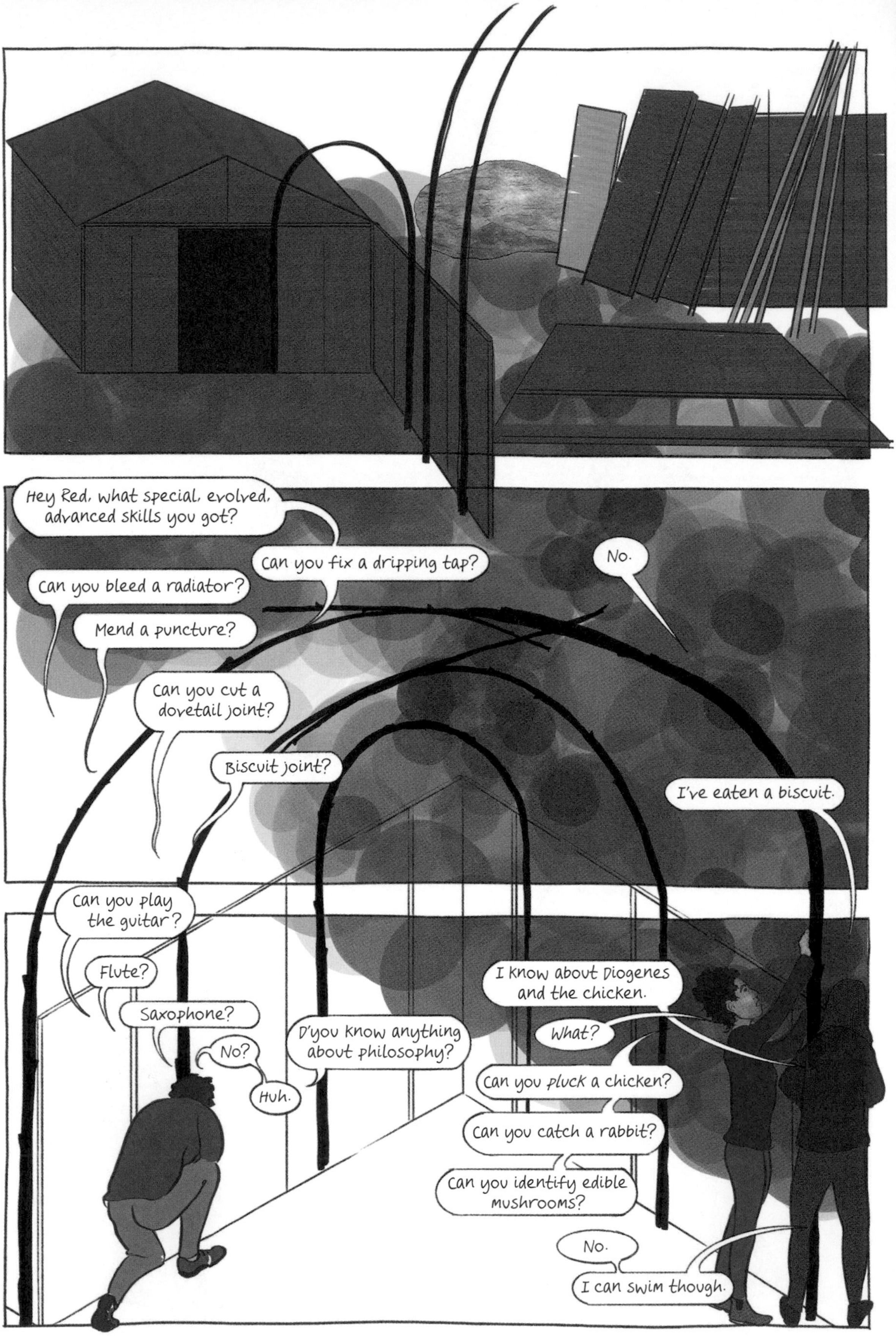
Hey Red, what special, evolved, advanced skills you got?
Can you fix a dripping tap?
Can you bleed a radiator?
Mend a puncture?
Can you cut a dovetail joint?
Biscuit joint?
No.
I've eaten a biscuit.
Can you play the guitar?
Flute?
Saxophone?
No?
Huh.
D'you know anything about philosophy?
I know about Diogenes and the chicken.
What?
Can you *pluck* a chicken?
Can you catch a rabbit?
Can you identify edible mushrooms?
No.
I can swim though.

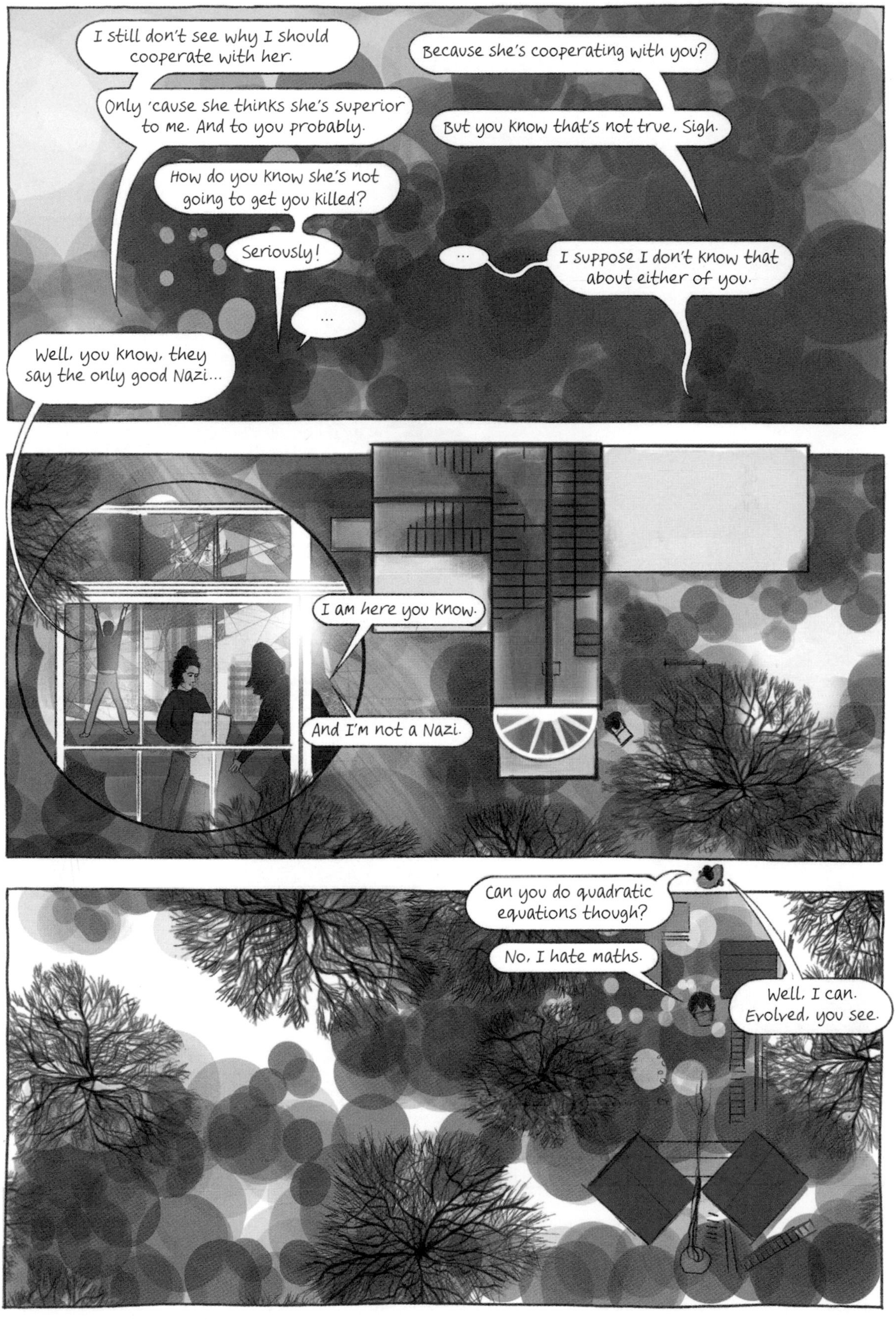

I still don't see why I should cooperate with her.
Only 'cause she thinks she's superior to me. And to you probably.
Because she's cooperating with you?
But you know that's not true, Sigh.
How do you know she's not going to get you killed?
Seriously!
...
I suppose I don't know that about either of you.
...
Well, you know, they say the only good Nazi...
I am here you know.
And I'm not a Nazi.
Can you do quadratic equations though?
No, I hate maths.
Well, I can. Evolved, you see.

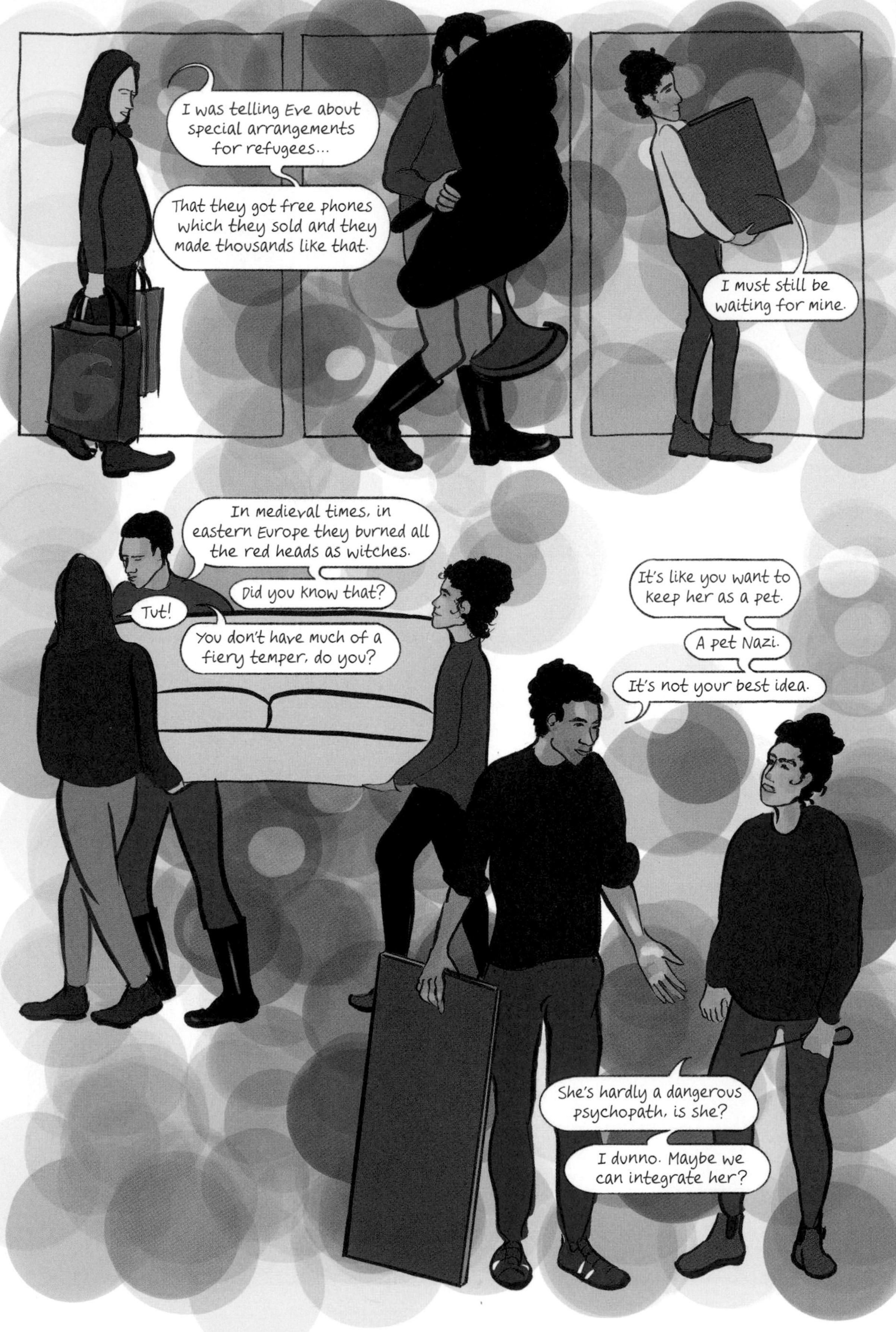
I was telling Eve about special arrangements for refugees...
That they got free phones which they sold and they made thousands like that.
I must still be waiting for mine.
In medieval times, in eastern Europe they burned all the red heads as witches.
Did you know that?
Tut!
You don't have much of a fiery temper, do you?
It's like you want to keep her as a pet.
A pet Nazi.
It's not your best idea.
She's hardly a dangerous psychopath, is she?
I dunno. Maybe we can integrate her?

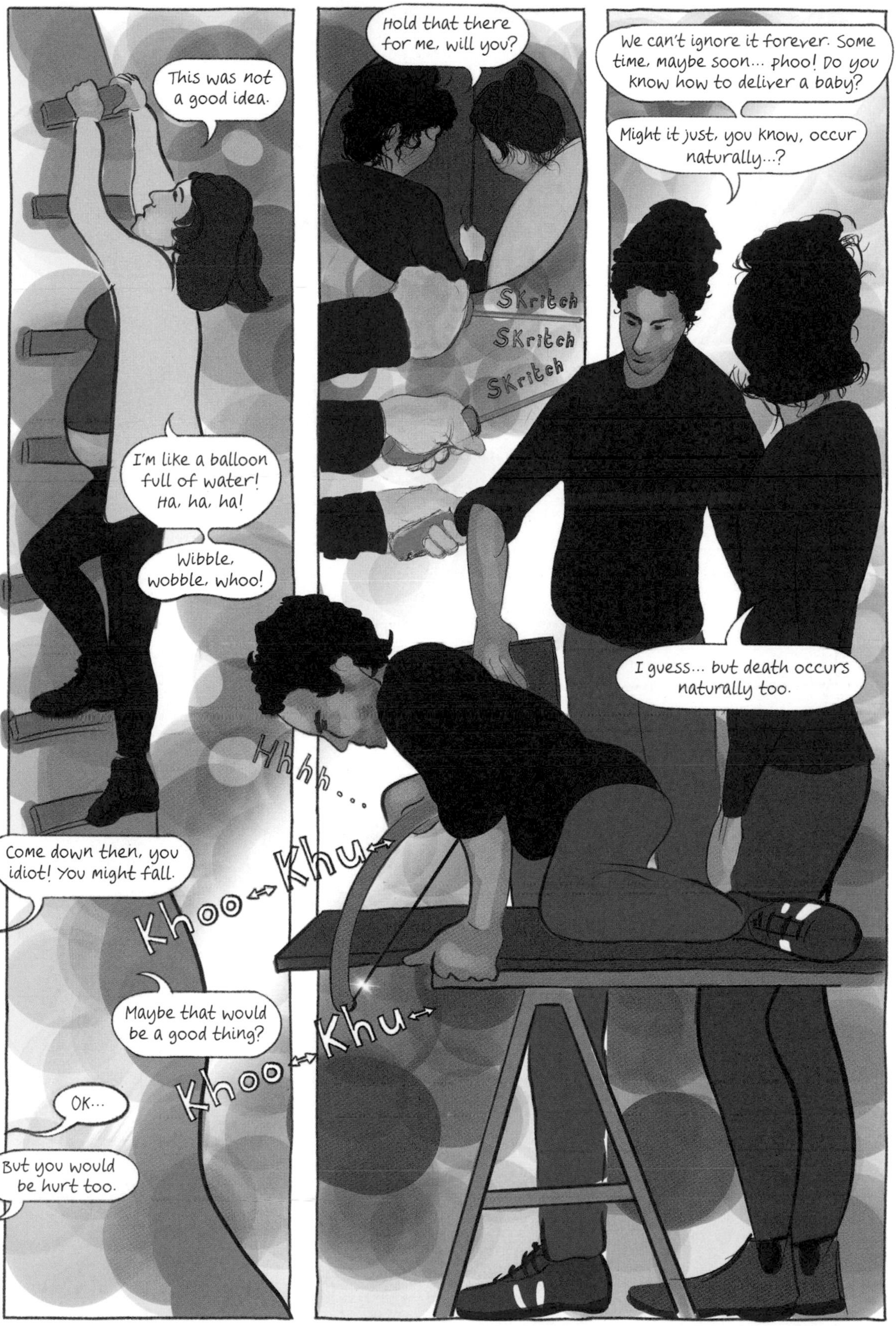

This was not a good idea.
I'm like a balloon full of water! Ha, ha, ha!
Wibble, wobble, whoo!
Come down then, you idiot! You might fall.
Maybe that would be a good thing?
OK...
But you would be hurt too.
Hold that there for me, will you?
SKritch
SKritch
SKritch
Hhhh...
Khoo↔Khu↔
Khoo↔Khu↔
We can't ignore it forever. Some time, maybe soon... phoo! Do you know how to deliver a baby?
Might it just, you know, occur naturally...?
I guess... but death occurs naturally too.

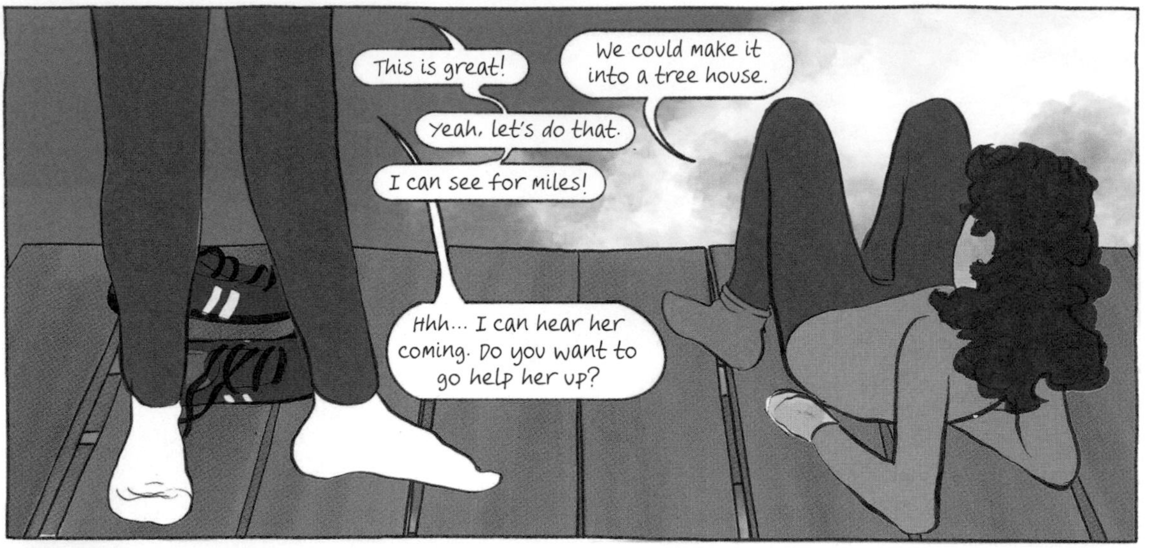
This is great!
We could make it into a tree house.
Yeah, let's do that.
I can see for miles!
Hhh... I can hear her coming. Do you want to go help her up?

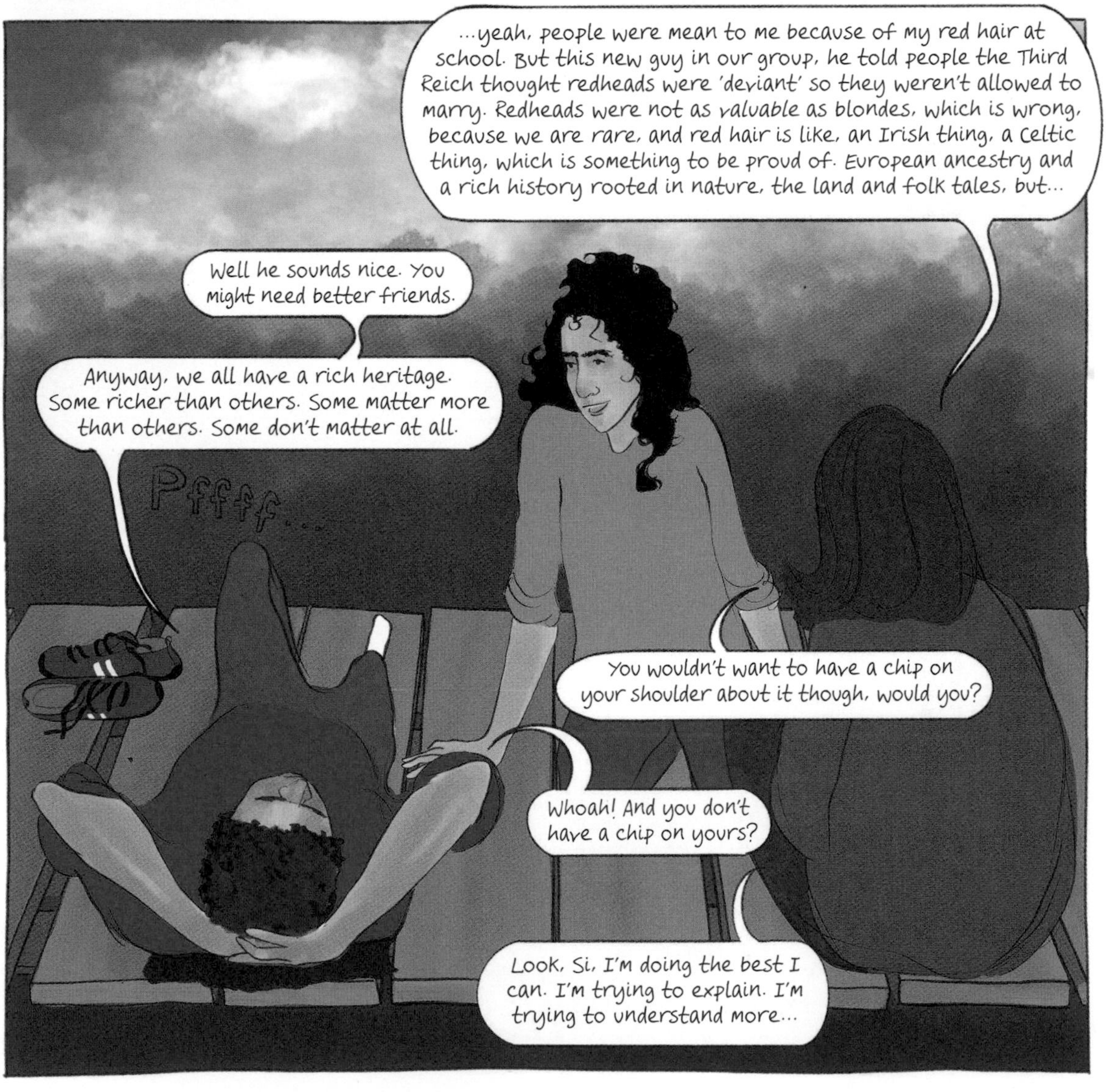
...yeah, people were mean to me because of my red hair at school. But this new guy in our group, he told people the Third Reich thought redheads were 'deviant' so they weren't allowed to marry. Redheads were not as valuable as blondes, which is wrong, because we are rare, and red hair is like, an Irish thing, a Celtic thing, which is something to be proud of. European ancestry and a rich history rooted in nature, the land and folk tales, but...
Well he sounds nice. You might need better friends.
Anyway, we all have a rich heritage. Some richer than others. Some matter more than others. Some don't matter at all.
Pffff...
You wouldn't want to have a chip on your shoulder about it though, would you?
Whoah! And you don't have a chip on yours?
Look, Si, I'm doing the best I can. I'm trying to explain. I'm trying to understand more...

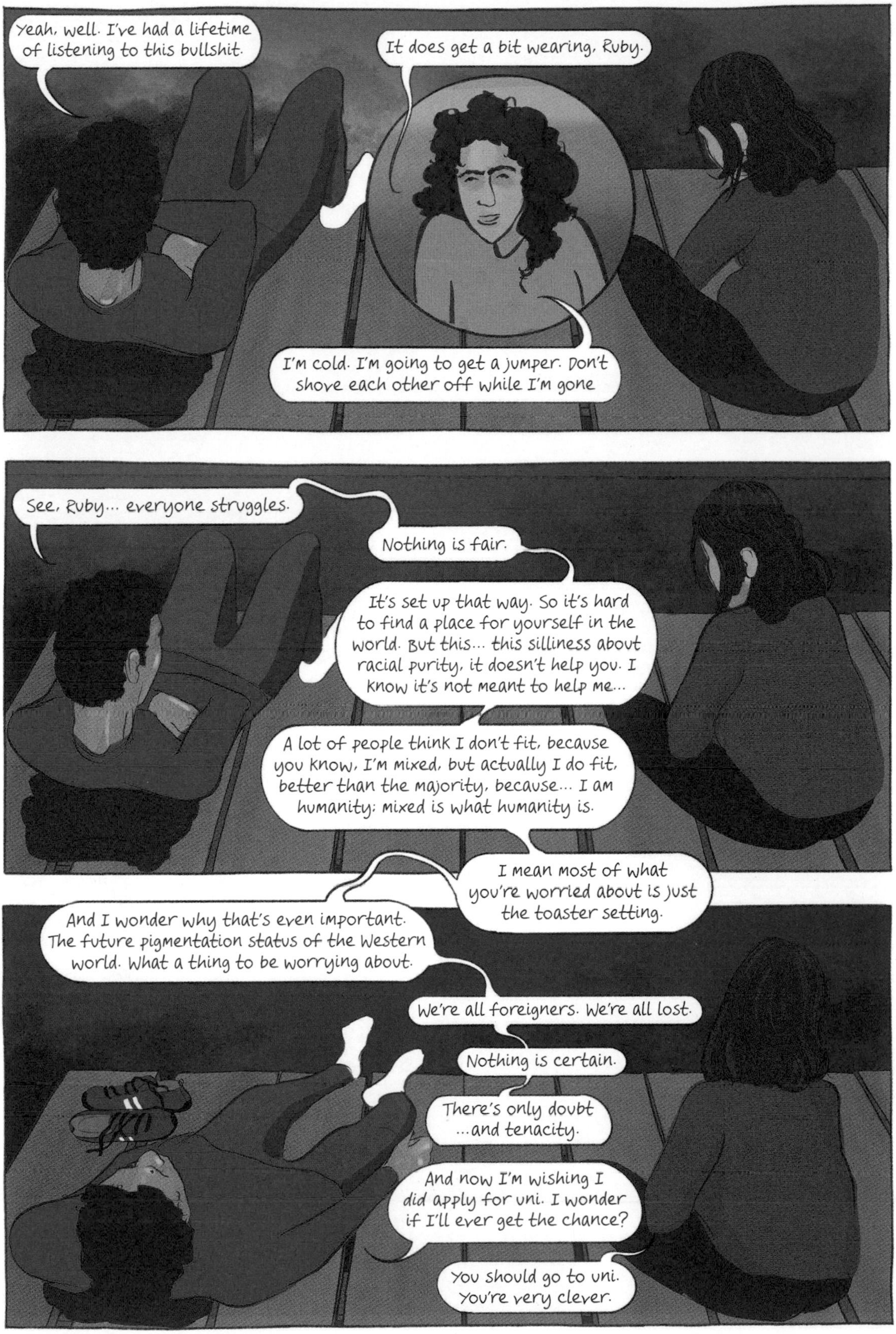
Yeah, well. I've had a lifetime of listening to this bullshit.
It does get a bit wearing, Ruby.
I'm cold. I'm going to get a jumper. Don't shove each other off while I'm gone
See, Ruby... everyone struggles.
Nothing is fair.
It's set up that way. So it's hard to find a place for yourself in the world. But this... this silliness about racial purity, it doesn't help you. I know it's not meant to help me...
A lot of people think I don't fit, because you know, I'm mixed, but actually I do fit, better than the majority, because... I am humanity: mixed is what humanity is.
I mean most of what you're worried about is just the toaster setting.
And I wonder why that's even important. The future pigmentation status of the Western world. What a thing to be worrying about.
We're all foreigners. We're all lost.
Nothing is certain.
There's only doubt ...and tenacity.
And now I'm wishing I did apply for uni. I wonder if I'll ever get the chance?
You should go to uni. You're very clever.

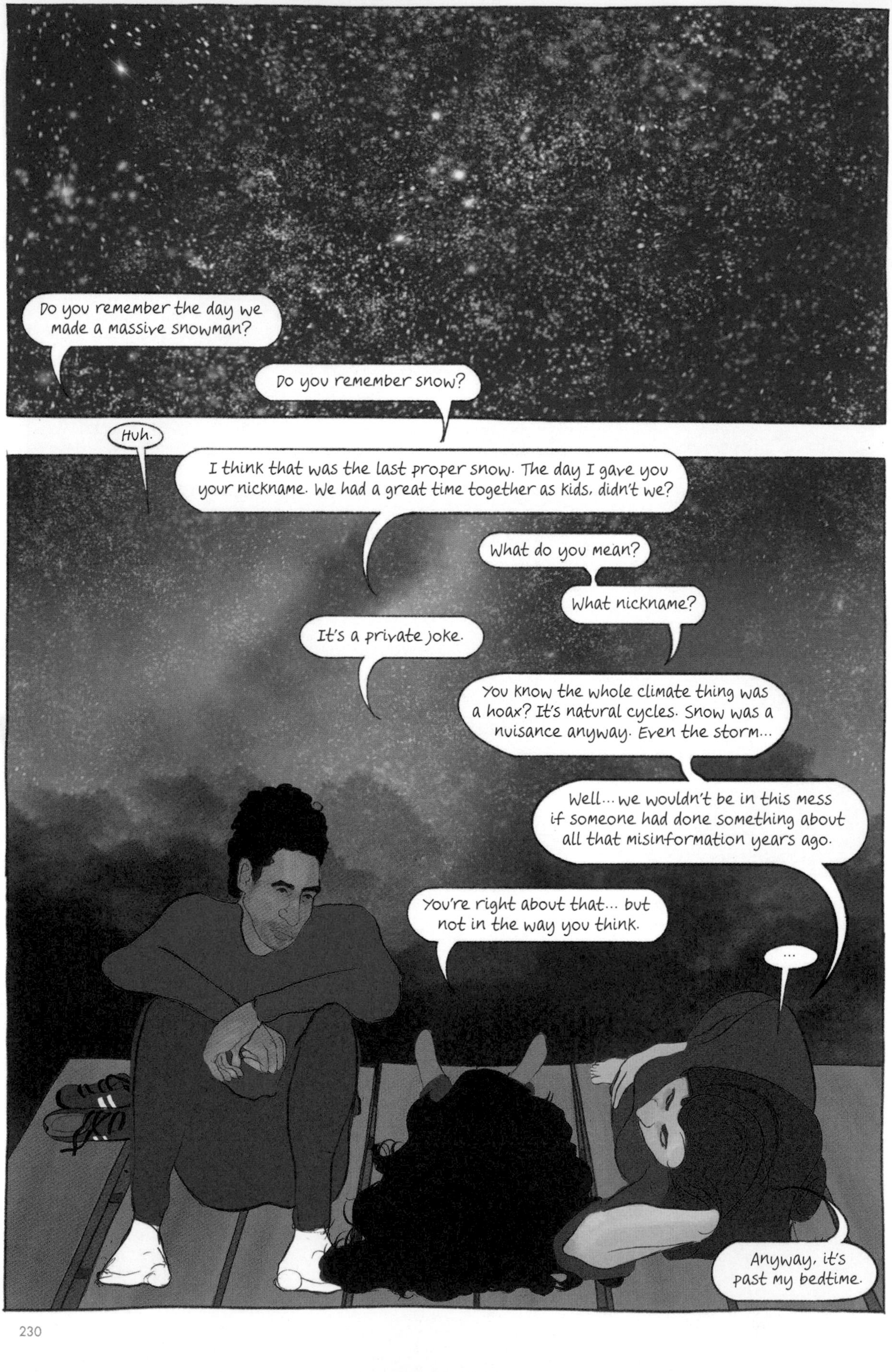
Do you remember the day we made a massive snowman?
Do you remember snow?
Huh.
I think that was the last proper snow. The day I gave you your nickname. We had a great time together as kids, didn't we?
What do you mean?
What nickname?
It's a private joke.
You know the whole climate thing was a hoax? It's natural cycles. Snow was a nuisance anyway. Even the storm...
Well... we wouldn't be in this mess if someone had done something about all that misinformation years ago.
You're right about that... but not in the way you think.
...
Anyway, it's past my bedtime.

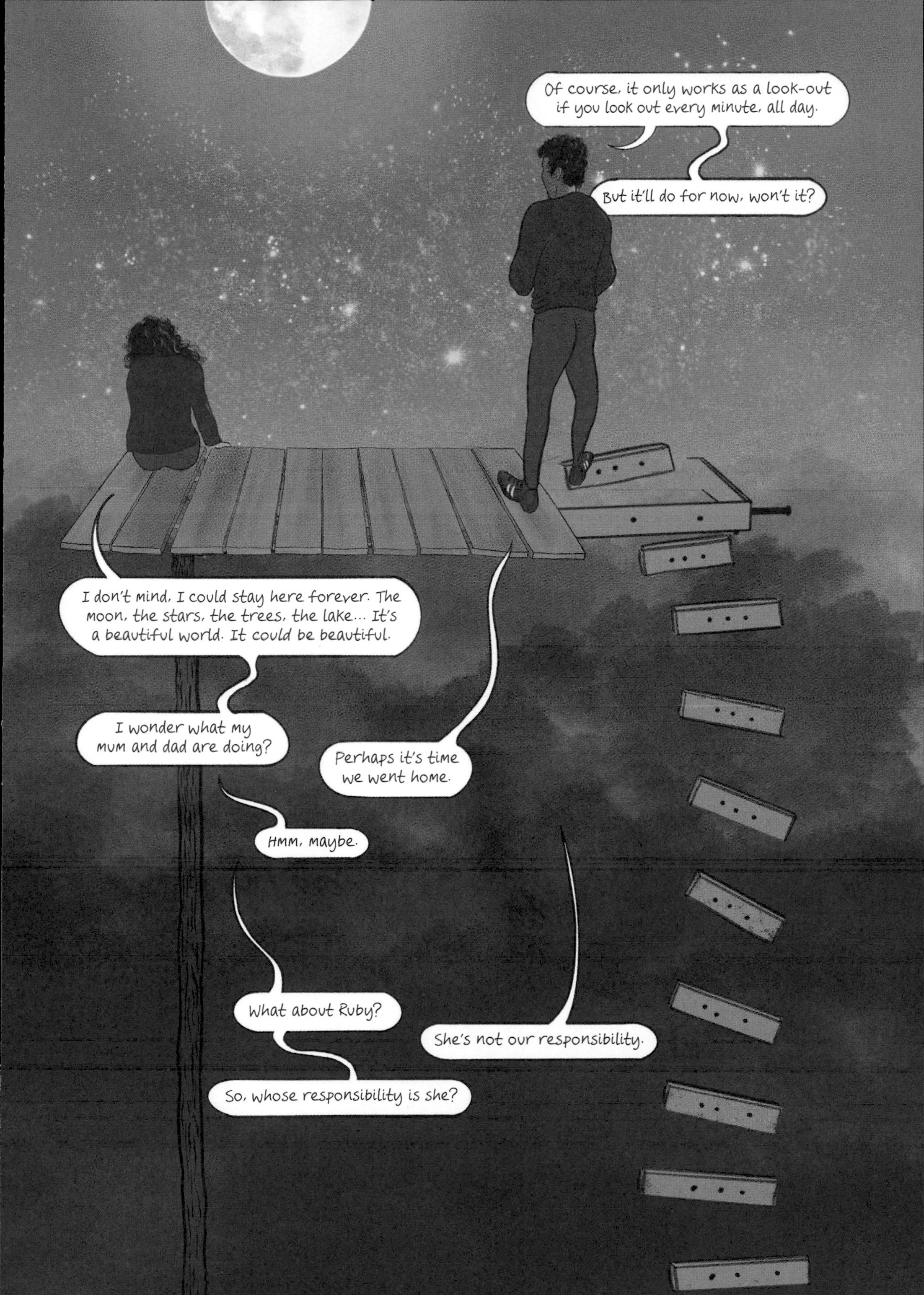
Of course, it only works as a look-out if you look out every minute, all day.
But it'll do for now, won't it?
I don't mind, I could stay here forever. The moon, the stars, the trees, the lake... It's a beautiful world. It could be beautiful.
I wonder what my mum and dad are doing?
Perhaps it's time we went home.
Hmm, maybe.
What about Ruby?
She's not our responsibility.
So, whose responsibility is she?

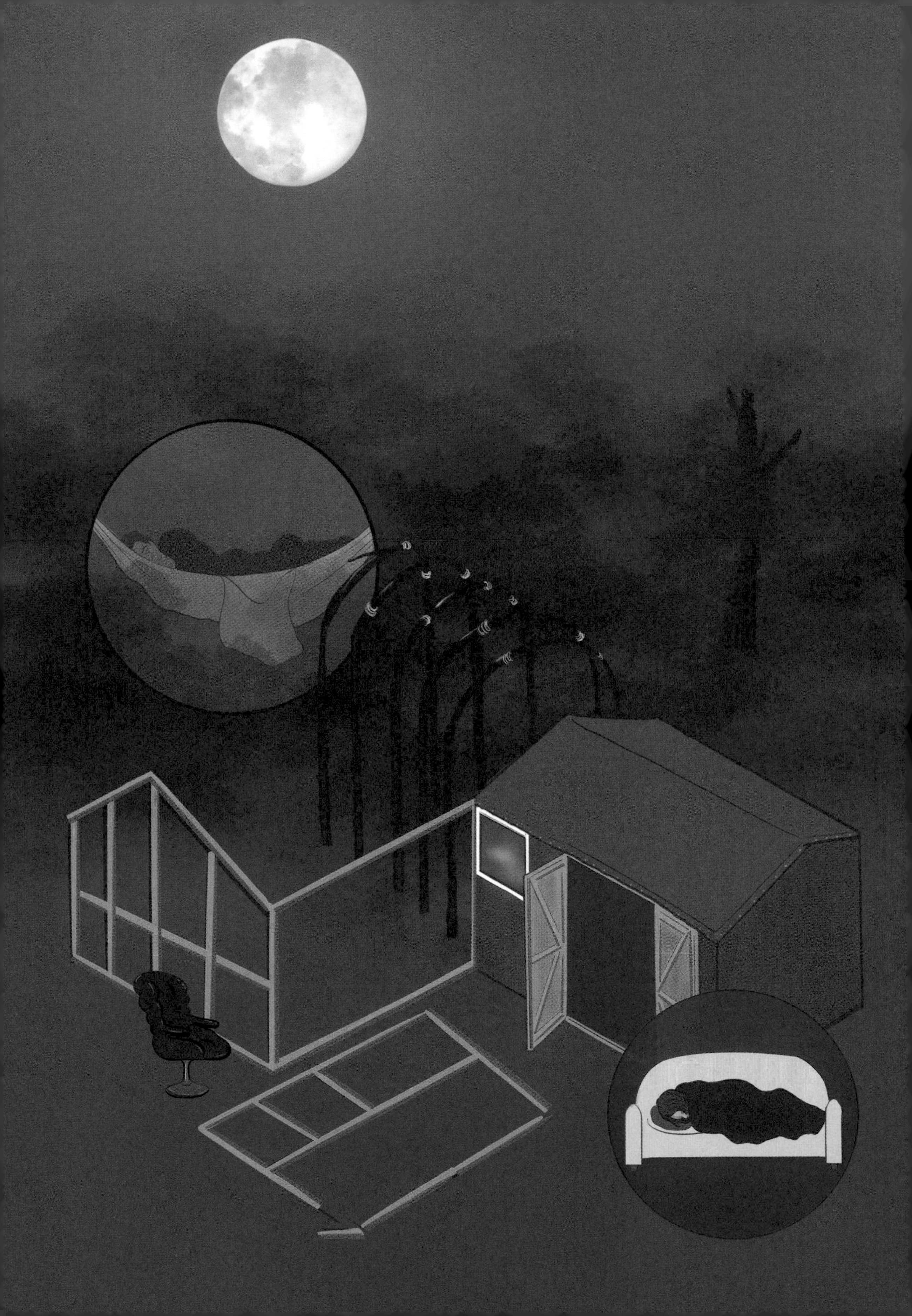

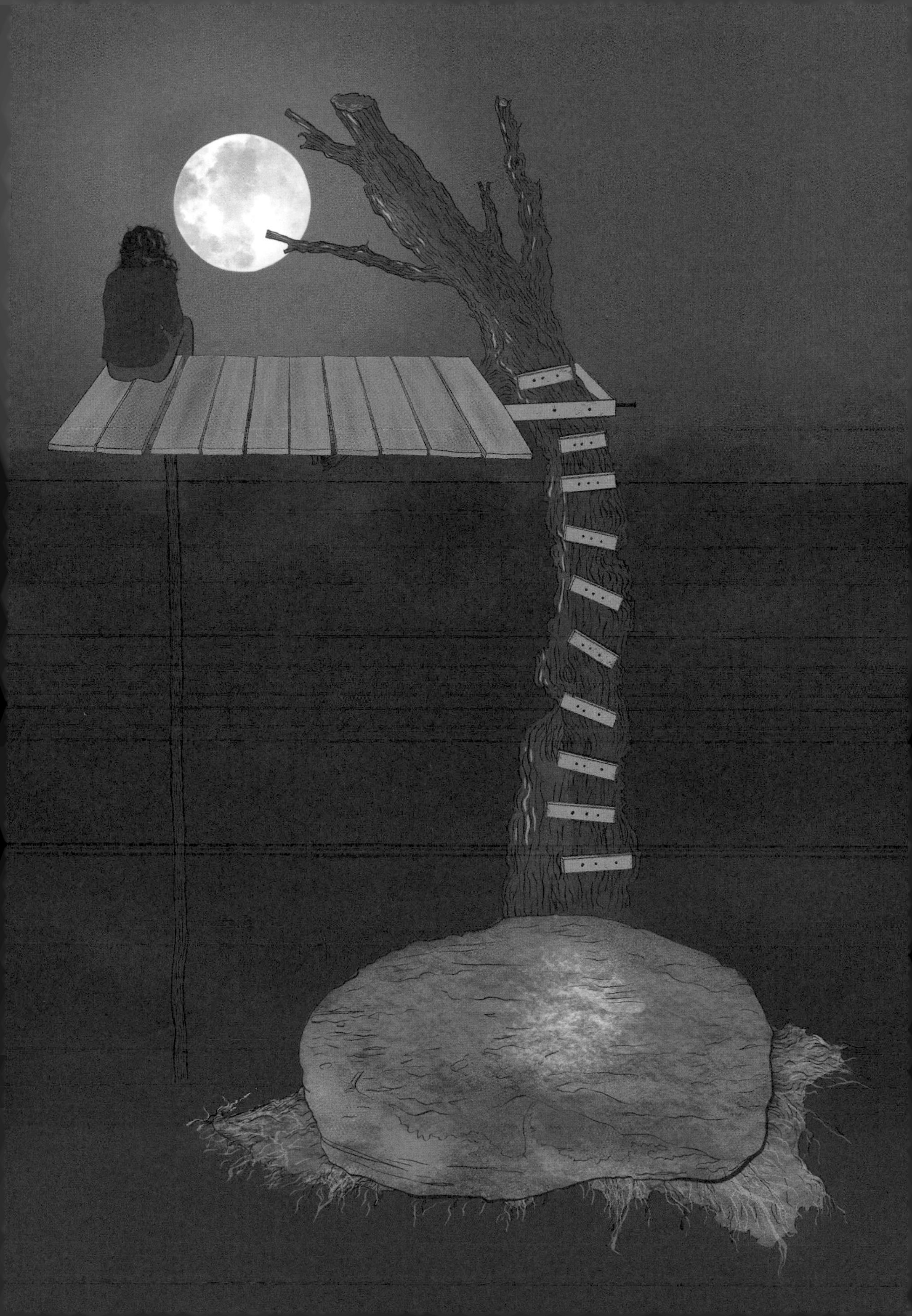

Tap tap tap
Khoo↔Khu↔
Khoo↔Kh...
Eve! Come quick, I can feel it kicking!
Tap tap tap
Hhhh...
Skritch
Skritch
Skritch
Tap tap tap
Mmm mm mm mm Mmm mm mm
Khoo↔Khu↔
Khoo↔Khu↔

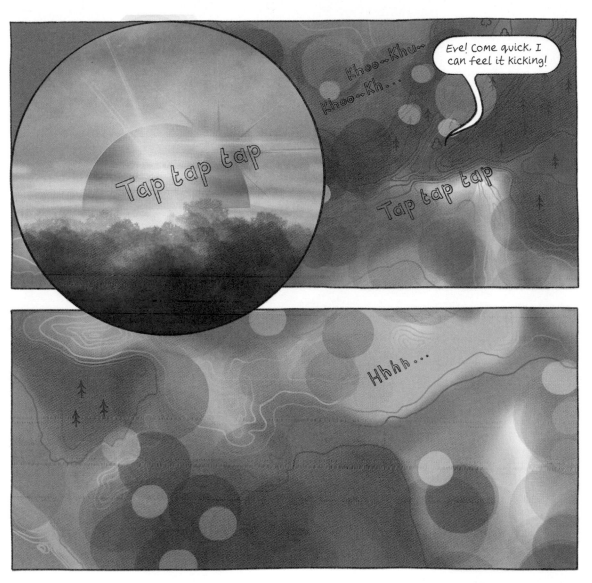

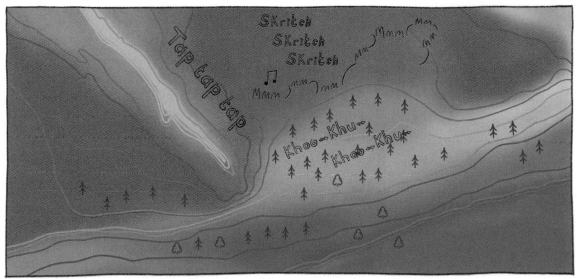

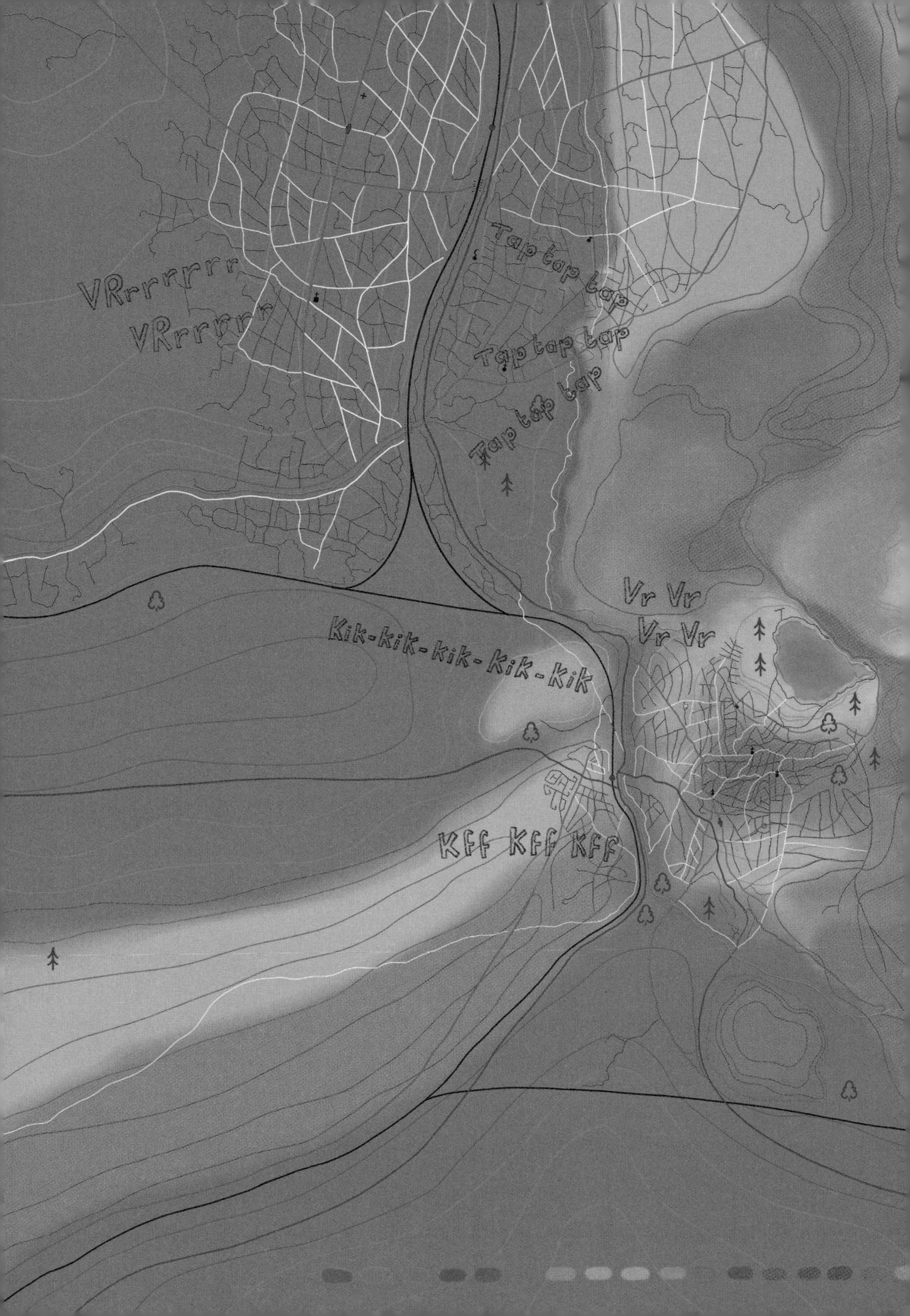
VRrrrrrr
VRrrrrrr
Tap tap tap
Tap tap tap
Tap tap tap
Tap tap tap
Vr Vr
Vr Vr
Kik-kik-kik-kik-kik
Kff Kff Kff

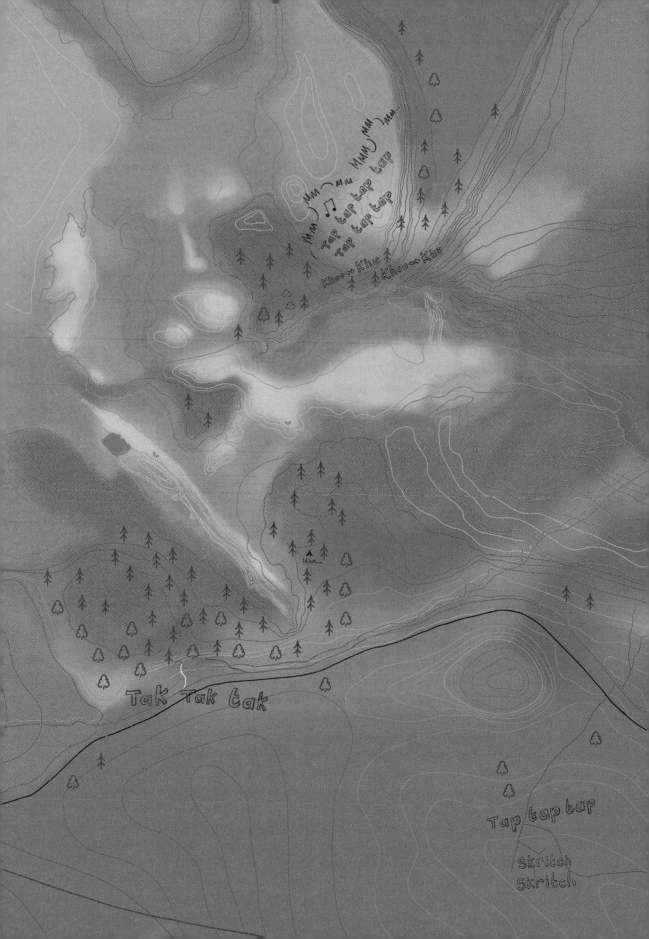

♩ MM MM MM MM MM
♪ Tap tap tap tap
Tap tap tap
Tap tap tap
Khoo Khu Khoo Khu

14km

Tak Tak tak

Tap tap tap

skritch
skritch

With thanks to Sarah for the wisdom and patience, Michael for the bottomless support, Ben for the instruction in teen colloquialisms, Alex for the music, Becky for holding my hand. Honourable mentions for Nico, Abby, Rose, Roger, Joanne and Jacky. Special thanks to everyone who has supported me and my work. There are so many of you. I'm full of gratitude, thank you from the bottom of my heart.

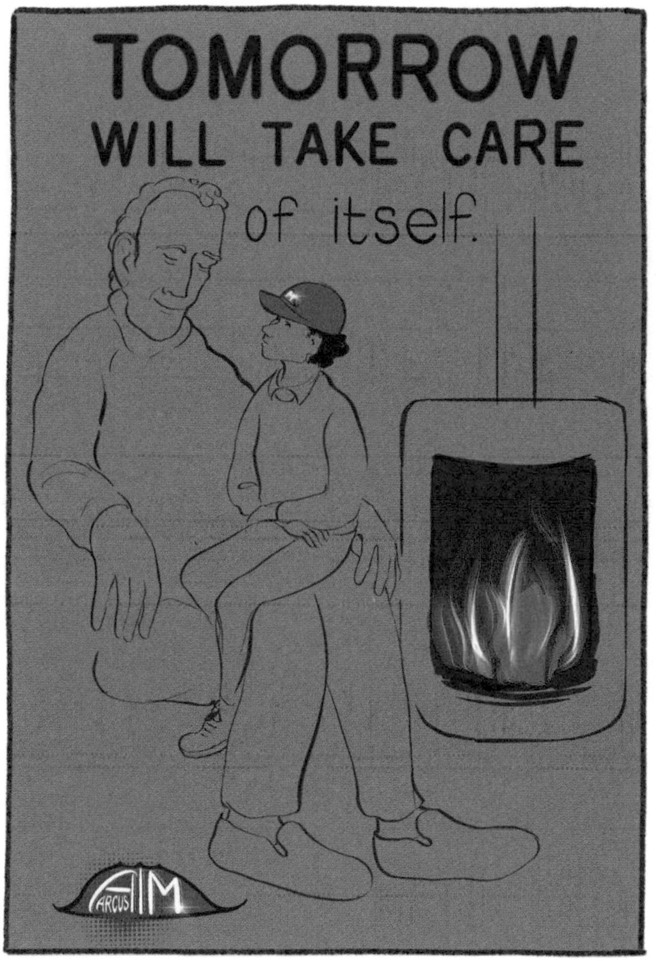
TOMORROW
WILL TAKE CARE
of itself.